Physical Education: Essential Issues

Physical Education: Essential Issues

edited by
Ken Green
and
Ken Hardman

⑤ SAGE Publications
London ● Thousand Oaks ● New Delhi

A SAGE Publications Company
1 Oliver's Yard
55 City Road
London EC1Y 1SP

SAGE Publications Inc
2455 Teller Road
Thousand Oaks, California 91320

SAGE Publications India Pvt Ltd
B-42, Panchsheel Enclave
Post Box 4109
New Delhi 110 017

British Library Cataloguing in Publication data

A catalogue record for this book is available from the British
Library

ISBN 0 7619 4497 4
ISBN 0 7619 4498 2 (pbk)

Library of Congress Control Number: 2004093138

Production by Deer Park Productions, Tavistock, Devon
Typeset by TW Typesetting, Plymouth, Devon
Printed in Great Britain by Athenaeum Press Ltd, Gateshead

Contents

For 'AJ'

and PE teachers like him everywhere

Contributors

Neil Armstrong is Professor of Paediatric Physiology, Director of the Children's Health and Exercise Research Centre and Head of the School of Sport and Health Sciences at the University of Exeter.

Professor Neil Armstrong
Children's Health and Exercise Research Centre
School of Sport and Health Sciences
University of Exeter
Heavitree Road
Exeter
EX1 2LU
Tel: 01392 264812
Fax: 01392 264706
Email: n.armstrong@exeter.ac.uk

Tansin Benn is Director of Learning and Teaching at the School of Education, University of Birmingham. Tansin trained and taught specialist physical education before moving into higher education to train teachers in 1981. Since then her career has expanded into teaching on PGCE, undergraduate and postgraduate programmes at the University of Birmingham, having a particular interest in gymnastics and dance in education. Since the mid-1990s her research interests have focused largely on the experiences of Muslim women both in teacher training and in their teaching careers.

Dr Tansin Benn
University of Birmingham
School of Education
Weoley Park Road
Selly Oak
Birmingham
B29 6LL
Tel: 0121 415 8391
Fax: 0121 414 5619
Email: t.c.benn@bham.ac.uk

Susan Capel is Professor and Head of Department of Sport Sciences at Brunel University. She was previously Reader in Education and Director of the Academic Standards Unit at

Canterbury Christ Church University College. Prior to that Susan was programme director for a Secondary PGCE course. Before entering higher education she taught physical education and geography in the UK and Hong Kong. Susan has a PhD in physical education from the USA and has published widely in a range of areas. She is a co-editor of *Learning to Teach in the Secondary School: A Companion to School Experience* and *Starting to Teach in the Secondary School: A Companion for the Newly Qualified Teacher*. She is also co-editor of *Issues in Physical Education*. From 2001–2003 Susan was President of the Physical Education Association of the United Kingdom (PEA UK).

Professor Susan Capel
Department of Sport Sciences
Brunel University
Uxbridge
Middlesex
UB8 3PH
Tel: 01895 816336
Fax: 01895 816340
Email: susan.capel@brunel.ac.uk

John Evans is Professor of Sociology of Education and Physical Education at Loughborough University, England. He teaches and writes on issues of equity, education policy, identity and processes of schooling. He is currently researching the relationships between formal education and eating disorders, with Dr Emma Rich. He has authored and edited a number of books and papers in the sociology of education and physical education and co-authored with Dawn Penney, *Politics and Policy in Physical Education* (E&FN Spon, 1999) and, with Brian Davies and Jan Wright *Body Knowledge and Control. Studies in the Sociology of Physical Education and Health* (Routledge, 2004).

Professor John Evans
School of Sport and Exercise Sciences
Loughborough University
Loughborough
LE11 3TU
Tel: 01509 222971
Fax: 01509 226301
Email: john.evans@lboro.ac.uk

Anne Flintoff is Reader in Physical Education and Education Development at Leeds Metropolitan University. She is part of the Gender, Race and Equity Research Group and teaches on undergraduate and postgraduate pathways in the sociology of PE and sport. Her major research interests include gender and physical education; contemporary youth sport policy; young people and active lifestyles; PE teacher education; gender and education;

feminist theory and sport. She has published widely in PE and sport studies, and is a member of the editorial board of *Physical Education and Sport Pedagogy*.

Dr Anne Flintoff
Reader in PE and Educational Development
School of Education and Professional Development
Leeds Metropolitan University
Carnegie Hall
Beckett Park
Leeds LS6 3QS
Tel: 0113 2832600
Email: a.flintoff@lmu.ac.uk

Ken Green lectures in the sociology of physical education, sport and leisure in the Chester Centre for Research into Sport and Society in the Department of Sport and Exercise Sciences, University College Chester. He is Editor of the *European Physical Education Review*.

Professor Ken Green
Chester Centre for Research into Sport and Society
Department of Sport and Exercise Sciences
University College Chester
Parkgate Road
Chester
CH1 4BJ
Tel: 01244 375444
Fax: 01244 380920
Email: kengreen@chester.ac.uk

Ken Hardman, formerly Reader in Education at the University of Manchester, currently holds Visiting Professorships at Akita University, Japan and University College Worcester. Immediate Past-President of the International Society for Comparative Physical Education and Sport and member of the Executive Board of the International Committee for Sport Science and Physical Education and the International Committee of Sport Pedagogy, Ken is a Fellow of the Physical Education Association UK, European Academy of Kinanthropology and Physical Education and Royal Society of Arts.

Dr Ken Hardman
Department of PE and Sport Studies
University College Worcester
Henwick Grove
Worcester
WR2 6AJ
Email: ken.hardman@tiscali.com

Jo Harris has 12 years' teaching experience of physical education in secondary schools and 15 years' lecturing experience in higher education. She is currently a Senior Lecturer in Physical Education and Director of the Teacher Education Unit at Loughborough University. She also lectures on masters degree courses and supervises research students. Her research focuses on the expression of health within the National Curriculum for Physical Education. Jo has produced numerous teaching resources and has delivered many in-service courses for physical education teachers. She contributed significantly to the work of the HEA Health and Physical Education Project based at Loughborough University for many years. She has presented at national and international conferences and has published articles in professional and academic journals. Jo is currently President of the Physical Education Association of the United Kingdom (PEA UK).

Dr Jo Harris
School of Sport and Exercise Sciences
Loughborough University
Loughborough
LE11 3TU
Tel: 01509 222971
Fax: 01509 226301
Email: j.p.harris@lboro.ac.uk

David Kirk joined Loughborough University in November 1998. He is currently Professor of Physical Education and Youth Sport. He also holds an Honorary Chair in Human Movement Studies at the University of Queensland, Australia and an Adjunct Chair in Physical Education at the University of Limerick, Ireland. David is Editor of the journal *Physical Education and Sport Pedagogy* (Carfax) and is a member of the advisory and editorial boards of several other leading journals. He received the IOC President's Prize in 2001 for his contribution to research in physical and sport education, and the outstanding Scholar Award in 2003 from the Research on Instruction and Learning in Physical Education Special Interest Group of the American Educational Research Association.

Professor David Kirk
School of Sport and Exercise Sciences
Loughborough University
Loughborough
LE11 3TU
Tel: 01509 223257
Fax: 01509 226301
Email: d.kirk@lboro.ac.uk

Joe Marshall lectures in physical education at Liverpool Hope University College. He is Book Review Editor for the *European Physical Education Review* and a member of the International Committee for Sports Science and Physical Education.

Dr Joe Marshall
Department of Sport Studies
Liverpool Hope University College
Hope Park
Liverpool
L16 9JD
Tel: 0151 291 3917
Fax: 0151 291 3164
Email: marshaj@hope.ac.uk

Mike McNamee is Senior Lecturer in Philosophy at the Centre for Philosophy, Humanities and Law in Health Care, School of Health Science, at the University of Wales Swansea. He has published and lectured widely in the philosophies of education and physical education, leisure and sport, in applied ethics, and has recently begun to work in the philosophy of health and medicine. He has co-edited the *Ethics of Leisure* (LSA publications, 1999), *Ethics and Sport* (Routledge, 1998) and the *Ethics of Educational Research* (Blackwell, 2002). He co-edits a book series in Ethics and Sport for Routledge. His latest edited book is *Philosophy and the Sciences of Exercise, Health and Sport* (Routledge, 2004). He is a former President of the International Association for the Philosophy of Sport and is the inaugural Chair of the British Philosophy of Sport Association.

Dr M. J. McNamee
Centre for Philosophy, Humanities and Law in Health Care
School of Health Science
University of Wales Swansea
Singleton Park
Swansea
Wales
SA2 8PP
Tel: 01792 602118
Email: m.j.mcnamee@swansea.ac.uk

Dawn Penney is a Senior Lecturer in the School of Education. Prior to her appointment at ECU, Dawn was a Senior Research Fellow at Loughborough University, UK and Research Fellow at the University of Queensland. Dawn has been involved in policy and curriculum research at national, state and school levels in the UK and Australia, focusing on development in health and physical education. Her publications include *Politics, Policy and Practice in Physical Education* co-authored with John Evans (Routledge, 1999) and *Gender and Physical Education. Contemporary Issues and Future Directions* (Routledge, 2002). Her most recent work has focused on the development of specialist schools in the UK and collaborative research with teachers engaged in curriculum development.

Dr Dawn Penney
School of Education
Edith Cowan University
2 Bradford Street
Mount Lawley 6050
Western Australia
Tel: +61 (08) 9370 6802
Fax: +61 (08) 9370 6215
Email: d.penney@ecu.edu.au

Ken Roberts is Professor of Sociology at the University of Liverpool. He is renowned for his work on social stratification and is widely regarded as the founding father of leisure sociology. He has published numerous articles as well as over 20 books, the most recent of which are *Class in Modern Britain* (Palgrave Macmillan, 2003) and *The Leisure Industries* (Palgrave Macmillan, 2004).

Professor Ken Roberts
Department of Sociology, Social Policy and Social Work Studies
Eleanor Rathbone Building
University of Liverpool
Bedford Street South
Liverpool L69 7ZA
Tel: 0151 794 2995/6
Fax: 0151 794 2997
Email: k.roberts@liverpool.ac.uk

Sheila Scraton is Professor of Leisure and Feminist Studies at Leeds Metropolitan University. She directs the Gender, Race and Equity Research Group, teaches on undergraduate and postgraduate pathways in leisure and sport studies and coordinates the Gender network across the University. Her major research interests include cross-national qualitative work on women and sport; sport, ethnicity and gender; women and football; older women and leisure; gender and physical education; leisure and feminist theory. She has published extensively in leisure and sport studies and is a member of the editorial board of *Leisure Studies* and the *Journal of Sport and Social Issues* and on the advisory board of *Sport, Education and Society*.

Professor Sheila Scraton
School of Education and Professional Development
Leeds Metropolitan University
Carnegie Hall

Beckett Park
Leeds LS6 3QS
Tel: 0113 2832600
Email: s.j.scraton@lmu.ac.uk

Andy Smith is a Researcher in the sociology of physical education, sport and leisure in the Chester Centre for Research into Sport and Society in the Department of Sport and Exercise Sciences, University College Chester.

Andy Smith
Chester Centre for Research into Sport and Society
Department of Sport and Exercise Sciences
University College Chester
Parkgate Road
Chester
CH1 4BJ
Tel: 01244 375444
Fax: 01244 380920
Email: andy.smith@chester.ac.uk

Nigel Thomas is Head of Sport and Exercise at Staffordshire University. He began his career in Higher Education following ten years working in local authority and governing body sports development roles, focusing specifically on the development of opportunities for young disabled people. His research interests include the media coverage of disability sport and the integration of children with special educational needs into mainstream physical education. He is currently completing his PhD on the 'policy process in disability sport'.

Mr Nigel Thomas
Head of Department
Sport and Exercise
Faculty of Health and Sciences
Staffordshire University
Leek Road
Stoke on Trent
Staffordshire
ST4 2DF
Tel: 01782 294019
Fax: 01782 294321
Email: n.b.thomas@staffs.ac.uk

Richard Winsley is a Researcher in the Children's Health and Exercise Research Centre and a Lecturer in the School of Sport and Health Sciences at the University of Exeter.

Dr Richard Winsley
Children's Health and Exercise Research Centre
School of Sport and Health Sciences
University of Exeter
Heavitree Road
Exeter
EX1 2LU
Tel: 01392 264724
Fax: 01392 264706
Email: r.j.winsley@exeter.ac.uk

Introduction

Ken Green and Ken Hardman

This book is aimed primarily at under- and postgraduate students pursuing entire programmes or discrete courses and modules in the broad area of physical education and sport in schools. It consists of a collection of what we consider to be essential readings – in the sense that they are contributions from eminent authors on a breadth of salient and enduring themes as well as contemporary issues – in physical education. Many of the authors are distinguished figures who have, over the last two decades, made substantial and distinctive contributions to our understanding of the process of physical education. By enduring themes we mean those aspects of physical education that have continued to be discussed, in a more or less contentious manner, throughout the history of the subject; for example, the nature and values of physical education and the relationship between the subject and physical activity and health. At the same time, the book explores contemporary issues in the form of relatively recent debates surrounding topics such as the growth of examinations in physical education and innovations and developments in teaching styles and formats.

The study of physical education has increasingly become multidisciplinary and inter-disciplinary and the book reflects this, incorporating philosophical, sociological, pedagogical and comparative perspectives on central themes and issues in the academic and professional study of physical education. In this respect the book offers readers ample opportunity to gain insight into the various disciplinary means by which we can develop a more adequate understanding of the subject.

While, at first glance, the text may appear oriented towards secondary school physical education in the United Kingdom, closer inspection reveals material that has direct relevance at an international level – either because the topics addressed are generic topics (physical activity, health-related exercise and pedagogy, for example) or because they offer comparative study (such as physical education in international context) or involve reference to international aspects of the topics under consideration (model-based teaching and assessment in physical education and the significance of social class for sport and physical education). Similarly, many of the themes and issues discussed are equally relevant to physical education at junior and senior levels of schooling.

We are acutely aware that, in attempting to provide such broad disciplinary and thematic coverage, an edited collection inevitably runs the risk of failing to satisfy anybody's requirements! At the same time, we appreciate that there are a number of themes and issues, as well as eminent authors that we have not managed to include. For this we can only apologise whilst accepting that the responsibility for this particular selection is entirely ours.

We trust that the book will provide a service to all those interested in the process of physical education. We wish to express our sincere gratitude to the individual chapter' authors who have gone to a great deal of trouble to provide stimulating, up-to-date contributions that can be considered essential readings for anyone involved in the domain of physical education. We particularly want to thank Marianne Lagrange and Emma Grant-Mills of Sage publications for their support in bringing the book to fruition. All that remains is to point out that the royalties from the sales of this book will go to the North-West Counties Physical Education Association (NWCPEA) – the parent-body of the *European Physical Education Review* of which this book's editors are current and immediate past editors – to support its work in furthering the study and practice of physical education.

Ken Green and Ken Hardman
2004

1 | The Nature and Values of Physical Education

Mike McNamee

There has always been an air of suspicion about those who think philosophically about the nature and values of physical education. On the one hand, physical education teachers are apt to claim that theirs is essentially a practical vocation; a calling to the teaching of physical activities that can help students to live better lives. What need have they of a philosophy? On the other hand, philosophers of education, notably in the liberal-analytical tradition, have often sought to cast a dim light on physical education, thinking it valuable (on good days at least) – but not educationally so. I shall try in this chapter to say something about the nature and values of physical education; the knowledge and the values that are inherent within its activities and those external ones which can be gained from them. The chapter revolves around a critique of some recent theoretically sophisticated attempts to discuss the nature and educational status of physical education by three philosophers David Carr (1997), Jim Parry (1998) and Andrew Reid (1996a, 1996b, 1997). I try to show where their arguments are both helpful but ultimately inadequate for the task of illuminating what physical education ought properly to consist of and how it might better prove its educational status and value. In particular, I try to show how it is absolutely necessary to think philosophically about the nature and values of activities that are thought to constitute physical education.[1]

ON ANALYTICAL PHILOSOPHY OF EDUCATION AND PHYSICAL EDUCATION

Before embarking on an account of the nature of physical education, and its knowledge and values claims, it is necessary to first take a short detour and second, offer an apology. First, it is necessary – if we are to have a reflective view of the philosophical terrain in which sense can be made of the concept of physical education – to understand a little of the nature of philosophical thinking. Second, the account here is itself situated within a particular tradition of thought. I do not speak of continental philosophy where there might be rich seams indeed for philosophers of physical education to plough. In particular, the work of phenomenologists[2] and hermeneuticists[3] have tremendous potential to offer understandings of our experiences in the activities that comprise physical education (whether in sport, games, play or even dance).

The manner in which this 'new' philosophy took a foothold in the UK and the USA – what came to be known as analytical philosophy of education – was nothing short of remarkable. The classic UK texts of the 1960s and 1970s bear testimony to it: Dearden's (1968) *Philosophy of Primary Education*, Hirst and Peters' (1970) *The Logic of Education* and Peters' (1966) *Ethics and Education* are paradigmatic. A cursory glance at their contents pages indicates their subject matter. Each philosopher bore down on their subject matter with microscopic linguistic scrutiny; precisely what was meant by concepts so central to education as 'authority', 'democracy', 'discipline', 'initiation', 'knowledge', 'learning', and so on. No educational concepts escaped their analytical scrutiny. A very similar movement was carrying the day in the USA where philosophers of education centrally saw themselves engaged in the same enterprise – and with surprisingly similar results given the cultural and geographical distance that set them apart. Despite the time that has elapsed since this highly original work, it is genuinely worthwhile to revisit their positions in order to better understand how (and perhaps how not) to think philosophically about physical education as an educational enterprise.

In the UK, Richard Peters developed the most powerful statement about the nature of education. In his inaugural lecture in 1965, he put forward a thesis that was to reach literally across the world through the old British Empire – many of whose educational lecturers were still taught in British universities – that education must be viewed, by all those who seriously investigate its nature, to comprise a certain logical geography. Briefly, his thesis was that education, properly conceived, referred to the initiation of the unlearned into those intrinsically worthwhile forms of knowledge that were constitutive of rational mind. Its shorthand was that education referred essentially to the development of rationality. Despite the hugely influential educational effects of muscular Christianity, physical education enjoyed little more than a Cinderella existence, even in British education, throughout the twentieth century. And now, it was surely not to be invited to the ball. The hegemony of that great thesis cast physical education well and truly into the educational hinterland. I shall now consider that thesis in a little detail.[4]

The particular picture of education favoured by analytical philosophers of education, then, is that of the British philosopher of education Richard Peters and, to a lesser extent, his close colleague Paul Hirst. I shall refer to their theses collectively as the Petersian conception of education. It is familiar enough to anyone who read any English language philosophy of education from 1965 to 1985. For Peters, the many uses of the word 'education' might be reduced to the central case and the philosophical task was to tease out criteria implicit in that case. This led Peters to develop his sophisticated account of education as the transmission of what was intrinsically worthwhile in order to open the eyes of initiates to a vaster and more variegated existence. That same worthwhile knowledge was

continuous with the various forms of knowledge that Hirst had delineated by
of epistemological criteria. The Petersian thesis was summarised thus:

♦ 'education' implies the transmission of what is worth-while to those who become
committed to it;

♦ 'education' must involve knowledge and understanding and some kind of cognitive
perspective, which are not inert; and

♦ 'education' at least rules out some procedures of transmission, on the grounds that they
lack wittingness and voluntariness on the part of the learner. (Peters, 1966: 45)

The first two conditions have been referred to as the axiological and epistemological
conditions by two other philosophers, Andrew Reid (1996a, 1996b, 1997) and David Carr
(1997), both of whom have sought to conceptualise physical education in similar ways, but
who have come to rather different conclusions about its educational potential. The third
criterion refers to the processes by which such transmission was ethically acceptable. I will
comment on the analytical and epistemological dimension of Carr's and Reid's articles and
then examine the axiological dimension of Reid's work which is the bedrock of his
justification for the educational status of physical education.

What is of significance in Reid (1996a, 1996b, 1997) is the idea that education, as conceived
in the Petersian mould, is narrow and restrictive. Despite a lack of argumentation, he
signifies a broader conception of education than is found in the accounts of philosophers
such as Peters, Hirst, Barrow or, for that matter, anyone housed within the liberal tradition.
These philosophers of education conceive of education as the development of individual,
rationally autonomous, learners. In their writings they sharply distinguish education from
other learning-related concepts such as 'socialisation', 'training' and 'vocation' in terms of
their content, scope, value and application. Reid's conceptualisation of a broader account
rests on the position of John White (1990) in his book *Education and the Good Life* where
educators aim toward the development of personal well-being grounded in rationally
informed desires of both a theoretical and practical kind. Education is thus subservient to,
and continuous with, the kinds of development that enable an individual to choose
activities, experiences and relationships that are affirmations of those informed choices.

By contrast, Carr is more traditional (in the liberal sense) in his account of education and
therefore physical education. Like Barrow and Peters before him, he marks the education-
training distinction by a thesis about mind. For the earlier writers in liberal philosophy of
education, all educational activities were broader and richer in scope than mere training
which was a form of instruction with limited, focused ends. Education properly conceived,
they argued, aimed at something much richer and more variegated. The educated mind did
not focus on things limited in scope, such as training for the world of work, but rather
helped learners to better understand their world, and their place within it. As it was often
said, education had no specific destination or goal as such; it was rather to travel with a new,
enlarged view. Necessarily, this educated view was informed by an initiation into the forms

of knowledge or rationality; aesthetic, mathematical, philosophical, scientific, religious, and so on. These were simply what being educated consisted in. Despite the fact that Carr recognises the value of practical as well as theoretical rationality, he undermines Reid's thesis about the importance of physical education conceived of as practical knowledge, and is driven back to the old liberal ground:

> The key idea here is the traditionalist one that certain forms of knowledge and understanding enter into the ecology of human development and formation – not as theories of a scientist or the skills of a golfer, but as the horizon of significance against which we are able to form some coherent picture of how the world is, our place in it and how it is appropriate for us to relate to others. Strictly speaking, it matters not a hoot on the traditionalist picture whether such received wisdom is theoretical or practical or located at some point in between; what matters is that there should be – in the name of education – some substantial initiation into this realm (or these realms) of human significance *alongside any training in vocational or domestic or merely recreational skills*. This is not to deny any proper normative conception of the latter, or that any pursuit of such skills may involve considerable rational judgement and discrimination; it is rather to insist that the sort of rationality they do exhibit may not and need not have anything much to do with education. Very roughly, one might put the point of the liberal-traditionalist distinction between educational and non-educational knowledge by observing that the former is knowledge which informs rather than merely uses the mind. (Carr, 1997: 201; emphasis added)

Thus, Carr's account is little more than a brave leap back to the Petersian position. Now, as with all philosophical argument, one can dispute a position on its own terms, one can deny the presuppositions of those terms or one can either assert or argue for a counter position. The middle option can be seen in any of a legion of writers[5] who attacked the liberal position for its normative presuppositions. Under the banner of ideological neutrality, it seemed to smuggle in an awful lot of values. Moreover, nearly every self-respecting sociologist of education (and physical education) cried that it entailed little more than a crystallisation of the kind of curriculum favoured by British grammar and public schools in the UK over the last 100 years or so. I shall not discuss the normative presuppositions in the liberal account of education. Instead, I will merely indicate here that I am persuaded by a less restricted account of the contents of education based on the notion of a worthwhile life which is not exhausted by those activities that, so to speak, inform the mind. I lay out the contours of such an account in the final section below.

There is a point of considerable agreement between Carr and Reid that is typical of the liberal theory of education, and it is one that is typically used against the educational advocates of physical education. Both writers are keen to hold on to the liberal ideal that education has its own ends. This of course cuts across the grain of 'common sense' thinking that it is the job of education to effect socialisation, or produce a more efficient workforce, and so on. Reid says that a broader view of what education entails – the introduction to cultural resources – must not simply be thought of as the development of qualities of mind:

The idea of *introduction to cultural resources* is to be taken here as an abbreviated way of referring to the complex and lengthy processes associated with the knowledge condition of education, with the teaching and learning which are required for effective appreciation and use of those resources. The sports and games which figure in physical education, then, are to be distinguished from work, the arts, intellectual illumination and so on in terms of their fundamentally hedonic orientation, but not in terms of their role as major cultural institutions, and thus (on the view which sees personal well-being and its component values in terms of socialisation and acculturation) in terms of their educational importance. (Reid, 1997: 15–6; original emphasis)

It seems, therefore, that Reid is not unhappy with the general model of education as initiation into sports and games as major cultural institutions.[6] As we have seen, Carr parts company with Reid on epistemological issues to do with the development of rational mind, though not only there. Despite recognising the value of such initiation, Carr pejoratively refers to sports and games (following Barrow, 1981) as merely a valuable part of one's schooling – but, note, not education. Carr's logical geography is restricted to the Petersian-liberal continent. Like many others before him, Reid wants to shift the ground of education away from the development of intellect as the sole basis and look also to a kind of 'pleasure principle'. Reid suggests that the nature and value of physical education is best characterised by a 'fundamentally hedonic orientation'. I shall consider these points in that order.

EPISTEMOLOGICAL ASPECTS

One major strand in physical education teachers' collective insecurity complex is to be found in epistemological aspects of their subject which, in the UK at least, has undergone significant professional changes. Central among those changes is the emergence of a graduate profession armed (supposedly) with a greater breadth and depth of theoretical knowledge. For my part, I harbour three suspicions about such claims. First, I am simply not sure if it is true that the development of an all-graduate profession has produced a teacher base that is characterised as having a broader and deeper knowledge base and I know of no empirical study to dis/prove the claim. Second, even if this were true, it does not follow necessarily that this would bring about better learning and teaching in physical education lessons. Third, over the last 20 years or so we have seen witnessed the introduction of significant elements of propositional knowledge into the school subject (taught in a fashion more typical of the classroom than the gymnasium) which has been incorporated systematically into syllabi, culminating in examinations.[7] Yet, it is not the mere snobbery of the physics or maths teacher that is problematic here. Carr, as we have seen above, gives it its most pithy statement: education comprises those forms of knowledge that do not merely use but, rather, inform rational mind. The distinction is both clear and elegantly put. But what follows from it? The answer is 'nothing necessarily'. Further exploration is required.

Reid claims that the family of activities of physical education are best conceived of as expressions of 'knowing how', to use Gilbert Ryle's famous phrase. That is to say, the activities and their knowledge contents are not merely the handmaiden of theoretical knowledge, but a species of knowledge in their own right. They are better captured under the title 'practical knowledge'. Similarly, Parry (1988) claims that it is the practical knowledge required for successful participation in physical education activities that satisfies the epistemological criterion of education. On a technical point, it could be argued that the phrase 'epistemological criterion' requires correction. Peters' remarks on the epistemological criteria of education are better subdivided thus: (a) the development of knowledge and understanding which are not inert; and that (b) such knowledge and understanding must be framed in some 'cognitive perspective'. This distinction is important since, among other objections, one could argue that the knowledge and understanding of the activities of physical education may well come to characterise part of one's way of viewing the world. The phrase 'having a healthy and active lifestyle' (of late, barbarously misused) might well capture the idea of a person considered physically educated; one whose knowledge was tied to action in important respects. It could be said that most adults 'know' what a healthier and more active lifestyle looks like but they are unable to incorporate it into their lives. On the stronger epistemological account, one could not be said *properly* to know this whilst acting in a contrary way. But it is really the second epistemological aspect – the cognitive perspective – that offends both Peters' and Carr's rationalism. Lest it be said that I am erecting a strawman, consider Peters' construction of the value of theoretical knowledge. Note that it is in contrast to theoretical knowledge that he dismisses, among other things, sports and games:

> To get attached to pets, people or possessions is a bad bet *sub specie aeternitatis*; for there is one thing we know about them – they will die or become worn out with use or age. No such fate awaits the objects of theoretical activities; for as long as there is an order of the world there will always be further things to find out about it. (Peters, 1966: 157)

> In so far as knowledge is involved in games and pastimes, this is limited to the hived off end of the activity which may be morally indifferent. A man (sic) may know a great deal about cricket if he is a devotee of the game; but it would be fanciful to pretend that his concern to find out things is linked with any serious purpose, unless the game is viewed under an aesthetic or moral purpose. Cricket is classed as a game because its end is morally unimportant. Indeed an end has almost to be invented to make possible the various manifestations of skill. (Peters, 1966: 158)

In a passage that should be etched on the hearts and minds of all physical education student teachers, he continues:

> Curriculum activities, on the other hand, such as science or history, literary appreciation, and poetry are 'serious' in that they illuminate other areas of life and contribute much to the quality of living. They have, secondly, a wide ranging cognitive content which distinguishes them from games. Skills, for instance, do not have a wide ranging cognitive content. There is very little to know about riding bicycles, swimming, or golf. It is largely a matter of knowing how rather than

of 'knowing that', of knack rather than of understanding. Furthermore, what there is to know throws little light on much else. (Peters, 1966: 159)

While Reid, therefore, presents a sophisticated account of practical knowledge and reasoning (ironically enough, following Carr and others), he fails to attack the proper target and to give an account for the specific epistemological aspects of the activities of physical education. It would seem to me that a more fruitful place to start would be to interrogate Peters' account of 'seriousness' which is used to demarcate knowledge considered educational from that which is not. Two brief sets of points can be made here. In what sense is the illumination of things other than themselves a necessary condition for what is said to be 'serious'? Why, furthermore, should wide-ranging cognitive content similarly be viewed as a logically necessary condition of educational activities? The criterion does indeed distinguish practices such as science from sport but, again, what follows from this? Second, note how the notion that certain ranges of knowledge contribute to the quality of living, gets sidelined thereafter. Surely this is one of the palpable claims that all physical educators would make as a hypothetical justification of the subject? As a matter of fact, one could survey the millions of people for whom sports and related practices are central to their quality of living. As a justification, of course, this form of argument is hypothetical since its success is contingent upon the satisfactions enjoyed by those persons. We should not need reminding that many children simply detest sports and games just as others come to love and care for them (both in spite of, and because of, the manner of a child's initiation into them).[8] If we agree the philosophical point that to be physically educated, what one knows must characterise the way one acts in the world, then as physical educators, it is our duty to both habitualise children into patterns of activity and engagement with social practices such as hockey and basketball, and to open up to our students the significant sporting inheritance of our cultures so that they too may come to savour its joys and frustrations *and* to know a little about that aspect of the cultures which sporting practices instantiate (for no one would seriously deny their enormous significance in modern societies).[9]

Thus Reid's exploration of the underlying logic of practical knowledge is, despite Parry's assertion, a worthwhile task. But Reid fails significantly to take that analysis further. This omission is manifest in his observation that there are profoundly complex kinds of practical knowledge required, for example, in playing Tchaikovsky or flying a plane. Howsoever these examples are used to illustrate the potential complexity of forms of practical knowledge, they are not representative of the kinds of knowledge definitive of physical education. Nor can they be used helpfully as analogues in such an argument. There is a further complication, moreover, in the contrast between the serious forms of knowledge and sports and games which relates to the ease with which children are initiated into cultural practices. Like physical education, the 'serious' educational subjects too have easy skills and techniques at their onset, yet these are the first steps in practices of immense rational sophistication in range and depth. Sports do not possess this range of cognitive complexity and it would be folly to argue that they do. Yet there is more to them than *mere* knack: a forward roll is a skill and so is a double twisting back somersault but compare the range of complexity. The capacity to generate immensely technical skills aligned to perceptive judgement and anticipation in a time-compressed manner is typical of any invasion game (though they too have their basic techniques). Sports skills are not comparable in density or range to classical music or philosophy. This is why Tchaikovsky's concertos or landing aeroplanes are inappropriate analogues. It might, however, be profitable to explore other areas of the curriculum that embody overt performative knowledge as opposed to intellectual ones with respect to the embodiment of that knowledge.

What has to be acknowledged in this debate is the exceptional difficulty in talking about sporting experiences especially where they refer significantly to the emotional dimension that accompanies success and failure. It is not so much that one can give a full account of action if only sports people were linguistically sophisticated (a point lamentably true of most media, post-performance, interviews); the point is that these descriptions occupy different worlds. A phenomenological account simply does not try to do the same thing as, say, a physiological or biomechanical one.[10] But that is a discussion for another day. This entire area has been largely neglected in the philosophy of physical education since David Best's (1978) and David Carr's work (1979) in the 1970s. Reid has done the profession a service by reminding us of their importance.

Characteristic of early analytical philosophers of education, however, Reid proceeds as if the logic of his philosophical analysis carries itself forward to a conclusion in the minds of any reasonable person (including policy makers, headteachers, and other curriculum tutors competing for scarce resources). Like so much earlier work in analytical philosophy of education Reid fails to accord sufficient weight to contextual particulars and specifically the power-related discourses of the school-as-institution (rather than mere concept) and the dominance of the academic therein. Reid merely gestures towards this problematic. Despite the clarity of his arguments regarding physical education, it is the widespread experiences of physical education teachers who have been demeaned by the hierarchical dominance, or positioning, of propositional over performative knowledge. I am certain that this is the core root of the professional insecurity that has always characterised the physical education profession, and which has culminated in the apparent 'academicisation' of our profession.

Finally, the greatest weakness in the epistemological aspect of Reid's account of physical education as education is his failure to offer a value argument for the kinds of knowledge representative of physical education. It is a point that Peters flagged up 30 years ago: 'It is one thing to point to characteristics of activities that are usually thought to be worth while; it is quite another to show why these sorts of characteristics make them worth while' (1966: 152).

Like any philosophical thesis, one may challenge the Petersian position by rejecting the manner in which it is presented rather than looking for inconsistencies or incoherence within it. One could, so to speak, reject the paradigm completely; that is to say, reject the very terms in which it is presented and the bases it presupposes. In doing so we could reconceptualise some or all of the notions of 'rationality', 'knowledge' or 'education' to find an account more conducive to physical education and its claims to proper educational status. Despite making a case for the necessary existence of practical rationality in educational matters, on Reid's case, physical educationists would still be left to argue whether the activities of physical education were *productive* of practical rationality and *why* the particular practical rationality employed or exemplified in the activities were of particular value. Equally unfortunate, we have seen how Carr's position appears little more than a retrenchmant into a broadly Petersian education. Reid's best hopes appear to be based on the pluralism of value conferred by the range of activities, but particularly in reference to their essentially hedonic character. While I think that it is clear that the range of activities represent a family (with some close relations and some more distant ones) I think the policies of both Carr and Reid are misguided. It is, therefore, to issues of axiology and physical education that I will now turn.

AXIOLOGY AND PHYSICAL EDUCATION

What Reid attempts, more generously than other liberal philosophers of education, is to connect the ways in which different kinds of knowledge in physical education activities embody different kinds of value. He sets out a fuller list of the sources of value and attempts to relate physical education to them. In addition to arguments about the value of theoretical knowledge, he articulates the following range: intellectual, ethical, aesthetic, economic, hedonic and health. As we have seen, anyone attempting to argue for the educational value of physical education on the grounds that the playing of games conferred a wide-ranging cognitive perspective on the world would be barking up the wrong tree. A more circumscribed claim regarding theoretical knowledge in physical education is plausible. Understanding sports and other forms of 'physical activities' from the appropriate field of theoretical standpoints (anatomy, biology, history, sociology, and so forth) illuminates the ways in which those activities can contribute to a worthwhile life. For example, I can benefit from knowing that steady state, medium intensity, exercise over 20 minutes' duration draws significantly upon aerobic rather than anaerobic metabolism and is therefore more appropriate to my maintaining lower levels of fat. Conversely, I may come to appreciate that circuit training is more conducive to anaerobic fitness and that by altering my body positions while performing sit-ups I may more specifically target my abdominal muscles and reduce the contribution of my hip flexors. Moreover, I may begin critically to appreciate the highly gendered atmosphere of the locker room or the deep offensiveness engendered by racist or anti-Semitic attitudes in some sports crowds. The point remains, however, that despite these benefits, the value-arguments for physical education ought not to be erected on *exactly* the same grounds as other curriculum subjects that are palpably different in nature. This inspires Reid's search for a broader range of values.

There is a sense in which Reid has brought this problem upon himself *because* of the way in which he conceives physical education. He recognises that no satisfactory account of the subject will flow simply from an examination of the ways in which the words 'physical' and 'education' are used. Rather, such an account must begin from an analysis of the historical practices and traditions that have been prominent in giving shape and form to physical education. Rather, Reid thinks the task is to elucidate

> the conceptual features of a set of well-founded educational practices and traditions. What is 'given', from this standpoint, is not some set of axioms or intuitions about the nature of 'physicality' and 'education', but what might rather be called physical education as a form of life, that is the practices and traditions of physical education as they have evolved historically and continue to evolve, in concrete social, cultural and institutional contexts. (1997: 10)

This is absolutely the right way to go about things. Not only should we look historically at those practices and traditions but also at their contemporary instantiations. But it is problematic to argue merely that physical education is the sum of its practices and traditions without also offering an account that articulates and brings together the disparate nature of those practices and traditions.[11] For which practices are we to opt? Into whose traditions ought we to initiate our young? Compare what values Rugby Union stood for only ten years ago with its new professional metamorphosis. To what extent does it represent the same kind of practice into which we once thought it worthwhile for our children to be initiated?[12] Is the ethos of girls' hockey or cricket really full of camaraderie as is stereotypically thought? What is entirely unhelpful, is to argue that what holds the different activities, their practices and traditions together, is the notion of hedonic pleasure.

In terms of ethical value, Reid points out the inherent normativity of physical education activities. Here, it must be pointed out, the diversity of what goes under the heading physical education renders generalisations problematic. In sporting games, the moral educational features are written into their very nature (that is to say, the regulative rules). Where games are taught properly, ethical notions such as equality, fairness, honesty and rule-abiding action necessarily arise. The extent to which these notions are merely caught rather than taught is another matter. Precisely, how these values infuse dance, health-related exercise, or orienteering is quite another matter and Reid's recognition of eclectic argumentation is helpful. Yet in his final paper (see Reid, 1997) there is a tendency to use only sporting games as the vehicle for his own justificatory argument. Reid makes two points that are designed to defuse the arguments of those who deny sports' ethical dimension. While I am in agreement with the point of arguing for the ethical dimension of sports I will dispute his specific argumentation below. Reid writes:

> The first relates to the discussion earlier on the relations between the constituents of our axiology, which concluded in favour of the priority of ethical values (when competing values are entertained). In the context of games teaching, this reflects the traditional principle that fair play, sportsmanship and respect for one's opponent take precedence over the competitive objectives of winning and avoiding defeat. The second point, likewise, concerns questions of priority. The position adopted in this paper . . . is that games and sports are forms of play, aimed essentially at promoting pleasure enjoyment, excitement, recreation, and the like; their primary

value, in short, is hedonic. Winning, from this point of view, is not, as is sometimes supposed, the ultimate goal of competitive games: enjoyment is, and competitive action, structured in highly specific ways by the operation of the norms, rules, codes, conventions and so on of the various particular sports and games, is the way in which the conditions of enjoyment are fulfilled, its possibilities realized. (1997: 12)

He continues: 'games themselves are, as essentially hedonic activities, fundamentally self-contained and in some sense non-serious . . . and this observation gives some weight to the scepticism sometimes expressed about the prospects for extending those ethical principles beyond the boundaries of the game'.

Here Reid answers Peters' question regarding the source of value. But is it a satisfactory one? I will make a few general points about Reid's general argument here, and then move specifically to the adequacy of his hedonic direction. First, Reid has failed to apply his own reasoning to his analysis of the logic of competitive games viz. their ethical dimension. He posits that where there is conflict between the competitive urge to win and other, ethical, principles such as fairness and honesty the latter should prevail. Yet he has already informed the reader that to play games logically entails the observance of such principles. This being the case there can be no such conflict, for where players are dishonest, or unfair or not rule-abiding (assuming they are breaking the rules, in being dishonest, or violent or disrespectful) they are *ipso facto* not playing the game. This point is commonly referred to as the 'logical incompatibility thesis'. Adherents of the thesis argue that to play a game one must play by the rules and to do otherwise is to be engaged in behaviours that are, by definition, not part of the game.[13]

Second, on an historical note, Reid's move can be compared with Robert Carlisle's (1969) doomed essentialistic argument.[14] Where Carlisle attempted to locate the educational status of physical education in terms of their essentially aesthetic character Reid opts for the hedonic. This sort of essentialism appears in marked contrast to his earlier recognition of the disparate nature of the constituent activities of physical education. Similarly, despite his earlier eclecticism, Reid appears to have turned physical education into competitive games. It is not a new sleight of hand; the National Curriculum for PE in the UK underwent such a reduction in the highly politicised policy formulation stages. And there are some clear benefits to such a strategy though there are burdens too. The dietary narrowness of competitive games has been the object of much rancorous debate and the breadth of modern physical education curricula is something welcomed not only by egalitarians of the left.[15] Nevertheless, from a philosophical point of view, it seems clear that if one were to conceptualise or justify physical education solely in terms of sports and games then this would beg questions as to the educational place of the other members of the family of activities that traditionally fall under the heading of physical education, in the UK at least. Furthermore, if one were to alter the conception of physical education it seems clear that one's arguments concerning the types of knowledge entailed therein, the aims, value and educational justification of the subject ought correspondingly to alter too. Reid's failure to acknowledge this is problematic since he later discusses at length the benefit of health values wrought by a physical education curriculum.[16] The precise picture of physical education Reid wants to defend is not specified though the contours are visible; a distaste for theoretical engagement; a predominance of sporting games; a reductionism to hedonic values. What Reid argues later is for a kind of eclecticism that blurs the emphasis on competitive sporting games. He urges that the full value of physical education is to be found in its manifold contributions to different sorts of value but that as a matter of logic, on his analysis, their value is essentially hedonic.

I have argued at length elsewhere (see McNamee, 1994) of the weakness of reducing sports and related practices to the value of felt pleasures and I will merely rehearse those arguments briefly here.[17] The central reason why the hedonic thesis should not be considered adequate is that it offers no criteria (and hence no logical basis over and above mere preference) against which to evaluate such practices or make subsequent policy decisions. If, for instance, we are concerned with the questions 'what practices are worth pursuing/providing/committing ourselves to?' we find ourselves without logical assistance since the first and last words of the hedonist's thesis are 'it gives me pleasure' or 'I enjoy it'. This response is sometimes referred to as a 'stopper'. It fails to provide any sort of logical answer to a sceptical questioner but stops them from further exploration. Of course, many children and adults who are committed to sports find the exercise of skilful acts deeply satisfying, fulfilling or pleasurable and attribute their value to nothing other than the experience or engagement in the activity. The language in which their accounts of the value of their experiences are often couched is hedonic in the sense that they refer exclusively to the subjective value of pleasurable feelings. Reid fails to instantiate in detail what the hedonic thesis amounts to.

By way of criticism, consider first those activities that are ill-characterised by felt pleasure. For instance, there may be many qualities, goods or values associated with, for instance, outdoor and adventurous activities in the winter time. It may be assumed, however, that fun or pleasure may not commonly be among them. These activities may come to be enjoyable but only after some considerable time and effort and this may only be afforded to a limited number of people who are genetically predisposed to them or who, through training, have come to be committed to them. Second, as Parry noted, the pursuit of pleasure itself does not demarcate any special class of activities except those logically thus defined. The corollary of the hedonic view would entail the justification of whatsoever people found pleasurable simply because they found it pleasurable. And the contents list of such an account could render some fairly unthinkable items for education. Third, pleasures differ in quality. The pleasures derived by a six-year-old child from engaging in simple motor actions are considered inappropriate for sixteen-year-olds who demand something more complex. To the best of my knowledge no one has explored this idea in the context of sport from a philosophical point of view yet the classification of games by Celia Brackenridge and John Alderson presupposes it.[18] It has been called the 'Aristotelian Principle' by John Rawls who writes:

other things equal, human beings enjoy the exercise of their realized capacities (their innate or trained abilities), and this enjoyment increases the more the capacity is realized, or the greater its complexity. The intuitive idea here is that human beings take more pleasure in doing something the more they become proficient at it, and of two activities they do equally well, they prefer the one calling on a larger and more intricate and subtle discriminations. (1972: 435)

Indeed the value of sports and games may themselves be considered time-related goods.[19] No one would want to deny that the satisfactions afforded by the successful grasping of timing a boast in squash or spotting a somersault are tremendously rewarding but are they always so, and is pleasure the right concept to denote the attendant satisfactions?

Every account of the value presupposes a particular *weltanschauung* and, moreover, a particular philosophical anthropology. Any particular and substantive account of the value of sports and related practices will therefore be related conceptually to an account of a person that is thought desirable for one to become. Sports and related practices thus become seen as one of a family of engineering processes (less deterministically, practices and traditions) that are constitutive of a person's becoming just that: a person. Each culture, indeed each epoch, has more or less tightly defined horizons that inform and are informed symbiotically by each other.

How are such horizons informed by the hedonic thesis? Let me start with a logical point. One cannot pursue pleasure in isolation. Pleasure is derived *through* actions and activities. A similar point is made by Nozick in one of his thought experiments, the 'experience machine'.[20] A thought experiment is a typical tool used by philosophers to get people to imagine a hypothetical scenario and then to show how this sheds light on a real case by analogy. So Nozick asks his readers, 'What else matters to us other than how life feels on the inside?' He asks us to consider whether we would hook ourselves up to a machine which simulates the feelings experienced when having any and all the wonderful experiences we desired. I have tried the experiment out with students over 20 years of lecturing. The vast majority, on the first run through of the argument opt to plug in. After considerable discussion many change their mind. The reasons for this are illuminating for our consideration of the value of physical education. In the experience machine one remains essentially passive. But *as* persons[21], we want to *do* certain things; to achieve the attendant satisfactions of being a successful teacher or pupil, cricketer, or athlete. To *be* such things is to be committed to various activities, roles and relationships which define the sort of persons we are. Plugging into the machine is a form of suicide. In a sense, we cease to be the same person since the relationship between our experiences and our acts no longer holds. Many of my students have used the language of merit: 'you don't deserve those experiences because you have not got the ability, or trained for years, or sacrificed your life to the goals of sport' they say. In the machine, all these pleasurable experiences would not be related to us in the strong way that flows from our being attached to particular plans and projects. On the contrary the status of those experiences would be contingent to, rather than definitive of, our identity. The experience machine effectively lives our lives for us. This is not the life of a person.

It should be noted that I have not denigrated the value of pleasure as an action guiding reason *per se*. It is in need of some focus if it is to be used in offering a sound account of the value of the activities, practices and traditions of physical education. Moreover, a value argument ought not to be built in terms of the pursuit of pleasure alone. Pleasure, as was noted above, can only be pursued through particular acts and activities.

All these arguments about the inadequacy of educational justification being based upon hedonic lines leaves untouched the philosophical questions concerning the nature of value itself and classes of value used to account for physical education. Parry discerned the blurring of the intrinsic/instrumental distinction by Linda Bain (in the USA) and Keith Thompson (in the UK).[22] Carr correctly offers a similar critique of Reid, and Peters before him, who employ the terms 'intrinsic', 'extrinsic', 'inherent' and 'instrumental' to refer to both the value of an activity and the motivational states of a person. It is helpful here to stipulate linguistic usage in the interests of conceptual clarity. Let the terms 'intrinsic' and 'extrinsic' refer to my motivations or valuing of an activity but preserve the terms 'inherent' and 'instrumental' to refer to the (potential) value of a given thing or activity. For one can be intrinsically motivated to bang one's head against a wall (i.e., where one did it for its own sake and sought no further end) whereas no one would want to maintain that it was an inherently valuable act. On the other hand, it could be argued that while sport was inherently valuable, any particular athlete only valued it instrumentally and therefore that their motivations were entirely extrinsic. Much confused debate in physical education has occurred precisely for the want of drawing these distinctions with care.

Though I have captured the heart of Carr's point here I have expressed it somewhat differently. Moreover, I want to say that the highest goods, after Plato,[23] should be called mixed goods; those which are inherently valuable *and* valuable as means to further valuable ends. Furthermore, we could extend the debate to consider not only the relationality between means and ends, but also between particular persons who have particular capacities, abilities, dispositions and potentialities, and those means and ends. The very same activity might be inherently valuable but, as a matter of fact, be valued intrinsically by one person, extrinsically by another, both by the same and or not at all by a third person.

Having set out the inadequacies of Reid's hedonic argument in terms of its inherent weaknesses, the essentialism his position embodies and, finally, the classification of value it rests upon, it is now incumbent upon me to offer the beginnings of an alternative picture of the nature and educational value of physical education.

PERSONS, PRACTICES AND PHYSICAL EDUCATION

Parry (1988) captured the bigger picture with respect to the nature and values of physical education when he urged upon the profession a fundamental re-examination of the central concepts education, culture and personhood.[24] He observed that any educational ideology could be challenged at a variety of levels: first, at the level of actual practices as legitimate expressions of the educational theory, or as efficient means to its goals; second, at the level of educational theory as a legitimate expression of the ideology; and, finally, at the level of ideology. The radical kind of conceptualisation was never fully taken up. But neither analytical philosophy of education nor the physical education profession at large is sympathetic to this dense continental philosophy that employs a language all of its own and seems antithetical to the common-sense strand of English-speaking analytical philosophy.[25] Parry urged a less cognitivist conceptualisation of education and personhood.

I have elsewhere attempted to answer that call by suggesting a conception of personhood based strongly around Charles Taylor's account which emphasised the human capacity not merely for weak, instrumental, evaluation (means–ends reasoning) but also for strong, qualitative, evaluation (ends–ends reasoning) and which also contains at its core the centrality of the emotions in the life of persons. I think that the move of situating a less rationalistic view of persons necessarily opens up a proper consideration of the role of the emotions in our lives and especially in sports where they are channelled, frustrated, exposed, and potentially explored in self-critical ways. But this has rarely been addressed either theoretically or in the professional education of physical educators where spaces for non-applied, or immediately relevant, professional matters are rarely created. Elsewhere I have attempted to situate that argument in a broader philosophical account about the nature of education, analytical philosophy of education, and an alternative account of value and the broader nature of practices that can inform one's identity and constitute an important component of one's evaluative picture of a worthwhile life.[26] I can only set out the skeleton of that argument here.

I would urge a less than radical evaluation of Petersian thinking; one that loosens the shackles tying education to the development of theoretical rationality embodied by the distinct forms of knowledge. I would not argue for a wholesale rejection of the thesis since, so it seems to me, education is concerned precisely with initiation into significant cultural practices. Neither would I set great store by those radical or revolutionary philosophers of education who are antithetical to the nature of authority as encapsulated by education and its constituent practices. This very thin conceptualisation is preferable at two levels to the position made famous by Peters and retained by Carr. In the first instance, it is preferable on normative grounds in that it recognises a plurality of conceptions of education that emerge from some shared understanding of the need for societies to seek the grounds of their own continuance. How is this to be done other than by capturing the hearts and minds (and lungs!) of its young? On analytical grounds, so open a position does not prescribe in precise terms how this is to be done though one would want, as Peters did, to proscribe certain procedures on ethical grounds. To set out the traditional liberal distinctions as Carr does, and as Peters did before him, renders him open to the simple charge of ideology; no matter how internally coherent the thesis, he is always open to counter-ideological critique. It seems that Parry, Reid and I point in a different direction but none of us have travelled down it any distance here. We have all signposted a less restricted account of education as the initiation into a range of cultural practices that have the capacity to open up the possibilities of living a full and worthwhile life. Reid has given us no clues as to a broader *weltanshauung* that informs the shared position against cognitive imperialism: he is merely at pains to stress the primacy of the hedonic. Parry has suggested some liberalised-Olympic thesis while I am inclined towards a communitarian position central to which would be a stronger recognition for the dominant role that social practices like sport play in the formation of our identities and values. I have suggested elsewhere a developed account of how sport can be characterised, within a broad communitarian framework, as a social practice broadly under MacIntyre's description of that term. I have also suggested how that thesis cannot unproblematically be translated into the context of sport as writers such as Peter Arnold have done. Furthermore, it will be clear from the position developed there that I see such practices as one of the foundational bedrocks of character and identity formation which is one of the crucial tasks that fall predominantly, though not exclusively to formal education.[27]

At an analytical level, then, rather than arguing that X is education or not-education on the grounds of a pre-eminent criterion: cognitive depth and breadth (or the capacity to inform rather than merely use the mind, as Carr pithily puts it) recognition must be made for the fact that there are competing conceptions of education. I would not wish to consort with the radical revision of education as an 'essentially contested concept'. If an essence at so basic a level as I have asserted is contestable, I see no grounds for calling it a concept, let alone a concept of education. Instead, as a matter of conceptual necessity, it seems to me that despite the fact that these conceptions embody particular evaluative commitments regarding the nature of persons and society, they all share the formal notion that education is the development of persons towards the living of full and valuable lives. The next step of the argument is to develop an account of persons and the kinds of things that make their lives worthwhile over and above Peters' intellectual pursuits. Persons, on the kind of account I am disposed to, are beings who have the capacity to develop, evaluate, and live out life-plans based on a combination of projects, relationships and commitments. Among this combination of activities are a variety of practices which are valuable by virtue of their internal goods and their capacity to secure external goods in particular and unique ways. The activities of physical education are exemplified by a certain range of sporting practices, which are taken as paradigmatic which can be characterised as mixed goods because they have the capacity to be valued not only for their internal goods but also for the particular manner in which they secure external goods. Physical education can, therefore, contribute to the living of full valuable lives for persons and is thus of educational value. I think this is precisely the kind of rationale that can be either be read *into* the work of the American physical educator, Daryl Siedentop (1986), with his enormously influential model of sport education or simply might be explored as a philosophical justification for at least some portions of that model.[28]

This kind of argument, it might be said, holds true only for those practices we recognise as sporting games or athletic activities (and I would add, *pace* Siedentop, dance too). While the argument is long on initiation into those practices that are partly definitive of a culture and its identity(ies) it is short on the kinds of individualised, health-related activities. Historically, there have been two strands in what is called physical education: sports and health (or in older times hygiene, posture, and so forth). It seems clear to me that a different type of justificatory argument is required to support each. Maybe Carr is right here to classify the latter activities (along with life saving and other 'anomalies' that fall to the task of physical educators) as valuable but not educationally valuable because of their lacking in what can be referred to as cultural significance or cultural capital. Time and space do not allow me to comment in any way here upon these other strands except to note the following. Those who look for *conceptual* unity are simply wasting their time. There is no meaningful essence to the concept in that way. As Reid remarks, one must look rather to culture-specific, historical and political factors that have shaped the professions. Dance is a cultural practice that employs large motor-skilled activity like tennis or football. Some forms of gymnastics require interpretative movements and proceed with music like dance. Sculpting bodies, like training for rugby or netball, often requires the kinds of regimes and exercises that are common. But these similarities are nothing more than that. If all that one can do is to point out commonalities then there is little that is philosophically interesting here for anyone attempting a conceptual analysis by necessary and sufficient conditions of linguistic usage. Reid's peroration towards value pluralism should extend so far as to recognise the inherent openness of the concept of physical education: pluralism in activities; pluralism in values. No universal criterion of demarcation can be raised that will help physical educators to select activities is available, and so we should simply stop looking. Instead we should enquire as to the types and natures of rituals that sports instantiate in our modern world. And if, as Wollheim argues,[29] traditions pass on what they possess, then we should see to it, as guardians of these great cultural rituals, that the values physical education has and gives are kept in good health.[30]

NOTES

1 This chapter is a revised version of a paper first published as 'Education, philosophy and physical education: analysis, epistemology and axiology' (McNamee, 1998b). In particular, I have omitted or diluted some of the more technical philosophical points that were made in the original article as well as connecting thoughts there with other material that I have published elsewhere in the ethics of sport, and more generally to other recent contributions to the field.

2 See, for example Whitehead (1990).

3 See, for example, Hogenova (2002).

4 Though the reader is invited to scan at least the veritable legion of writers that have written more and less charitably about it. See for examples of these, respectively, Cooper (1986) and Kleinig (1983).

5 Again, for just one example among many, see Kleinig (1983).

6 Most writers, oddly enough, in the philosophy of physical education, are in agreement with this view. This may well have something to do with the fact that sports typically have conservative forces – notably in the idea of rule-following, and the transmission of dominant norms, via physical activity to the socialisation of the

players/athletes/dancers involved. I shall comment later, though only briefly, on this value-conserving function. For much more specific insights, one might look to sociologists of physical education (notably Evans and Penney, 2002) to highlight these latent political functions.

7   This is itself part of that wider trend which might be called 'certificationism' – if I may be excused for introducing a word that looks dangerously postmodern.

8   In a celebrated remark, Peters once observed that 'education cannot be forced upon unwilling minds'. Without recourse to dualism one should also remark that it cannot likewise be forced upon unwilling bodies (or persons with both physical and mental aspects, if you prefer to avoid dualistic, specifically Strawsonian language). See Strawson (1959).

9   Although my point here is somewhat abstractly stated, it seems to me that this is precisely the kind of philosophical orientation that guides the work of Daryl Siedentop in his model of Sport Education and which Kirk (2002) has recently elaborated.

10   On which see Whitehead (1990).

11   The term practice is used in a special way in recent philosophy. It is derived from the work of Alisdair MacIntyre (1985). I note that this way of talking of sports activities is gaining ground in mainstream physical education discourse (Almond, 1996; Kirk, 2002; Siedentop, 2002). Their account, like some philosophers of sport, rarely seeks to acknowledge the problems of considering sports as social practices as opposed to, say, architecture or farming. For an account of some of these subtleties see McNamee (1994, 1995).

12   I am not implying that the 'professionalisation' of that sport has necessarily wrought a morally poorer game. It strikes me that, in the particular case of rugby, we may well witness less violence and more legal but exceptionally harmful aggression. Is that progress? Moreover, I am not at all clear that the phrase 'professionalisation' best characterises the kinds of development we have witnessed in elite, finance-driven, sports.

13   A fuller discussion of this debate can be found in Lehman (1982) and Morgan (1987).

14   See Carlisle (1969).

15   An excellent collection housing a variety of egalitarian criticisms of traditional curricula and pedagogy is Evans and Davies (1993). See especially the editor's introduction, of the same title, pp. 11–27.

16   I have made some critical philosophical remarks about the tenuous relationship involved here while the movement was at its height in McNamee (1988) though I no longer hold to the justificatory argument that I set out there.

17   See McNamee (1994).

18   Brackenridge and Alderson (1982) unpublished. I have benefited from several long discussions with Rod Thorpe on this point in the context of sports.

19   For a discussion of this concept see Slote (1989).

20   Nozick (1974) see especially pp. 42–5.

21   The terms 'person' and 'personhood' are rather special ones in moral philosophy. See McNamee (1992) and Meakin (1982, 1990) for competing analyses and applications of them in physical education contexts.

22   See Bain (1976) and Thompson (1983).

23   See Plato (1974).

24   A footnote is required here as a matter of intellectual honesty. When Parry published the article that is reprinted with additions in this journal I was a doctoral student of his. The subsequent thesis 'The Educational Justification of Physical Education' owes a very significant debt to his intellectual guidance. A portion of one of the chapters sought to satisfy one of his perorations: McNamee (1992).

25   A more recent attempt to offer a phenomenological account of the sports experience (particularly what is often referred to as 'peak experience') from a Heideggerian perspective can be found in Standish (1998).

26   See the unpublished doctoral dissertation cited above, University of Leeds, 1992.

27   See McNamee (1995). With respect to conceptualising social relations more generally see, McNamee (1998a).

28   See his classic Siedentop (1986) and most recently Kirk (2002) and Siedentop (2002). In saying this I am in no way committing myself to what can sometimes be read into Siedentop's earlier work regarding the uncritical

socialisation into dominant forms of sometimes ethically corrupt (viz. homophobia, racism, sexism, and so forth) values. See also McNamee (1995).

29 See Wollheim (1993).

30 I am extremely grateful to Graham McFee for his incisive and generous observations and criticisms on an earlier version of this essay.

REFERENCES

Almond, L. (1996) *The Place of Physical Education in Schools*. 2nd edn. London: Kogan Page.

Bain, L. (1976) 'Play and intrinsic values in physical education', *Quest*, 26: 75–80.

Barrow, R. (1981) *The Philosophy of Schooling*. London: Harvester.

Best, D. (1978) *Philosophy and Human Movement*. London: George Allen and Unwin.

Brackenridge, C. and Alderson, J. (1982) 'A classification of sports', British Association of Sports Science Conference.

Carlisle, R. (1969) 'The concept of physical education', *Proceedings of the Philosophy of Education Society of Great Britain*, 3: 1–11.

Carr, D. (1979) 'Aims of physical education', *Physical Education Review*, 2 (2): 91–100.

Carr, D. (1997) 'Physical education and value diversity: a response to Andrew Reid', *European Physical Education Review*, 3 (2): 195–205.

Cooper, D. (ed.) (1986) *Education, Values and Mind*. London: Routledge and Kegan Paul.

Dearden, R.F. (1968) *The Philosophy of Primary Education*. London: Routledge and Kegan Paul.

Evans, J. and Davies, B. (1993) 'Equality, equity and physical education', in J. Evans (ed.), *Equality, Education and Physical Education*. London: Falmer Press. pp. 11–27.

Evans, J. and Penney, D. (2002) 'Introduction', in D. Penney (ed.) *Physical Education. Contemporary Issues and Future Directions*. London: Routledge. pp. 3–13.

Kirk, D. (2002) 'Junior sport as a moral practice, *Journal of Teaching in Physical Education*, 21: 402–8.

Hirst, P.H. and Peters, R.S. (1970) *The Logic of Education*. London: Routledge and Kegan Paul.

Hogenova, M. (2002) 'Legality and legitimacy in sport', *European Journal of Sport Science*, 2 (1): 1–6. *http://www.humankinetics.com/EJSS/viewarticle.cfm?aid=120*   *http://www.humankinetics.com/EJSS/viewarticle.cfm?aid=120*

Kleinig, J. (1983) *Philosophical Issues in Education*. Sydney: Croom Helm.

Lehman, C. (1982) 'Can cheaters play the game?', *Journal of Philosophy of Sport*, 8: 41–6.

McIntyre, A. (1985) *After Virtue. A Study in Moral Theory*. London: Duckworth.

McNamee, M.J. (1988) 'Health-related fitness and physical education', *British Journal of Physical Education*, 19 (2): 83–4.

McNamee, M.J. (1992) 'Physical education and the development of personhood', *Physical Education Review*, 15 (1): 13–28.

McNamee, M.J. (1994) 'Valuing leisure practices: towards a theoretical framework', *Leisure Studies*, 13 (1): 288–309.

McNamee, M.J. (1995) 'Sporting practices, institutions, and virtues: a critique and a restatement', *Journal of Philosophy of Sport*, XXII: 61–82.

McNamee, M.J. (1998a) 'Contractualism and methodological individualism and communitarianism: situating understandings of moral trust', *Sport, Education and Society*, 3 (3): 161–79.

McNamee, M.J. (1998b) 'Education, philosophy and physical education: analysis, epistemology and axiology', *European Physical Education Review*, 4 (1): 75–91.

Meakin, D.C. (1982) 'Moral values and physical education', *Physical Education Review*, 5 (1): 62–82.

Meakin, D.C. (1990) 'How physical education can contribute to personal and social education', *Physical Education Review*, 13 (2): 108–119.

Morgan, W.P. (1987) 'Formalism and the logical incompatibility thesis', *Journal of Philosophy of Sport*, 14: 1–20.

Nozick, R. (1974) *Anarchy, State and Utopia*. Oxford: Blackwell.

Parry, S.J. (1988) 'Physical education, justification and the national curriculum', 11 (2): 106–18.

Parry, S.J. (1998) 'Physical education as Olympic education', *European Physical Education Review*, 4 (2): 153–167.

Peters, R.S. (1966) *Ethics and Education*. London: Allen and Unwin.

Plato (1974) *The Republic*, 2nd edn. (trans.) D. Lee. London; Penguin, pp. 102–4.

Rawls, (1972) *A Theory of Justice*. Oxford: Oxford University Press.

Reid, A. (1996a) 'The concept of physical education in current curriculum and assessment policy in Scotland', *European Physical Education Review*, 2 (1): 7–18.

Reid, A. (1996b) 'Knowledge, practice and theory in physical education', *European Physical Education Review*, 2 (2): 94–104.

Reid, A. (1997) 'Value pluralism and physical education', *European Physical Education Review*, 3 (1): 6–20.

Siedentop. D. (1986) *Sport Education*. Champaign, IL: Human Kinetics.

Siedentop. D. (2002) 'Content knowledge for Physical Education', *Journal of Teaching in Physical Education*, 21 (4): 409–18.

Slote, M. (1989) *Goods and Virtues*. Oxford: Clarendon Press.

Standish, P. (1998) 'In the zone: Heidegger and sport', in M.J. McNamee and S.J. Parry (eds) *Ethics and Sport*. London: Routledge. pp. 256–69.

Strawson, P.F. (1959) *Individuals*. London: Methuen.

Thompson, K. (1983) 'The justification of physical education', *Momentum*, 2 (2): 19–23.

White, J.P. (1990) *Education and the Good Life*. London: Kogan Page.

Whitehead, M. (1990) 'Meaningful existence, embodiment and physical education', *Journal of Philosophy of Education*, 24(1): 3–13.

Wollheim, R. (1993) *The Mind and its Depths*. London: Harvard University Press.

2 | Policy, Power and Politics in Physical Education

Dawn Penney and John Evans

Policies are everywhere and always, it seems, likely to change. Policies new and old are very much a part of our daily lives and everyday thinking. Sometimes we are all too aware of their influence, at other times not. Yet, like it or not, policy frames and forms the fabric of our personal and professional lives. The time that the school bell rings and the children arrive, the length of the school day, the number of pupils in the classroom, their sex and social class, the quantity and quality of the resources (human and physical) available for teaching, the content of the curriculum, even the colour of the paint on the sports hall walls – all may be the products of policy; of someone's (an individual's, institution's, local or central government's) authoritative decision about how 'things' should be. Those decisions are never arbitrary nor neutral. Policy decisions are always intentioned and inevitably involve an 'allocation of values' (Easton, 1953; Prunty, 1985). Consequently they are often difficult and emotive processes, involving struggles and contests over interests, goals and aspirations, over whose voices should be permitted 'a hearing' and what status will be accorded to them at various points in the policy process.

The taken-for-granted routines of physical education (PE) may be the residue of recent or more distant policy processes; of struggles and contests that are no longer apparent amid the hubris of the day; that have become a forgotten blur as attention has shifted to ways of working with and within the implications, boundaries, possibilities and constraints of policy. Where one stands, or is positioned in the policy process, will determine one's experience and interpretation of policy. Variously, we will be more or less aware that policies (in their many forms) will reflect prevailing expediencies – social, political, economic and ideological – arising either within particular institutions, or locally, nationally, perhaps even internationally. Thus, any analysis of policy in PE must consider not only how past policy on education has helped frame and form contemporary PE but also how institutional, local, national and global circumstances either alone or together, intersect in this process. If we are to gain an understanding of why we do what we do in the way of teaching, learning, curriculum development, and much else, in contexts of PE, we need to look beyond the immediate and the obvious in the decision-making process.

We write this chapter as sociologists of education and PE rather than, for example, political economists or political scientists – who have had rather more to say about issues of government, administration, politics, policy and *sport* than researchers in PE (see Houlihan, 2003). However, in our view, recent developments in policy research in the sociology of education go beyond conventional analysis to offer potentially innovative ways of approaching policy, that may be especially helpful if we have interests in better understanding how power and p/Politics are expressed in the practices and rituals of PE and furthermore, how elements of those practices and rituals can be effectively challenged. Our analysis is, however, underscored by one of the main tenets of a political economy perspective, that, 'within capitalist societies, economic, political and cultural power is distributed unequally, since those societies are based upon quite fundamental inequities in the labour market involving the extraction of surplus value. Social class relations represent fundamental relations of exploitation and oppression within such societies' (Arnot, 2002: 127). These relations may be compounded by gender, ethnicity, disability, age and sexuality. How PE policy and practice are implicated in processes such as these is, therefore, prominent among our concerns.

Our view – like that of others who write within the sociology of education from the standpoint of 'education policy sociology' – is not, then, a view of the democratic process as one in which policy is produced through mutual agreement by 'the great and the good', while 'authority to produce it is invested in elected representatives, (often supported by technical expertise), consigning all else and all others to the domains of [simplistic, uncontested] implementation and consumption' (Gale, 2003: 51). As we have emphasised previously, we view policy as a complex, ongoing, always contested process, in which there are struggles over values, interests and definitions, reflecting fundamental conceptions of how society and within it, individuals, schools, knowledge are and ought to be (Evans et al., 1993; Penney and Evans, 1999). In contexts of unequal distributions of power and the differential position of various individuals in the policy process, consensus may not always be deemed desirable, or necessarily possible to achieve. Our concern is therefore with both 'the *who* and the *how*' (Gale, 2003) of policy – and their symbiosis. Who is involved and allowed to be involved, in what capacities and at what times, how individuals, groups or associations are included in various contexts as policy makers, whose voices, interests and values are permitted a hearing (a tokenistic hearing, a 'serious' hearing and/or an 'authoritative' hearing).

RETHINKING POLICY

How we conceptualise policy will depend on the analytical framework from which it is perceived, and will also have a bearing on how it is approached in research terms (see Halpin and Troyna, 1994; Ozga, 2000; Penney, 1997). Over the last two decades, in the UK and elsewhere, a plethora of education policy emerging from central governments (some of it specifically relating to PE teaching and teacher education for PE) has provided unprecedented stimuli for the development of research concerned with education policy. The

Education Reform Act (ERA) of 1988 was described by Troyna (1994: 2) as providing 'the most important shot in the arm to the study of education policy in Britain'. Since the ERA, development of policy-focused research has continued apace, its theoretical and empirical orientations generating much debate and some critical scrutiny (see, for example, Grace, 1984; Henry, 1993; Lingard, 1993; Whitty, 1997).

What we now refer to as 'education policy sociology' attempted to address a two-fold neglect in the study of politics and policy in education (Raab,1994). First, a failure on the part of 'political science' and 'policy studies' to produce a body of research specifically relating to education, and second, educational researchers' failure prior to the 1990s to focus on policy matters. In the UK, Stephen Ball (1990) and his colleagues (Bowe et al., 1992; Gervitz et al., 1995) did much to counter the latter tendency and challenge the authority of the traditional 'managerial' and 'bureaucratic' perspectives on policy that had historically dominated research concerned with social and educational administration and organisation (see Ham and Hill, 1984). At the heart of the renewed debate were the matters of how we think about 'policy' and 'practice' and their inter-relationship. Traditionally, the image has been of a firm distinction between two arenas, two sets of individuals, engaged in separate and fundamentally different activities, and related sequentially and hierarchically to one another. From this perspective agencies and individuals associated with central government are viewed as having an essentially direct and determining influence over what happens in schools. Teachers are portrayed as a final link in a chain of decision making. They are positioned in a passive role, to act on the whims of powerful others outside schools. Meanwhile pupils remain out of view, rarely deemed worthy of comment in relation to the 'how' or 'who' of policy. The image portrayed is of a transmission of policy to those whose task it is to translate it, in an essentially direct manner, into practice.

Even with the expanding body of work emerging under the auspices of education policy sociology, research in education and PE has still rarely mounted much in the way of a convincing challenge to these established images and understandings of policy. A number of studies have addressed the role and authority of central governments, or other agencies and agents of the state, in the production of policy statements, texts and documents (see, for example, Dudley and Vidovich, 1995; Fletcher, 1984; Graham with Tytler, 1993; Kirk, 1992). These studies have revealed the particular interests and values inherent in the agendas of decision makers outside schools. In parallel, other studies have directed attention to policy/curriculum development as it materialises in schools (see for example Hoyle, 1986; Sabatier, 1993; Sparkes, 1988). These have provided a so called 'bottom-up' view of the policy–practice relationship, emphasising the active role of the practitioner in policy and curriculum change, and the degree to which policies in education are influenced and shaped by what happens in schools. Thus, the focus has tended to be primarily (if not exclusively) on *either* the 'macro' *or* the 'micro' and concerned with the actions of different organisations, institutions and individuals. Both bodies of work have made important contributions to understandings of policy. Yet by their selective focus, they have left the defining distinction between policy and practice and between policy makers and practitioners essentially unchallenged. The artificial and inaccurate temporal and spatial boundaries between 'making' and 'implementation', 'makers' and 'implementors' have remained intact. Established conceptualisations of policy and practice have effectively been reaffirmed. Reflecting upon the contribution of 'implementation studies' to policy analysis, Ham and Hill (1984: 95) made the point that:

> Its very strength in stressing the importance of the implementation process as distinguishable from the policy-making process, and deserving of study in its own right, has tended to lead to the weakness of overemphasising the distinctiveness of the two processes. There has been a tendency to treat policies as clear-cut, uncontroversial entities, whose implementation can be quite separately studied.

It was against this backdrop that 'new' and still relatively 'experimental' work (Raab, 1994) in education policy sociology emerged, seeking to present a more complex and inherently more 'realistic' view of policy. The challenge has been to engage with the ways in which policy is socially constructed, mediated and 'flows' within and between agencies, individuals, sites and fields of practice in complex social systems. Analyses have attempted to bridge the 'gap' between macro and micro analyses by presenting and investigating policy 'as process and not merely substance' (Raab, 1994: 24). Policy is then viewed as dynamic, ongoing and always subject to contestation and adaptation across and within the many sites that we might variously associate with policy 'making' and 'implementation'. It is no longer static or fixed in either temporal or spatial terms. It is 'struggled over, not delivered, in tablets of stone, to a grateful or quiescent population' (Ozga, 2000: 1). Policy is *continually* made and remade at and 'between' sites throughout the process – although with an important caveat. Transformations of policy are also constrained; always framed to a greater or lesser degree (and directly and indirectly) by the actions of others.

The attention of analysts has thus shifted, to a focus on connections rather than distinctions between policy and practice (making and implementation; makers and implementors). Notions of policy being all too simplistically transmitted have been replaced by the acknowledgment that always and inevitably transmission involves at least some element of transformation. There has been a clear response to concerns that the conceptual isolation of policy making from implementation obfuscates ongoing creativity, and the complexity and number of influences and individuals that are variously involved with policy.

CAN WE COPE WITH COMPLEXITY?

Once we view policy from this new perspective, we have to then be prepared to take up the empirical and conceptual challenges that it presents – for us to explore and be able to represent the relationships both within and between multiple sites and/or levels ('macro', 'meso' and 'micro' (Hargreaves, 1986)) of decision making and action in the process. It demands that we engage with not just two, but many arenas, organisations and individuals that we may regard as centrally or peripherally involved at various points in the progressive policy development-enactment process. Furthermore, the new perspective necessitates that we also extend our view, inquiry and analysis to arenas that we may actually think of as outside of the policy network with which we are concerned. In 1989, Reynolds was undoubtedly justified in reflecting somewhat critically on the tendency for research concerned with practice to be confining its attention to classrooms, rather than extending its view to 'the schools, the LEAs[1] or other educational sectors that are most involved in framing policy changes' (Reynolds, 1989: 191). However, education policy researchers now face challenges that are of a different order and on a grander scale. In short, the terrain on which education policy is developed and played out is not a fixed one. Throughout the 1990s and into the twenty-first century there have been immense changes in the boundaries and composition of policy arenas and the positioning of various organisations and agencies within them. Some previously central features/facets of the policy terrain have visibly shifted to the margins – or disappeared from view. The field has a different look. Boundaries have been extended to embrace some organisations and interests more fully. Other boundaries have been contracted, thereby marginalising or excluding particular organisa-tions and the interests that they represent. Some of these changes have very openly been by (policy) design. Others have seemed more incidental or opportunist in nature. Those involved in teaching, teacher education and/or research in PE, in England and elsewhere in recent years, will have little difficulty relating to these dynamics. The effects of the changes are reflected in the limited degree to which teachers and teacher educators now feel able to influence the curriculum and teaching of PE in schools.

Looking at education as a whole, similar changes in policy dynamics can be identified. Many recent initiatives (and not only in England) have been concerned explicitly with extending the sector, with talk of new learning 'networks', 'communities', more 'partnership' activities, more active involvement of 'other' organisations and individuals in shaping the form and focus of education practices. Teaching and learning activities are themselves being extended or relocated to workplace and community contexts. These trends can be expected to continue as further emphasis is placed upon the creation of opportunities for elements of examination and certified courses of study to be undertaken in a work placement or community volunteer context (see Department for Education and Skills (DfES), 2003a, 2003b). Both teachers and learners are being encouraged to move more between and across different contexts in an endeavour to enhance the coherency, relevance and potentially, appeal of teaching/learning experiences. For example, the 'Playing for Success' initiative has used English premier league soccer clubs and subsequently other high profile sports clubs as venues for literacy and numeracy learning support directed particularly towards boys deemed in educational terms, as 'at risk' of underachievement in and/or disengagement from their schooling (see DfES, 2003a and *http://www.dfes.gov.uk/playingforsuccess/*).

In relation to PE in England, we might reflect upon the extent to which individuals and organisations that may once have been regarded as outside an education policy network (particularly sport/sport development organisations) are now repositioned not merely within that network, but central to it. The interaction between policies and policy arenas (that previously we were perhaps aware of, but had not fully embraced in either our conceptualisations or empirical studies) has progressively been made more explicit. The overlap between PE and *sport* policy development is no longer incidental and nor are those in authority content for it to now be left to chance. Rather, overlap is intended to be an integral, prioritised component of the policy process, at all its stages/phases (see for example, Department for Culture, Media and Sport (DCMS), 2000, 2001). At a central government level this has been reflected in various ways. There have been an increasing number of joint policy statements/publications issued by departments respectively responsible for education, sport and health. Cross or inter-departmental/agency working groups have become commonplace and the expectation of dual and/or collaborative activities, roles and responsibilities written into remits for schools and teachers. The publication of *A Sporting Future for All. The Government's Plan for Sport* (DCMS, 2001) arose to a large degree (and of necessity) from multiagency consultation. Subsequently, a cross-site, multi-agency policy commitment has been evident in efforts directed towards implementation of the plan, with for example, the DCMS and DfES co-authoring the publication *A Sporting Future for All. The Role of Further and Higher Education in Delivering the Government's Plan for Sport* (DCMS/DfES, 2001). The same partnership has more recently issued *Learning Through PE and Sport. A Guide to the Physical Education, School Sport and Club Links Strategy* (DfES/DCMS, 2003), a publication that is clearly intended to give a concise and overtly collaborative 'steer' to the development of PE and sport in schools and junior clubs in England.

Meanwhile, at a local and institutional level, 'partnership based' work and the re-negotiation of roles and responsibilities within this, is similarly very much the order of the day. These expectations have been most vividly expressed (and at the same time advanced) by the Specialist Sports College and School Sport Coordinator initiatives.[2] Together these initiatives have changed the PE-sport policy terrain in England on an arguably unprecedented scale. Those schools designated as Specialist Sports Colleges have assumed a position of centrality and influence in (redefined) local networks of schools and community organisations, with other organisations obliged to take up a new position within those networks, or risk missing out on a share of the major investments destined for them.

The current (physical) education policy context is, therefore, increasingly both more complex and extensive in relation to the sites, organisations and interactions that it accommodates. It is a context that renders a conceptualisation of the policy process as a 'chain image' (Hill, 1980) inherently problematic. A chain implies that the policy process is always and inevitably sequential and characterised by linear progression forward. With the ever-increasing scope and complexity of policy contexts comes a need to revisit the adequacy and appropriateness of conceptualisation of 'policy-as-a-process'. We might well question whether the term 'process' is itself now problematic. Does it generate an artificial sense of neatness, order, momentum and rationality, where no such characteristics are evident or easily observed?

Following Stephen Ball and his colleagues (Ball, 1990; Bowe et al., 1992) we have previously spoken of the policy process as being multi-staged, involving the production of many texts (not the transmission of a single fixed text), each of which is always a hybrid of those from which it is derived. The changes may be very obvious and strategic or in contrast, subtle and sometimes largely subconscious. One of the points that we have stressed is that policy analyses need to consider texts in a broad and holistic manner. Highly formalised written or spoken texts are by no means the only texts with which we should be concerned. Rather, we need to acknowledge and incorporate into our analyses understandings that texts also take on (modified) mental and corporeal forms. A formal written document is read and in that process reformed in our minds. We produce our own abbreviated and/or expanded version (what we remember, have consciously 'noted' and/or developed thoughts 'around'), interpreting and applying content in a particular way, decontextualising and then recontextualising content, meaning and values. This hybrid text is then our reference point for further communicating or enacting policy, with further textual 'slippage' (Bowe et al., 1992) destined to occur.

In addition we have emphasised that the interpretation and modification (reduction and/or expansion) of texts always occurs in and in relation to specific contexts. There is an ever-present and unavoidable interplay between texts and contexts (social, cultural, economic, institutional, historical). Texts are not only shaped by contexts; they simultaneously shape (reproduce and/or change) those contexts. This constant interplay means that 'slippage' is unlikely to follow clear patterns. Various contextual issues will become influential at particular sites and times. Consequently 'slippage' will appear erratic and diverse, and is also likely to highlight two points in relation to policy. First, that the boundaries to the policy process are always fluid. The development and 'implementation' of a policy may be influenced (deflected, diverted, accelerated, halted) by seemingly unrelated policies or issues. It may be financial considerations that provide the linkage, since 'Even policies with [apparently] little direct impact upon each other will be 'rivals' for scarce resources' (Hill, 1980: 106). In other instances, a situation may develop in which 'surrounding' policies retain a dominant influence upon the ways in which new policies are interpreted and responses formulated. For example, amid new policy initiatives for schools, performance leagues tables remain an ongoing (and sometimes obstructive) policy reference point (see Adnett and Davies, 2003). In part this reflects the second point: that polices cannot be divorced from developments that have preceded them. In education policy we are never starting with a blank page. As Hill (1980: 11) emphasised: 'There is a cumulative process to be analysed in which policies create needs for other policies, opportunities for other policies, and new social situations for further political responses.' Policies are 'to a considerable extent products of other policies' (1980: 11). In our analysis of the development of and revisions to the National Curriculum for Physical Education (NCPE) in England through the 1990s we pointed to powerful ways in which this 'cumulative' characteristic was evident and influential. The initial framework for the curriculum of PE accorded identified 'areas of activity' (for example, games, gymnastics, swimming) a central organisational position, and this remained 'the framework' for all subsequent proposals and thinking in the development of a NCPE.

So, having emphasised the fluidity of the process, but added this cautionary note about the extent and nature of that fluidity, we can now go on to consider how, when and where 'slippage' occurs. In parallel, we will seek to gain some purchase on what determines the nature and extent of policy slippage.

DISCOURSE GETS TO THE DETAIL

Policy texts are never neutral or socially disinterested. Rather, they include and privilege certain interests and ideologies, while subordinating or excluding others. It is inevitable and unavoidable. All interests cannot be present to the same degree. Producing any text thus involves both selection and compromise. Consider, for example, the time and attention that is currently being directed towards matters of health and physical activity in relation to the curriculum of PE. Why is this so? What are the implications for what teachers teach and pupils experience as 'PE'? How is the development of a 'health-focused' PE informed and influenced by the disciplines that underscore the training of PE teachers? How are such developments related to the interests of the multi-million pound health and leisure industries that operate outside schools? Whose interests will any of the curricula and/or pedagogical changes serve? (Evans et al., 2004). How will 'planned for' changes be deflected and/or compromised by other dominant interests – specifically in the production of sport performance in and via PE? Recent comments from Sue Campbell, Chief Executive of the Youth Sport Trust, who has progressively succeeded in positioning herself firmly 'in the midst' of the PE and school sport policy process at a national level in the UK[3], are interesting in this regard. Her reflections on the 'failing' of British athletes at the world athletics championships in France and the state of 'chaos' in the organisation and administration of sport in Britain provide a backdrop for the comment that 'We're putting a good deal of money into sport. You wouldn't put money into a business for an ever lower return . . . we've got to recognise that if we want government investment, we've got to deliver' (Campbell; cited in Mott, 2003).

A longstanding issue thus returns to the fore: What is PE for? What is PE in schools expected and/or assumed to be able to 'deliver'? After the World Athletics Championships, the Rugby World Cup and in the run up to the Athens Olympics, attention may well be firmly upon the elite sport arena. But soon enough this will be accompanied by talk of a crisis of child obesity and/or physical inactivity, and/or youth crime, drug use and social exclusion. We may smile wryly at the flippancy here, but a glance at the many policy statements that already abound relating to PE and school sport in schools confirms the underpinning reality that this is an openly contested and extremely 'crowded' (Houlihan, 2000) policy arena.

The concept of discourse is a key tool in any exploration and understanding of the questions that we have posed in relation to the interests being served or equally, overlooked in and by PE. It is a concept that is now widely, but often inconsistently (see Luke, 1995), used in sociological and educational research and that is central to our ongoing endeavours to explore the ways in which values and interests are encoded in contemporary PE policies (see also Evans et al., 2004). It helps us to investigate not only the origins of policies in broader social formations (for example, in capitalism and the formations of social class and patriarchy (see Apple, 1993)) but also the particular form that a policy text may take at specific points in time and different sites in the policy process. It enables us to investigate the precise nature of 'slippage' throughout the process and explore the moments of contestation and struggle, reinforcement and rejection, stability and change. What remains and is actively retained, what disappears from view or is reconfigured as hybrid texts are produced by various individuals, with differing degrees of authority and influence in relation to subsequent readings. All of this relates to discourse. Thus discourse enables us to interrogate the values and interests inherent in texts, those that texts effectively omit or marginalise, and simultaneously engages us with the 'why' of the inclusions and exclusions.

Getting to grips with what discourse 'is', is no easy task. Of central concern in theories of discourse are 'language and meaning', matters that 'have often been taken for granted in policy analysis in the past' (Taylor, 1997: 25). Our use of the term discourse is influenced by poststructural social theory and in particular by the analyses of contemporary culture by Michael Foucault (1972, 1977, 1980). He emphasises the

> *constructing* character of discourse, that is how, both in broader social formations (i.e., epistemes) and in local sites and uses discourse actually defines, constructs and positions human subjects. According to Foucault (1972, p.49) discourses 'systemically form the objects about which they speak', shaping grids and hierarchies for the institutional categorisation and treatment of people. (Luke, 1995: 8; emphasis added)

In this view discourse is not only about what is said, but also what is *not* said. It constructs certain possibilities for thought and expression in and via texts – and the absent as well as the present is significant in this regard: 'Texts include traces of words and concepts not [visibly] present, and that which is not present makes possible that which is present' (Cherryholms, 1988; cited in Sparkes, 1992: 273). Discourses order and combine words in particular ways and exclude or displace other combinations (Ball, 1990). In so doing, they promote certain interests while displacing others. It is important to keep in mind that texts will always contain multiple discourses. The relative visibility of different discourses will vary, as will the precise combinations and inter-relationships. It is these characteristics that give any single text its particular form and dominant meaning in the particular context of reading. This latter comment reflects that the concept of discourse allows us to explore the content of texts but also and importantly, the discursive fields within which they arise and are understood, transmitted and transformed. Thus we are prompted to consider how discourses dominant in educational and political arenas outside schools, for example, of competitive individualism or cultural restoration (Penney and Evans, 1999) or 'obesity and ill-health' (see Evans et al., 2004), shape interpretations of and responses (on the part of teachers and pupils) to PE texts. We thereby see evidence of not only local or national, but also global social, economic and ideological influences.

WHO HAS WHAT SAY IN POLICY MATTERS?

The 'arrangements for policy' (Hill, 1980) (development and implementation) are an integral part of policies, critical in creating particular conditions that shape their development and subsequent expression. We have illustrated this in the way in which particular arrangements for policy established in and by the ERA were critical in shaping the development and content of the National Curriculum (and NCPE specifically) in England and Wales (Evans and Penney, 1995; Penney and Evans, 1999). In so doing, we also confronted the matter of inequality in policy and observed the way in which a conceptualisation of the process as one of sequential, essentially even flow through a series of linkages is rendered problematic if not redundant. In reality, 'varying responsibilities and degrees of autonomy are involved, and individuals in the chain may be bypassed' (Hill, 1980: 83). Furthermore, as indicated above, with increasingly complex policy networks we should no longer be thinking in strictly linear terms.

In our analysis of contemporary PE policy in England and elsewhere we have also repeatedly emphasised that discourses are 'about what can be said, and thought, but also about *"who can speak where, when and with what authority"*' (Ball, 1990: 17; emphasis added). Formal arrangements for policy have a critical influence in relation to these matters. At one level opportunities for and constraints upon involvement are explicitly mapped out by particular arrangements. For example, certain individuals will enjoy the 'privilege' of appointment to policy consultation or working groups. But the appointment will undoubtedly be a bounded one, with the remit and timescale for comment (and thus the 'scope for influence') likely to be predetermined and all too often very clearly restrictive. Certainly, there is a need to recognise that we cannot merely take arrangements at 'face value'. Notable constraints upon 'involvement' are often subtly embedded in particular policy arrangements – but so too are opportunities for involvement to be extended, for positions/positioning in the policy process to be resisted and/or renegotiated. Purdon's (2003) analysis of consultation processes associated with the development of a national framework of continuing professional development for teachers in Scotland provides some illustration of notions of (hidden) control and constraint. Some of the characteristics that Purdon highlights may well mirror those experienced in other policy contexts. For example, she reports a delayed and 'fairly low-key' launch of website based consultation documents (2003: 426). We might smile at the consequential low response, and Purdon's comment that 'Given that there are approximately 75,000 registered teachers, 3,000 schools, 32 local authorities, and six teacher education institutions in Scotland, not to mention numerous education-related organisations and bodies, 58 responses would not seem to be a particularly large response to a national consultation exercise' (2003: 426). Furthermore, as Purdon also notes, there are aspects of policy arrangements into which we rarely have any insight – for example, of how responses from different origins are treated, how different types of response are viewed, and whether, therefore, some sources and/or categories are accorded a higher status in the policy process than others.

None of the arrangements for policy can be deemed neutral. Control of the 'flow of information' – out from the centre and back towards it – is very significant in relation to policy as a process. But the control of the flow is never total. Individuals work within but also around arrangements for policy. Meetings and conversations (formal and informal, in person and electronic) may provide contexts in which new issues may be raised and the attention of those more influential than oneself drawn to matters of personal interest in relation to policy. Just as there is slippage in policy content, so there may also be slippage in relations. 'Given' roles and remits will be variously accepted or resisted, adapted and exploited. Also (and of particular note in relation to our previous emphasis of a changing policy terrain), individuals may actively seek out new roles and/or positions in an endeavour to reposition themselves more centrally in the process (Penney, 2003).

THE BALANCING ACT: SLIPPAGE AND STABILITY

Amid the emphasis of complexity, fluidity and scope for slippage, there remains, nevertheless, a need to note continuity – and furthermore, to be able to articulate what underpins and maintains it; meaning that for all the apparent policy activity, there is also stability and order in education and PE. While any analysis of policy must recognise the potential for change, it also has to remain sensitive to the continuities that run through the process, and recognise that aspects of policies may remain unchanged and/or unchallenged and/or unchallengeable. In PE we cannot escape the fact that in important respects, people have been saying very similar things for a very long time – most obviously about the need for fundamental change in the curriculum of PE (Corbin, 2002; Crum, 1983; Locke, 1992; Penney and Chandler, 2000). Furthermore, we can reflect that despite the introduction of a NCPE in England and Wales and all the talk of change and reform, key inequities have gone unchanged and unchallenged in education and PE. It remains the case that the scope and quality of a pupil's and teacher's experience of PE will be variously influenced by a host of material constraints that serve to deflect or compromise concerns for individual learning needs and interests. Ironically, this was an anticipated outcome of the implementation of the NCPE. Embedded in many policy developments are expectations that some things will (and are supposed to) remain the same. The development of the NCPE was no exception. Throughout this development it was acknowledged that any recommendations would have to accommodate the differential resourcing of PE across schools in England, and reaffirm existing, politically and publicly recognisable versions of PE curricula (see Evans and Penney, 1995; Penney and Chandler, 2000; Penney and Evans, 1999). Thus, there was a strong reaffirmation throughout the policy process of the 'taken for granted' structure and 'core content' of the PE curriculum and a relative absence of any significant shift in thinking about PE, its curriculum, teaching, learning and social significance. This led us to restrain our talk of 'flexibility' and 'scope for slippage' in the policy process and instead emphasise the presence of continuity, constraint and control (Penney and Evans, 1997).

Recognising both the changes and continuities in the policy process demands that we again take a closer look at the nature of texts, what is involved in their production and transmission, and who has the 'authority' and 'power' to determine agendas and to decide what is to count as worthwhile knowledge. In seeking a better and perhaps more sophisticated understanding of policy we have suggested that we might usefully employ the concept of *frame*, drawn from the work of Bernstein (1990, 1996) and Lundgren (1977). Both Bernstein and Lundgren attempted to articulate the conceptual link 'between teaching and levels above teaching' (Lundgren, 1977: 82), to identify factors that limited teachers (and pupils)' freedom to develop different pedagogies, and register the strength of constraints and/or possibilities in teaching and curriculum development. It is a concept that helps us explore 'who controls what' in pedagogical and policy processes and specifically, articulate the relational balance between 'freedom' and 'control' experienced by individuals and agencies at various policy sites – the potential for, but also boundaries to, the slippage that it is possible to pursue and achieve. It seeks to capture the influence of 'discourses surrounding discourses' (Apple, 1982) in the policy process and the complex ways in which 'old', extant and well established frames of thought and action become embedded (consciously or not) in contemporary thinking.

'Frame' thus seeks to capture the ways in which the actions of individuals at various policy sites are restricted and to a degree directed by a complex range of factors, but in particular, by preceding events in the policy process. For example, in the development of the NCPE in England and Wales we observed teachers being permitted little say in the shaping of a curriculum that they would be charged to 'deliver'. Many of the decisions made at the early tages of the policy process by government ministers or their appointed agents retained a critical influence throughout the process, and set limits to what teachers could do and think in PE (see Evans and Penney, 1995; Penney and Evans, 1999). The process can thus be seen to involve the creation and progressive reinforcement of frames or boundaries within which slippage is possible. In a subtle but powerful way certain continuities are maintained. Focus remains on some issues and is kept away from others that are deemed and positioned beyond the boundaries of legitimate debate. Thus, we have pointed to the significance of *discursive frames* in the policy process, but also located these in dynamic relation with *political*, *ideological* and *economic* frames (Penney, 1994; Penney and Evans, 1999).

WHERE AND WHAT IS 'POWER' IN THIS POLICY GAME?

Talk of 'power' in relation to policy returns us to questions of who is involved and has what say in the construction of education policy and defining its agendas; of what values are being pursued and in whose interests; of what underpins the dominance of particular voices and discourses. What constitutes power in these terms? Is it the ability to 'be heard', to negotiate a position via which to achieve that and thereby bring particular discourses into play, and/or to achieve their acceptance? How and why does one (an individual, group or association) succeed or fail in such endeavours?

The preceding discussion has highlighted certain characteristics of the policy process. We have emphasised the dynamic interactions between different (and often seemingly unrelated) policies, and the involvement of many sites and individuals in determining how policies issued by central government are ultimately reflected in the practices of schools, teachers and more particularly, the curriculum of PE. Yet despite our commitment to deconstruct the divide between policy 'making' and 'implementation' ('makers' and 'implementors') and to emphasise the 'creative' dimension at play throughout the policy process, we remain very aware that individuals are not equally equipped with the 'resources' of knowledge, authority and status, to enter into and be active within these processes. At one level the multifaceted aspects of frame (discursive, political, economic) enable us to pursue the origins and distribution of power and specifically, the scope for different sites and individuals (locally, nationally, internationally) to define policy content and the mechanisms of its 'production'. At another level we are prompted to pursue the nature of power itself in relation to policy. Throughout our research and in various sites in the education system, we have seen that power was not only about discourse but also about one's position and status in the policy process (see also Ball, 1993). We have identified different dimensions to power; discursive, structural, economic, and also seen that power is 'not a commodity or an object', but rather, is *relational*. It is about a balance between freedom and constraint, agency and structure. At all sites and throughout the policy process it is apparent that 'there is agency and there is constraint in relation to policy – this is not a sum-zero game' (Ball, 1993: 13). In Ball's view, policy analysis 'requires not an understanding that is based on constraint **or** agency but on the changing relationships between constraint *and* agency' (1993: 13–14).

We contend that any consideration of this relationship must engage with structural issues and 'arrangements for policy' (Hill, 1980). Both matters have an important 'positioning' effect, in terms of authority and relationships in the policy process and serve to set limits upon the part that it is possible to play, the issues that it is possible to raise or pursue. But again, following Ball (1993) we add the caveat that, policies are not all encompassing or defining, they do not and cannot normally tell you what to do. Rather, 'they create circumstances in which the range of options available in deciding what to do are narrowed or changed. A response must still be put together, constructed in context, off-set against other expectations' (Ball, 1993: 12).

The value of the concept of frame lies in its engagement with fundamental issues of agency and structure, 'freedom' and constraint, context and opportunity. Frame thus prompts us to explore the relationships between (a government's ideologically driven) expectations and their bearing upon the range of options (for a PE curriculum) that can be discussed, recognised and enacted in schools. In the case of the NCPE in England these options were 'framed' discursively, in terms of their differential status and visibility, and in relation to the power relations that they then reproduced and endorsed via their enactment in schools. In pursuing these issues, the work of Bernstein (1971, 1990, 1996, 2000) has been particularly helpful and central to our analyses. It has helped us illustrate that differences in the use of and access to particular discourses (relating, for example, to PE and sport) acts to distinguish and privilege specialist contexts, defining them as bounded contexts in relation with others. 'Power' lies in the relation, in the boundary maintenance that underpins the definition of a specialist context. This conceptualisation enables us to critically explore the form, content and focus of attention in contemporary PE and to pose questions of what and whose interests are being served by the ongoing reproduction of established knowledge boundaries in PE and in education more broadly. It may be tempting and indeed, more comfortable to believe that we are each somehow detached from processes such as these, but we are not. We are all implicated in maintaining positions that reaffirm inequitable differences and hierarchy. Acknowledging this is essential when considering the complex interactions between policy, knowledge, social and cultural identity and pedagogical practices/experiences. Bernstein's powerful analysis of the dynamics between policy, identity and pedagogy directs us to pay attention not only to the ways in which pedagogical contexts shape teachers and children's identities and consciousness, but also that teachers are both framed by the discursive structures, requirements and resources of the curriculum and its delivery, and are themselves framing the learning opportunities made available to children.

In considering policy proposals relating to PE we thus need to be aware that the way in which the curriculum is 'classified' and 'framed' (Bernstein, 1971, 1990, 1996, 2000) will impact the developing identities of teachers, children and young people. It will shape not only what they learn to value as physical culture, but also how they, *vis-à-vis* their culture, class, sex or ability, are positioned in relation to physical culture and to the subject matter of PE. Teachers and pupils learn what elements of and whose physical cultures are valued in and by the curriculum; and whose skills and abilities are recognised and whose go unnoticed. Sometimes very subtly and at others very obviously, we see how the curriculum and teaching of PE relates to wider social values, structures and opportunities.

The influence and importance of policy in PE cannot, therefore, be understated. Furthermore, in the study of policy we have to remain committed to a position that conceptually and empirically explores the dynamic balance in the relative ability of individuals (groups and associations) to shape, as well as be shaped by policy (BERA, 2002). There are fundamental tensions in our analysis, between identifying opportunities or 'spaces' for innovation, while indicating that the direction and scope of change may be more or less strongly framed. Individuals may construct their own interpretations and responses to policy but not in contexts of their own making, or necessarily with awareness of what and who informs and has acted to frame their own and others' texts. Apple's attempt to conceptualise this relational balance of power is helpful here. He emphasises that 'the powerful are not *that* powerful. The politics of official knowledge are the politics of accords or compromises' (1993: 10). At the same time he reminds us that compromises are, 'not compromises between or among equals. Those in dominance almost always have more power to define what counts as a need or a problem and what an appropriate response to it should be' (1993: 10). For Taylor et al. (1997: 153) the relationship between policy and change 'is an ambiguous one, given that change occurs regardless of policy interventions, and that policy can result intentionally or otherwise in little or no change'. Amid what we have portrayed as a complex and ongoing set of transformations, there are key and often seemingly very dominant elements of reproduction. The processes are simultaneous and intertwined. Such is the dynamic of 'policy-as-a-process'.

CONCLUSION

This chapter is testimony to the fact that the complexities of policy are as difficult to describe as they are to adequately explain. However, we continue to emphasise the need to seek to engage with the complexities rather than avoid them. Change – specifically for greater equity and inclusion in education and PE – relies on that engagement. And these are not just issues for research, though to be sure there is agenda enough here for those interested in the study of policy and PE. We need further debate on how we might productively conceptualise policy in all its varied forms, and on how we can study it empirically in ways that do justice to its complexity. This is no small order. How are we to engage in research that traverses the multiple terrains over which policy 'moves', while embracing different sites and levels of action? We have barely scraped the surface of these issues in this chapter. Indeed, we need to broaden our agendas, to include issues of g/Government, administration and o/Organisation, topics and sites of socio-political activity that have rarely been mentioned in contemporary research in PE. These are not just research matters, they are central to our professional understandings of PE and of what it will take to provide forms of practice (a curriculum, pedagogy, forms of assessment) that are both more meaningful to more pupils and are educationally worthwhile.

ACKNOWLEDGEMENT

This chapter has drawn upon previous work published in Chapters 2 and 7 of *Politics, Policy and Practice in Physical Education*, by Dawn Penney and John Evans (1999).

NOTES

1 Local Education Authorities.
2 See DfES/DCMS (2003) *http://www.standards.dfes.gov.uk/specialistschools* and the Youth Sport Trust website *http://www.youthsporttrust.org/yst_schools.html* for details of these initiatives.
3 Sue Campbell became the Chief Executive of the newly created Youth Sport Trust in 1995 and subsequently was appointed as the 'non-political' Government Adviser of PE and sport in schools, working across multiple government departments (DfES and DCMS, in particular) in this role. She has now also taken up the role of chairman (sic) of 'UK Sport'.

REFERENCES

Adnett, N. and Davies, P. (2003) 'Schooling reforms in England: from quasi-markets to co-opetition?', *Journal of Education Policy*, 18 (4): 393–406.

Apple, M.W. (1982) *Education and Power*. London: Ark.

Apple, M.W. (1993) *Official Knowledge*. London: Routledge.

Arnot, M. (2002) *Reproducing Gender, Essays on Educational Theory and Feminist Politics*. London: RoutledgeFalmer.

Ball, S.J. (1990) *Politics and Policy Making in Education. Explorations in Policy Sociology*. London: Routledge.

Ball, S.J. (1993) 'What is policy? Texts, trajectories and toolboxes', *Discourse*, 13 (2): 10–17.

BERA (2002) *Educational Policy and Research Across the UK*, Report of a BERA colloquium held at the University of Edinburgh, 7–8 November 2002. Southwell: BERA, Commercial House, Notts, NG25 0EH.

Bowe, R. and Ball, S.J. with Gold, A. (1992) *Reforming Education and Changing Schools*. London: Routledge.

Bernstein, B. (1971) 'On the classification and framing of educational knowledge', in M.F.D. Young (ed.) *Knowledge and Control: New Directions in the Sociology of Education*. London: Collier Macmillan.

Bernstein, B. (1990) *The Structuring of Pedagogic Discourse. Volume IV Class, Codes and Control*. London: Routledge.

Bernstein, B. (1996) *Pedagogy, Symbolic Control and Identity. Theory, Research, Critique*. London: Taylor and Francis.

Bernstein, B. (2000) *Pedagogy, Symbolic Control and Identity. Theory, Research, Critique. Revised Edition*. Oxford: Rowman and Littlefield Publishers, Inc.

Corbin, C. (2002) 'Physical activity for everyone: what every physical educator should know about promoting lifelong physical activity', *Journal of Teaching in Physical Education*, 21: 128–44.

Crum, B.J. (1983) 'Conventional thought and practice in Physical Education: problems of teaching and implications for change', *QUEST*, 45: 336–356.

Department for Culture, Media and Sport (DCMS) (2000) *A Sporting Future for All*. London: DCMS.

Department for Culture, Media and Sport (DCMS) (2001) *A Sporting Future for All. The Government's Plan for Sport*. London: DCMS.

Department for Culture, Media and Sport (DCMS)/Department for Education and Skills (DfES) (2001) *A Sporting Future for All. The Role of Further and Higher Education in Delivering the Government's Plan for Sport*. London: DCMS.

Department for Education and Skills (DfES) (2003a) *A New Specialist System: Transforming Secondary Education*. London: DfES.

Department for Education and Skills (DfES) (2003b) *14–19: Opportunity and Excellence*. London: DfES.

Dudley, J. and Vidovich, L. (1995) *The Politics of Education Commonwealth Schools Policy 1973–95*. Melbourne, Australia: The Australian Council for Educational Research Ltd.

Easton, D. (1953) *The Political System*. New York: A.A Knopf.

Evans, J. Davies, B. and Wright, J. (2004) (eds) *Body Knowledge and Control. Studies in the Sociology of Physical Education and Health.* London: Routledge.

Evans, J. and Penney, D. (1995) 'The politics of pedagogy: making a national curriculum physical education', *Journal of Education Policy,* 10 (1): 27–44.

Evans, J. and Penney, D. and Bryant, A. (1993) 'Theorising implementation: a preliminary comment on power and process in policy research', *Physical Education Review,* 16 (1): 5–22.

Fletcher, S. (1984) *Women First: The Female Tradition in English Physical Education, 1880–1980.* London: Athlone.

Gale, T. (2003) 'Realising policy: the who and how of policy production', *Discourse,* 24 (1): 51–67.

Gerwitz, S. Ball, S. and Bowe, R. (1995) *Markets, Choice and Equity in Education,* Buckingham: Open University Press.

Grace, G. (1984) *Education and the City. Theory, History and Contemporary Practice.* London: Routledge.

Graham, D. with Tytler, D. (1993) *A Lesson for us all. The Making of the National Curriculum.* London: Routledge.

Halpin, D. and Troyna, B. (1994) (eds) *Researching Education Policy. Ethical and Methodological Issues.* London: The Falmer Press.

Henry, M. (1993) 'What is policy? A response to Stephen Ball', *Discourse,* 14 (1): 102–5.

Hill, M. (1980) *Understanding Social Policy.* Oxford: Basil Blackwell.

Ham, C. and Hill, M. (1984) *The Policy Process in the Modern Capitalist State.* London: Wheatsheaf Books.

Hargreaves, A. (1986) 'The macro–micro problem in the sociology of education', in M. Hammersley (ed.) *Controversies in Classroom Research.* Milton Keynes: Open University Press.

Houlihan, B. (2000) 'Sporting excellence, schools and sports development', *European Physical Education Review,* 6 (2): 171–94.

Houlihan, B. (2003) 'Politics, power, policy and sport', in B. Houlihan (2003) (ed.) *Sport and Society.* London: Sage.

Hoyle, E. (1986) *The Politics of School Management.* London: Hodder and Stoughton.

Kirk, D. (1992) *Defining Physical Education. The Social Construction of a School Subject in Postwar Britain.* London: The Falmer Press.

Lingard, R. (1993) 'The changing state of policy production in education: some Australian reflections on the state of policy sociology', *International Studies in the Sociology of Education,* 3 (1): 25–49.

Locke, F.L. (1992) 'Changing secondary school physical education', *QUEST,* 44: 361–72.

Luke, A. (1995) 'Text and discourse in education: an introduction to critical discourse analysis', in M. Apple (ed.) *Review of Research in Education.* Washington: American Educational Research Association.

Lundgren, U.P. (1977) *Model Analysis of Pedagogical Processes.* Stockholm Institute of Education: CWK Gleerup.

Mott, S. (2003) 'The state of British sport', *Daily Telegraph,* 13 September 2003, p. 1, 6–7.

Ozga, J. (2000) *Policy Research in Educational Settings. Contested Terrain.* Buckingham: Open University Press.

Penney, D. (1994) 'No change in a new ERA? The impact of the Education Reform Act (1988) on the provision of PE and sport in state schools'. Ph.D dissertation, University of Southampton.

Penney, D. (1997) 'Playing different games, speaking different languages: policy 'makers', practitioners and researchers in health and physical education', in J. Wright (ed.) *Researching in Health and Physical Education.* Faculty of Education. University of Wollongong, Australia.

Penney, D. (2003) 'Countering control: challenging conceptualisations of educational research', *Curriculum Perspectives,* 23 (1): 60–64.

Penney, D. and Chandler, T. (2000) Physical education: what future(s)? *Sport, Education and Society,* 5 (1): 71–87.

Penney, D. and Evans, J. (1997) 'Naming the game: discourse and domination in physical education and sport in England and Wales', *European Physical Education Review,* 3 (1): 21–32.

Penney, D. and Evans, J. (1999) *Politics, Policy and Practice in Physical Education.* London: FN Spon/Routledge.

Prunty, J. (1985) 'Signposts for a critical educational policy analysis', *Australian Journal of Education,* 29 (2): 133–40.

Purdon, A. (2003) 'A national framework of CPD: continuing professional development or continuing policy dominance?' *Journal of Education Policy,* 18 (4): 423–37.

Raab, C.D. (1994) 'Where we are now: reflections on the sociology of education policy', in D. Halpin and B. Troyna (eds) *Researching Education Policy. Ethical and Methodological Issues.* London: The Falmer Press.

Reynolds, D. (1989) 'Better schools? Present and potential policies about the goals, organisation and management of secondary schools', in A. Hargreaves and D. Reynolds (eds) *Education Policies: Controversies and Critiques.* London: The Falmer Press.

Sabatier, P.A. (1993) 'Top down and bottom up approaches to implementation research', in M. Hill (ed.) *The Policy Process: A Reader.* London: Harvester Wheatsheaf.

Sparkes, A.C. (1988) 'The micropolitics of innovation in the physical education curriculum', in J. Evans (ed.) *Teachers, Teaching and Control in Physical Education.* London: The Falmer Press.

Sparkes, A.C. (1992) 'Writing and the textual construction of realities: some challenges for alternative paradigms research in physical education' in A.C. Sparkes (ed.) *Research in Physical Education and Sport: Exploring Alternative Visions.* London: The Falmer Press.

Taylor, S. (1997) 'Critical policy analysis: exploring contexts, texts and consequences', *Discourse: Studies in the Cultural Politics of Education,* 18 (1): 23–35.

Taylor, S., Rizvi, F., Lingard, B. and Henry, M. (1997) *Educational Policy and the Politics of Change.* London: Routledge.

Troyna, B. (1994) 'Reforms, research and being reflexive about being reflective', in D. Halpin and B. Troyna (eds) *Researching Education Policy. Ethical and Methodological Issues.* London: The Falmer Press.

Whitty, G. (1997) 'Education, policy and the sociology of education', *International Studies in Sociology of Education,* 7 (2): 121–137.

3 Physical Education[1] in Schools in European Context: Charter Principles, Promises and Implementation Realities

Ken Hardman and Joe Marshall

In the decade of the 1970s, two intergovernmental inspired initiatives heralded internationally important developments in school physical education, which bore widespread political significance in standard setting policy principles: the Council of Europe's European Sports Charter, adopted by Ministers responsible for Sport at their first conference in 1975 under the title of *European Sport for All Charter* (Council of Europe, 1975); and the United Nations Educational, Scientific and Cultural Organisation's (UNESCO) *Charter for Physical Education and Sport* (UNESCO, 1978) adopted in 1978 at the 20th session of the General Conference in Paris. Less widely known perhaps, but nevertheless equally important in its political significance, was a precursor to these two Charters emanating from a voluntary sector national umbrella organisation in the then West Germany (Federal Republic of Germany): the German Sport Federation's Sports Charter (Deutscher Sportbund (DSB) 1966) was made public in 1967. The links between the DSB Charter and those of the Council of Europe and UNESCO are clearly demonstrated in biological, educational and social functions ascribed to physical education and sport in modern society and in the statements noting physical education's indispensability in individuals' upbringing and education and advocating the role of education authorities in ensuring inclusion of physical education lessons in the school curriculum in all types of school (DSB, 1966). Other links are seen in the Charter's call for multisectoral cooperative support in fostering and promoting an inclusive programme for all based on partnerships, the construction of facilities in schools and appropriately trained personnel to deliver curricular, extra-curricular and out-of-school physical education and sport-related activity as well as a decisive role for research in sport and physical education (DSB, 1966).

The original European Sport for All Charter first formulated by the Council of Europe in 1966 was officially launched on 20 March 1975, endorsed and officially adopted in September 1976. As its title suggests, the Charter was oriented towards sport, the definition of which excluded physical education at school. However, as the then Sports Council

(1977) pointed out, the intimate relationship between sport and physical education and the dependency of sport for all programmes on foundations laid down at school signify that they are commonly rooted hence, the policy principles of the ministerial Resolution (76) 41 of September 1976 are also relevant to physical education. Ministers adopted revisions to the European Sport for All Charter on 24 September 1992 (Recommendation No. R(92) 13 rev; number of articles increased from 8 to 12) and on 16 May 2001 (13 Articles additionally to include a *Revised Code of Sport Ethics*). Among its aims, the 1992 version of the Charter sought to ensure opportunity of physical education instruction for all young people. Like the DSB, the Council of Europe envisaged a multisector approach to provision for all with cooperation between governmental and non-governmental agencies including voluntary organisations and partnerships with commercial enterprises. This inclusion policy principle embraced availability of dual use facilities and programmes of activities, training of qualified teachers, opportunities to engage in sport after the period of compulsory education and providing sports ethics' education from primary school on as well as promoting research and disseminating findings at appropriate levels (Council of Europe, 2001).

The UNESCO 1978 Charter emanated from the first International Conference of Ministers and Senior Officials responsible for physical education and Sport (MINEPS I) in 1976, at which it was agreed to develop a declaration, recommendation or charter proclaiming the right for everyone to have access to physical education and sport programmes. In the event, the 1978 Charter declared that an essential condition in the exercising of 'human rights is that everyone should be free to develop and preserve his or her physical, intellectual and moral powers, and that access to physical education should consequently be assured and guaranteed for all human beings' (UNESCO, 1978). Like its Council of Europe counterpart, the UNESCO Charter addressed policy principle issues ranging from access to the role of public authorities and non-governmental bodies in encouraging educationally valued physical education and sport activities, provision of qualified and trained personnel, adequate facilities and equipment, design and delivery of physical education and sport programmes, a corporate multisector contribution to promotion and encouragement of physical education and sport and the role and functions of research, information and documentation dissemination.

The Council of Europe and UNESCO Charters set policy norms for provision and, indeed, over the years, both of these intergovernmental agencies have sought to establish themselves as catalysts for cooperation and renewal in which the development and promotion of standard-setting norms are key areas for action, which are expected to inform and filter into national legislation and practice. The use of standard-setting instruments can be seen as an example of the potential effectiveness to achieve equality of opportunities to access education. However, the very nature of the broad idealism expressed in the Charters means that it is easy for member states to simply pay 'lip-service' to the principles contained within them. In essence, the Council of Europe and UNESCO Charters comprise recommendations to national governmental and non-governmental agencies to take account of their respective inherent principles when elaborating physical education and sports-related policies. Specifically the Council of Europe (2001) called upon governments to 'take the steps necessary to apply the provisions of . . . [the] Charter . . .' and UNESCO (1978) urged 'governments . . . to put [its International Charter] into practice'. However, even as these Charters were calling for guaranteed access to physical education and sport in schools, reports were raising doubts surrounding the provision for, and implementation of, school physical education and these gathered momentum across all continental regions of the world as the century progressed.

In the 1980s attention was being drawn to concerns and problems arising in physical education in schools and its perceived low priority in education systems worldwide became increasingly apparent in the 1990s. In the USA in 1987, the *Journal of Physical Education Recreation and Dance (JOPERD)* dedicated an issue to the marginalised and threatened position of physical education within the American educational system. In introducing this dedicated issue, Griffey (1987) observed that secondary physical education was 'suffering from reduced support, resource cutbacks, a lack of understanding by administrators and teachers in other subject areas, misunderstanding by the public . . . and reduced time requirements for physical education in America's schools' (1987: 21). Manifestations of an ostensibly deteriorating situation were subsequently witnessed in a number of conference themes (e.g. 'Crisis in Physical Education', Deakin University, Geelong, Australia 1991 and 'Critical Crossroads – Decisions for Middle and High School Physical Education', Orlando, USA, 1992), a range of national and international journal articles reporting on the perilous position of physical education in schools and several national and international surveys as well as ongoing analyses of national and international documentation regularly reported by Hardman (1993, 1994, 1996, 1998a, 1998b). The extent of the concern generated by the serious situation of school physical education caused international agencies such as the World Health Organisation (WHO, 1998) and 'Sport for All' Movement (Barcelona Declaration, 1998) as well as regional continental organisations such as the European Union Physical Education Association, (EUPEA, Madrid Declaration, 1996) and the All-African Association for Health, Physical Education, Recreation, Sport and Dance (Johannesburg Declaration, 1999) respectively to issue Position, Policy and Advocacy and Declaration Statements in support of physical education in schools. In the middle of the 1990s, the situation worldwide was well summed up in the then Canadian Association of Health, Physical Education, Recreation and Dance Association (CAHPERD) President's assertion that physical education was not seen as a priority, that it was under severe attack and facing competition for time within the school curriculum with budget reductions 'impacting negatively on the time and resources required to teach a quality physical education programme' (Mackendrick, 1996: 2).

In 1996, Wilcox gathered data from professional leaders in physical education in his *Status of Physical Education in the World Today Survey*, which were utilised to highlight challenges facing the profession. He found that the physical education profession was suffering from low general self-esteem, that physical education was not thought to be of central importance to the mission of the national ministries responsible for the subject, that the status of physical education was not equal to that of other subjects, that physical education faced scepticism regarding its academic value and inadequacy of provision and poorly maintained facilities (Wilcox, 1998). In Europe, the EUPEA 25 country survey (Loopstra and Van der Gugten, 1997) indicated that while in some countries within the region, especially in central and eastern Europe, there were some encouraging developments in curriculum time allocation, the subject appeared to be under greater threat than it had been at the beginning of the decade. The survey revealed that only three countries were providing two hours per week for physical education at primary and secondary levels (ages 6–18) and only 9 out of 25 countries were offering two hours per week for the 6–12 years age group. A majority of countries reported inadequate training in physical education for primary school teachers, undervaluing the contribution of the primary school phase curriculum as well as insufficient curriculum time, especially for primary age groups and the 17–18 years age group, and insufficient monitoring of the quality of physical education.

Against this background of widespread concerns over the subject's seemingly tenuous position, a worldwide survey of the state and status of school physical education was undertaken by Hardman and Marshall on behalf of the International Council of Sports Science and Physical Education (ICSSPE). The survey's findings reaffirmed the perilous position of physical education revealed in earlier investigations and brought an UNESCO concessionary response that the principles of the International Charter had not filtered down into practice with physical education and sport not yet established as a national priority. A year after the publication of the Worldwide Survey *Final Report* (Hardman and Marshall, 2000), a Council of Europe Committee for the Development of Sport (CDDS) 'Working Group of Experts' on Access of Children to Physical Education and Sport picked up the investigative baton. The Working Group resolved to examine the situation of school physical education and sport in the 48 member states of the Council of Europe with a view to providing informed recommendations for discussion and action at the Informal Meeting of Ministers responsible for Sport in Warsaw, Poland, 12–13 September 2002. In the event, the ministerial *Conclusions* acknowledged a serious decline in the quality and the time allocated to physical education and sport for children and young people in schools as well as inadequate opportunities to participate in recreational sport out of school. Additionally, they indicated a need to study ways in which the provision of physical education and sport can be improved in Council of Europe member countries for all children and young people, including those with disabilities. According to the Deputy Secretary-General of the Council of Europe in her Warsaw Informal Ministerial Meeting Opening Address 'the crux of the issue is that there is too much of a gap between the promise and the reality' (De Boer-Buquicchio, 2002: 2). It is this issue that is the focus of this chapter: the promises inherent in the Council of Europe and UNESCO Charters' policy principles and the reality of implementation in schools for which we draw from data generated by several international (Wilcox, 1996, published 1998; and EUPEA, Loopstra and Van der Gugten, 1997), national (National Association of Head Teachers (NAHT) England and Wales, 1999;

Speednet, Primary Schools in England, 1999; Sport England, *Young People and Sport*, 2000; and Deutscher Sportlehrerverband, Helmke and Umbach, Germany, 2000), and regional (Sollerhed, southern Sweden, 1999, and Fairclough and Stratton, North West England Primary Schools, 2000) surveys. In the main, however, illustrative exemplars of findings are drawn from common areas and aspects of school physical education-related matters addressed in the three most recent international surveys, i.e. Worldwide (Hardman and Marshall, 2000), Council of Europe, CDDS (Hardman, 2002) and European Union (Marshall, 2002) and their respective underpinning literature reviews (governmental and non-governmental reports, international and national academic and professional journal articles, institutional and individual statements, web network sites, etc.) in order to provide a more comprehensive and balanced overview of the situation in Europe. 'Comprehensive' in respect of number of countries and educationally autonomous states and provinces included and 'balanced' with regard to nature and type of sources accessed but in particular the profile of the surveys' questionnaires' respondents, which is centrally relevant to the case for 'promise' and 'reality'. Respectively the respondents to questionnaires, administered as part of these three international surveys', comprised:

◆ Worldwide survey – government level policy makers and administrators, advisory professionals, physical education teachers and academic scholars;

◆ Council of Europe (CDDS) survey – CDDS representatives;

◆ European Union (EU) survey – physical education teachers.

In seeking to examine the extent of EU countries' compliance with the principles of the UNESCO International Charter of Physical Education and Sport, Marshall (2002) identified a number of distinct areas of benchmark indicators.[2] Five of these indicators (access, including curriculum time allocation, subject status, programme content, teaching personnel and resource provision encompassing facilities and equipment and finance) have been adopted here to provide a structure for presenting the case on 'promise' and 'reality'.

ACCESS TO PHYSICAL EDUCATION IN SCHOOLS

Both the Council of Europe (Article 1) and UNESCO (Article 1) Charters refer to assurance of opportunities of access to, and participation in, physical education and entrust public sector central agencies, supported wherever necessary by non-governmental organisations, with the realisation of the Charters' provisions.

All Council of Europe member states have a compulsory general education system, in which physical education is either an obligatory school subject for both boys and girls for at least some part of the compulsory schooling years or is taught as a matter of general practice. However, despite this official commitment to entitlement of access to physical education in schools through state legislation, such provision is far from being assured, particularly in contexts of localised implementation of the curriculum. In terms of years and class stages (but not in lesson 'hours' per week) with few exceptions, physical education features equally alongside the core subjects of 'mother' language (including literature) and mathematics.

In the CDDS survey, all countries apart from Italy (prevalence of the principle of didactical autonomy and/or inadequate specialist knowledge of teachers responsible for delivery) and Malta indicated that physical education is implemented or delivered in accordance with statutory prescriptions or guideline expectancies. Exemption granted on presentation of a medical certificate from compulsory physical education classes was only acknowledged by Belarus but such exemption practice on medical grounds is recognisably widespread throughout the region. An issue here is that exemption is rarely sought, if ever, from other curricular subjects except perhaps for religious education in some countries. However, while the Worldwide and EU surveys pointed to a high proportion (almost 90 per cent) of European countries with statutory requirements and apparent implementation in line with legal prescriptive or guideline expectations for physical education, there are suggestions that physical education is often dropped to make way for other subjects or at best there is minimal provision. The Wilcox, EUPEA and other national and regional surveys also found the latter to be the case. The surveys' data infer that while in many countries legal requirements for physical education in schools seem to be in place, actual implementation does not meet with statutory obligations or expectations. This 'gap' between official policy and regulations and actual practice is geographically widespread and pervasive factors contributing to it are seen in devolvement of responsibilities for curriculum implementa- tion, loss of time allocation, lower importance of school physical education in general, lack of official assessment, financial constraints, diversion of resources elsewhere, inadequate material resources, deficiencies in numbers of properly qualified personnel and attitudes of significant individuals such as head teachers.

Southern European and Mediterranean countries exhibit considerable disparities between state legal policy requirements and implementation. Although there is widespread justification in Cyprus for physical education, its actual situation 'in schools may contrast with the official recognition attached to it by the authorities . . . Physical education lessons are abandoned when time is required for reading and mathematics or for revision purposes and tests on academic work' (Yiallourides, 1998: 41). In some schools in Spain, compulsory physical education lessons in the final school years are replaced by optional lessons despite governmental level indicators of required physical education throughout the years of compulsory education.

Examples from elsewhere in the European region show the discrepancies between statutory (or expected) requirement and implementation and especially in countries where curricu- lum responsibility falls under the administrative management of education districts or individual schools and are, therefore, subject to local interpretations. In England, the timetable may not reflect the amount of physical education actually done, because many individual teachers do not choose to teach it, or suspend teaching when they have other, 'higher', priorities (Speednet, 1999). In Ireland 'Many primary schools do not offer the required time for PE (and the) level implementation is not uniform. [A] majority of senior students in secondary schools receive little or no PE ... PE is not given equal time or resources with other subjects' (Senior Inspector of Physical Education). Within some countries mainly in northern and western Europe, curriculum implementation falls under the administrative managerial responsibility of education districts or individual schools and are, therefore, subject to local and wide variations. In Finland for example, we are informed that 'Legal status is the same, but in practice not. The freedom of curriculum planning at schools has led to situations where implementation of physical education is not done according to the regulations concerning the weekly lessons' (University Professor). Similar concerns over local variations have also been frequently expressed in Sweden, where the implementation of physical education is dependent upon the decisions of each headteacher, to whom ultimately the responsibility for the delivery of physical education has been handed down (Ericsson, 2001).

PHYSICAL EDUCATION CURRICULUM TIME ALLOCATION

UNESCO's International Charter for Physical Education and Sport and the European Sports Charter do not specify any requirements for the amount of time that should be allocated to physical education within schools beyond time set aside that is deemed to be 'appropriate' (Council of Europe Charter, Article 5.i). It is, therefore, not unsurprising that the various surveys' findings reveal marked variations in the amounts of physical education curriculum time prescribed or expected and actually delivered in schools. 'Guaranteed' access does not equate with equal amounts of access, testimony to which are the variations of timetable allocation. Even within a relatively small geographical region, there are marked variations in the amount of access that is given to physical education, which brings into question the effectiveness of the Charters as standard-setting instruments and the roles of the Council of Europe and UNESCO in ensuring that even the basic human right of assured access to physical education is being met in schools.

In the period 1991–2001, many European states introduced reforms in education but they do not appear to have impacted significantly on the area of school physical education and sport. Generally, the legal status of physical education remained unchanged. Some increases in curriculum time allocation occurred in Andorra, Belarus, Greece, Lithuania, Poland, Portugal, Slovakia, Slovenia and the Ukraine but conversely decreases in time allocation were evident elsewhere, examples of which are to be seen in northern Europe. Educational reforms in Finland divested responsibility for curricular matters to schools thus, providing scope for potential local variations in state-guided stipulations, one consequence of which was a decrease in the amount of mandatory physical education and an increase in options. In Norway, the two school reforms (1994 and 1997) led to reduction of time allocation (although recently policy makers have signalled an intention to reinstate the time lost in the mid-1990s' reform changes). Even in Sweden with its strong historical physical education traditions, there were substantial reductions in physical education time allocation (Sollerhed, 1999). The decade of the 1990s also saw reductions in primary school physical education time allocation in Austria and The Netherlands, where physical education was also curtailed in Vocational Schools. In Switzerland a new Article in the Law brought in change from three hours compulsory to 'generally 3 hours compulsory. We have to fight against the cut of 1 lesson per week in different cantons' (Physical Education Teacher). Since German (re)-unification in 1990, Helmke and Umbach's national survey (2000) has revealed reductions as high as 25 per cent in timetable allocation for physical education at all class stages (except class 11). Belgian Wallonia (technical and vocational school classes), Bulgaria and Malta also report reductions in time allocation in the 1990s. In *England*, one-third of primary schools suffered reductions in physical education in the year 1998–99 to make time for literacy and numeracy work (Speednet, 1999). Pressure from other subjects for timetable space and examination requirements for facilities meant that the reduction of curriculum time for physical education resulted in insufficient time in some schools to deliver the national curriculum. Reductions were mooted in Ireland and Portugal (September 1998). In Portugal the education ministerial suggestion to reduce physical education curriculum time allocation in both elementary and secondary schools with a possibility even of loss of status as a core subject was shelved after widespread national and international expressions of concern.

PHYSICAL EDUCATION SUBJECT STATUS

Implicit within the UNESCO Charter is that physical education is accorded equivalent status to that of other subjects as part of a balanced curriculum (Article 2.3); in the Council of Europe Charter, such status is not specifically ascribed but sport (and physical education is subsumed within it) is regarded 'as an important factor in human development' (Article 1). However, as intimated earlier, underlying several of the examples of discrepancies and problems in the provision and delivery of physical education appears to be a suggestion that physical education is not regarded on a par with other so-called academic subjects.

The Worldwide, Council of Europe and EU surveys suggest that in around 94 per cent of countries, physical education seems to have attained the same or a similar legal status to other subjects. This figure, however, may be somewhat misleading because of interpretations of the meaning(s) attached to 'legal status'; for example 'core' or 'principal' as opposed to 'foundation' or 'subsidiary' status as in some western European countries. Furthermore, as pointed out previously, while physical education features pervasively alongside key subjects such as language and mathematics as a school curriculum subject, it is allocated less 'hours' or lessons hence, it is accorded lower status.

The view that there is a hierarchical 'pecking order' of subjects (Gowrie, 1996) with physical education occupying 'a low position on the academic totem pole . . . [and held] in low esteem' Jable (1997: 78) is mirrored in a Luxembourg teacher's comment that 'our academic programme is so heavy that all other lessons (gym, music, painting) are considered secondary' and a specific reference made by a teacher in Austria to both traditional and new technology subjects: 'physical education has not the same status that other academic subjects have (e.g., technical/science subjects and computers)'. This lower subject status and esteem is only acknowledged (in the CDDS survey) in Armenia, Italy, Malta, the Netherlands and Norway. Overall, the CDDS survey points to physical education teachers enjoying the same status as other subject teachers; in Georgia and Slovenia they are adjudged to have higher status; and only in Austria is there an indicator of lower status for physical education/sport teachers in some schools. However, these findings on subject and physical education teacher status stand in contrast to published literature assertions that physical education suffers low status and esteem. Data from the other surveys also suggest that the actual status of physical education in relation to other school subjects is lower than that accorded within the legal framework and so, underscore the literature. As Wilcox (1998) found, physical education faces considerable scepticism regarding its academic value: it is generally seen to be a 'distraction'. The regard of physical education as a non-productive educational activity and that it is academic subjects, which are the important stepping-stones to a successful future, is a common feature.

In central and eastern Europe, where since the so-called 'silent' or 'velvet' revolution' of 1989–90 there has been a reorientation in the concept of school physical education, in spite of government directives on physical education as a curriculum requirement, a number of negative features are endemic in several countries. Many Bulgarian headteachers are said to be 'too much occupied with other engagements to be able to pay attention to the PE of the pupils' and while 'other teachers understand the necessity of sport [they] think that their subject is more important for their children' (Physical Education Professor). In Poland, a physical education lecturer contends that 'the aims and goals of school physical education are misunderstood by national and local educational authorities', a situation, which leads to it frequently being 'treated as a subject of the second category by other teachers' and cancellation of lessons; it is a subject about which 'there is a very low consciousness in society', with 'parents mostly not interested both in the programme and the level of teaching'. A similar situation exists in Hungary, where 'health and physical fitness . . . aren't on the top among the parents rank of values; more important is the learning performance of the students because of the continuation of studies in higher education' (Associate Professor). In Russia, low status is reflected in 'lack of sports halls and proper equipment/facilities . . . and declining financial support' (Physical Education Lecturer).

In western Europe, national level agencies in Germany such as the Standing Conference of Ministers of Culture (KMK) and the DSB have periodically articulated the significant and essential importance and indispensability of physical education; however, its 'general importance is diminishing in critical times. Physical education is dispensable'! (Physical Education Professor). This diminished importance and dispensability is perhaps seen in a North Rhine-Westphalian physical education teacher's view that the status of physical education is undermined when 'many medical certificates allow non-participation in sports'. It is also evident in parental predisposition to favouring academic subjects with time spent on physical education perceived as a threat to academic achievement and/or examination performance: generally in Germany, 'public protests (especially from parents) are expected to be not so strong as if "academic" subjects were cancelled' (Physical Education Lecturer) and in Lower Saxony specifically 'there is absolutely no protest from parents, when PE lessons are cancelled. There is always a protest if lessons in e.g. maths, German, English, etc. are cancelled. Occasionally parents demand that PE lessons are "converted" to maths etc.' (Physical Education Teacher). A similar situation exists in France where 'unfortunately parents don't protest [when physical education lessons are cancelled] and it [physical education] is not considered as fundamental' (Physical Education and Sport Teacher); moreover, its supposed status as a mere antidote to academic subjects is reflected in a French physical education teacher's view that 'a lot of them [other subject teachers] think that PE is not important, except for students to let off steam after or before intellectual classes'. In Belgium, greater value in Flanders is attached to academic subjects with physical education more generally associated with recreation (Physical Education Professor) and in Wallonia 'PE is a subject, which is considered of far less importance than other academic subjects in the school' (Physical Education Teacher). In Luxembourg, another physical education teacher expressed similar sentiments: 'Legally PE is part of the national curriculum. In practice, PE is perceived as not important; it is just play time, time off from serious school subjects.' Thus, in theory it has the same status but other subject teachers believe themselves 'more important, PE comes always after academic lessons. Pupils are punished that means no PE lesson. When teachers have problems to finish the programmes of French for example they cut PE lessons.' In Austria, a physical education teacher maintains that 'physical education has not the same status that other subjects (e.g., technical/science subjects and computers) have'. In northern Europe, the status of physical education in Norway is problematically related to its legal status, which leads to less curriculum time allocation than for other subjects. This lower status is confirmed through central school policy (University Sport Pedagogue) and is affirmed in the belief among physical educators in the country that physical education is seen to be inferior to other subjects with headteachers seeing physical education 'OK as recreation, but not really necessary' (Primary School Teacher). This viewpoint is echoed on the other side of the North Sea in a Scottish Principal Teacher's comment that 'Sport is a release. It is a therapy session for pupils. It gets them away from the pressures, which other subjects bring. PE gives them a chance to switch off their brain and run around for an hour and a half. It is just relief' (cited in Gowrie, 1996: 48). Mediterranean and Iberian countries exhibit similar characteristics. In Italian primary schools, physical education is often regarded as free play and in the upper level of secondary schools, it has a lower status than other subjects (High School Teacher); an Italian physical education teacher also expresses the view that 'legally PE is like the other subjects, but often it is the Cinderella of the school'. As a Spanish physical educator observed, 'physical education is seen as leisure time'. In Portugal, physical education is regarded as non-academic and 'under adverse conditions, PE is included in the "sacrificed" subjects together with the so-called "non-academic" subjects' (University Professor). In Cyprus, physical education and physical educators are seen to be of lesser importance with inadequate parental encouragement (many regard it as a waste of time) and academic subject teachers regard physical educators as 'having lower status and their work in the field is not fully appreciated' (Yiallourides, 1998: 37). A Greek Cypriot sports administrator brackets education ministry officials with school headteachers in not 'valuing physical education. They have in mind that the students have only a brain.' In Malta, a physical education teacher asserts that Maltese headteachers 'give a lot of lip service, but when it comes to effective support this is virtually non-existent' and even parents 'look at it as a waste of time' as indeed they also do in Greece, where another physical education teacher alleges that they 'don't really care about the lessons of physical education, and it is considered as a break and not as a real lesson with a pedagogical means'. These examples confirm the existence of prestige differentiation between physical education and other subjects. Even in countries where it has achieved examination accreditation status, it remains at the lower levels of the prestige scale within schools. Physical education's practical orientation is not appreciated for its potential to contribute to the educational experience of children. In Scotland, a female pupil has commented:

> More credit is given to what you can do with your mind rather than what you can do with your body. It has a stigma attached to it, which gives you an impression that developing your intelligence is the really big aim, which the school is trying to achieve (Gowrie, 1996: 47).

One indicator of subject status is frequency of cancellation of lessons. In the CDDS survey, over 75 per cent of the countries indicated that physical education lessons are not cancelled any more frequently than other subjects and only seven countries acknowledged that lessons are cancelled more often than those of other subjects. Evidence from the other international, and supported by the national and regional, surveys brings another reality that the low status and esteem of the subject are detrimental to its position, because in many countries physical education lessons are cancelled more often than so-called academic subjects.

Apart from its attributed low subject status, other reasons given for the cancellation of physical education include the use of the dedicated physical education lesson space for examinations, concerts and as dining areas. The negative impacts of ceremonial occasions are a feature in Malta when hall space is required for prize-day practices, Christmas concerts and spiritual exercises during Easter (Physical Education Lecturer). In many countries the approach of the end of the school term/semester or year is marked by the cancellation of physical education lessons to make way for teaching of other subjects in preparation for examinations. Several Scottish physical education teachers observe that lessons are cancelled particularly during examination times: 'our programme is adversely affected when we lose two-thirds of our indoor teaching area; . . . the games hall is used for exams and prize giving which can disrupt PE programmes'. In England a primary school teacher reports adverse effects on the physical education programme because of loss of space to other school ceremonial functions and state required tests associated with national curriculum standard attainment targets (SATS):

> half way through November we have to start practising for the Christmas concert so the stage goes up; between four and five weeks PE is lost. The SATS, and all their preparation take up about three weeks, there's little time to fit PE in and much of the SATs are carried out in the hall. Towards the end of the Summer Term we have another wretched concert to prepare for, and again we use the hall; about 3–4 weeks. If you calculate this lost time it amounts to about the equivalent of a whole term. What message are we giving children about the purpose and value of PE? How many other PE co-ordinators are banging their heads against the wall like me? (E-mail from Oxford teacher cited in Davies, 2001)

PHYSICAL EDUCATION CURRICULUM CONTENT

The UNESCO Charter (Article 2) articulates a clear commitment to pupils' exposure to a broad and diverse range of activities within physical education lessons. The justification for this is based upon the notion that physical education should not be synonymous with just one particular activity area and, therefore, pupils should have opportunities to experience and be educated in an array of physical activities. The situation in the Council of Europe Charter is less clear because of terminological confusion surrounding what is meant by the term 'sport'. However, sport is seemingly used on the one hand in an inclusive generic sense and on the other hand is set alongside recreation and physical education, for which Articles 5 and 6 seek assurance of programmes' availability. The commitment to a broad and diverse physical education curriculum was examined across Europe.

The CDDS, EU and Worldwide surveys variously sought information on areas specifically related to the physical education curriculum. Pervasive throughout Europe are official policy statements on school physical education curriculum aims, which variously relate to all-round physical, motor competence skills and psycho-social development, active life-style promotion and life-span physical activity engagement *inter alia*; they are to be achieved through participation in a diverse and yet balanced range of activities (usually athletics, dance, games, gymnastics, outdoor adventure pursuits and swimming), which make up the content of the curriculum. In some countries (Austria, Belgium, Ireland, the Netherlands, Scotland and Sweden) policy documents specifically note that their physical education programmes should offer activities beyond simply games or sports. However, from the analysis of CDDS survey data on curricular aims, themes and content, the reality is that there is a clear orientation towards sports-dominated programmes, in which competitive games, especially team games, have a significant presence in both primary and secondary schools, and in which track and field athletics are generally present. This is contrary to trends and tendencies in out-of-school settings among young people. In Italy a number of schools do not offer outdoor adventure-based activities or swimming and in all of the schools surveyed in Spain swimming was not offered. Nonetheless, as in other parts of the world, physical education curricula in some countries and regions appear to be undergoing change with signs that its purpose and function are being redefined to accommodate other and/or broader educational outcomes. Links between physical education with health education and with personal and social development are occurring in some countries: in the Nordic group, for example, agreement has been reached (though not yet adopted by governments) on a united commitment to a health focus in physical education programmes. New, non-traditional activities are being incorporated into some physical education programmes (fitness-based activities such as aerobics and jazz gymnastics and popular culture 'excitement' activities such as snow-boarding and in-line skating, etc.). Nevertheless, in spite of these recent physical education curriculum-related developments, all the international surveys point to a sustained broad-spread predisposition towards games and development of competitive sports skills.

TEACHING PERSONNEL FOR PHYSICAL EDUCATION

Articles 5 and 9 of the Council of Europe Charter refer respectively to ensuring the training of qualified teachers and encouragement of the development of training courses. In the UNESCO Charter, Article 4 is devoted to qualified personnel responsible for the delivery of physical education and sport programmes and to voluntary personnel who might also contribute. Personnel who take professional responsibility must be capable of taking physical education and sport activities that are suited to the needs and requirements of the pupils in order that their safety is not jeopardised. The acquisition and development of the necessary relevant skills are acquired in teacher training programmes and updated throughout a teacher's career through in-service (INSET) or continuing professional development (CPD) programmes.

In many countries, the adequacy of teacher preparation for physical education is arguable and initial teacher training can present a problem even in economically developed countries. Generally throughout the European region, physical education/sport teaching degree and diploma qualifications are acquired at universities, pedagogical institutes, national sports academies or specialist physical education/sport institutes. For primary school teaching, qualifications tend to be acquired at pedagogical institutes but not exclusively so; for secondary school teaching, qualifications are predominantly acquired at university level institutions. In approximately half of the countries, physical education teacher graduates are qualified to teach a second subject. Though not applicable to all countries, a common scenario across Europe is the practice of having qualified 'specialist' physical education teachers at secondary level and 'generalist' teachers at primary level. Some countries do have specialist physical educators in primary schools but the variation is wide and there are marked regional differences: in central and eastern Europe, around two-thirds of countries have specialist physical educators in primary schools compared with a third of countries in western Europe. In some countries, the primary school generalist teacher is often inadequately or inappropriately prepared to teach physical education and *initial* teacher training presents a problem with minimal hours allocated for physical education teaching training.

The following examples may not be typical within each country, but they do indicate some problematic issues and they do represent some of the concerns articulated in other European countries. A physical education teacher in Austria remarks 'in primary schools teachers are not trained well – they often just go for a week or do German or mathematics instead of PE'. In Norway and Sweden, it is possible to teach physical education in primary schools stages without any prior training; no wonder that a Swedish physical education professional protests 'Generalists keep the PE level low!' (EUPEA, 2002). An Office of Standards in Education (OFSTED) Report indicated that in England 'On average post-graduate trainees do 23 hours and undergraduates 32 hours. But some do as little as seven-and-a-half' (cited in *Times Higher Education Supplement*, 1999: 2). This limited amount of training preparation is also evident in Ireland, where a physical education professional comments 'primary schools teachers have not a broad enough PE training to be teaching it'. In Malta the inadequacies extend to secondary schools for 'there is still a large number of unqualified people who hold teaching posts . . . who do not know what they are doing' (Physical Education Lecturer).

Close to two-thirds of teachers in Europe undertake required INSET/CPD, but there are several countries where it is not required: Spanish Andorra, Bosnia-Herzegovina, Czech Republic, Finland, Greece, Iceland, Italy, Luxembourg, the Netherlands, Norway and Slovenia. There are substantial variations in frequency and time allocated for INSET/CPD. Frequency ranges from choice through nothing specifically designated, every year, every two years, every three years to every five years. Duration of INSET/CPD also reveals differences in practice between countries: those with annual training range from 12 to 50 hours, from 3 to 25 days; biennial and triennial training courses of 4 weeks; and five years range from 15 days to 3 weeks or 100 hours over the five-year period. In some countries, inadequate promotional infrastructure and finance can inhibit participation in INSET/CPD: a Swedish physical educator reports 'often I have to find in-service training myself and I have also often to pay for it with my own money'. Situations like this are unlikely to encourage participation on INSET courses; equally barriers imposed by the school may prevent participation. One teacher in Scotland reported: 'As the only member of staff in the school trained to teach physical education means that there is no cover for physical education while I am away on in-service training. So (it is) often impossible to attend.' It is clear that the commitment made by education authorities to provide INSET is not, by itself, sufficient to ensure participation by teachers, and raises questions as to whether the quality of physical education delivery may be undermined by the low take-up of training. Voluntary INSET Course attendance has raised concerns that those teachers most in need of the help and support may not be participating and that this 'hit or miss' nature is not particularly conducive to effective delivery of physical education. A paradox within the compulsory/

voluntary INSET/CPD debate is exemplified in a Scottish teacher's observation: 'I recently attended a trampoline course and a lifesaving course. Though both courses were voluntary, the implications of not attending in terms of the dangerous nature of activities and possible litigation implications if there was an accident meant that the courses were almost compulsory.'

A consistent feature of all the surveys on the issue of further professional development of teachers involved in physical education teaching is countries across Europe indicate a need for in-service training and there is a recognition in some countries that in-service and resource materials have been minimal and have been exacerbated by a marked decline in physical education advisory/supervisory service numbers.

There is very limited use of volunteer personnel in teaching physical education/sport classes. Andorra (secondary schools), French Andorra (primary schools), Austria, Finland, Malta and Slovakia do use volunteer personnel mainly in an assistant capacity for demonstrations or techniques and with small group supervision or one-to-one support. In Italy, volunteers are utilised only as a necessity; in the Czech Republic there are exceptional occasions when a coach or trainer is involved with sport in a school. In Austria, Czech Republic, Malta and Slovakia training of volunteers is externally sourced, though Slovakia also has school-based training. Finland and Italy do not require training of volunteers. On the issue of supervision of volunteer personnel, only Slovakia does this on a constant basis, whereas Austria and Malta indicate that supervision never occurs and French Andorra, Czech Republic and Finland supervise on an occasional basis.

RESOURCES FOR PHYSICAL EDUCATION

Facilities and equipment

Arguably effective learning and teaching in physical education is in part reliant upon the provision of facilities and equipment. Both Charters (Council of Europe, Articles 4 and 5; UNESCO, Article 5) urge appropriate provision for physical education with adequate and sufficient material in schools and that government and non-governmental agencies should co-operate in planning and provision. The international surveys and the literature reveal deficiencies in the provision of facilities and equipment in schools for the subject.

In Europe, physical education is commonly faced with the challenge of inadequate facilities and poor maintenance of existing teaching sites but there are marked subregional and intra-country differences and there are specific facility problems in small, in particular, rural schools. A physical education teacher in Finland, for example, refers to 'regional differences (being) still big, especially in grades 1–6 at small schools and in the countryside'. The findings of the international surveys indicate an east–west divide between largely central and eastern and to a lesser extent in southern European countries and the rest of Europe in facility provision. Generally in northern, western and some regions in southern European countries quality and quantity of facilities and equipment are regarded as at least adequate and in some instances excellent. In central and eastern European countries as well as in southern Italy, Malta and Portugal, there are reports of inadequacies in both quality and quantity of facilities and equipment. In Italy, several physical education teachers refer to 'inadequacy of structures and equipment for physical education'; and 'structures could be improved, equipment could be improved'. In Malta 'in a great number of primary and secondary schools, the facilities are virtually non-existent except for school yards; where there are gymnasiums, they are mostly 30–40 years old and are not in very good condition' (Physical Education Lecturer).

Because of the challenges of inadequate facilities and their poor maintenance, the actual implementation of physical education classes can be made difficult and the quality of the lessons provided can be less than adequate. Former 'socialist bloc' countries in general show signs of depleted and deteriorating provision since the revolutionary weeks of 1989–1990. Specific exemplars reveal the extent of facility and equipment inadequacies: in Azerbaijan, many outdoor and indoor spaces are unusable in winter, some schools do not have sports halls and there is insufficient money to replace damaged equipment (Government Official); in Bulgaria, there is a particular shortage of 'gym apparatus . . . [and] . . . balls for basketball, volleyball, handball, football' (Professor of Physical Education); and in the Czech Republic 'bad conditions, especially in big cities where old school buildings, often without sports grounds or gymnasium' prevail (University Physical Education Lecturer).

The problem appears to stretch beyond the traditional divides of developed and developing nations. While it could be reasonably argued that there are higher expectations over levels and standards of facilities and equipment in economically developed countries, examples from other European regions illustrate the point. Hart (1999) comments that the levels of sports provision in many English and Welsh schools is grossly inadequate and that playing fields suffer from low levels of maintenance and drainage problems. The consequence of sharing the school hall for assemblies, dining areas, school concerts and examinations means that a quarter of primary schools cannot provide adequate time for physical education. Even in hitherto economically sound Germany, a physical education teacher in North Rhine Westphalia observes that there is 'no money to equip/maintain/build [new] sports halls, pupils don't take care of the equipment [so it doesn't last long]. You have to improvise a lot [make the best out of the situation]'.

Finance

The Council of Europe seeks financial resource availability from public funds for the fulfilment of the aims and purpose of its Charter (Article 12) and the UNESCO Charter (Article 10) calls for fiscal measures to support the delivery of physical education and sport through the appropriate provision of resources.

Funding of physical education with its initial high capital costs of facilities and recurrent maintenance, apparatus and equipment costs is a contentious issue in many countries. In times of financial constraints on government spending, three-quarters of countries in the CDDS survey indicate that physical education is not usually likely to suffer from budget cuts or reductions. Those countries indicating cuts, or that reductions would be likely, cited a number of consequential impacts on school physical education and sport: Austria and Iceland – reduced number of lessons; Finland – decrease of school club activity; Malta – reductions because it is not regarded as a 'top subject'; and Sweden – variable impacts at local levels. From the Worldwide and EU surveys, an overall different continental and regional picture emerges: over half of European countries indicate cuts or reductions in physical education with around two-thirds of central and eastern European countries indicating a situation of declining financial support in recent years.

In some countries (for example Belgium), commentators (Carreiro da Costa and Piéron, 1997) have highlighted the integration of physical education with other subjects or areas such as fine arts, health, social and personal development as a direct consequence of policies based in economic realities and rationalisation of curricula. A widely reported impact of funding limitations is on swimming. The considerable financial investment of maintaining, or gaining access to, swimming facilities exposes this important component of physical education to cancellation of lessons, reductions or even omission from curricula in some countries. Three illustrations serve as exemplars: (i) the Netherlands, where 'due to financial reductions, school swimming has been cancelled as an obligatory part of the PE curriculum' (Physical Education Teacher); (ii) Denmark, where 'formerly swimming was a compulsory subject for all pupils. Many communities tend unfortunately to save the money. Today only two-thirds of all pupils get adequate swimming lessons' (Physical Education Lecturer); and (iii) England and Wales, where Slater (2000: 21) cites 'cuts in school budgets, increased transport and admissions costs to community pools, use of specialist tuition as well as increased pressures on lesson times' as responsible for reductions in teaching of swimming.

Financial considerations have had a number of other adverse impacts on physical education in Europe, the most common of which relate to material and personnel resources (including professional development), typified in the west of the region by an Irish Senior Physical Education Inspector's comment that 'facility provision and teachers' employment are adversely affected by financial constraints. Many schools have been built with no indoor PE facilities' and a Scottish Physical Education Teacher's intimation that 'as money is tight at the moment all of the in-service training will probably be cancelled'. Moving eastwards in the region, a Physical Education Teacher in the German Land of Lower Saxony complains that financial support to physical education is 'Lousy. Below average. Most of the school budget goes to ruddy computers' and a Professor of Physical Education in Bavaria alludes to employment of lower-waged instructors: 'Non-professional instructors are intended to be employed as PE teachers at schools as their wages are lower ... The financial and economical situation is still unstable. The willingness to invest in the physical education in schools is not very high.' An Austrian Physical Education Teacher observes that his school 'has a low budget – therefore, the financial support for PE is very limited. There is too (little) money to buy new equipment' and in another school, a Physical Education Teacher alleges that 'we annually collect money from students in order to keep our equipment up to date'. A similar picture is evident in Slovakia, where a Physical Education Lecturer refers to 'problems with lack of finances for maintenance sports facilities and for reconstruction and acquisition of new sports materials. There are schools existing also without sufficient sports facilities . . . there is a decrease of financial areas to PE.' This central European scenario is also seen in Poland where a Physical Education Lecturer reports 'an essential lack of money for the improvement of already existing equipment and places as well as for the purchasing of new equipment, necessary for proper work' and again further east in the region in Estonia, where 'one of the main problems: the equipment is very expensive. Also, most of the facilities require reconstruction' (Physical Education Lecturer).

Devolvement of responsibility for financial expenditures to local school levels in some countries makes it difficult to discern whether this form of distribution is beneficial or detrimental to the quality of support to individual subjects. Smith (1998) alleges that support to physical education in France can be particularly mixed and can range from excellent to poor between neighbouring schools. In Belgium, level of support to physical education can to be linked to the goodwill of head teachers (Physical Education Professor). If the educational priorities of head teachers or local authorities do not indicate or attach little value to physical education, then it is unlikely that it will be allocated an equal amount of financial support.

INTERNATIONAL COOPERATION: POST-BERLIN SUMMIT INTER- AND NON-GOVERNMENTAL ORGANISATIONS' INITIATIVES

While the Council of Europe deems necessary cooperation at continental regional and international level to fulfil its Charter's aims, UNESCO places greater emphasis on the role of international community in the promotion and development of physical education and sport. Article 10 of the UNESCO Charter focuses on international cooperation as 'a prerequisite for the universal and well-balanced promotion of physical education and sport' with national, international and regional intergovernmental and non-governmental organisations giving 'physical education and sport greater prominence in international bilateral and multi-lateral co-operation', indicating that such collaboration will 'encourage the development of physical education and sport throughout the world'.

It is a matter of historical record that the Hardman and Marshall worldwide survey led to the World Summit on Physical Education, 3–5 November 1999 in Berlin organised by ICSSPE with patronage and support from the IOC, UNESCO and WHO. The Berlin Summit brought together policy makers, administrators, researchers and physical education practitioners from around the world to share information on the situation of, and case for, physical education in schools. It culminated in the formulation of Action Agendas and an Appeal to UNESCO General Conference and the Ministers with responsibility for Physical Education and Sport (MINEPS III) meeting in Punta del Este, Uruguay (30 November–3 December 1999).

The so-called 'Berlin Agenda' called for governmental and ministerial action to implement policies for physical education as a human right for all children in recognition of its distinctive role in physical health, overall development and safe, supportive communities. Furthermore, in making the case for quality physical education, it called for investment in initial and in-service professional training and development for well-qualified educators and support for research to improve the effectiveness and quality of physical education. These were issues, which were repeated in an *Appeal to the General Conference of UNESCO*: the General Conference was urged to commit to developing strategies for effective implementation of and properly resourced physical education programmes, to mobilise intergovernmental and non-governmental organisations, public and private sectors to cooperate in the promotion and development of physical education and was requested to invite the Director General of UNESCO to submit the World PE Summit's *Appeal* to the MINEPS III meeting in Punta del Este, 30 November–3 December 1999. Subsequently, the Punta del Este Declaration endorsed the Berlin Agenda for Action and encouraged member states to implement it through incorporation in school programmes or, as a minimum, meeting with any legal requirements with respect to physical education programmes in school curricula (refer Doll-Tepper and Scoretz, 2001). The Ministers reiterated the importance of physical education as an essential element and an integral part in the process of continuing education and human and social development, expressed concern that, in spite of the expansion of elite sport and sport for all programmes in recent years, opportunities for children to participate in physical education had been significantly curtailed and noted that the time required for physical education in schools was not being respected and was even being substantially reduced in many countries because of changing priorities. In essence, MINEPS III was acknowledging that member states were not wholly complying with the 1978 UNESCO Charter.

The Berlin World Summit on Physical Education was instrumental in placing physical education on the world political agenda. The Declaration of Punta del Este (1999) was an encouraging initial development, but restructuring within UNESCO hitherto has hindered implementation. The restructuring subsumed physical education and sport as one of three sections (and without a specific budget) grouped under the Education Sector/Division of Quality Education/Section 'Education for Personal Well-being'. Under such circumstances, it is difficult to see how UNESCO can fulfil its role as focal point of the UN for matters related to physical education and sport.

In the first post-MINEPS III meeting of CIGEPS held in Athens (April, 2000) the work of implementing the Declaration of Punta del Este was set about but UNESCO's financial situation in general and that of physical education in particular (reduced to one-sixth of the amount available in 1988) inhibited any ambitious programmes and activities. Nonetheless, a UNESCO 'Round Table Meeting' of Ministers and Senior Officials of PE and Sport met in Paris, 10 January 2003 to address three thematic topics: school physical education; protection of young athletes; and anti-doping measures in sport. Along with proposals related to protection of young athletes and anti-doping, the *Communiqué* adopted by representatives from 103 countries noted that in many countries physical education is being increasingly marginalised within education systems even though it is instrumentally important for health, physical development, social cohesion and intercultural dialogue. To reverse this trend, the 'Round Table' participants committed themselves to working for implementation of MINEPS III policy principles and the full recognition of the place of physical education and sport both within and outside education systems, thus, adhering to the UNESCO 1978 Charter principles. The fact that this commitment to implement policy principles was more than three years on from the Punta del Este Declaration is perhaps a stark reminder of the limitations of UNESCO's spheres of influence! The commitment is to be pursued through actions to bring about curriculum, sports facilities and equipment, status of physical education and initial and in-service teacher training improvements together with cooperation of partners, specifically the family, schools, sporting associations and clubs, communities, local and other relevant authorities, public and private sectors. The participants requested the UNESCO Director-General to draw the United Nations' Secretary-General's attention to the importance of physical education and sport and to the desirability of debating this topic in the General Assembly. Furthermore, they sought to have the *Communiqué* transmitted for follow-up action to UNESCO's Member States, to the Intergovernmental Committee on Physical Education and Sport (CIGEPS), to the General Conference of UNESCO (with the proposal that an International Year for Physical Education and Sport be proclaimed for submission to the UN General Assembly)[3] and to the Fourth International Conference of Ministers and Senior Officials Responsible for Physical Education and Sport (MINEPS IV) in Athens in August 2004 (*http// www.unesco.org*, 2003).

The UNESCO *Communiqué* echoes some of the set of *Conclusions* agreed by the European Ministers at their Informal Meeting in Warsaw in September 2002, mentioned in the introductory statement. However, the *Conclusions*, (Bureau of the Committee for the Development of Sport, 2002a, 2002b) essentially embracing issues of quality[4] and delivery (curriculum content, facilities and equipment, teacher training), inclusion, more active lifestyles and an associated variety of pan-European programmes, implementation of a range of measures grouped around perceived spheres of influence (home and family, school, local and wider community collaborative provision and flexible programmes), development of relevant and appropriate national policies, intergovernmental cooperation, sharing informa-tion, research findings and national experiences in promotion of physical activity, were more detailed and prescriptive. It remains to be seen what impact, if any, the ministerial deliberations may have. It is encouraging to see physical education and sport in schools on the Council of Europe political agenda but the status of Conclusions is below those of

Recommendations and Resolutions and hence, is far removed from any form of mandatory requirement of member states.

As well as intergovernmental initiatives since the Berlin Physical Education Summit, a number of European non-governmental organisations have begun to address issues and concerns surrounding physical education in schools. Two examples will suffice as illustrations. In October 2002, the European Non-governmental Sports Organisation (ENGSO) held a two-day forum in Malta, in which access to physical education in schools and the role of non-governmental organisations in contributing to a sustainable future for school physical education were main themes discussed. ENGSO pledged its support for physical education in schools through appropriate partnership advocacy initiatives and demonstrated interest in the EUPEA's recently published *Code of Ethics and Good Practice Guide for Physical Education* to inform its own planned code of ethics and practice for personnel involved in sport. A landmark for EUPEA itself, founded in 1991 to promote physical education all over Europe, was its 1st Symposium, 9 November 2002 in Brussels, Belgium on the topical theme of 'Quality Physical Education'. Nearly 200 delegates from 35 countries attended the Symposium from which a number of perceived challenges emerged. These challenges embrace minimal time requirements, balanced programmes, inclusion strategies and policies, teacher education and competencies, in-service training and planned continuing professional development, ways and means of disseminating good practice and understanding frameworks used by young people to interpret physical education in contexts of national and cultural diversity across Europe. In summarising the deliberations of the Symposium, EUPEA Vice-President Chris Laws (2002) concluded that in striving for a relevant physical education curriculum there is a role for all European Physical Education Associations to act to provide 'quality experiences for all children'. Clearly there is concurrence here with the UNESCO *Communiqué* and the Council of Europe's ministerial *Conclusions*.

CONCLUDING COMMENTS

Arguably, the data from the extensive literature and investigative surveys provide a distorted picture of school physical education in Europe. Without doubt, there are examples of positively implemented programmes and good practices in physical education in most, if not all, countries across the region. Furthermore, there is an array of individual and institutional endeavours to optimise the quality of physical education delivery and so enhance the experiences of children in schools. Equally there is evidence to generate continuing disquiet about the situation. It is clear that in too many schools in too many countries children are being denied the opportunities to experience quality physical education provision. Such denial of opportunities is inconsistent with the policy principles of the Council of Europe and UNESCO Charters and does bring into question the effectiveness of the two Charters as appropriate standard-setting instruments; perhaps the justification lies in fundamental purposes of the Charters ostensibly to reduce inequalities between countries and ensure minimum standards of provision.

The positive/negative messages are mixed and continue to be so as testified by reports in the Minutes of the EUPEA Forum meeting in Brussels, 8 November 2002. Physical education representatives pointed to an improving national situation in the Czech Republic, Poland and Slovenia and discussions on increasing physical education curriculum time allocation in Croatia and Denmark. At the same time, it was indicated that in France it is difficult to maintain school sport every Wednesday and that there is a problem with physical education evaluation in the final year of secondary schools: teachers find it difficult to do; and in Ireland that intentions to introduce higher quality and more time for physical education under proposed curriculum reform may be compromised because 'there is not a lot of room for increased time allocation, since the government introduced two new subjects in an already tight programme' (BVLO, 2002).

The overview of research findings also reveals mixed messages when it comes to compliance within a continental regional context to the principles of the Council of Europe and UNESCO Charters. Examination of official policy documentation reveals a high degree of compliance with the principles of both Charters. However, it has to be said that the broad and often non-specific nature of the Charters makes it easy for countries to appear to be meeting with the principles. At policy level there are instances where compliance is less than adequate: for example, physical education not being compulsory over all school years as well as pan-European concerns over the devolving of resource provision to local levels, which lead to marked variations in provision. There is a sense of *déjà vu* about the 'mixed messages' situation. The 1997 EUPEA Survey (Loopstra and Van der Gugten) revealed a similarly confused scenario. On the one hand, the survey indicated some encouraging developments mainly in central and eastern European countries but a number of threats and marginalisation on the other hand.

The evidence indicates that many national governments have committed themselves through legislation to making provision for physical education but they have been either slow or reticent in translating this into action through actual implementation and assurance of quality of delivery at the national level. Deficiencies are apparent in curriculum time allocation, subject status, financial, material and human resources (particularly in primary school teacher preparation for physical education teaching), as well as the quality and relevance of the physical education curriculum and its delivery. Of particular concern are the considerable inadequacies in facility and equipment supply, frequently associated with under-funding, especially in central and eastern European and in some parts of countries in southern Europe, where economically developing regions predominate. More generally, there is disquiet over the falling fitness standards of young people, rising levels of obesity among children of school age and high youth dropout rates from physical/sporting activity engagement, which are occurring concomitantly with the perceived decline in the position of physical education in schools and its questionable quality. It seems that the disquiet is exacerbated by insufficient and/or inadequate school–community coordination and problems of communication in some countries (see Hardman, 2002).

The Worldwide and EU surveys revealed in countries across Europe that there is a narrow and unjustifiable conception of the role of physical education merely to provide experiences, which serve to reinforce achievement-orientated competitive sport, thus limiting participatory options rather than expanding horizons. Cross-analysis of relevant responses to questions on curriculum aims and content in the CDDS survey also revealed that generally throughout the region, a competition/performance curriculum model prevails. This observation is also indirectly supported in the minimal attention paid to broader pedagogical and didactical activities in physical education and an overwhelming predisposition of countries to cite competitive sport-oriented programmes (e.g., sports competition structures, sports talent development and provision of specialist facilities) as examples of best practice and the problem of reconciliation of elite sport and regular schooling. In this context, it is unsurprising that pupil interest in physical education declines throughout the school years and young people become less active in later school years. While it may not be pervasively the case in every Council of Europe member state that there are decreasing numbers of participants from school-based and post-school life sports-related activity, it *is* the case in too many countries not only in the region but also in other parts of the world.

A fundamental question is what should be done to secure a sustainable future for school physical education and sport? One answer is to accept the situation for what it is and suffer the consequences. The other is to confront the situation and address available options to help resolve some of the problems not only in Europe but also globally. Whatever the direction for resolution, there is little point in 'fiddling' while physical education in particular 'burns'. As comparativists, we are acutely aware of the dangers of generalising and making specific suggestions and/or prescriptions for universal applicability because while globally we might be able to see trends and tendencies and, unquestionably, similarities, there are also differences and variations based in politico-ideological, socio-cultural, economic values and norms and ecological settings. Thus, policy and practice, more often than not, are subject to localisation and/or local interpretations; what might be relevant in one country might not be relevant in another. As the Council of Europe Informal Meeting's *Conclusions*, UNESCO's Round Table *Communiqué* and the EUPEA Vice-President's reference to the role of national Physical Education Associations in quality physical education provision clearly articulate, the emphasis has to be on action and advocacy to meet with the challenges at international, national and local levels.

The Berlin Physical Education Summit, *Agenda for Action for Government Ministers*, the Punta del Este *Declaration*, the Council of Europe's Warsaw Meeting *Conclusions* and UNESCO's Round Table Communiqué together with various WHO, IOC and some national governments' initiatives demonstrate that there is now an international consensus that issues surrounding physical education in schools deserve serious consideration in order to solve existing and future problems. It is imperative that watching briefs on what is happening in physical education and sport across Europe (beyond the Forum of European Physical Education Association's efforts to monitor the situation) are maintained. Both the Council of Europe's ministerial *Conclusions* and the UNESCO Round Table *Communiqué* called for monitoring systems to be put into place to regularly review the situation of physical education in each country. Indeed, the Council of Europe referred to the introduction of provision for a pan-European survey on physical education policies and practices every five years as a priority! (Bureau of the Committee for the Development of Sport, 2002a, 2002b). Policy as well as idealistic and sometimes politically inspired rhetoric can, and do, mask the truth. In spite of official documentation on principles, policies and aims, actual implementation into practice exposes the realities of situations. 'Promises' need to be converted into 'reality' if threats are to be surmounted and a safe future for physical education in schools is to be secured. Otherwise with the Council of Europe Deputy Secretary General's intimation of a gap between 'promise' and 'reality', there is a real danger that the Informal Ministers' meeting's agreed Conclusions will remain just that – more 'promise' than 'reality' in too many countries across Europe and compliance with Council of Europe and UNESCO Charters will continue to remain compromised.

NOTES

1   'Physical education' is applied generically to encompass other terminological descriptors for this school curricular subject such as 'physical culture', 'movement', 'human motricity', 'physical education and sport', 'sport', 'sport education' and 'sport pedagogy' utilised in various European countries.
2   Benchmark is 'a means by which to measure standards of performance against those achieved by others with broadly similar characteristics' (SCAA, 1997: 8).
3   The proposed International Year on PE and Sport is now confirmed as 2005.
4   The final (revised) *Conclusions* refer to 'quality' with an undefined time allocation. This replaced the initial draft, which specified a long-term aim of 'a minimum of 180 minutes per week of structured lesson time' (Bureau of the Committee for the Development of Sport, 2002a); the consensus among ministerial representatives was that 180 minutes was unrealistic and for at least one country's representative was unacceptable.

REFERENCES

N.B. In the interests of confidentiality, names of questionnaire respondents, whose comments have been quoted in the text, have been withheld from the list of references.

Bureau of the Committee for the Development of Sport (2002a) *Draft Conclusions on Improving Physical Education and Sport for Children and Young People in all European Countries*, MSL-IM16 (2002) 5 Rev.3. 16th Informal Meeting of European Sports Ministers, Warsaw, Poland, 12–13 September, Strasbourg: Council of Europe.

Bureau of the Committee for the Development of Sport (2002b) *Draft Conclusions on Improving Physical Education and Sport for Children and Young People in all European Countries. Revised by the Drafting Group*, MSL-IM16 (2002) 5 Rev.4. 16th Informal Meeting of European Sports Ministers, Warsaw, Poland, 12–13 September, Strasbourg: Council of Europe.

BVLO (2002) *Minutes of 13th EUPEA Forum Meeting*, Brussels, 8 November.

Carreiro da Costa, F., and Pieron, M. (1997) 'Teaching the curriculum: policy and practice in Portugal and Belgium', *The Curriculum Journal*, 8 (2): 231–247.

Council of Europe (1975) *European 'Sport for All' Charter*, European Sports Ministers' Conference, Brussels, Belgium.

Davies, H. (2001) 'Across the sectors', *British Journal of Teaching Physical Education*, 32 (3): 34.

De Boer-Buqicchio, M. (2002) *Opening Address*. 16th Informal Meeting of the European Ministers responsible for Sport, Warsaw, 12 September.

Deutscher Sportbund (1966) *Charta des Deutschen Sports*, Frankfurt: DSB.

Doll-Tepper, G., and Scoretz, D. (2001) *Proceedings, World Summit on Physical Education*, Schorndorf: Verlag Karl Hofmann.

Ericsson, S. (2001) *Finnish National Report Submitted to EUPEA Board Meeting*, Madrid, Spain, May.

EUPEA (1991) *Madrid Declaration*. Madrid: EUPEA.

EUPEA (2002) *Forum*, Brussels, November.

Fairclough, S., and Stratton, G. (2000) *Physical Education Curriculum and Extra-curriculum Time as a Consequence of the Relaxed Physical Education Orders and National Literacy Strategy: A Survey of Primary Schools in the North-west of England*, Paper presented at the European College of Sports Science Congress, Jyväskylä, Finland, 19–23 July.

Gowrie, R. (1996) 'Watching from the sidelines: the prestige of physical education in the Scottish secondary school', *Scottish Journal of Physical Education*, 24 (2): 44–54.

Griffey, D.C. (1997) 'Trouble for sure – a crisis perhaps. Secondary school physical education today', *JOPERD*, 58 (2): 20–21.

Hardman, K. (1993) 'Physical education within the school curriculum', in J. Mester (ed.), *'Sport Sciences in Europe 1993' – Current and Future Perspectives*, Aachen: Meyer and Meyer Verlag. pp. 544–60.

Hardman, K. (1994) 'Physical education in schools', in F.I. Bell and G.H. Van Glyn (eds), *Access to Active living*. Proceedings of the 10th Commonwealth and International Scientific Congress, Victoria, Canada, University of Victoria. pp. 71–76.

Hardman, K. (1996) *The Fall and Rise of Physical Education in International Context*. Symposium Paper, Pre-Olympic and International Scientific Congress, Dallas, Texas, 9–14 July.

Hardman, K. (1998a) *School Physical Education: Current Plight and Future Directions in International Context*. Paper presented at the 11th Commonwealth and International Scientific Congress, Kuala Lumpur, 3–8 September.

Hardman, K. (1998b) *Threats to Physical Education! Threats to Sport for all*. Paper presented at the I.O.C. VII World Congress 'Sport for All', Barcelona, Spain, 19–22 November.

Hardman, K. (2002) *Council of Europe Survey. Committee for the Development of Sport (CDDS) European Physical Education/Sport Survey. Report on Summary of Findings*. Strasbourg: Council of Europe.

Hardman, K., and Marshall, J.J. (2000) *World-wide Survey of the State and Status of School Physical Education, Final Report*. Manchester: University of Manchester.

Hart, D. (1999) 'No gym generation', *Daily Mail*, 5 March: 17.

Helmke, C., and Umbach, C. (2000) *Anmerkung zur Übersicht 'Sportunterricht in Deutschland (Stand 01/2000)*, Baunatal: Deutscher Sportlehrerverband E.V.

http://www.unesco.org/bpi/eng/unescopress/2003/03-02e.shtml.

Jable, J.T. (1997) 'Whatever happened to physical education?', *Journal of Interdisciplinary Research in Physical Education*, 2 (1): 77–93.

Laws, C. (2002) *Report on 1st EUPEA Symposium*, Brussels, 9 November 2002 (personal communication).

Loopstra, O., and Van der Gugten, T. (1997) *Physical Education from a European Point of View*, EU–1478.

Mackendrick, M., (1996) 'Active living+quality daily physical education=the perfect solution', *CAHPERD Journal*, 62 (1): 2.

Marshall, J.J. (2002) 'School physical education: the extent of compliance with the UNESCO Charter for Physical Education and Sport in the European Union'. PhD dissertation, University of Manchester, Manchester.

National Association of Head Teachers. (1999) *Survey of PE and Sport in Schools. Report*. Haywards Heath, NAHT, Thursday 4 March.

SCAA – School Curriculum and Assessment Authority (1997) *Target Setting and Benchmarking in Schools – Consultation Paper*, Hayes, Middlesex: SCAA Publications.

Slater, J. (2000) 'Schools fail to take the plunge – TES and the CCPR survey', *Times Educational Supplement*, 21 July: 21.

Smith, P. (1998) 'The French experience: a report on the current provision for physical education in North-east France', *Bulletin of Physical Education*, 34 (3): 12–18.

Sollerhed, A-C. (1999) 'The status of physical education in the Swedish school system', *Paper, ICHPER.SD 42nd World Congress, 'Developing Strategies of International Co-operation in Promotion of HPERSD for the New Millennium'*, Cairo, Egypt 2–8 July.

Speednet (1999) *Effects of the Suspension of the Order for National Curriculum Physical Education at Key Stages 1 and 2 on Physical Education in Primary Schools During 1989. Interim Summary of Findings*, National Speednet Survey, Press Release, 19 August.

Sports Council (1977) *Council of Europe. European Sport for All Charter*. London: Sports Council.

Sports Department of the Directorate General IV – Education, Culture and Heritage, Youth and Sport, Council of Europe (2001) *European Sports Charter and Code of Sports Ethics*, Strasbourg: Council of Europe.

Times Higher Educational Supplement (1999) 8 January: 2.

UNESCO (1978) *Charter for Physical Education and Sport*. Paris: UNESCO.

Wilcox, R. (1998) 'Shared scepticism and domestic doubts: globalization, localization, and the challenges to physical education in the world today', in R. Naul, K. Hardman, M. Piéron and B. Skirstad (eds), *Physical Activity and Active Lifestyle of Children and Youth*, Schorndorf: Verlag Karl Hofmann: 108–14.

Yiallourides, G. (1998) *Factors influencing the attitudes of 9–14-year-old Cypriot pupils towards physical education*. PhD dissertation, University of Manchester, Manchester.

4 | Physical Activity, Physical Fitness, Health and Young People

Richard Winsley and Neil Armstrong

The health benefits of being physically active in adulthood are well known. The evidence suggests that being a physically active adult can help in both the prevention and treatment of many common, but serious, health conditions such as high blood pressure, poor blood lipid profile, insulin resistance, obesity and some forms of cancer (US Department of Health and Human Services,1997). While the evidence supports the goal of encouraging all adults to be physically active on a daily basis, whether children can enjoy the same health benefits from being physically active has been the subject of much debate.

HEALTH STATUS, PHYSICAL ACTIVITY AND AEROBIC FITNESS IN YOUNG PEOPLE

It is important to understand the relationships between physical activity, aerobic fitness and health. Physical activity is a complex behavioural variable that varies from day to day, in intensity, frequency and duration, and consists of both unavoidable activity (for example, walking to work/school) and voluntary activity (for example, sports, recreation). Aerobic fitness on the other hand is a quantifiable physiological variable that reflects the ability of the individual's cardiopulmonary and muscular systems to use oxygen to produce energy for movement. Adults who are physically active generally have superior levels of aerobic fitness than their sedentary peers, but with children there is only a weak relationship between aerobic fitness – peak oxygen uptake (peak VO_2) – and physical activity level, with correlations of about $r = 0.16$ being typical (Morrow and Freedson, 1994). The reasons are unclear, but the genetic contribution to peak VO_2 and the fact that few children habitually experience the physical activity levels associated with improvements in peak VO_2 are likely candidates. Finally, health is the state of physical, mental and social well-being and not merely the absence of disease or infirmity. These three components interact with each other (see Figure 4.1) but the influence of the inter-relationships varies between adults and children.

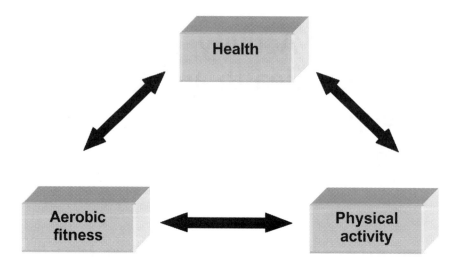

Figure 4.1 *The interactions of physical activity, aerobic fitness and health*

PHYSICAL ACTIVITY, AEROBIC FITNESS AND HEALTH

The health effects of physical activity and high aerobic fitness during childhood have been studied less frequently than with adults but evidence of the relationship between physical activity and/or aerobic fitness with health issues such as obesity, hypertension, hyper-lipidaemia, skeletal health and psychological well-being is accumulating.

Obesity

The prevalence of juvenile obesity is increasing in many western countries, the UK being no exception. Published data on the prevalence of obese and overweight children in the UK varies with the definition used – currently there is no consensus – yet the reported figures suggest that between 2 to 15 per cent of UK children are obese and 18.2 to 23.6 per cent are overweight (Chief Medical Officer, 2002). Not only does overfatness in childhood produce its own inherent health problems at that time but may lay the foundation for health problems in adult life (Bar-Or, 2003). Regrettably, the evidence suggests that overfatness during childhood, and particularly during adolescence, tracks into adulthood. This empha-sises the importance of addressing and reversing overfatness in young people.

Although the logical inference would be that overweight/obese children are less physically active than their lean peers, the data are in fact equivocal. Many studies have reported that overfat children tend to be less physically active than their leaner peers but others have shown no significant difference in activity levels between the two groups. In young people who are overfat, the most efficient way to lose excess body fat is through a multidisciplinary approach comprising diet, exercise and behavioural change interventions. Exercise alone programmes produce a small reduction in body fat percentage in obese young people of between 1 to 4 per cent, but the multifaceted approach brings about more substantial reductions of typically 5 to 20 per cent (Bar-Or and Baranowski,1994). Importantly, the fat reduction occurs not only in the subcutaneous fat, but also in the fat surrounding the internal organs (visceral fat), which is positively correlated with increased cardiovascular disease. In obese youngsters, a positive effect of physical activity on both blood lipids and glucose metabolism has been noted (Armstrong and Welsman,1997). An appropriate exercise programme for the treatment and prevention of obesity, adapted from the recommendations of Bar-Or (1995), is outlined below:

- emphasise exercise that uses large muscle groups;
- emphasise duration rather than intensity;
- raise daily energy expenditure by 10 to 15 per cent (approx. 200–300 kcal);
- include activities to promote muscle strength;
- include daily (habitual) physical activities;
- increase volume of physical activity progressively;
- ensure all physical activities are enjoyable for the child.

Blood pressure

The majority of young people have normal blood pressures and relationships between physical activity level and blood pressure in normotensive young people remain to be proven (Riddoch and Boreham, 2000). Some studies have reported a favourable relationship between the two variables but when differences in body fatness are statistically accounted for, such relationships become weak or non-significant.

In general, putting normotensive children through an exercise training programme has no effect on lowering either their systolic (SBP) or diastolic blood pressures (DBP). However, for young people with hypertension, exercise-training studies have been shown to bring about reductions in both SBP and DBP. Endurance type exercise is seen to be the most effective in reducing blood pressure, but both endurance and resistance type exercise are suitable to maintain the reductions (Armstrong and Welsman,1997).

Blood lipids

Intervention studies provide little compelling evidence that physical activity enhances the blood lipid or lipoprotein profile of normolipidaemic young people. For example, Stoedefalke et al. (2000) conducted a three times per week, 20-week endurance training programme with teenage girls but failed to evoke any significant changes in blood lipid or lipoprotein profile. Cross-sectional observational studies generally report no significant association between physical activity or fitness and blood lipids once adjustments have been made for body fatness. However, trained or highly physically active young people tend to have higher high-density lipoprotein cholesterol levels than their untrained or less active peers (Armstrong and Welsman, 1997).

Skeletal health

Peak bone mass is achieved during the third decade of life, therefore increasing bone mineral density (BMD) during childhood and adolescence may help to reduce the risk of osteoporosis in adult life. Factors such as hormonal status and genetics play an important role in influencing BMD, but nutrition and physical activity levels are key modifiable determinants of BMD. To ensure that the BMD is at optimal levels, adequate and suitable nutrition is vital throughout childhood and adolescence. The positive effects of calcium intake and physical activity on skeletal health may be independent but it is possible that calcium is an important enabling factor for the effects of physical activity on BMD.

Well-controlled studies of the effect of physical activity on BMD are sparse and the results are equivocal. However, active young people have a 5 to 15 per cent greater BMD than their less active peers and comparisons of trained and untrained subjects have provided evidence of a positive association between participation in weight-bearing sports and BMD (Riddoch and Boreham, 2000). Current data do not allow an evidence-based exercise prescription for the promotion of skeletal health but expert opinion suggests the promotion of lifetime participation in weight-bearing physical activities supplemented by resistance training (Armstrong and Welsman, 1997).

Psychological health and well-being

Physical activity improves self-esteem and reduces anxiety, stress and depression. The mechanisms by which it influences young people's psychological well-being are not fully understood and the specific effects of various types of physical activity on mental health have not been documented (Tortolero et al., 2000). However, an appropriate behavioural goal may be for children and adolescents to adopt active lifestyles. As enjoyable experiences are more likely to foster future participation, young people should be encouraged to develop a repertoire of motor skills so that they may achieve success in a range of activities and feel confident enough in their own abilities to want to pursue more active lifestyles.

The main health benefits of being physically active in childhood and adolescence are:

◆   reduces body fatness;
◆   aids management of obesity;

- lowers high blood pressure;
- increases bone mineral density;
- enhances psychological well-being.

CAN EXERCISE TRAINING IMPROVE FITNESS IN CHILDREN?

The trainability of the different aspects of fitness – strength, stamina and flexibility – in children has been investigated previously, with encouraging findings. It is possible to bring about an increase in children's aerobic fitness by putting them through an endurance exercise training programme, but the gains in fitness are smaller than those seen in adults. Typically, the gains in adult peak VO$_2$ may be approaching 25 per cent, but in children, such gains are commonly between 2 to 10 per cent. Prepubertal children in contrast, often fail to show any increase in aerobic fitness. As with adults, any gains in aerobic fitness are lost if the new level of physical activity is not maintained (Armstrong and Welsman, 1997; Mahon, 2000).

Young people respond to resistance type exercise with increased muscle strength and muscle hypertrophy. The gains are particularly noticeable in adolescence, when the hormonal environment may aid strength acquisition. Although some studies have reported that strength training in prepubertal children is ineffective, an appropriately designed programme can indeed elicit gains in strength, these predominately arising from neuromuscular adaptations rather than through muscle hypertrophy. Such neuromuscular changes include improved motor unit activation and motor coordination. The structure and content of the resistance training programme needs to be carefully considered when working with children, this is to ensure both the safety of the child and to give dispensation for the level of physical maturation of the young person (Mahon, 2000).

The use of flexibility training may involve either or both static and ballistic type movements. Although ballistic type stretching is currently popular with adults, especially athletes, the increased potential for muscle damage makes it unwise to practice with children. Thus, static stretching exercises are the recommended format to use with children. This type of flexibility exercise has been shown to be effective in increasing flexibility, and should, therefore, be an integral part of any training programme (Armstrong and Welsman, 1997).

The main fitness benefits of being physically active in childhood and adolescence are:

- increases aerobic fitness;
- increases muscular strength;
- improves flexibility.

In summary, the evidence suggests that being physically active in childhood brings with it positive health and fitness outcomes. Although these relationships are not as well-documented as with adults, where there is evidence of a relationship, the effects are favourable.

CURRENT RECOMMENDATIONS FOR PHYSICAL ACTIVITY

Until recently, widely recognised recommendations for young people's activity levels were not available but two Consensus Conferences have provided useful guidelines.

In 1993, an International Consensus Conference on Physical Activity Guidelines for Adolescents was convened, 'to develop empirically based guidelines that can be used by clinicians in their counselling, as well as by policy makers with responsibility for youth health promotion' (Sallis and Patrick, 1994: 303). A systematic review of the scientific literature was presented at the conference and the following recommendations emerged:

◆ all adolescents should be physically active daily, or nearly every day, as a part of play, sports, work, transportation, recreation, physical education or planned exercise, in the context of the family, school and community activities;

◆ adolescents should engage in three or more sessions per week of activities that last 20 minutes or more at a time and that require moderate to vigorous level of exertion.

In 1998, the Health Education Authority initiated a process of expert consultation and review of the evidence surrounding the promotion of health-enhancing physical activity for young people (Biddle et al., 1998). The policy framework that was developed acknowledged that neither the minimal nor the optimal amount of physical activity for young people could be precisely defined at that time but proposed the following recommendations:

◆ all young people should participate in physical activity of at least moderate intensity for one hour per day;

◆ young people who currently do little activity should participate in physical activity of at least moderate intensity for at least half an hour per day;

◆ at least twice a week, some of these activities should help to enhance and maintain muscular strength and flexibility, and bone health.

DO CHILDREN MEET CURRENT RECOMMENDATIONS FOR PHYSICAL ACTIVITY?

The assessment of young people's physical activity patterns presents unique challenges to the researcher. A range of tools are available – questionnaires, activity diaries, pedometers, accelerometers, doubly labelled water, heart rate monitors – all of which have their benefits and drawbacks. With young people, the technique used must be socially acceptable, it should not burden the subject with cumbersome equipment, and it should minimally influence the subject's normal physical activity pattern. Intensity, frequency and duration of activities should be recorded if a true picture of the children's habitual and planned physical activity is to be gained. It is also recommended that at least three separate days are monitored, including one weekend day (Armstrong and Van Mechelen,1998).

STUDIES FROM THE UK

Armstrong et al. (1990) continuously monitored heart rates, as a surrogate measure for physical activity, over three school days in 163 girls and 103 boys, aged 11–16 years. In order to interpret the data a subsample of children was brought to the laboratory to exercise on the treadmill at various velocities. Walking briskly at 6 km.h^{-1} (1.67 m.s^{-1}) produced a mean heart rate of approximately 140 b.min^{-1}. The data were then analysed to determine the number of young people who spent sustained periods with heart rates above this threshold (see Table 4.1).

Table 4.1   *Percentage of young people aged 11–16 years old sustaining 20- or 10-minute periods with heart rates above 139 b.min^{-1}*

	Sustained periods of 20 minutes with heart rate >139 b.min^{-1} during three days of weekday monitoring		Sustained periods of 10 minutes with heart rate >139b.min^{-1} during three days of weekday monitoring	
	Boys (%)	Girls (%)	Boys (%)	Girls (%)
0	76.7	87.7	35.9	51.5
1	14.6	10.4	26.2	20.9
2	4.9	1.2	14.6	15.3
3 or more	3.9	0.6	23.3	12.3

Source: Data taken from Armstrong et al., 1990.

These data clearly indicated that the majority of children was not experiencing the equivalent of a 20-minute brisk walk in any three-day period, with a sizeable proportion not even taking a single 10-minute brisk walk. Subsequent research of the activity patterns over a weekend revealed an even more discouraging picture, with 70.7 per cent (boys) and 93.3 per cent (girls) not experiencing a single 10-minute period of exercise with a heart rate greater than 139 b.min^{-1}.

A decade later the same research team repeated the study in a group of 52 boys and 42 girls from the same school and environment (Welsman and Armstrong, 2000). Disappointingly, their data indicated a similar picture to that reported in 1990 (see Table 4.2). Weekend monitoring again echoed the findings of a decade earlier. Of the boys, 71 per cent did not

Table 4.2 *Percentage of young people aged 11–15 years old sustaining 20- or 10-minute periods with heart rates above 139 b.min^{-1}*

| | Sustained periods of 20 minutes with heart rate > 139 b.min^{-1} during three days of weekday monitoring | | Sustained periods of 10 minutes with heart rate > 139 b.min^{-1} during three days of weekday monitoring | |
	Boys (%)	Girls (%)	Boys (%)	Girls (%)
0	67.3	88.1	28.8	54.8
1	13.5	7.1	21.2	4.8
2	13.5	4.8	28.8	21.4
3 or more	5.7	0.0	21.2	19.0

Source: Data taken from Welsman and Armstrong, 2000.

experience a single 10-minute sustained period with heart rate greater than 139 b.min^{-1}, encouragingly the proportion of girls had dropped to 60.9 per cent, but this may be explained by the slightly younger aged group sampled in comparison with the original sample.

Following the Health Education Authority Conference, Armstrong (1998) reanalysed heart rate data on over 1,000 children and adolescents, and demonstrated that the majority of young children (aged 6–10 years) satisfied their less stringent recommendation and accumulated a daily total of at least 30 minutes with their heart rate above 139 b.min^{-1}, although more boys than girls did so. However, there was a marked decline during the teenage years in the percentage of young people who achieved this target, with boys outscoring girls at all ages.

Other UK-based studies support the above findings that significant numbers of children lead relatively sedentary lives and rarely experience sustained periods of moderate or vigorous physical activity during the weekdays or weekends (Armstrong and Van Mechelen, 1998).

A common finding is that boys are significantly more active than girls, a trend echoed in other European countries. Whether this is explained through socio-cultural factors rather than physiological ones remains to be confirmed, but regardless of the explanation for such a difference, the long-term health implications of inactivity for both sexes remains a matter of concern.

In relation to younger children (less than 11 years old) a review of the published studies indicates that low levels of sustained moderate to vigorous physical activity are present in this group as well, but to a lesser extent to that recorded in the older children (Armstrong and Van Mechelen, 1998).

STUDIES FROM EUROPE

Children's physical activity patterns have also been studied in many European countries: Belgium, Finland, Sweden, Norway, Germany and the Netherlands. These studies have used a range of different measurement tools and physical activity categorisations, thus making comparisons between them difficult. In general, the European data tell a similar story to that seen in the UK, with many children demonstrating low levels of physical activity.

A large-scale study was conducted by WHO (King and Coles, 1992) on children aged 11, 13 and 15 years. The researchers assessed how many times per week the children exercised out of school to the point where they got out of breath or sweated. The data from European countries (Figure 4.2) indicate a sizeable proportion of European teenagers exercise less than once a week outside school, with boys tending to be more active than girls and for a decrease in participation with increasing age.

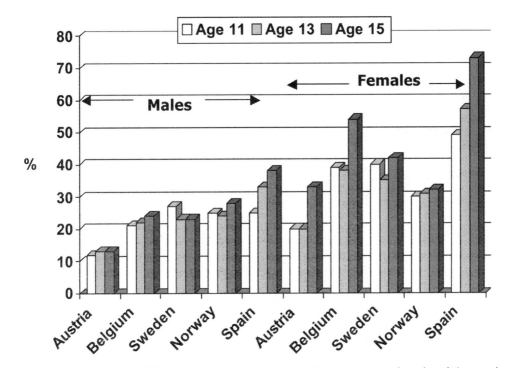

Figure 4.2   *Percentages of European students who exercise once a week or less (King and Coles, 1992)*

ARE TODAY'S CHILDREN LESS ACTIVE THAN THEIR PREDECESSORS?

Unfortunately a large-scale longitudinal assessment of children's activity patterns has not been performed, thus information from other sources are needed to answer this question. Durnin (1992) analysed energy intake data of UK children from the 1930s to 1980s and demonstrated a progressive decline in the energy intakes of young people in the UK. Over the same time frame the body mass of young children has stayed relatively stable; thus with energy intakes declining but body mass staying the same, the logical explanation is that energy expenditure must have declined over the last 50 years.

TRACKING OF PHYSICAL ACTIVITY BEHAVIOURS

Childhood physical activity is also important from a behavioural perspective, as the health status of adults may have its origins in behaviours established during childhood. No prospective study of physical activity has followed children into adult middle-age and beyond but a comprehensive review of the literature reported that physical activity tracks at low to moderate levels from adolescence to adulthood (Malina, 1996). The Allied Dunbar National Fitness Survey (Activity and Health Research, 1992) reported that of adults who were 'active now', only 2 per cent had been inactive as teenagers, indicating that inactive children are unlikely to become active adults. It is, therefore, concluded that activity during childhood and youth may form the foundation for activity behaviours in later life.

In summary there is convincing evidence to suggest that many children and teenagers lead sedentary lives. With physical activity behaviours learnt in childhood and adolescence tracking into adulthood, the challenge is to promote physical activity at a young age and then foster these behaviours through into adult life.

Below is a summary of young people's physical activity patterns:

- young people seldom experience sustained periods of moderate to vigorous physical activity;
- girls are less active than boys;
- both sexes become more inactive as they get older;
- inactive children are unlikely to become active adults.

YOUNG PEOPLE'S AEROBIC FITNESS

There is a public misconception that children's aerobic fitness is poor. This may have arisen because a physiological variable (aerobic fitness) is thought of synonymously with a behavioural variable (physical activity). As the previous section illustrated, children's activity patterns are indeed of concern but are children's aerobic fitness levels also poor?

The ability to perform exercise lasting more than 1–2 minutes is dependent on the body's ability to produce energy via aerobic processes. This system reflects the integration of the pulmonary, cardiovascular and muscular systems to allow a person to take air into the lungs, extract the oxygen from this air, transport the oxygen around the body and deliver it to the muscles where it is used to produce energy for movement. Peak VO_2 – the highest oxygen uptake elicited during an exercise test to exhaustion – is the best single indicator of young people's aerobic fitness.

In their review paper, Armstrong and Welsman (1994) assembled peak VO_2 data determined by treadmill running for 3,703 male and 1,234 female children aged between 8 and 16 years and reported that peak VO_2 when measured in absolute terms ($L.min^{-1}$), shows a positive increase with age for both sexes. This increase is due largely to the normal growth related increase in body size towards adulthood. Although both boys and girls increase their absolute peak VO_2 with age, there exists a significant sex difference in aerobic fitness from at least age 10 years. Before the age of 10 years there is little reported difference between the peak VO_2 ($L.min^{-1}$) between the sexes, but it was noted that boys' peak VO_2 ($L.min^{-1}$) was 12 per cent higher at 10 years, rising to 37 per cent higher at 16 years. The lower levels of peak VO_2 observed in females have been attributed to their lower stroke volumes, smaller quantity of muscle mass and lower level of haemoglobin (Armstrong and Welsman, 2000).

To compare two individuals of differing body sizes, it is common to express peak VO_2 ($L.min^{-1}$) in relation to body size ($mL.kg^{-1}.min^{-1}$). In so doing, the pattern of age related changes in aerobic fitness alters. Rather than a progressive increase, boys demonstrate a consistent level of aerobic fitness in relation to their body size, but girls show an age related decline; aged 6–16 years, boys' peak VO_2 remains at about 50 $mL.kg^{-1}.min$, but girls' drops from 45 to 40 $mL.kg^{-1}.min^{-1}$. The reduction in females' body size related aerobic fitness is partially attributed to a greater accumulation of body fat through puberty in comparison with boys (Armstrong and Welsman, 1994).

The appropriateness of dividing absolute peak VO_2 by body mass to remove the influence of different body sizes has been questioned, and as such the use of allometric scaling techniques has been advocated (Armstrong and Welsman, 1997). After partitioning out body size using allometric principles, VO_2 increases progressively in males from prepuberty through to adulthood and from prepuberty to circumpuberty in females. This indicates that there may be an independent effect of maturity on aerobic fitness that is separate from changes in body size (Armstrong and Welsman, 2000).

From the preceding discussion it is clear that care must be taken when making judgements about children's aerobic fitness; when aerobic fitness is expressed relative to body size, children's aerobic fitness is at least as good as that of most adults. Not only do the peak VO_2 values of UK children compare favourably with those from other countries, but the evidence shows that children's aerobic fitness has changed very little since some of the earliest research reported in the 1930s (boys) and 1950s (girls). There is no scientific evidence to indicate that young people's peak VO_2 has declined over the last 50 years (Armstrong and Van Mechelen, 1998).

CONCLUSION

The preceding discussion has indicated that aerobic fitness and physical activity in young people are independent variables and must be interpreted as such. There is no evidence that UK children's aerobic fitness is low or deteriorating from generation to generation. The health and fitness benefits from being physical active are not as marked as observed with adults, but are favourable nonetheless. The current level of physical activity experienced by many children is, however, cause for concern and shows no signs of improving. Encouraging our school children to become more physically active, will promote potential health benefits during childhood, and may facilitate a positive attitude towards physical activity which will be sustained throughout adult life.

REFERENCES

Activity and Health Research (1992) *Allied Dunbar National Fitness Survey*. London: Sports Council and Health Education Authority.

Armstrong, N. (1998) 'Young people's physical activity patterns as assessed by heart rate monitoring', *Journal of Sports Sciences*, 16: S9–S16.

Armstrong, N., Balding, J., Gentle, P. and Kirby, B. (1990) 'Patterns of physical activity among 11 to 16-year-old British children', *British Medical Journal*, 301: 203–5.

Armstrong, N. and Van Mechelen, W. (1998) 'Are young people fit and active?', in S. Biddle, J. Sallis and N. Cavill (eds), *Young and Active?* London: Health Education Authority. pp. 69–97.

Armstrong, N. and Welsman, J.R. (1994) 'Assessment and interpretation of aerobic function in children and adolescents', *Exercise and Sports Sciences Reviews*, 22: 435–76.

Armstrong, N. and Welsman, J.R. (1997) *Young People and Physical Activity*. Oxford: Oxford University Press.

Armstrong, N. and Welsman, J.R. (2000) 'Development of aerobic fitness', *Pediatric Exercise Science*, 12: 128–49.

Bar-Or, O. (1995) 'Obesity', in B. Goldberg (ed.), *Sports and Exercise for Children with Chronic Health Conditions*. Champaign, Illinois: Human Kinetics. pp. 335–53.

Bar-Or, O. (2003) 'The juvenile obesity epidemic: Strike back with physical activity', *Sports Science Exchange 89*, 16 (2)

Bar-Or, O. and Baranowski, T. (1994) 'Physical activity, adiposity, and obesity among adolescents', *Pediatric Exercise Science*, 6: 348–60.

Biddle, S., Sallis, J. and Cavill, N. (eds) (1998) *Young and Active?* London: Health Education Authority.

Chief Medical Officer's Annual Report (2002) Department of Health Publications. London: HMSO.

Durnin, J.V.G.A (1992) 'Physical activity levels past and present', in N. Norgan (ed.), *Physical Activity and Health* Cambridge: Cambridge University Press. pp. 20–27.

King, A.J.C. and Coles, B. (1992) *The Health of Canada's Youth*. Ottawa: Ministry of Health and Welfare.

Mahon A (2000) 'Exercise training', in N. Armstrong and W. Van Mechelen (eds), *Paediatric Exercise Science and Medicine*. Oxford: OUP. pp. 201–22.

Malina, R.M. (1996) 'Tracking of physical activity and physical fitness across the lifespan', *Research Quarterly for Exercise and Sport*, 67 (Suppl 3): 48–57.

Morrow, J.R., and Freedson, P.S. (1994) 'Relationship between habitual physical activity and aerobic fitness in adolescents', *Pediatric Exercise Science*, 6: 315–329.

Riddoch, C.J. and Boreham, C. (2000) 'Physical activity, physical fitness and children's health: current concepts', in N. Armstrong and W. Van Mechelen (eds), *Paediatric Exercise Science and Medicine*. Oxford University Press: Oxford. pp. 243–52.

Sallis, J.F. and Patrick, K. (1994) 'Physical activity guidelines for adolescents; Consensus statement', *Pediatric Exercise Science*, 6: 302–314.

Stoedefalke, K., Armstrong, N., Kirby, B.J. and Welsman, J.R. (2000) 'Effect of training on peak oxygen uptake and blood lipids in 13 to 14-year-old girls', *Acta Paediatrica*, 89: 1290–94.

Tortolero, S.R., Taylor, W.C. and Murray, N.G. (2000) 'Physical activity, physical fitness and social, psychological and emotional health', in N. Armstrong and W. Van Mechelen (eds), *Paediatric Exercise Science and Medicine*. Oxford: Oxford University Press. pp. 273–93.

US Department of Health and Human Services (1997) *Physical Activity and Health: A Report of the Surgeon General*. Atalanta, GA: US Department of Human Services, Centers for Disease Control and Prevention, National Center for Chronic Disease Prevention and Health Promotion.

Welsman, J.R. and Armstrong, N. (2000) 'Physical activity patterns in secondary schoolchildren', *European Journal of Physical Education*, 5: 147–57.

5 | Health-related Exercise and Physical Education

Jo Harris

This chapter will review health-related exercise developments within the school curriculum and identify enduring themes and contemporary issues. At the outset, it is important to clarify the meaning of 'health-related exercise' (HRE) both within and beyond the school setting. In broad terms, HRE is physical activity associated with health enhancement and disease prevention (Health Education Authority, 1998: 2). More specifically within an educational context, HRE refers to: 'the teaching of knowledge, understanding, physical competence and behavioural skills, and the creation of positive attitudes and confidence associated with current and lifelong participation in physical activity' (Harris, 2000: 2).

Of course, the close relationship between physical education (PE) and health is hardly a new concept. PE was driven by this objective at the beginning of the twentieth century (Sleap, 1990) although other objectives such as skill development and self-discovery later came to the fore, at the expense of a concern for health. Nevertheless, health once again became an important objective of the PE curriculum in the early 1980s, and since then there has been a well documented and active interest by many physical educators in promoting health-related physical activity in schools in the UK (Almond, 1989; Williams, 1988).

There is little doubt that the school is an appropriate setting for the promotion of health-related learning and behaviours, not least because there is the potential for sustained exposure to an environment which can positively influence the behaviour of virtually all children for about 40–45 per cent of their waking time (Fox and Harris, 2003). It is known that school-based intervention studies have positively influenced young people's health, fitness and physical activity levels, as well as their knowledge, understanding and attitudes towards physical activity (Almond and Harris, 1998; Cale and Harris, 1998; Harris and Cale 1997; Stone et al., 1998).

PE is considered to play a key role in the promotion of health and activity in young people (Armstrong 2002; Cale, 2000a; Cardon and De Bourdeaudhuij, 2002; McKenzie, 2001; Shephard and Trudeau, 2000). Indeed, McKenzie (2001) views PE as the most suitable vehicle for the promotion of active, healthy lifestyles among young people while Green (2002: 95) refers to the 'taken-for-granted role of PE in health promotion'. Both Green

(2002) and Harris and Penney (2000) have noted how government policy in recent years has identified PE and school sport as important in educating and providing opportunities for young people to become independently active for life (Department of Health (DoH), 1999; Department for Culture, Media and Sport (DCMS/DfEE), 2001). This is exemplified by the following significant statement: 'The government believes that two hours of physical activity a week, including the National Curriculum for Physical Education and extra-curricular activities, should be an aspiration for all schools' (Department for Education and Employment (DfEE) and Qualifications and Curriculum Authority (QCA), 1999b: 17).

A further example is the government's PE, School Sport and Club Links Strategy which is designed to transform PE and school sport, and carries with it an investment of £459 million over three years (DfES and DCMS, 2003). These examples are clearly encouraging in terms of the future provision and quality of health-related learning and activity opportunities for young people.

Although it is accepted that PE represents much less than 2 per cent of a young person's waking time and, therefore, cannot in itself satisfy the physical activity needs of young people or address activity shortfalls (Fox and Harris, 2003), there is a strong belief that PE can affect leisure time physical activity through positive activity experiences and exercise education (Vilhjalmsson and Thorlindsson, 1998). It is, therefore, essential to carefully consider how PE can most effectively contribute to promoting active lifestyles and providing opportunities for all pupils to experience appropriate levels of physical activity (Cardon and De Bourdeaudhuij, 2002). In this respect, the content and delivery of the health-related learning in the PE programme within the context of the National Curriculum, as well as the provision of activity opportunities within and beyond the school, are critical.

REVIEW OF HRE WITHIN THE NATIONAL CURRICULUM

The first National Curriculum for Physical Education (NCPE) formally addressed health issues (Department of Education and Science (DES) and The Welsh Office (WO), 1992) and identified HRE as a component of the cross-curricular theme of health education (National Curriculum Council, 1990). However, its position and mode of expression in the curriculum were unclear (Harris, 1997a). At the time, some feared that the area would be marginalised or overlooked as it was not afforded the status of a separate programme of study but was instead identified as a theme to be delivered through the activity areas (Cale, 1996; Fox, 1992; Penney and Evans, 1997). These fears were all but confirmed by Harris' (1997a) research which revealed the teaching of HRE in PE in secondary schools to be characterised by much confusion and considerable variation in practice, resulting in limited systematic expression of health. In short, HRE meant different things to different people, and it was evident that health promotion as a key goal of PE was neither universally accepted nor well understood (Harris, 1995).

In these early days of the NCPE, the absence of an activity area for HRE was interpreted by some to indicate that HRE should be delivered solely through the activity areas (Oxley, 1994). However, Harris and Almond (1994) pointed out that the National Curriculum should permit scope for professional judgement regarding how best to deliver content within the context of different schools. Consequently, a number of different approaches to the delivery of HRE have emerged (that is to say, permeation/integration; focused/discrete; combination), each with specific strengths and limitations (see Table 5.1). Cale (2000a) has revealed a combination of approaches to be the most common (that is to say, focused units of work in PE, integration through the activity areas, and delivery within other areas of the curriculum) which suggests that HRE is now being addressed in a more explicit and structured manner in schools. However, the critical issue remains the effectiveness of the learning more than the particular approach adopted (Harris, 2000).

Subsequent revisions of the NCPE (Department for Education (DfE) and the WO), 1995; Department for Education and Employment (DfEE) and Qualifications and Curriculum Authority (QCA), 1999a) have arguably provided a stronger positioning of health-related issues which implies a more explicit prompt for the area to be addressed in curriculum planning and delivery (Fox and Harris, 2003). For example, 'knowledge and understanding of fitness and health' is now one of four aspects of the NCPE through which learning is developed at each key stage. A more explicit approach to HRE is also evident in *Curriculum Wales 2000* which provides a detailed programme of study for HRE at each key stage, and incorporates 'exercise activities' (non-competitive forms of exercise, such as step aerobics, jogging, weight-training, cycling, circuit-training and skipping) as one of four areas of experience at Key Stage 4 (Welsh Assembly, 1999). Similarly, in England, in line with a call from government for the broadening of provision within the PE curriculum to enhance lifelong learning and healthy lifestyles, the compulsory requirement to study games activities for 14 to 16-year-olds was removed (DfEE and QCA, 1999a).

Not before time, these developments have opened the doors to more flexible, creative and relevant provision of PE for older pupils. Indeed, Green (2002) acknowledges the trend identified by Roberts (1996b) of schools beginning to respond to the changing lifestyles and activity interests of young people and supplementing the traditional PE diet with a broader range of activities. This was acknowledged in an OFSTED summary of secondary school physical education reports (2000–02) which made a positive reference to the provision of more indoor alternative activities such as aerobics, fitness, badminton, volleyball and access to accredited courses, as well as changes to gender groupings and kit requirements (OFSTED, 2002: 2).

SUPPORTING THE TEACHING OF HRE IN SCHOOLS

In response to ongoing concerns over the expression of health in PE, and teachers' relatively limited knowledge and understanding of the area (Almond and Harris, 1997; Cale, 1996; Fox, 1992; Harris, 1997a), an HRE working group comprising representatives from schools,

Table 5.1 *Approaches to HRE within the National Curriculum*

Approach	Strengths	Limitations
Permeation/Integration An integrated approach in which HRE is taught through the PE activity areas (i.e., through athletics, dance, games, gymnastics, swimming, and outdoor and adventurous activities).	HRE knowledge, understanding and skills can be seen as part of and integral to all PE experiences. Children learn that all physical activities can contribute towards good health and can become part of an active lifestyle.	HRE knowledge, understanding and skills may become 'lost' or marginalised among other information relating to skills and performance; there may be an overload of information for pupils; much liaison is required to ensure that all pupils receive similar information from different teachers; the approach may be somewhat ad hoc and piecemeal.
Focused/Discrete An approach involving teaching HRE through specific focused lessons or units of work either within a PE or health education programme. During PE lessons, the main focus is the learning concept rather than the activity itself.	A specific focus can help to ensure that HRE does not become lost or take second place to other information; there is less likelihood of HRE being regarded as an assumed 'by-product' of PE lessons; HRE is perceived as important through having its own time slot and identity; the value and status of the associated knowledge, understanding and skills is raised.	HRE may be seen in isolation and not closely linked to the PE activity areas; the HRE knowledge, understanding and skills may be delivered over a period of time with long gaps in between which is problematic in terms of cohesion and progression (e.g., one short block of work per year); the knowledge-base may be delivered in such a way as to reduce lesson activity levels (e.g., through 'sitting down' lessons with too much talk).
Combined/Multi-method Any combination of permeation, focused and topic-based approaches is possible.	A combination of approaches can build on the strengths of different approaches and, at the same time, minimise their individual limitations; it can ensure that value is placed on HRE and that the area of work is closely linked to all PE experiences and other health behaviours.	Combined approaches may be more time consuming initially to plan, structure, implement and coordinate within the curriculum.

higher education, the advisory service, and key sport, health and PE organisations was established in 1997 to produce good practice guidelines on HRE for primary and secondary teachers. The published resource provided an interpretation of the health and fitness requirements of the NCPE in England and Wales expressed in the form of learning outcomes, and incorporated links with aspects of related subjects such as Personal, Social and Health Education (PSHE) and Science (Harris, 2000). The learning outcomes are placed in four categories (safety issues; exercise effects; health benefits; activity promotion) to clarify the range of coverage and the progression of learning within and across the key stages. Table 5.2 presents examples of these learning outcomes for Key Stage 2 (7–11 years) and Key Stage 3 (11–14 years) pupils.

Reassuringly, a study conducted with 500 secondary schools revealed that the HRE guidance had a positive impact on many PE teachers' knowledge, attitudes and confidence, and on their planning, content, evaluation, organisation and delivery of HRE (Cale et al., 2002). However, it was less successful in changing teachers' philosophies and teaching methods. Clearly, resources by themselves are limited in their ability to bring about 'real' change. To quote Sparkes (1994), what results represents 'innovation without change' in that new ideas are taken on board but only at a superficial level, or they are integrated within already well established philosophies and paradigms.

During and since the development of the guidelines on HRE, resources have been produced to reflect and exemplify the consensus guidance. Examples include Fit for TOPs for primary teachers of PE (Youth Sport Trust et al., 1998) and Fit for Life for secondary PE teachers (Youth Sport Trust, 2000). Furthermore, the YMCA has produced a series of 'health and fitness' resources to support the teaching of HRE at Key Stage 4 in secondary schools (Elbourn and YMCA Fitness Industry Training, 1998; Elbourn et al., 1998a, 1998b, 1998c; YMCA, 2000, 2002). These resources provide primary and secondary teachers of PE with a much needed and long awaited support structure to assist them in designing and delivering effective HRE programmes in schools. Nevertheless, it cannot be assumed that teachers are aware of these resources and are able to access them, or that the resources and/or associated training will necessarily be successful in bringing about changes in philosophical approaches underpinning the content and delivery of current programmes.

Resource? readily available?

PARALLEL HEALTH-RELATED DEVELOPMENTS OF SIGNIFICANCE

A parallel health-related development of much significance was the launch of the Health Education Authority's (HEA) (now the Health Development Agency (HDA)) policy framework for the promotion of health-enhancing physical activity for young people 'Young and Active?'(HEA, 1998). This framework identifies the Education Sector as one of the key organisations which has a role to play in promoting health-enhancing physical activity and includes a series of key recommendations for schools, including:

Table 5.2 *Examples of HRE Learning Outcomes for Pupils 7–14 years*

Category of HRE learning outcomes	HRE learning outcomes at Key Stage 2 (7–11 years)	HRE learning Outcomes at Key Stage 3 (11–14 years)
Safety issues	Know the purpose of a warm up and cool down and recognise and describe parts of a warm up and cool down.	Know the value of preparing for and recovering from activity and the possible consequences of not doing so, and explain the purpose of and plan and perform each component of a warm up and cool down.
Exercise effects	Experience and explain the short-term effects of exercise (e.g., increase in rate and depth of breathing to provide more oxygen to the working muscles; increase in the heart rate to pump more oxygen to the working muscles; varied feelings and moods).	Monitor and explain a range of short-term effects of exercise on body systems (e.g., cardiovascular system – changes in breathing and heart rate, temperature, appearance, feelings, recovery rate, ability to pace oneself and remain within a target zone).
Health benefits	Know that exercise strengthens bones and muscles (including the heart) and keeps joints flexible.	Know a range of long-term benefits of exercise on physical health (e.g., reduced risk of heart disease, osteoporosis, obesity, back pain).
Activity promotion	Be aware of their current levels of activity; know when, where and how they can be active in school and outside.	Be able to access information about a range of activity opportunities at school, home and in the local community, and know ways of incorporating activity into their lifestyles.

◆ schools should recognise the importance of health-related exercise within the National Curriculum and ensure that the requirements are fully implemented in practice;

◆ health-related exercise should take the form of an effectively planned, delivered and evaluated programme of study;

◆ professional development, training and support services, including FE and HE colleges, should provide appropriate training (including initial teacher and in-service training) that includes the teaching of health-related exercise (Health Education Authority, 1998: 8).

In addition, the policy framework contained the following recommendations about how active young people (that is to say, all people aged 5–18 years) should be:

Primary recommendations

◆ All young people should participate in physical activity of at least moderate intensity *for one hour per day*.

◆ Young people who currently do little activity should participate in physical activity of at least moderate intensity for *at least half an hour per day*.

Secondary recommendation

◆ *At least twice a week*, some of these activities should help to enhance and maintain muscular strength and flexibility and bone health (Health Education Authority, 1998: 3).

These recommendations are significant and timely. They represent a concise response to the key question 'how active should young people be?' and they provide a consistent message for young people and for adults involved in caring for and working with young people. Disappointingly though, many PE teachers appear to be unaware of these recommendations as they are rarely integrated within schemes and units of work. Teachers of PE and PSHE (Personal, Social and Health Education) clearly need to be informed of these exercise recommendations and their implications for practice, as well as their limitations (Cale and Harris, 1993, 1996).

Further significant developments within the education sector include the expansion of the Specialist Sports Colleges infrastructure and the School Sport Co-ordinator partnerships, and QCA's PE and School Sport (PESS) investigation into the impact of high quality PESS on young people and schools. Each of these developments has now become an element of the government's Physical Education, School Sport and Club Links (PESSCL) Strategy (DfES and DCMS, 2003) and the potential influence of these programmes collectively is promising in terms of sharing good practice among schools in relation to innovative HRE programmes and increasing the number of young people who benefit from being active.

LIMITED AND LIMITING INTERPRETATIONS OF HRE WITHIN PE

With respect to enduring themes, research has highlighted examples of narrow interpretations of HRE that often equate the area with some or all of the following: vigorous activity such as cross-country running; fitness testing; safety and hygiene issues such as warming up and cooling down, lifting and carrying equipment, and taking showers (Harris, 1997b). Such narrow interpretations are worrying as they have the potential to lead to undesirable practices such as: forced fitness regimes; directed activity with minimal learning; inactive PE lessons involving excessive theory or teacher talk; dull, uninspiring drills; or an over-emphasis on issues relating to safety and hygiene (Harris, 2000). Furthermore, the knowledge base associated with HRE is not always fully acknowledged and consequently activity-based units (for example, blocks of work on aerobics, cross country, circuit-training) may be delivered with minimal learning and limited pupil involvement. Evidence also suggests that physiological issues, such as the physical effects of exercise and fitness testing tend to dominate HRE courses in schools (Harris, 1995, 2000). Indeed, one could argue that many health-related programmes designed, taught and evaluated in schools are oriented more towards 'fitness for sports performance' than 'fitness for healthy lifestyles'.

This is perhaps not surprising given that Green (2002) and Penney and Evans (1999) have observed that both teachers and government appear to view sport, and particularly team games, as the primary focus of PE and the primary vehicle for the promotion of ongoing involvement in health-promoting, active lifestyles. Certainly, despite successive revisions of the NCPE, and notwithstanding the loosening of the constraint towards games at Key Stage 4 within Curriculum 2000 (DfE and WO, 1995; DfEE and QCA, 1999a), competitive sports and team games with an emphasis on performance still dominate the curriculum (Fairclough et al., 2002; Penney and Evans, 1999; Penney and Harris, 1997). In addition, changes in the terminology towards 'fitness' and 'training,' evident within the new requirements (DfEE and QCA, 1999b), further highlight the continued and powerful influence of the focus on sport and performance in PE (Hargreaves, 2000; Penney and Evans, 1997, 1999).

This is despite the fact that the relevance and appeal of competitive sports and team games to many youngsters in the UK has been questioned (Fairclough et al., 2002; Fox and Harris, 2003; Green, 2002; Roberts, 1996a) and concern has been expressed that the continued emphasis and privileging of 'traditional PE' may be turning many young people off physical activity participation (Fox and Harris, 2003; Harris and Cale, 1998; Roberts, 1996a). Green (2002: 97) suggests that much official and semi-official government rhetoric concerning school sport and PE fails to acknowledge participatory trends in young people towards lifestyle activities and non-competitive, more recreational sporting forms, and away from competitive performance-oriented sports. Green (2002) suggests that this results in a substantial disservice to physical educators committed to promoting lifelong participation by proposing an inappropriate response. Similarly in the USA, Douthitt and Harvey (1995:

34) consider that the PE profession has 'been trying to force youth into a PE curriculum mold which does not include sensitivity to individual psycho-emotional needs and preferences'.

Indeed, this is partly exemplified by the prevalence of fitness testing in schools (American College of Sports Medicine, 2000; Harris, 1995; Cale and Harris, 2002) despite controversy about its value and place in the curriculum (American College of Sports Medicine, 1988; Armstrong, 1987, 1989; Cale and Harris, 2002; Harris, 2000; Harris and Cale, 1997; Physical Education Association, 1988; Rowland, 1995). A key concern with testing in PE lessons is, of course, the amount of time spent on it without necessarily positively influencing either pupils' activity levels or their attitudes towards physical activity (Cale and Harris, 2002; Harris and Cale, 1997). Indeed, Rowland (1995) considers programmes of field testing children to be antithetical to the goal of promoting physical activity in children, demeaning, embarrassing and uncomfortable to those children about which there is most concern, and believes that they serve to reinforce the notion that exercise is competitive and unpleasant. To assist PE teachers in critically evaluating the place of fitness testing in the curriculum, the HRE guidance material (Harris, 2000) identifies the main issues associated with testing and recommends that any testing should: promote activity; develop understanding; be safe and developmentally-appropriate; be individualised; and be enjoyable. The national PESS programmes both in England and in Wales include plans to develop resources on monitoring pupils' health, activity and fitness through developmentally-appropriate procedures linked to criterion referenced standards. These resources should do much to help teachers overcome the limitations of commonly practised fitness testing, and maximise the benefits that pupils can obtain from being involved in informative, individualised and positive monitoring of health, activity and fitness.

Linked to this are concerns over the low level of moderate to vigorous physical activity during PE lessons (Babiarz et al., 1998; Curtner-Smith et al., 1995; Fairclough, 2003; Stratton, 1996, 1997) although it is known that intervention studies have successfully shown that PE can be made more active for pupils, and teachers can make a difference to the amount of activity achieved during lessons (for example, McKenzie et al., 1996, 1997; Sallis et al., 1997; Simons-Morton et al., 1991). However, Harris and Cale (1998) caution how increasing activity levels within PE prompts a range of potential responses including those that may be misguided and undesirable. For example, some teachers may respond by forcing pupils into 'hard, uncomfortable' exercise, such as arduous cross-country running or fitness testing, at the expense of developing understanding and physical and behavioural skills and enhancing attitudes through positive activity experiences. Likewise, Fairclough (2003) also suggests that by employing interventions and activities aimed to increase pupils' heart rates (see, for example, Baquet et al., 2002), other teaching objectives within PE may be compromised. Cale and Harris (1998) believe that such examples serve only to simplify the complex nature of health enhancement and overlook the multifaceted nature of exercise education and activity promotion.

STRENGTHS AND AREAS FOR DEVELOPMENT

An analysis of health-related learning within the PE curriculum reveals that the PE profession addresses some areas of learning well but there are areas which are less well addressed. These areas of strength and areas for development are summarised in Table 5.3.

Table 5.3 *Strengths and limitations of health-related learning in PE*

HRE: Strengths What does the PE profession do well?	HRE: Areas for development What does the PE profession do less well?
Addressing safety issues, e.g. providing a safe learning environment; warming up.	Understanding health benefits, e.g. explaining the links with energy balance and healthy weight management; emphasising the social and psychological benefits of activity.
Explaining exercise effects, e.g. describing the effects of exercise on heart rate and breathing rate.	Promoting activity, e.g. routinely informing all pupils where they can do more activity; informing pupils about how active they should be; monitoring involvement in activity.

This is supported by the findings of a critical document analysis of OFSTED inspection reports (1997–2000) of 33 secondary schools in the Midlands, focusing on the 'knowledge and understanding of health and fitness' aspect of the PE curriculum, which revealed variations in both the quantity and quality of the comments and inconsistencies in the range of the statements. In summary, the comments were generally narrow in scope, focusing predominantly on 'safety issues' and 'exercise effects', with minimal attention to 'health benefits' and 'activity promotion'. Typical comments included:

> Pupils know the value of a warm-up activity, such as stretching, to prevent muscles tearing. Some pupils know and locate the muscles in their legs to be stretched, for example, the hamstrings and calf muscles (11–14 school; November 1999).

> Fitness knowledge is appropriate, with all students able to conduct their own warm-up and stretching exercises (14–18 years; January 1997).

> Most know the names of large muscle groups and can locate them accurately (11–18 school; September 2000).

The analysis indicated a limited expression of 'health and fitness' within OFSTED inspection findings, reflecting a narrow interpretation by teachers and/or inspectors of health-related issues within physical education. For example, while some health-related topics and concepts were adequately addressed in inspection reports, if not overdone (for example, warming up), others were neglected (for example, cool down; health benefits of exercise; exercise recommendations for young people; the role of physical activity in healthy weight management; personal exercise programming). The comments within OFSTED inspection reports reflected the physiological domination of health-related PE programmes and their limited attention to social and psychological issues. For example, it was rare to find statements relating to pupils' learning about the health benefits of physical activity, how active they should be, and about opportunities to be active in the community. This is disappointing, especially given the increasing profile of 'health' in the public domain and concerns about sedentary lifestyles, low activity levels and increasing obesity levels. It would seem that by focusing on such a narrow range of health-related issues, OFSTED inspectors are doing little to encourage teachers to move the area forward. This clearly has implications for the future expression of health within physical education.

DISPARATE AGENDAS FOR PE AND PUBLIC HEALTH

It remains evident that physical education has not yet fully acknowledged, addressed or embraced its potential contribution to public health. Furthermore, PE does not appear to be perceived by significant others as a major contributor to public health. For example, 'physical activity' is frequently absent from National Healthy School Standard (NHSS) developments in schools and PE teachers are usually not centrally involved in such initiatives. The NHSS is one component, along with the 'Wired for Health' website and Strategies for Safer Travel to School, within the Healthy Schools Programme (DoH, 1999) which is a key part of the government's drive to improve standards of health and education and to tackle health inequalities. The Healthy Schools Programme aims: 'to make children, teachers, parents and communities more aware of the opportunities that exist in schools for improving health' (*www.wiredforhealth.gov.uk*).

Principally, a 'healthy school' seeks to achieve healthy lifestyles for the entire school population by developing supportive environments conducive to the promotion of health. Wired for Health is a series of websites which provides health information for a range of audiences, including pupils. The following websites: *www.welltown.gov.uk* (for 5–7-year-olds); *www.galaxy-h.gov.uk* (for 7–11-year-olds); *www.lifebytes.gov.uk* (for 11–14-year-olds); and *www.mindbodysoul.gov.uk* (for 14–16-year-olds), include messages about physical activity such as:

> A lot of young people are active for a total of 30 minutes a day. This may sound okay but actually it's not enough to keep your heart and body in good health. You should be aiming for at least one hour per day of moderate intensity physical activity. Activities like brisk walking, cycling and dancing are all excellent examples of moderate activity. Moderate activity makes you feel warmer and slightly out of breath. (*www.lifebytes.gov.uk*)

> Once you know how much activity you should be aiming for and the types of activity you can do, how are you going to find time and opportunity to do it all? After all, you're at school all

day, and have homework and other commitments in the evening. Sound familiar? Check out the excuse busters. (*www.mindbodysoul.gov.uk*)

In addition to these developments, a number of recommendations to guide physical activity promotion within schools have been published in recent years (Harris, 2000; HEA, 1998; National Audit Office, 2001; National Heart Forum, 2002; Centers for Disease Control and Prevention, 1997, 2000; Morrow et al., 1999). These recommendations identify the need for a whole school approach to physical activity promotion, targeted physical activity interventions, and further research into school-based approaches to promote physical activity. However, it is disappointing that the PE profession is not more centrally involved in whole-school initiatives to promote health, and that many PE teachers remain unaware of the NHSS programme and its component parts as these could be used to reinforce and develop learning in and through PE and school sport. It is also a pity that comparatively limited attention appears to have been paid to the formally recognised concept of an 'Active School' which maximises opportunities for children and adults associated with the school to be active by exploring all opportunities and avenues to promote physical activity (Cale, 1997; Fox, 1996; Fox and Harris, 2003; National Heart Forum, 2002).

With respect to the notion of disparate and possibly conflicting agendas for PE and public health, it would appear that PE tends to reflect and reinforce concepts relating to fitness, sport and performance, while health education is more closely associated with health, activity and participation. Consequently, PE teachers tend to be viewed outside the PE profession as sports teachers or coaches, more interested in performance and excellence, than participation and health. Furthermore, and perhaps surprisingly, rather than promoting equity and inclusion, Harris and Penney (2000) found that health-related PE programmes often reflected, expressed and reinforced gendered practices.

Clearly, in order to promote health and activity, the way in which health-related information and activity experiences are presented is critical. PE should involve enjoyable, positive and meaningful exercise experiences, a practical knowledge base and caring teaching strategies (Fox and Harris, 2003). There should also be a clear emphasis on the beneficial short- and long-term effects of exercise, improved functional capacity, weight management, and psychological well-being associated with exercise participation. Fox (1993) reminds us that merely highlighting the risks of inactivity is ineffective as teenagers believe that they are either immortal or immune from such risks. Young people need to be helped to shift from dependence on the teacher to independence, by acquiring the necessary understanding, competence and confidence to be active independently (Harris, 2000). This needs to be taught, not relied upon to be 'caught'. Smith and Biddle (1995) and Harris (1995, 2000) have pointed out that limited attention is paid in schools to socio-cultural, environmental and behavioural factors influencing children's participation in activity. Yet, it is commonly accepted within health promotion that knowledge alone is insufficient to bring about behaviour change (Douthitt and Harvey, 1995) and that simply encouraging children to be more active takes no account of key socio-cultural, environmental and behavioural factors (Smith and Biddle, 1995).

Teachers who do address these factors within the curriculum typically adopt educational or behavioural approaches to the promotion of physical activity, presenting arguments for and relevant information about physical activity, and possibly involving pupils in learning self-management and regulatory skills such as goal setting, programme planning, self-reinforcement and monitoring or time management to encourage participation in physical activity. These skills are considered critical to lifestyle change and activity independence (Corbin, 2002). However, this approach has major limitations as it holds the individual totally responsible for their activity behaviour, and fails to acknowledge other factors in the social environment which influence physical activity. In recognition of such limitations, there has been growing interest and support for environmental or ecological approaches to physical activity promotion in recent years (Sallis et al., 1998). For example, many aspects of the school can either promote or inhibit the adoption of an active lifestyle, and understanding gained through the 'formal' curriculum can be reinforced and supported or completely undermined by the 'hidden' curriculum. Thus, to increase the likelihood of physical activity promotion being successful and leading to sustainable behaviour change, it needs to be more than just a curriculum activity focusing on individual behaviour change strategies (Cale, 1997).

So why is the PE profession not more successful in terms of fostering lifelong activity in young people (Douthitt and Harvey, 1995; Harris and Cale, 1998)? Possible contributory reasons include limited PE time and low subject status. The time allocated to PE in the UK has consistently been among the lowest in Europe (Cale, 2000a; Harris, 1994; Fairclough and Stratton, 1997; Morrow et al., 1999) and the health and PE curricula are generally seen as competing with core subjects (for example, maths/numeracy; English/literacy) and in times of high academic priority, viewed as more expendable (Fox and Harris, 2003). Hardman and Marshall's (2000) international study of school PE similarly highlighted issues of restricted or decreasing curriculum time for PE, low subject status and negative attitudes of significant others such as headteachers and parents towards PE. More encouragingly, however, the government's recent PE, School Sport and Club Links Strategy aims to increase the percentage of school children in England who spend a minimum of two hours each week in high quality PE and school sport within and beyond the curriculum from 25 per cent in 2002, to 75 per cent by 2006 (DfES, 2003). Yet, even with increased PE time, there can be no guarantee that health and activity promotion will become central features of the curriculum. Fox and Harris (2003) highlight how, despite a stronger positioning of health issues within the curriculum in recent years, the effect may be minimal because many teachers continue to prefer to focus on competitive sport in the curriculum.

Additional reasons for the somewhat narrow approach to HRE may be PE teachers' limited health-related (Cale et al., 2002; Harris, 1995; OFSTED, 1996) and physical activity promotion knowledge (Cale, 2000b; Cardon and De Bourdeaudhuij, 2002), despite a positive attitude towards physical activity and fitness goals (Cale, 2000b; Kulinna and Silverman, 2000). Cardon and De Bourdeaudhuij (2002), for example, revealed that many PE teachers were not sufficiently aware of the health-promoting role of PE, and Cale

(2000b) reported that a number had limited understanding of the concept and how it could be approached in their school. Of course, the above may partly be explained by the fact that few physical educators have been adequately trained to address health-based work and physical activity promotion (Cardon and De Bourdeaudhuij, 2002; Harris, 1997a; Fox and Harris, 2003; Pate et al., 1999). Corbin (2002: 132) reminds us that children 'do activity in different ways than adults' and Fox and Harris (2003) describe young children's activity as 'kiss-and-chase' or 'kick-and-run' type bursts of energy and teenagers' activity as more adult-like, involving sustained moderate activity through sports or exercise. It is also evident that young people's activity occurs in a range of settings, in a variety of modes, and at particular times of the day including: active transport to and from school; informal play during school breaks and lunchtimes; informal play after school; formal sports, PE and exercise training; active jobs (Fox and Harris, 2003: 187).

Finally, in terms of constraining factors within the PE profession, Fox and Harris (2003) suggest that the structure and funding of initial teacher training courses often serve to limit prospective teachers' experience of health-related exercise within the curriculum. Furthermore, the approach many PE teachers adopt to the area is inevitably influenced by the highly scientised sports science courses (which typically focus on a bio-physical conception of the body and of health) from which PE teachers normally graduate (Colquhoun, 1994).

CONTEMPORARY ISSUES

A contemporary issue associated with HRE relates to future plans for the 14–19 curriculum. The government's Green Paper *14–19: Extending Opportunities, Raising Standards* states that there should be an emphasis on physical fitness, health and well-being during the 14–19 stage in PE. The Qualifications and Curriculum Authority (QCA)'s website (*www.qca.org.uk/pess*) contains guidance on key objectives and signs of success. The key objectives are considered to be:

◆ to improve pupils' knowledge and understanding of fitness, health and well-being;

◆ to improve pupils' commitment to healthy, active lifestyles;

◆ to increase pupils' involvement in healthy, active lifestyles.

Examples of 'signs of success' which teachers might expect to see from their pupils when there has been an increased emphasis on fitness, health and well-being at Key Stage 4 are presented in Table 5.4.

In response to concerns that the traditional PE programme is neither relevant nor appealing to a large proportion of older pupils, and taking into account psycho-social factors influencing young people's participation, Fox and Harris (2003) identified a number of features which, in their view might produce more successful programmes. These features included:

Table 5.4 *Examples of 'signs of success': fitness, health and well-being at Key Stage 4*

Key objectives of increasing the emphasis on fitness, health and well-being	Examples of signs of success You will see pupils who:
Knowledge and understanding of fitness, health and well-being	◆ can explain more clearly what H, F and WB are and the relationships between them; ◆ can explain more clearly the value and benefits of being involved in healthy, active lifestyles; ◆ have a greater understanding of the barriers to getting involved and how to overcome them.
Commitment to healthy, active lifestyles	◆ are clearer about the targets and goals they want to set for themselves; ◆ show an increased interest in joining or setting up clubs and groups; ◆ show a greater interest in how they travel to school and consider alternatives to car travel.
Involvement in healthy, active lifestyles	◆ have clearer exercise and health plans that they monitor and evaluate regularly; ◆ take part in organised physical activity groups and clubs more often and effectively; ◆ choose healthy travelling and eating options more often.

Source: www.qca.org.uk

◆ introducing more individual sports and fitness activities;

◆ providing activities acceptable to a range of adolescent subcultures;

◆ teaching the 'why' of physical activity in the curriculum;

◆ helping youngsters to develop self-management skills that equip them to make lifestyle changes;

◆ creating a learning environment in which young people can develop a sense of responsibility.

Relatively little systematic research has been undertaken on the effectiveness of school-based approaches to the promotion of young people's physical activity, particularly in the UK and mainland Europe (Almond and Harris, 1998; Fox and Harris, 2003; Harris and Cale, 1997). This lack of rigorous evaluation has meant that there has been little opportunity to build an evidence base regarding programme effectiveness and successful mechanisms for change. Consequently, no definitive guidelines are available for schools outlining which types of programmes and strategies are most successful and why. Fox and Harris (2003) suggest that until such an evidence base is constructed, the design and delivery of effective health and activity promotion initiatives are likely to remain uninformed, undirected and sporadic.

It is good news then that current government initiatives (DfES and DCMS, 2003) incorporate monitoring and evaluation procedures to determine their impact on pupils and to ascertain whether high quality PE and school sport has influences which extend beyond the gymnasium and playing field. Hence the government agenda on learning through PE and school sport (as opposed to learning in PE and school sport) and the focus on whole-school improvement and the promotion of healthy, active lifestyles.

CONCLUSION

Despite an improving picture of health in PE and a number of key health-related developments, it is suggested that many schools are still not maximising their potential in terms of promoting lifelong healthy, active lifestyles. Indeed, some responses by schools to combat sedentary lifestyles and rising obesity figures, may be misguided and could consequently dissuade some young people from being more active. However, the government's major investment of funding through the PESSCL Strategy provides much hope in England of enhanced status and increased time for PE and school sport, additional professional development to help teachers effectively address health-related learning and promote health and activity, and increased confidence to transform PE and school sport programmes so that they are central to whole school improvement, and relevant and appealing to children. It would seem that the time for PE has finally arrived and it us up to the PE profession to make the most of it for the sake of its own future and for the benefit of today's young people.

REFERENCES

Almond, L. (1989) 'New wine in a new bottle – implications for a national physical education curriculum', *British Journal of Physical Education*, 20 (3): 123–5.

Almond, L. and Harris, J. (1997) 'Does health related exercise deserve a hammering or help?', *British Journal of Physical Education*, 28 (2): 25–7.

Almond, L., and Harris, J. (1998) 'Interventions to promote health-related physical education', in S. Biddle, J. Sallis and N. Cavill (eds) *Young and Active? Young People and Health-enhancing Physical Activity – Evidence and Implications*. London: Health Education Authority. pp. 133–49.

American College of Sports Medicine (ACSM) (1988) 'Opinion statement on physical fitness in children and youth', *Medicine and Science in Sport and Exercise*, 20 (4): 422–3.

American College of Sports Medicine (ACSM) (2000) 'Exercise testing and prescription for children, the elderly, and pregnant women', in ACSM's *Guidelines for Exercise Testing and Prescription*, 6th edition. Lippincott Williams and Wikins. pp. 217–34.

Armstrong, N. (1987) 'A critique of fitness testing', in S. Biddle, (ed.), *Foundations of Health Related Fitness in Physical Education*. London: Ling Publishing House. pp. 19–27.

Armstrong, N. (1989) 'Is fitness testing either valid or useful?' *British Journal of Physical Education*, 20: 66–7.

Armstrong, N. (2002) Promoting physical activity and health in youth: The active school and physical education. Abstract presented at the 12th Commonwealth International Sport Conference, 19–23 July 2002. Manchester, Association of Commonwealth Universities, pp. 37–40.

Babiarz, B., Curtner-Smith, M.D. and Lacon, S.A. (1998) 'Influence of national curriculum physical education on the teaching of health-related exercise: A case study in an urban setting', *Journal of Sport Pedagogy*, 4: 1–18.

Baquet, G., Berthoin, S. and Van Praagh, E. (2002) 'Are intensified physical education sessions able to elicit heart rate as a sufficient level to promote aerobic fitness in adolescents?', *Research Quarterly for Exercise and Sport*, 73 (3): 282–8.

Cale, L. (1996) 'Health related exercise in schools – PE has much to be proud of!', *British Journal of Physical Education*, 27 (4): 8–13.

Cale, L. (1997) 'Physical activity promotion in schools – beyond the curriculum', *Pedagogy in Practice*, 3 (1): 56–68.

Cale, L. (2000a) 'Physical activity promotion in secondary schools', *European Physical Education Review*, 6 (1): 71–90.

Cale, L. (2000b) 'Physical activity promotion in schools – PE teachers' views', *European Journal of Physical Education*, 5 (2): 158–167.

Cale, L. and Harris, J. (1993) 'Exercise recommendations for children and young people', *Physical Education Review*, 16 (2): 89–98.

Cale, L. and Harris, J. (1996) 'Understanding and evaluating the value of exercise guidelines for children', in R. Lidor, E. Eldar and I. Harari (eds), *Proceedings of the 1995 AIESEP World Congress*, Wingate, Israel, pp. 161–6.

Cale, L. and Harris, J. (1998) 'The benefits of health-related physical education and recommendations for implementation', *Bulletin of Physical Education*, 34 (1): 27–41.

Cale, L. and Harris, J. (2002) 'National fitness testing for children – issues, concerns and alternatives', *British Journal of Teaching Physical Education*, 33 (1): 32–4.

Cale, L., Harris, J. and Leggett, G. (2002) 'Making a difference? Lessons learned from a health-related exercise resource', *Bulletin of Physical Education*, 38 (3): 145–60.

Cardon, G. and De Bourdeaudhuij, I. (2002) 'Physical education and physical activity in elementary schools in Flanders', *European Journal of Physical Education*, 7 (1): 5–18.

Centers for Disease Control and Prevention (1997) 'Guidelines for school and community programs to promote lifelong physical activity among young people', *Morbidity and Mortality Weekly Report*, 46: RR-6.

Centers for Disease Control and Prevention (2000) *Promoting Better Health for Young People through Physical Activity and Sports. A report to the President from the Secretary of Health and Human Services and the Secretary of Education.*

Colquhoun, D. (1994) 'Health and physical education in the health promoting school', *Healthy Lifestyles Journal*, 41 (1): 32.

Corbin, C.B. (2002) 'Physical activity for everyone: what every physical educator should know about promoting lifelong physical activity', *Journal of Teaching in Physical Education*, 21: 128–44.

Curtner-Smith, M.D., Chen, W. and Kerr, I.G. (1995) 'Health-related fitness in secondary school physical education: a descriptive-analytic study', *Educational Studies*, 21 (1): 55–66.

Department for Culture, Media and Sport (DCMS) and DfEE (2001) *A Sporting Future for All. The Government's Plan for Sport.* London: DfCMS/DfEE.

Department for Education and the Welsh Office (DfE and WO) (1995) *Physical Education in the National Curriculum.* London: HMSO.

Department for Education and Employment and Qualifications and Curriculum Authority (DfEE and QCA) (1999a) *Physical Education. The National Curriculum for England.* London: HMSO.

Department for Education and Employment and Qualifications and Curriculum Authority (DfEE and QCA) (1999b) *The National Curriculum. Handbook for Secondary Teachers in England.* London: HMSO.

Department for Education and Skills (DfES) and Department for Culture, Media and Sport (DCMS) (2003) *Learning Through PE and Sport. A Guide to the Physical Education, School Sport and Club Links Strategy.* London: DfES.

Department of Education and Science and the Welsh Office (DES and WO) (1992) *Physical Education in the National Curriculum*. London: HMSO.

Department of Health (DoH) (1992) *The Health of the Nation. A Strategy for Health in England*. London: HMSO.

Department of Health (DoH) (1999) *Our Healthier Nation*. London: HMSO.

Douthitt, V.L. and Harvey, M.L. (1995) 'Exercise counseling – how physical educators can help', *Journal of Physical Education, Recreation and Dance*, 66 (5): 31–5.

Elbourn, J. and YMCA Fitness Industry Training (1998) *Planning a Personal Exercise Programme*. London: YMCA Fitness Industry Training.

Elbourn, J., Brennan, M. and YMCA Fitness Industry Training (1998a) *Exercise Technique Resource Pack*. London: YMCA Fitness Industry Training.

Elbourn, J., Brennan, M. and YMCA Fitness Industry Training (1998b) *Assisting a Circuit Training Instructor*. London: YMCA Fitness Industry Training.

Elbourn, J., Brennan, M. and YMCA Fitness Industry Training (1998c) *Assisting an Exercise to Music Instructor*. London: YMCA Fitness Industry Training.

Fairclough, S. (2003) 'Physical activity lessons during key stage 3 physical education', *British Journal of Teaching Physical Education*, 34 (1): 40–5.

Fairclough, S. and Stratton, G. (1997) 'Physical education curriculum and extra curriculum time: A survey of secondary schools in the North West of England', *British Journal of Physical Education*, 28 (3): 21–4.

Fairclough, S., Stratton, G. and Baldwin, G. (2002) 'The contribution of secondary school physical education to lifetime physical activity', *European Physical Education Review*, 8 (1): 69–84.

Fox, K. (1992) 'Education for exercise and the national curriculum proposals: a step forwards or backwards?', *British Journal of Physical Education*, 23 (1): 8–11.

Fox, K. (1993) 'Exercise and the promotion of public health: more messages for the mission', *The British Journal of Physical Education*, 24 (3): 36–7.

Fox, K. (1996) 'Physical activity promotion and the active school', in N. Armstrong (ed.) *New Directions in Physical Education*. London: Cassell Education. pp. 94–109.

Fox, K. and Harris, J. (2003) 'Promoting physical activity through schools', in J. McKenna and C. Riddoch (eds) *Perspectives on Health and Exercise*. Basingstoke: Palgrave Macmillan. pp. 181–201.

Green, K. (2002) 'Physical education and the 'couch potato society' – part one', *European Journal of Physical Education*, 7 (2): 95–107.

Hardman, K. and Marshall, J. (2000) 'The state and status of physical education in the international context', *European Physical Education Review*, 6 (3): 203–29.

Hargreaves, J. (2000) 'Gender, morality and the national physical education curriculum', in J. Hansen and N. Nielsen (eds) *Sports, Body and Health*. Odense: University Press.

Harris, J. (1995) 'Physical education: a picture of health?', *British Journal of Physical Education*, 26 (4): 25–32.

Harris, J. (1997a) *Physical Education: A Picture of Health? The Implementation of Health-related Exercise in the National Curriculum in Secondary Schools in England*. PhD dissertation, Loughborough University.

Harris, J. (1997b) 'A health focus in physical education', in L. Almond (ed.) *Physical Education in Schools* (2nd edn). London: Kogan Page. pp. 104–20.

Harris, J. (2000) *Health-related Exercise in the National Curriculum. Key Stages 1 to 4*. Champaign, IL: Human Kinetics.

Harris, J. and Almond, L. (1994) Letter in response to OFSTED inspector's view of HRE in the National Curriculum, *Bulletin of Physical Education*, 30 (3): 65–8.

Harris, J. and Cale, L. (1997) 'How healthy is school PE? A review of the effectiveness of health-related physical education programmes in schools', *Health Education Journal*, 56: 84–104.

Harris, J. and Cale, L. (1998) 'Activity promotion in physical education', in K. Green and K. Hardman (eds) *Physical Education, A Reader*. Oxford: Meyer and Meyer. pp. 116–31.

Harris, J. and Penney, D. (2000) 'Gender issues in health-related exercise', *European Physical Education Review*, 6 (3): 249–73.

Health Education Authority (1998) *Young and Active? Policy Framework for Young People and Health-enhancing Physical Activity*. London: HEA.

Kulinna, P.H. and Silverman, S. (2000) 'Teachers' attitudes toward teaching physical activity and fitness', *Research Quarterly for Exercise and Sport*, 71 (1): 80–4.

McKenzie, G. (2001) 'Physical activity and health: school interventions', Abtracts of the 6th Annual Congress of the European College of Sports Science, 24–28 July, p. 17.

McKenzie, T.L., Nader, P.R., Strikmiller, P.K., Yang, M., Stone, E. and Perry, C.L. (1996) 'School physical education: effect of the child and adolescent trial for cardiovascular health', *Preventive Medicine*, 25: 423–31.

Morrow, J.R., Jackson, A.W. and Payne, V.G. (1999) *Physical Activity Promotion and School Physical Education. President's Council on Physical Fitness and Sports Research Digest*, 3 (7): 1–7.

National Audit Office (2001) *Tackling Obesity in England*. London: The Stationary Office.

National Curriculum Council (1990) *Curriculum Guidance 5: Health Education*. London: HMSO.

National Heart Forum (2002) *Young@Heart: A Healthy Start for a New Generation*. London: National Heart Forum.

Office for Standards in Education (OFSTED) (1996) *Subjects and Standards. Issues for School Development Arising from OFSTED Inspection Findings 1994/95. Key Stages 3 and 4 and Post 16*. London: HMSO.

Office for Standards in Education (OFSTED) (2002) *Secondary Subject Reports 2000/01: Physical Education. HMI 381*. London: HMSO.

Pate, R.R., Small, M.L., Ross, J.G., Young, J.C., Flint, K.H. and Warren, C. W. (1999) *School Physical Education. NASPE Speak II Advocacy Kit*, pp. 19–26.

Penney, D. and Evans, J. (1997) 'Naming the game: discourse and domination in physical education and sport in England and Wales', *European Physical Education Review*, 3 (1): 21–32.

Penney, D. and Evans, J. (1999) *Politics, Policy and Practice in Physical Education*. London: E and FN Spon.

Penney, D. and Harris, J. (1997) 'Extra-curricular physical education: More of the same for the more able?', *Sport, Education and Society*, 2 (1), 41–54.

Physical Education Association (PEA) (1988) 'Health-related fitness testing and monitoring in schools. A position statement on behalf of the PEA by its Fitness and Health Advisory Committee', *British Journal of Physical Education*, 19 (4/5): 194–5.

Qualifications and Curriculum Authority website: <*www.qca.org.uk*>

Roberts, K., (1996a) 'Young people, schools, sport and government policy', *Sport, Education and Society*, 1 (1): 47–57.

Roberts, K., (1996b) 'Youth cultures and sport: the success of school and community sport provisions in Britain', *European Physical Education Review*, 2 (2): 105–15.

Rowland, T.W. (1995) 'The horse is dead; let's dismount', *Pediatric Exercise Science*, 7: 117–20.

Sallis, J.F., Bauman, A. and Pratt, M. (1998) 'Environmental and policy interventions to promote physical activity', *American Journal of Preventive Medicine*, 15 (4): 379–97.

Sallis, J.F., McKenzie, T.L., Alcaraz, J.E., Kolody, B., Faucette, N. and Hovell, M.F. (1997) 'The effects of a 2-year physical education programme (SPARK) on physical activity and fitness in elementary school students', *Sports, play and active recreation for kids. American Journal of Public Health*, 87: 1328–34.

Shephard, R.J. and Trudeau, F. (2000) 'The legacy of physical education: influences on adult lifestyles', *Pediatric Exercise Science*, 12: 34–50.

Simons-Morton, B.G., Parcel, G.S., Baranowski, T., Forthofer, R. and O'Hara, N.M. (1991) 'Promoting physical activity and a healthful diet among children: results of a school-based intervention study', *American Journal of Public Health*, 81: 896–991.

Sleap, M. (1990) 'Promoting health in primary school physical education', in N. Armstrong, (ed.) *New Directions in Physical Education Volume 1*, Champaign, IL: Human Kinetics. pp. 17–36.

Smith, R.A. and Biddle, S.J.H. (1995) 'Psychological factors in the promotion of physical activity', in Biddle S.J.H. (ed.) *European Perspectives on Exercise and Sport Psychology*, Champaign, IL: Human Kinetics. pp. 85–108.

Sparkes, A. (1994) Curriculum change: on gaining a sense of perspective, in N. Armstrong, and A. Sparkes (eds) *Issues in Physical Education*. London: Cassell.

Stone, E.J., McKenzie, T.L., Welk, G.J., and Booth, M.L. (1998) 'Effects of physical activity interventions in youth: review and synthesis', *American Journal of Preventive Medicine*, 15 (4): 298–315.

Stratton, G. (1996) 'Children's heart rates during physical education lessons: a review', *Pediatric Exercise Science*, 8: 215–33.

Stratton, G. (1997) 'Children's heart rates during British physical education lessons', *Journal of Teaching in Physical Education*, 16: 357–67.

Vilhjalmsson, R. and Thorlindsson, T. (1998) 'Factors related to physical activity: a study of adolescents', *Social Science and Medicine*, 47: 665–75.

Welsh Assembly (1999) *Curriculum 2000*. Cardiff: Welsh Assembly.

Williams, A. (1988) 'The historiography of health and fitness in physical education', *British Journal of Physical Education Research Supplement*, 3: 1–4.

Wired for Health Website (2003) <*http://lwww.wiredforhealth.gov.uk*>

YMCA Fitness Industry Training (2000) *Teaching about HRE in a Fitness Room at Key Stage 4*. London: YMCA.

YMCA Fitness Industry Training (2002) *Teaching about HRE through Exercise to Music/Aerobics at Key Stage 4*. London: YMCA.

Youth Sport Trust, YMCA Fitness Industry Training and English Sports Council (1998). Fit for TOPs. Loughborough: Youth Sport Trust.

Youth Sport Trust (2000). Fit for Life. Loughborough: Youth Sport Trust.

6 | Extra-curricular Physical Education in Secondary Schools in England and Wales: Reflections on the 'State of Play'

Ken Green

Traditionally, extra-curricular physical education (PE) in England and Wales has been 'almost exclusively oriented towards competitive team games' (Daley, 2002: 44) and, one might add, sport. Despite this fact, over the course of the last decade or so, governments and the sports lobby[1] have repeatedly expressed their dissatisfaction with the alleged demise of sport in schools in England and Wales, in general, and extra-curricular PE provision in particular (see, for example, Ahmed et al., 2003; Carvel, 1999; Department for Culture, Media and Sport (DCMS), 2000; DCMS/Strategy Unit, 2002; Department of National Heritage (DNH), 1995; English Sports Council, 1997; Leisure Opportunities, 1999; Townsend and Revill, 2003). Oft-repeated claims by the media and politicians 'that extra-curricular physical education in state schools in England and Wales is an increasingly rare feature of PE provision' (Penney and Harris, 1997: 42) have manifested themselves in active political interest at the level of central government policy towards extra-curricular PE (Green, 2000). This chapter will provide a broad outline of the state of extra-curricular PE in secondary schools in England and Wales – challenging a number of common-sense assumptions in the process – before attempting a brief explanation of why extra-curricular PE remains relatively conventional in content and form. Finally, some of the more salient issues surrounding this supposedly fundamental aspect of secondary school PE will be explored in the conclusion.

DEFINING EXTRA-CURRICULAR PE

Attempts at definition are important not least because different authors and organisations display a tendency to utilise different terms even when appearing to discuss similar, sometimes identical, things. Government agencies have a tendency to refer to extra-curricular *sport* (see, for example, Mason, 1995; Sport England, 2003a, 2003b) rather than *physical education*, and define it as 'sport organised by the school but out of school lesson time' (Sport England, 2003a: 86). Yet, when dealing with provision for extra-curricular *sport*, Sport England can frequently be found referring to 'sports and *physical activities*' (2003a: 66; my italics). The Sports Council for Wales (SCW) (2003) and Littlefield et al. (2003), on the other hand, talk of extra-curricular *activities* rather than sports or physical education. For SCW 'extra curricular activity is defined as any activity organised by the school at lunchtime, after school or at the weekend' (SCW, 2003: 9). Daley (2002) concurs with this definition, referring to extra-curricular physical activities in preference to either extra-curricular sport or, for that matter, physical education. In contrast, the government's inspection and advisory service – the Office for Standards in Education (OFSTED) (2001) – talk of after-school physical or sporting activities. For their part, PE teachers use the terms 'extra-curricular PE', 'extra-curricular activities', 'extra-curricular sport' or even just plain 'extra-curricular' interchangeably (Green, 2000). All in all, extra-curricular PE is probably most adequately defined, along with Penney and Harris (1997: 42), as 'the provision of activities outside of the formal PE curriculum, most often after school and at lunch times, but also in some schools, at weekend and/or before school (by PE teachers)'. The point of this definitional outline is that Penney and Harris' conception of extra-curricular PE includes physical activities that would not, conventionally, be deemed sports as such. Talk of defining extra-curricular PE would be of no more than academic interest if it were not for the fact that different definitions or conceptions of this ostensibly central aspect of the subject tell us something about the theory and practice of extra-curricular PE and, of particular significance, the actual and potential place of physical activities and sport, as well as PE teachers and coaches, therein.

THE STATE OF EXTRA-CURRICULAR PE

Provision

In marked contrast to the portrayal of extra-curricular PE in official and semi-official government publications, the picture emerging from much research (see, for example, Bass and Cale, 1999; Fairclough and Stratton, 1997; Green, 2000; Mason, 1995; Penney and Harris, 1997; SCW, 1995, 2003; Sport England, 2003a, 2003b) is one of extra-curricular provision as 'a strong and developing area of PE in state schools in England and Wales' (Penney and Harris, 1997: 42). In 1997, Penney and Harris (1997: 42) noted that 'almost without exception' secondary schools in England were 'providing activities after school and at lunch-times and many also . . . at weekends'. By the end of the 1990s, Bass and Cale (1999: 45) felt able to claim that extra-curricular activities continued to 'thrive in many schools' while, at the turn of the millenium, Daley (2002) suggested that most secondary schools were offering extra-curricular physical activities outside of formal lessons. Sport

England (2003b) observed that all 63 secondary schools in their 2002 survey of *Young People and Sport in England* had provided extra-curricular sporting and physical activities for their pupils.

According to Sport England (2003a), between 1994 and 2002, there has been a steady climb in the percentage of secondary schools in England reporting an increase in the number of sports and physical activities offered to pupils. At each survey point (1994, 1999, 2002) over half (51, 54, and 55 per cent respectively) of schools reported such an increase. In 2002, a total of 89 per cent of schools reported that the number of sports and physical activities provided in extra-curricular PE had either stayed the same (34 per cent) or increased (55 per cent) over the previous three years (Sport England, 2003b). This, it was suggested, reflected 'the increase in extra-curricular sport reported by young people' (Sport England, 2003a: 66). In terms of time, SCW (2002) reported that, in Wales, the overall time devoted by teaching staff to extra-curricular activities each week had increased since 1997/98 to an average of approximately 30 hours per school.

In the midst of a widespread perception of growth and development in extra-curricular PE provision, it is important to introduce a note of caution, in the form of dissenting voices: 'A few PE teachers' in the Sport England (2003b: 112) survey felt that there had been a decline in provision in England in recent years while 9 per cent of schools took the view that the number of sports and physical activities on offer had, in fact, decreased.

Levels of participation

Notwithstanding the seemingly widespread provision of extra-curricular PE in secondary schools in England and Wales, estimates of actual rates of participation among pupils tend to vary. In the mid-1990s, for example, Mason (1995: 61) observed that while 'virtually all schools' in the 1994 Sport England survey 'provided at least some extra-curricular activity', most of this activity was undertaken 'by very small proportions of pupils'. Sport England's 2002 survey reported 41 per cent of young people of secondary school age participating at least once in extra-curricular PE at some time or other (Sport England, 2003b). While this figure was down 8 per cent from 49 per cent in 1999, it remained almost identical to the 42 per cent participating in 1994 (Sport England, 2003a). Thus, three-fifths (59 per cent) of secondary age pupils in Sport England's most recent survey had not taken part in extra-curricular PE at all in the previous year (Sport England, 2003b). More optimistic estimates of participation rates for extra-curricular PE can, however, be found. In Daley's (2002) smaller-scale study, for example, 'approximately half of the pupils surveyed reported that they … participate[d] in some form of physical activity outside of PE lessons and during the school day' (2000: 42). Indeed, as if to demonstrate the uncertainty surrounding participation rates for extra-curricular PE – and in marked contrast to the figure of 40 to 50 per cent of young people taking part suggested by Sport England and Daley – SCW reported that in Wales, in 2000, almost three-quarters (72 per cent) of young people of secondary age 'had participated in extra-curricular PE at some point' (SCW, 2001: 9): the same level, interestingly enough, as in SCW found in their earlier (1999) study. Whatever the 'true' figure, as Littlefield et al. (2003: 219) observe of Scotland, it is probably the case that the figures 'hide large differences between schools and regions'. This is certainly true for Wales, where SCW (2001: 4) reported 'considerable variations' among young people 'in the range and nature of (extra-curricular) activities undertaken across Wales and between local authorities'.

If, as appears more likely on balance, no more than 50 per cent of young people (in England at least) take part in extra-curricular PE, then around half or more of secondary-age youngsters are doing none at all. Daley (2002) suggests that the numbers of pupils taking part in extra-curricular PE has always been low and continues to be so despite an upward trend through the 1990s. 'Most pupils', Daley (2002: 38) observes, 'are given the opportunity to participate in physical activities outside of formal physical education lessons, but . . . many choose not to do so'. Indeed, an analysis of participation rates by year groups in the Sport England (2003a, 2003b) and SCW (2003) studies reveals that, in secondary schools, participation drops as pupils move from lower- through to upper-school; that is to say, from years 7–9 to years 10–11.

In relation to trends within the secondary phase, the gender dimension of participation in extra-curricular PE is especially deserving of attention. In Wales, boys' and girls' participation in extra-curricular PE 'at all' during 2000 remained very similar for Years 7 to 9 but showed a marked decline thereafter. Indeed, in Year 7, girls' participation was marginally higher (84 per cent) than boys (83 per cent), while levels remained the same (at 74 per cent) in Year 8 but reversed in Years 9 (to 72 per cent for boys and 69 per cent for girls) before the gap widened substantially in Years 10 and 11 – wherein boys' participation remained steady in the low to mid-70 per cent category while girls' involvement dropped from about three-quarters (74 per cent) at Year 8 to just over half (53 per cent) at Year 11 (SCW, 2003). In England, 41 per cent of Year 7–9 girls took part in extra-curricular PE; a figure which reduced relatively little to 35 per cent in years 10 and 11. Interestingly, this figure of 35 per cent was only 1 per cent below that of boys (36 per cent) (Sport England, 2003b). It is noteworthy, however, that whereas boys' participation remains in the 40–49 per cent percent range through Key Stages 1–3 (that is to say, from primary through to secondary schooling) – only dropping to 36 per cent at Key Stage 4) – with girls the pattern is far more changeable moving from 28 per cent at Key Stage 1 to a substantial high of 55 per cent at Key Stage 2 (upper primary school) then steadily decreasing through 41 per cent at Key Stage 3 (years 7–9: the lower secondary years) to the figure of 35 per cent at Key Stage 4 (upper secondary school). The significance of these patterns lies not simply in the fact that participation in extra-curricular PE declines as secondary-age young people get older but the realisation that 'the overall decreases that are seen with age' are, in effect, 'driven by falling participation rates among girls' (SCW, 2003: 14) in particular.

Frequency of participation

In terms of frequency of participation in extra-curricular PE, half of the heads of PE departments in Cale's (2000) study of 50 secondary schools in central England expressed the view that only 'between 5 and 30 per cent of pupils regularly took part in the extra-curricular activities their departments offered' (2000: 75). This estimate is broadly in line with findings from recent Sport England (2003b) and SCW (2003) surveys. In England, 34 per cent of secondary age pupils take part in extra-curricular PE at least once per week, 23 per cent on two or more days per week and 15 per cent on three or more days per week. In Wales, 43 per cent of secondary age pupils are said to be 'taking part at least once a week' (SCW, 2003: 9): made up of approximately 17 per cent once a week, 17 per cent two to three times a week, and 8 per cent three times a week or more. Participation once a week or more in Wales declines steadily from 51 per cent for Year 7 pupils through to 38 per cent for Year 11 pupils. Corresponding figures for England indicate a drop from approximately 43 per cent for Years 7–9 to to 35 per cent for Years 10–11 (Sport England, 2003b). According to Sport England (2003a: 64) this pattern of participation across the year groupings has 'remained fairly consistent year-on-year' since 1994. 'Encouragingly', they add, the proportion of secondary-age youngsters participating in extra-curricular PE on four days or more per week has increased [to 9 per cent] since 1994 (Sport England, 2003a).

In terms of frequency of participation among boys and girls of secondary age, Daley's (2002: 42) study found that 'boys were involved in extra-curricular activities on more occasions and for longer periods of time each week than girls'. However, the 2002 Sport England (2003b) survey suggests that the 'frequency' gap between the sexes is a good deal closer than one might expect with the figures for participation only drawing apart substantially at five days or more per week (7 per cent for boys compared with 2 per cent for girls). The figures for one day or more per week are far closer: 36 per cent for boys versus 32 per cent for girls. In this regard, Flintoff and Scraton (2001) note that most of the young women in Wright's (1996; cited in Flintoff and Scraton, 2001) study were physically active out of school and observe that 'it seems that more women than ever before are taking part in physical activity in out of school contexts' (2001: 5). This notwithstanding, they suggest that a 'gap' remains 'between PE programmes and young women's active leisure lifestyles out of school' (Flintoff and Scraton, 2001: 18).

Types of sports and physical activities on offer

It is evident that alongside the growth in provision and participation in extra-curricular PE over the last decade or more there has been a marked diversification in the variety or breadth of sport and physical activities on offer. According to Sport England (2003a: 63), young people in England 'are taking part in a wide variety of extra-curricular sport': over 45 sports in 2002 and this increase in the number of sports and physical activities on offer is said to be a major factor in the apparent 'increase in the number of pupils taking part' (Sport England, 2003b: 117) in extra-curricular PE.

The change towards a broadening of provision notwithstanding, extra-curricular PE continues to be characterised by a large amount of continuity. Sport England (2003a: 63) point to 'a level of consistency in the types of extra-curricular sports that schools are offering young people'. Sport and team games continue to dominate extra-curricular provision. The only non-sports in the top 14 extra-curricular PE activities in secondary schools in England in 2002 were gymnastics (including trampolining), dance, cross-country, swimming and climbing and other outdoor pursuits. In England, the top seven (with 5 per cent or more 11–16 year olds involved) sports or physical activities provided in extra-curricular PE in 2002 in secondary schools were pretty-much the same as 1994 and were, indeed, *sports*:[2] namely, football, athletics, netball, rounders, hockey, rugby and cricket (Sport England, 2003a). These were closely followed by tennis, basketball, gym, dance, cross-country, climbing and swimming. In England, in 2002, football was 'the most popular extra-curricular sport' for secondary age youngsters with 11 per cent of young people taking part (Sport England, 2003a: 65). Interestingly, football was the joint-second most popular extra-curricular PE activity for girls (aged 5–16) behind netball (Sport England, 2003a). Elsewhere in the UK, in Scotland, Littlefield et al. (2003) report that, whereas games are offered by over 80 per cent of secondary schools, individual sports are only offered by approximately half that number – just over 40 per cent.

It is particularly interesting to note the consistent patterns (over Sport England's three data collection points of 1994, 1999 and 2002) in participation trends in particular types of activity as young people move from primary to secondary schooling. Perhaps unsurprisingly, the sports that show a marked increase in participation rates in extra-curricular PE are, for the most part, sports and activities traditionally associated with the expanded provision for, and greater focus upon, sport at secondary level (that is to say, games such as rugby, hockey, rounders, athletics and basketball). A notable omission from that list is football which repeatedly experiences a drop-off in participation as youngsters move from primary to secondary school (Sport England, 2003a). Other activities that experience a decline in participation as youngsters move to secondary school include netball, gym, dance, cross-country and, interestingly, given the dearth of pools in primary schools, swimming.

In terms of types of activity, it is true to say that some extra-curricular activities (most notably football) are offered to girls as well as boys. In Wales, SCW identifies what it refers to as 'positive trends' in the extra-curricular provision for girls 'of traditionally male dominated sports such as football and rugby' and 'the likelihood of schools having at least some girls teams in these sports' (SCW, 2002: 4) despite the percentage of schools offering such activities on a regular basis remaining low. Similarly, 'the increase in football as an extra-curricular sport' in England 'is common to both boys and girls' (Sport England, 2003a: 63). Nevertheless, beyond this noteworthy exception, the types of extra-curricular PE participated in by boys and girls has 'remained fairly consistent (in England) over the last eight years' (Sport England, 2003a: 64). Netball remains the most popular extra-curricular activity among secondary girls in England with football first choice for boys. It remains the case that boys are, typically, 'offered a wider range of activities than that on offer to girls' and 'most schools offer activities like rugby exclusively to boys and netball exclusively to girls' (SCW, 1995: 32).

It is in extra-curricular PE, Penney and Harris suggest, where the 'fundamental link', as they describe it, between PE and sport 'is arguably most visible' (1997: 42) in both official pronouncements as well as the views and practices of PE teachers themselves (Green, 2000). In the light of claims regarding the alleged decline of sport in schools it is noteworthy that a common feature of research into extra-curricular PE in the 1990s (see, for example, Bass and Cale, 1999; Cale, 1997, 2000; Fairclough and Stratton, 1997; Penney and Harris, 1997; SCW, 1995) was the identification of a strong sporting orientation or 'bias' (Penney and Harris, 1997) amid burgeoning extra-curricular provision. Despite the evident vitality of extra-curricular PE when measured in terms of *quantity*, concern had been expressed regarding the *quality* or nature of that provision (see, for example, Bass and Cale, 1999; Penney and Harris, 1997). Such concerns have to do with the *kinds* of activities on offer – what Penney and Evans (1998) term the 'privileged' position of school sport within PE – and for *whom* they are intended rather than how *much* extra-curricular PE is available *per se*.

The title of Penney and Harris' (1997) paper ('Extra-curricular physical education: More of the same for the more able?') indicated that their concern was not, so much, with the amount of extra-curricular PE nor, for that matter, the commitment of PE teachers to extra-curricular PE, for both of these were and remain demonstrably non-issues. Rather, their specific interest was with the 'content, organisation and delivery' of extra-curricular PE (Penney and Harris, 1997: 41). Penney and Harris (1997) were, in particular, concerned with the manner in which extra-curricular PE was, in their eyes, 'dominated by traditional team games', typically had 'a competitive focus' and was highly 'gendered' (1997: 43). Accordingly, they argued that this 'particular focus' resulted in extra-curricular PE '*offering limited opportunities to only a minority of pupils*' (original emphasis). That a sporting orientation, if not 'bias', existed was highlighted by SCW's (1995) observation that 'coached and competitive sport had gained disproportionately in the time devoted to it in extra-curricular activities in comparison to recreational sporting activity' (Penney and Harris, 1997: 44). Schools in Wales were running more representative sides in a wider range of sports in the mid-1990s than ever before (SCW, 1995). In 1997, Penney and Harris (1997) pointed up the continuing imbalance in favour of sport and argued that, in the process of becoming ever-more performance oriented, extra-curricular PE had become increasingly biased towards, thereby favouring, the minority of pupils with sporting ability at the expense of the majority of ostensibly less-able pupils. In the early years of the twenty-first century it remains the case that the bulk of extra-curricular time continues to be devoted to coached and competitive sport (SCW, 1995, 2003; Sport England, 2003a, 2003b). Indeed, Sport England observe that while, overall, young people engage in a wide range of sports and physical activities, 'there are only four sports that have been participated in by more than 5 per cent of all pupils' (2003b: 107): football (15 per cent), netball (7 per cent), athletics (6 per cent) and cricket (5 per cent).

In the light of an alleged 'sporting bias' one additional aspect of in extra-curricular PE provision is worthy of mention: namely, the involvement of outside agencies.

Involvement of outside agencies

Sport England (2003b: 111) point out that in their most recent survey, two-thirds (68 per cent) of secondary schools 'have called on other organisations to help teach or lead sports out of school time'. This has been the case, in particular, with football. Notwithstanding the fact that SCW report 'increasing involvement of non-teaching staff in the delivery of extra-curricular activity' (SCW, 2002: 4), it is interesting to observe that the increased provision of extra-curricular sports and physical activities in England over the course of the last decade or so is only partly attributable to greater levels of involvement among existing as well as new teaching staff – whether physical educationalists or not. Increased involvement from coaches, specialists and sports organisations were viewed as 'the main reason for the increase in the number of sports and physical activities arranged by the school out of lesson time' (Sport England, 2003a: 66) over the three years 1999 to 2002. This is worthy of note, not least because 'increased workloads' and 'fewer staff helping or willing to take clubs' (2003b: 114) – cited as the main reasons for what a small minority of PE teachers perceive as recent and likely future decreases in the number of activities on offer in extra-curricular PE – may well mean increased opportunities for the utilisation of coaches and sports development officers (Green, 2003). While, the number of sports development officers, in particular, involved in extra-curricular PE in secondary schools in Wales appears to have fallen between 1997 and 2000, many remained involved in 1999/2000.

Before concluding with an exploration of some of the more salient issues surrounding extra-curricular provision, I want to offer a tentative explanation for the shape and character of this aspect of secondary school PE in secondary schools in England and Wales.

EXPLAINING EXTRA-CURRICULAR PE

Despite sometimes feeling their professional (and, frequently, personal) lives to be more or less dominated, on occasions blighted, by it many teachers appear to view extra-curricular PE as the 'high point' of their PE teaching lives (Green, 2003). If one were to be critical one might be inclined to argue that it is when the constraints of National Curriculum Physical Education, classroom management and such like are diminished that teachers' 'real' 'philosophies'[3] of PE become apparent. It is in extra-curricular PE that one sees most clearly the extent of many teachers' commitment to competitive sport and, in particular, traditional team games. How might one best explain this? Elsewhere I have endeavoured to explain the apparent sporting bias inherent in extra-curricular PE in terms of how 'sporting ideologies and practices come to be embedded in the normative behaviour of PE teachers' (Green, 2000: 179) coupled with the manner in which constraints at the local and national level serve to reinforce such a predisposition.

In making sense of the apparent sporting bias of extra-curricular PE (Penney and Harris, 1997) it is important to appreciate that for very many PE teachers, sport (and especially traditional team games) is an important aspect of their lives: they often have strong emotional ties to sport and it forms a significant dimension of their individual identities (Green, 2000). Added to this PE teachers are, broadly-speaking, a self-selecting group. For many, PE teaching represents an opportunity for them to continue their association with sport – an area of life in which they have had extensive and positive experiences: it appears 'a "natural" progression from enjoying, and being succesful at, sport while at school' themselves (Green, 2000: 191). PE teachers, expecially males, tend also to be a self-replicating group. PE teaching mentors in schools – if less so teacher trainers in initial teacher training institutions – exhibit a tendency towards conservatism which manifests itself in the passing on of skill-oriented and sport dominated (extra-) curricular programmes (Green, 2000).

Occupational socialisation into PE teaching 'on the job', it is argued, is likely to reinforce any tendency newly-qualified teachers may have to view PE – and especially extra-curricular PE – as synonymous with sport. This is further exacerbated by the legacy of school traditions (in the form of 'custom and practice') as well as the expectations of headteachers, governing bodies and even parents and pupils, as well as the status concerns of PE colleagues, that incoming teachers are greeted with (Green, 2000). In ideological terms, such expectations, it must be said, are frequently pushing at an open door as far as PE teachers' predispositions towards placing team games and competitive sport at the heart of the subject is concerned.

CONCLUSION

Opportunities for extra-curricular PE in secondary schools in England and Wales appear to have grown over the last decade, with correlative increases in the percentage of all young people involved therein (Sport England, 2003a, 2003b; SCW, 2002). Nevertheless, it remains the case that somewhere around half of secondary age youngsters may seldom, if ever, engage with extra-curricular PE provision with, at best, only around 15 per cent taking part three times or more each week. While there can be little doubt that levels of participation in extra-curricular PE are lower than physical educationalists would want them to be the question remains: are they lower than one might reasonably expect? And, if so, 'low' in what terms: absolutely or relatively? The 50 per cent reported by Daley (2002) might be considered high if one were to view sport and physical activity as having limited appeal as a leisure or spare-time activity! It is interesting to note that Daley (2002: 43) herself recognises that while 'many pupils do not participate in extra-curricular physical activities, the same appears to be true for other types of non-physical activities (for example, music and arts clubs) where pupils also reported low participation rates'. Indeed, when compared with young people's participation in extra-curricular PE at primary school level the figures do not appear so low (Sport England, 2003a). In short, participation levels can only be considered low by those whose higher expectations are based upon optimistic views of the potential appeal of extra-curricular PE. This said, there do appear to be grounds for optimisim in the form of increased participation in sport and physical activity among young people in their leisure time outside school.

Not only has extra-curricular PE grown, it has also broadened and diversified somewhat. Nevertheless, it retains a quite conventional, not to say conservative, character and, in remaining largely independent of developments such as the National Curriculum Physical Education, remains a relatively autonomous element of PE (Green, 2000). It is conventional in remaining dominated by sport and team games and a performance orientation. It remains conservative in the sense that when PE teachers have a greater degree of freedom to choose what they do – in the name of extra-curricular PE, in this case – both male and female PE teachers tend to opt for sport and games. This is particularly true for male PE teachers. Perhaps unsurprisingly, therefore, extra-curricular PE tends to reflect traditional forms of gender stereotyping (Green, 2000; Penney and Harris, 1997). Indeed, it is evident that more gender differentiation is to be found in extra-curricular PE than curricular PE and this is true in terms of participation as well as provision.

One of 'the main reasons' for the 'past', as well as what PE teachers perceive to be the likely 'future' increases in provision of, and participation in, extra-curricular PE is, according to Sport England, 'increased involvement from coaches, specialists and sport organisations' (2003b: 112). Unsurprisingly, perhaps, it was anticipated that 'increased involvement from coaches, specialists and sports organisations' would 'act as a catalyst' (2003b: 115) for the expected increase in participation in extra-curricular PE. Whatever the scale or form of involvement of coaches and sports development officers there may be a number of unintended consequences of involving outside agencies in extra-curricular PE. First, while, on the whole, PE teachers appear very receptive to it, the involvement of coaches, sports development officers, and outside agencies generally in extra-curricular PE implies that there is no *a priori* need for a specialist teaching qualification in order to be involved in PE. This might, in turn, be seen as undermining claims for the kinds of specialist professional knowledge and status which has been something of a preoccupation for PE teachers in recent years. Second, as purveyors of specialised sporting knowledge to extra-curricular PE, coaches and sports development officers will inevitably aquire positions of relative power in relation to PE teachers for as long as the latter feel they need the expertise of the former. Thus, an unintended consequence of developing links with and involving outside agencies may well be a weakening of the status and power of PE teachers in relation to the provision of extra-curricular PE and, ultimately, PE itself.

A particularly prominent issue in relation to extra-curricular PE has to do with the issue of whether it can can provide the 'fundamental link' (Penney and Harris, 1997), that many expect of it, between curricular PE and young people's involvement in sport and physical activity in their spare time? In effect, can extra-curricular PE do anything to bridge the 'clear disparity' (Sport England, 2003b: 6) between what young people are experiencing in curricular PE and what they are choosing to do out of school in a manner that will enhance and reinforce their ongoing involvement in sport and physical activity? While Sport England (2003a, 2003b) and SCW (2002, 2003) data bear out Roberts' (1996) claim that schools have been extending and enhancing, rather than cutting back on, their provision of sports and physical activities in extra-curricular (as well as curricular) PE, nevertheless, provision continues to be largely focused around competitive sports in general and team-games especially; making Penney and Harris' (1997) description of extra-curricular PE as 'more of the same for the more able' as pertinent now as it was seven years ago. In this respect, there is clear scope for extra-curricular PE to become more user-friendly. The substantial increase in young people's participation in sport and physical activity over the last decade or more (Sport England, 2003a) is largely attributable to the popularity of recreational physical activities (for example, health and fitness gym-work, swimming, cycling, badminton, tennis, ice-skating and skateboarding) alongside smaller increases in team sports (such as football – among girls especially – and basketball). In short, young people's leisure participation is typically characterised by a *blend* of 'lifestyle activities' alongside more competitive, less recreational performance-oriented team games and sports. Extra-curricular PE is only likely to form a bridge between school physical education and young people's future leisure lives if emphasis is given to developing extra-curricular provision in the direction of their preferred participation forms and styles. There is evidently room for improvement in three broad areas:

1. A better 'match' in the *aims* and *purposes* of extra-curricular PE – towards an emphasis upon the intrinsic pleasure of sport and physical activities rather than preoccupation with levels of performance and achievement.

2. A better 'match' in *format* – between the more recreational, informal manner in which many young people (and, for that matter, adults) prefer to take part and the way in which extra-curricular PE is provided.

3. A better 'match' of *activities* – between those offered in extra-curricular PE and those that 'track' into young people's leisure.

Regardless of the reality of current levels of participaton in extra-curricular PE among young people, PE teachers in England and Wales expect the number of secondary pupils taking part in extra-curricular PE to increase over the next three years (Sport England, 2003b: 112). Notwithstanding the optimism brought on by recent increases in both provision and participation, as things stand there remains a good deal of room for improvement in the latter. This may only be achievable, however, to the extent that physical educationalists embrace the need for greater change in the former – in the direction of young people's preferred leisure-time sports and physical activities.

ACKNOWLEDGEMENT

I am grateful to Andy Smith (Chester Centre for Research into Sport and Society, University College Chester) for his comments on an earlier draft of this chapter.

NOTES

1 That is to say, governing bodies of sport and those quasi-autonomous non-governmental organisations (QUANGOs) – such as Sport England, the Sports Council for Wales and the Central Council for Physical Recreation – who perceive themselves as representing the interests of sport.
2 In the more specific sense of the term sport: competitive, physically vigorous and institutionalised activities.
3 By 'philosophies' I mean the aphoristic or everyday views PE teachers hold upon the nature and purposes of PE (see Green, 2003).

REFERENCES

Ahmed, K., Revill, J. and Hinsliff, G. (2003) 'Official: fat epidemic will cut life expectancy', *The Observer*, 9 November, 2003, p. 1.
Bass, D. and Cale, L. (1999) 'Promoting physical activity through the extra-curricular programme', *European Journal of Physical Education*, 4 (1): 45–64.
Cale, L. (1997) 'Physical activity promotion in schools: beyond the curriculum', *Pedagogy in Practice*, 3: 56–8.
Cale, L. (2000) 'A whole school approach to physical activity promotion', *European Physical Education Review*, 6 (1): 71–90.
Carvel, J. (1999) '£60 m sport fund to fire pupils' will to win', *The Guardian*, 21 June, p. 9.
Daley, A. (2002) 'Extra-curricular physical activities and physical self-perceptions in British 14–15-year-old male and female adolescents', *European Physical Education Review*, 8 (1): 37–49.
Department for Culture, Media and Sport (DCMS) (2000) *A Sporting Future for All*. London: DCMS.
Department for Culture, Media and Sport (DCMS)/Strategy Unit (2002) *Game Plan: A Strategy for Delivering Government's Sport and Physical Activity Objectives*. London: DCMS/Strategy Unit.
Department of National Heritage (DNH) (1995) *Sport: Raising the Game*. London: DNH.
English Sports Council (ESC) (1997) *England, the Sporting Nation: A Strategy*. London: ESC.
Fairclough, S. and Stratton, G. (1997) 'PE curriculum and extra-curricular time: a survey of secondary schools in the north-west of England', *British Journal of Physical Education*, 28: 21–4.
Flintoff, A. and Scraton, S. (2001) 'Stepping into active leisure? Young women's perceptions of active lifestyles and their experiences of school physical education', *Sport, Education and Society*, 6 (1): 5–21.
Green, K. (2000) 'Extra-curricular physical education in England and Wales: a sociological perspective on a sporting bias', *European Journal of Physical Education*, 5 (2): 178–207.
Green, K. (2003) *Physical Education Teachers on Physical Education: A Sociological Study of Philosophies and Ideologies*. Chester: Chester Academic Press.
Leisure Opportunities (1999) 'Brooking talks on sport', *Leisure Opportunities*, 1–13 September, 242: 2.
Littlefield, R., Green, B., Forsyth, S. and Sharp, B. (2003) 'Physical education in Scottish schools – a national case study', *European Journal of Physical Education*, 8 (2): 211–27.
Mason, V. (1995) *Young People and Sport*. London: Sports Council.
Office for Standards in Education (OFSTED) (2001) OFSTED *Subject Reports 1999–2000*. London: HMSO.

Penney, D. and Harris, J. (1997) 'Extra-curricular physical education: more of the same for the more able?', *Sport, Education and Society*, 2 (1): 41–54.

Penney, D. and Evans, J. (1998) 'Dictating the play: government direction in physical education and sport policy development in England and Wales', in K. Green and K. Hardman (eds) *Physical Education: A Reader*. Aachen: Meyer and Meyer Verlag. pp. 84–101.

Roberts, K. (1996) 'Young people, schools, sport and government policy', *Sport Education and Society*, 1 (1): 47–57.

Sports Council for Wales (SCW) (1995) *The Pattern of Play: Physical Education in Welsh Secondary Schools*. Cardiff: SCW.

Sports Council for Wales (SCW) (1999) *A Strategy for Welsh Sport – Young People First*. Cardiff: SCW.

Sports Council for Wales (SCW) (2001) *Widening the Net? Young People's Participation in Sport 1999/2000*. Cardiff: SCW.

Sports Council for Wales (SCW) (2002) *Swimming Against the Tide? Physical Education and Sports Provision in Secondary Schools in Wales*. Cardiff: SCW.

Sports Council for Wales (SCW) (2003) *Secondary School Aged Children's Participation in Sport 2001*. Cardiff: SCW.

Sport England (2003a) *Young People and Sport in England: Trends in Participation 1994–2002*. London: Sport England.

Sport England (2003b) *Young People and Sport in England, 2002: A Survey of Young People and PE Teachers*. London: Sport England.

Townsend, M. and Revill, J. (2003) 'Massive backing for sport campaign', *The Observer*, 5 October 2003, p. 9.

7 | Teachers, Teaching and Pedagogy in Physical Education

Susan Capel

How physical education is taught is as important as its content for pupils' learning. How physical education is taught, or the pedagogy, is the focus of this chapter. Pedagogy has been defined as 'any conscious activity by one person designed to enhance learning in another' (Watkins and Mortimore, 1999: 3) and it is this definition that is used in this chapter.

Research (for example, Evans et al., 1987; Evans and Clarke, 1988; Evans and Penney, 1993; Kirk, 1993; Laws and Aldridge, 1995; Penney and Harris, 1998; Sparkes, 1992) has shown that many physical education teachers have not changed the way they teach physical education, despite innovations in the curriculum, including the introduction of a National Curriculum for Physical Education (NCPE) in England in 1992 (Department of Education and Science/Welsh Office (DES/WO), 1992), and its subsequent revisions and developments in 1995 (Department for Education (DfE), 1995) and 2000 (Department for Education and Employment/Qualifications and Curriculum Authority (DfEE/QCA), 1999). In relation to the introduction of the NCPE (DES/WO, 1992) Evans et al. (1996: 165) claimed that the 'noise of education reform and the weight of education legislation of recent years pressing teachers to engage in curriculum change have done very little to alter the way in which physical education is taught in schools'. They suggested that pupils, particularly boys, may be denied the educational experiences they need and deserve by some teachers adopting conservative, uni-dimensional pedagogical activities. One reason for lack of change in the teaching of physical education has been suggested by Hargreaves (1989) and Sparkes (1991a, 1991b) as resistance to change due to the incompatibility of teachers' values and beliefs with a specific innovation. Jewett et al. (1995) noted that greater resistance is likely when teachers believe that their personal and professional goals are incompatible with the innovation and when they believe their pupils will not benefit. Sparkes (1987) suggested that this may result in teachers changing what they say but not what they do in their curriculum.

This chapter looks at what teaching approaches are used by physical education teachers and at the influence of physical education teachers' values and beliefs on the teaching approaches adopted. It then looks at how values and beliefs are formed, focusing on socialisation, before considering the impact of values and beliefs on the subject knowledge which prospective teachers bring with them to their initial teacher education (ITE) courses.

The chapter concludes by looking at the role of reflection in enhancing teachers' pedagogical practice.

TEACHING APPROACHES

What do we know about teaching approaches recommended for use in physical education? Kane (1976), Underwood (1988) and Wright (1995) identified differences in teaching approaches used in physical education, either due to the demands of different activities or different intended learning outcomes. Assuming a direct link between teaching approach and intended learning outcome, a teaching approach is selected to enable the aims and intended learning outcomes in a lesson or section of a lesson to be met. Indeed, it has been recommended (DES, 1985; DES/WO, 1992; DfE, 1995) that in order to achieve the range of learning outcomes identified in the NCPE, teachers should employ a variety of teaching strategies (across and within lessons) to cater for differences in pupils' abilities, attainment, needs and ages. The requirements of planning, performing and evaluating in the NCPE in 1992 and 1995 (DES/WO, 1992; DfE, 1995) and of the four strands – acquiring and developing skills; selecting and applying skills, tactics and compositional ideas; evaluating and improving; and knowledge and understanding of fitness and health – in the NCPE 2000 (DfEE/QCA 1999) require teachers to focus on both the learning process, for example, to compare, make judgements, analyse, review, adapt, refine, interpret, design, evaluate (DfE, 1995; National Curriculum Council (NCC), 1992; see also, Mawer, 1999; Murdoch, 2004) as well as the acquisition of skills. These require different teaching approaches.

However, does practice match recommendations? Based on evidence collected in schools, the Office for Standards in Education (OFSTED) (1995a) and OFSTED (Wales) (1995b) suggested that pupils learn best and most where teachers are flexible and able to mix teaching approaches with respect to pupils' ability and need and to subject matter. They also argued that a limited pattern of curriculum design and delivery restricts pupil learning. Likewise, the Scottish Qualifications Authority (SQA, 1999) advised that indirect constructivist teaching approaches are the most effective teaching and learning environment.

Some research has focused on the use by physical education teachers of formal and informal approaches to teaching. Research evidence led Mawer (1999: 98) to suggest that direct teaching approaches such as the practice style of (Mosston and Ashworth (2002) may be effective for learning motor skills) whereas reciprocal teaching styles may be effective for learning aspects of social development) and cooperative approaches may facilitate interpersonal and social skills development.

Results of a study by Penney and Evans (1995) suggested a predominance of teacher-centred teaching. Heads of physical education departments reported a combination of 'formal' (described as teacher centred, didactic, highly structured in organisation and mode and oriented towards precisely defined goals set by the teacher) and 'informal' (described as teaching that is pupil-centred and oriented towards guided discovery and problem solving) teaching approaches being used in their department for each of the areas of activity in the NCPE. However, these approaches were not used evenly across areas of activity. In athletics activities, outdoor and adventurous activities and games 'formal' teaching was prevalent, while in dance and to a lesser degree in gymnastics 'informal' teaching was prevalent. Likewise, when analysing the teaching styles used in NCPE, Curtner-Smith (2001) found that up to 74 per cent of teacher time was spent in 'teacher directed practice' teaching styles (those which emphasise control, with the teacher making decisions related to planning, delivery and evaluation). A maximum of 7 per cent of time was spent in more shared, problem-solving teaching environments.

Alexander and Luckman (2001) found that in relation to teaching a sport education season, teachers perceived they adopted less direct teaching styles. Teachers also reported placing less emphasis on learning skills and more emphasis on the development of personal and social skills, knowledge and understanding, values and attitudes and pupil self-management skills. Thus, they believed that there was a shift in pupils learning towards personal and social skills and that motor skill and fitness outcomes were less achievable. Results also showed that teachers perceived that sport education made a positive contribution to their repertoire of pedagogical skills. These results suggest that there is room within existing physical education programmes to incorporate 'different content (sport) and pedagogy (less teacher-directed; more student managed) which can emphasise collaboration and cooperation within a competitive structure' (2001: 260).

Thorburn and Collins (2003) reported many teachers fluctuating between different teaching approaches when teaching analysis of performance in one Scottish examination qualification. They also found that the most frequent solution to concern about the lack of development in pupils' written answers on analysis of performance was the adoption by many teachers of more directed teaching approaches, thereby assuming greater control over the teaching environment. Some teachers taught to the examination, encouraging superficial learning through focusing on repetition and following instructions, to the detriment of actively solving problems. However, trial and error resulted in a few teachers moving beyond reproductive teaching styles to productive teaching styles that involved pupils in active cognitive situations such as problem solving. (These teachers encouraged deep learning, by setting challenging tasks and linking learning with experience. Thorburn and Collins (2003) suggested that *what* is meant by concepts in analysing performance should be taught at the beginning of the course, which can be supported by practical experience to show *why* these concepts are important. This links to the need for declarative knowledge – characterised by the awareness of 'knowing that', which helps learners to understand information and ideas, to support the development of procedural knowledge (see, for example, Abrahams and Collins, 1998). They suggested that adopting more teacher-directed approaches was determined by short-term course requirements and pupils' grades (which, in turn, determined the quality of pupils' learning experiences) and by pressure on teachers in terms of general workload, amount of course content to be covered and assessment procedures to be completed.

Kane (1976) emphasised that it was probably ill-advised to make any attempt to characterise teachers as having a particular style. However, he identified that 'in general' women teachers preferred guided discovery and problem-solving approaches while men teachers appeared to prefer direct and guided discovery styles. He also reported that 'the profile of women and younger teachers appeared to demonstrate a stronger commitment to open and less structured styles' (Kane, 1976: 85). Likewise, studies (for example, Flintoff, 1995, 2003; Harris and Penney, 2002; Waddington et al., 1998) have highlighted that the subject expertise and pedagogical strategies of some secondary physical education teachers is influenced strongly by gender.

Thus, there are a range of teaching approaches that can be used although, as Rink (2001) stressed, the effectiveness of different teaching methodologies is contested. Further, it seems that physical education teachers generally use more formal than informal teaching approaches. The teaching approaches adopted by any one teacher, however, are influenced by their own perspective on physical education. For example, Curtner-Smith (1999) identified teachers in his study as holding three broad interpretations of the NCPE: conservative, innovative, and eclectic, depending on their perspective. A 'sporting perspective' (Sparkes, 1991b) of physical education was held by teachers with a conservative interpretation. The main concerns of this group of teachers were improving sporting performance and producing successful school teams in traditional British team games. Their teaching, therefore, mainly used direct styles of teaching to teach the skills and strategies of games. An 'idealistic perspective' of physical education which 'tends to be egalitarian, child-centred, progressive, and concerned with the personal and social development of pupils via self-paced individual activities' (Sparkes, 1991b: 4) was held by teachers with an innovative interpretation. They used a range of traditional and non-traditional activities and teaching styles to enable a range of objectives, including cognitive, social, health-related and performance objectives, to be achieved and to provide opportunities for all pupils to develop a leisure interest. Their main concern was with the learning process; teaching pupils to 'plan, perform and evaluate' through physical activity. This group of teachers was enthusiastic about changes they had made to their curricula and teaching styles as a result of the introduction of the NCPE (Curtner-Smith, 1999). A perspective of physical education that incorporated elements from both the conservative and innovative interpretations was held by teachers with an eclectic interpretation. These teachers used mainly direct teaching styles which focused mainly on improving pupils' performance, but taught a range of activities to enable pupils to develop a leisure interest.

These perspectives are influenced by the values and beliefs held by physical education teachers. So, what are these values and beliefs?

TEACHERS' VALUES AND BELIEFS

Values and beliefs rely heavily on evaluations that are affective and personal, therefore they depend more on subjective rather than objective evidence. Research on physical education teachers' value orientations by Ennis and colleagues has identified five value orientations which may be held by physical education teachers: disciplinary mastery; learning orientation; social responsibility (in an earlier version of the scale this was social reconstruction); ecological integration; and self-actualisation. Different teachers place high priority on different value orientations. In a study by Ennis et al. (1992), 56.8 per cent of 90 teachers placed a high priority on social reconstruction and 7.6 per cent placed a high priority on disciplinary mastery. Ennis and Chen (1995) found that teachers who worked in rural schools placed a higher priority on learning process and disciplinary mastery, while teachers who worked in urban schools placed a higher priority on self-actualisation and social responsibility.

Regardless of gender, experience or activity background, Curtner-Smith and Meek (2000) found that, in a sample of 64 physical education teachers, highest priority was given to the learning process, disciplinary mastery and social responsibility value orientations, with lowest priority given to self-actualisation and ecological integration value orientations. They identified the value orientation given highest priority by the greatest number of teachers as social responsibility. However, this was also given the lowest priority by the greatest number of teachers. Self-actualisation was given a low priority by the smallest number of teachers, while self-actualisation and ecological integration were the two orientations for which the greatest number of teachers had neutral priority.

Ennis and Chen (1995) and Ennis and Zhu (1991) found that teachers who gave high priority to social orientation and learning process were likely to give low priority to self-actualisation, ecological integration and social responsibility. A moderate positive correlation has been found (Curtner-Smith and Meek, 2000; Ennis and Chen, 1995; Ennis et al., 1992; Ennis and Zhu, 1991) between the value orientations of disciplinary mastery and learning process; a strong negative correlation between disciplinary mastery and self-actualisation, disciplinary mastery and social responsibility, learning process and ecological integration and learning process and social responsibility; and a moderate negative correlation between learning process and self-actualisation. Ennis and Chen (1995) highlighted the inverse relationship between value orientations which place some emphasis on content and those which place emphasis on affective orientations.

However, it is not clear whether values and beliefs are held strongly or not by individual teachers, that is, whether values and beliefs are based on ethical or other practical, empirical or theoretical principles of teachers or whether they are idiosyncratic or arbitrary (for example, I know what I like or that seems like a good idea). Green (2000; 2002) highlighted the predominantly arbitrary or idiosyncratic nature of five prominent what he called 'philosophies' (or ideologies) held by physical education teachers: sport; health; academic value; education for leisure; and sport for all. He stressed that these 'philosophies' are 'what might best be described as a mishmash of views on physical education: sometimes overlapping, sometimes contradictory, frequently ill thought through and typically confus-ed', rather than 'integrated, coherent sets of ideas' (Green, 2000: 123). This related to Green's assertion that teachers simply *do*, and are not philosophising very much about, physical education. Their 'doing' appears to interact with the way they think about and teach physical education – their predispositions influenced by their past experiences. Thus, these practical 'philosophies' are based on prior physical education and sporting experien-ces. Further, the 'philosophies' of many physical education teachers incorporated several dimensions, although for many physical education teachers there was one dominant dimension and several additional dimensions. For many male physical education teachers whose 'philosophy' contained more than one dimension, most emphasis was placed on sport and the development of sporting skills, although health and education for leisure were also included, albeit the promotion of health was implicitly related to sport. Other physical education teachers emphasised personal and social education. Green (2000) also found that 'philosophies' of physical education change over time, with 'older philosophies' such as sport performance retained, but supplemented by 'newer philosophies' such as health, education for leisure and sport for all (Hendry at al., 1993; Scraton, 1992) and academic value.

But what factors determine physical education teachers' philosophies, values and beliefs and how does this impact on subject knowledge? The next part of the chapter looks at the importance of socialisation.

OCCUPATIONAL SOCIALISATION

Lawson (1986: 107) defined occupational socialisation as 'all kinds of socialisation that initially influence persons to enter the field of physical education and later are responsible for their perceptions and actions as teacher educators and teachers'. In addition, he observed three distinct types of socialisation – acculturation, professional socialisation and organisa-tional socialisation – which are likely to mould physical education teachers perspectives about their subject and their pedagogical practices (Lawson, 1983a, 1983b).

Acculturation begins at birth and is based on observations and experiences during childhood and adolescence and interactions with significant people. Some of the most important observations and experiences are school in general (Hutchinson, 1993; Lawson, 1983a, 1983b; Lortie, 1975; Placek et al., 1995) and physical education in particular (Curtner-Smith, 1999; Evans and Williams, 1989; Green, 1998; Schempp, 1989), as well as sport (both in an out of school) (Curtner-Smith, 1999; Dewar and Lawson, 1984; Dodds et al., 1992; Templin, 1979) and interactions with physical education teachers and other adults responsible for coaching/teaching sport and physical activity (Mawer, 1996). Through these observations and experiences, prospective physical education teachers become familiar with pedagogical practices and begin to make judgements about what constitutes quality of teaching (Schempp, 1989). These influence the understanding of prospective physical education teachers' about what it means to be a physical education teacher before they enter initial teacher education (ITE). This 'has a distinct and traceable influence on an individual's future decisions, practices, and ideologies as a teacher' (Schempp and Graber, 1992: 333).

Research (for example, Dewar and Lawson, 1984; Dodds et al., 1992; Evans and Williams, 1989; Green, 1998; MacDonald et al., 1999; Templin, 1979) has shown that love of sport attracts many physical education teachers to the profession. However, the type and level of sport and physical activity experience are important. Lawson (1983a: 7) noted that 'sport has been identified as a carrier of conservative values', which led him to hypothesise that teachers who had participated in traditional sport at a high level were likely to hold a conservative orientation towards physical education, whereas teachers who had participated in non-traditional sports and other types of physical activity were more likely to have an innovative orientation towards physical education. This hypothesis was supported by results of studies by Ennis and colleagues, but not by results of a study by Curtner-Smith and Meek (2000), which showed that teachers who had participated mainly in traditional games and sports placed a significantly higher priority on the value orientation of social responsibility than teachers who participated mainly in non-traditional activities or had participated equally in traditional and non-traditional activities. On the other hand, teachers who had participated in non-traditional activities or had participated equally in traditional and non-traditional activities (described as an eclectic background) placed a significantly higher priority on the learning process than teachers with a traditional activity background. Lawson (1983a, 1983b) also noted that the different physical education and sport experiences during childhood of many prospective male and female physical education teachers and societal attitudes towards male and female sport in general are likely to impact on physical education teachers' philosophies, values and beliefs and lead to different perceptions of physical education teaching and pedagogical practices.

Lawson (1983a: 4) defined professional socialisation as 'the process by which . . . teachers acquire and maintain the values, sensitivities, skills, and knowledge that are deemed ideal for physical education teaching'. Research suggests that values and beliefs about physical education developed during childhood and adolescence are not easily changed and that ITE has relatively little impact on student teachers (Curtner-Smith, 1999; Evans, 1992; Evans et al., 1996; Green, 1998; Placek et al., 1995). In fact, many student teachers confirm their values and beliefs in ITE rather than modify them (Doolittle et al., 1993; Solmon and Ashy, 1995). However, there is some evidence to suggest that ITE may have an influence if student teachers values and beliefs are challenged. For example, Schempp and Graber (1992: 336) suggested that 'only when recruits encounter teacher educators with alternative orientations is a dialectic likely to emerge and enable change to take place'. O'Bryant et al. (2000) noted that, if teacher educators have a better understanding of student teachers' perceptions, values and beliefs about teaching physical education, they may be better able to socialise them for their role as physical education teachers.

Organisational socialisation was defined by Van Maanen and Schein (1979: 211) as 'the process by which one is taught and learns the ropes of a particular organisational role'. Lawson (1983a, 1983b) identified the workplace, particularly early in a teachers career, as important in supporting or restricting beginning teachers practice. This is because schools are highly 'custodial bureaucracies' (Lawson, 1983b) in which 'basic assumptions and beliefs are shared . . . as the correct way to perceive, think, and feel' (Schein, 1988: 6), which can result in beginning teachers adopting the prevailing values and beliefs of the school. This may result in pedagogical practices and perspectives learned during ITE, which are incompatible with those operating in the school, being 'washed out' (Zeichner and Tabachnik, 1981).

Thus, socialisation determines the philosophies, values and beliefs of prospective physical education teachers. It also determines the subject knowledge with which teachers enter ITE courses. For example, Amade-Escot (2000) highlighted findings from a series of studies that suggest that pedagogical content knowledge is composed of intimately linked and integral knowledge, beliefs and experiences; is embedded in the practice of teaching; has undergone long-term evolution in relation to professional competence; and is dependent on contextual factors. The next section looks at subject knowledge and then the influence of values and beliefs on subject knowledge and on teaching approaches.

TEACHERS' KNOWLEDGE BASE

Shulman (1986, 1987) has been a key figure in identifying the knowledge that teachers need for effective teaching. He identified seven knowledge bases:

1.   Content knowledge.
2.   General pedagogical knowledge.
3.   Curriculum knowledge.
4.   Pedagogical content knowledge.
5.   Knowledge of learners and their characteristics.
6.   Knowledge of educational contexts.
7.   Knowledge of educational ends, purposes, values and philosophical and historical influences.

Others have identified other knowledge bases. For example, because teaching demands a large investment of self, Turner-Bissett (1997) identified knowledge of self as a crucial element in the way teachers themselves understand the nature of the job. This has some effect on student teachers' ability to deliberate, or reflect, on their own practice, which in turn impacts on their development.

For Wilson et al. (1987), a significant part of learning to teach requires student teachers to re-learn content knowledge for the purposes of teaching and to develop their pedagogical content knowledge so that they are able to facilitate the learning of others. Further, although student teachers may gradually develop in respect of each of Shulman's knowledge bases, each one is dependent upon the other in terms of effective teaching to promote learning. The interaction between these knowledge bases is complex, as sometimes several knowledge bases inform teaching decisions, selection of materials, teaching approaches and organisational strategies.

Calderhead and Shorrock (1997) highlighted the importance of the extent and quality of teachers' content knowledge, particularly in relation to teaching practices and professional development. Depth of knowledge influences pedagogical choices that beginning teachers make. Government surveys (for example, Her Majesty's Inspectorate (HMI, 1987)) have highlighted that if subject knowledge is insecure, restricted practices are likely. Teaching unfamiliar material is difficult and teachers use a variety of tactics to cope with this task, ranging from trying to avoid teaching material they do not know very well to relying on secondary sources such as a textbook to provide the content knowledge. Teachers' lack of content knowledge can also affect the teaching approach. In teaching content about which they are uncertain, teachers may choose to use a directed approach rather than one that encourages problem solving or asking questions.

In a study of student physical education teachers in the USA, Graber (1995: 164) stated that: 'When student teachers have limited subject matter [content] knowledge and are unfamiliar with the details of particular activities, they will be unable to make informed choices about how to teach that subject matter'. She found that: how student teachers had learned an activity themselves shaped how they then taught it; one single powerful person could shape a student teacher's beliefs in terms of content knowledge as much as an entire ITE course; and student teachers knew they needed to combine content knowledge with pedagogical strategies but did not understand how to do so. Thus, student teachers' experiences are central to developing content knowledge and understanding.

Capel and Katene (2000) investigated PGCE student teachers' perceived level of subject knowledge in the six NCPE areas of activity. Results showed that most of the student teachers felt most confident in the games area of activity and lacked confidence in areas such as dance and outdoor and adventurous activities (OAA). This was attributed to their prior experiences, qualifications and knowledge of activities on entry to the PGCE course. Further, they identified a number of activities in which student teachers did not perceive an increase in their subject knowledge over the year, for example, football for male and netball for female student teachers. These activities were those in which the highest percentage of student teachers perceived good subject knowledge early in their ITE course. They speculated that lack of perceived increase in subject knowledge could have been due to student teachers having more confidence in teaching these activities, therefore they did not perceive the need to improve their knowledge or were less receptive to learning. Consequently, they may have spent less time and/or put in less effort to gain knowledge in these activities, relying on what they already knew or concentrating on gaining knowledge in activities in which they perceived weaknesses. This could be linked also to their values and beliefs about these activities.

Wilson et al. (1987) concluded that depth of content knowledge appears to influence whether teaching is effective. Teachers are more likely to be able to stress conceptual understanding and systematic knowledge (the 'whys') if they have greater knowledge of syntactic structures and conceptual understanding of a subject, therefore are more likely to be able to teach pupils how to think through problems in the subject. Teachers without such knowledge may focus on 'how to do' an activity, for example, memorising predictable problems. Thus, pupils may differ in their conceptual understanding, but not in their skills, when taught by teachers with deeper understanding. Ennis and Mueller (1991) found that expert teachers are more likely than beginning teachers to draw on a richer and more extensive depth of content knowledge. However, it is not clear whether depth of content expertise comes mainly from their own background in sports performance and/or coaching (Amade-Escot, 2000), or from pedagogical content knowledge (Shulman, 1986).

Student teachers are often struggling at a basic level, in acquiring content knowledge itself. They need to understand the importance of content knowledge for teaching and the consequences of lack of knowledge. Learning to teach must, therefore, be conceptualised as both developing content knowledge and how to communicate the content effectively to pupils (pedagogical knowledge). Without solid content knowledge, student teachers have difficulty in making the transition between acquiring content knowledge and making it accessible for the learner. Further, student teachers must develop the ability to acquire new knowledge throughout their careers. This requires, among other things, the ability to reflect on and learn from experience. Student teachers may need to be taught this skill.

THE INFLUENCE OF VALUES AND BELIEFS ON SUBJECT KNOWLEDGE AND ON TEACHING APPROACHES

Work in the area of subject knowledge has looked at beliefs about subject knowledge. One type of belief that beginning teachers hold is related to the content that they teach. Grossman et al. (1989) and McDiarmid et al. (1989) have argued that student teachers' beliefs about content knowledge are as powerful and influential as their beliefs about teaching and learning, as they appear to influence both what they choose to teach and how they choose to teach it. Hence, it is essential that there are opportunities for reflection on ITE courses. However, McDiarmid et al. (1989) argued that there are problems in trying to achieve this. Notably, time constraints on ITE courses result in student teachers' content knowledge being taken for granted with the focus being on the development of pedagogical knowledge and skills.

Some work has identified the impact of different value orientations on the teaching approaches used by teachers. For example, results of a study by Ennis et al. (1990) on the extent to which the value orientations of 25 primary school teachers influenced their reactions to an in-service course on movement education as measured by changes in written lesson plans found that some concepts in the movement framework were sensitive to teacher value orientations. Lesson plans written by teachers with strong social reconstruction and weak disciplinary mastery value orientations included more opportunities for pupils to engage in shared decision making than did lesson plans of other teachers.

CONCLUSION

This chapter has looked at the teaching approaches used by physical education teachers and the impact of values and beliefs on the teaching approaches of any one teacher. It has also looked at the impact of socialisation on the values and beliefs and on the knowledge bases of physical education teachers and how these impact on their pedagogies. The chapter highlights the interaction of a number of factors which influence all aspects of teaching and learning. We have a good understanding of some of the reasons why teachers adopt the teaching approaches they do. However, we have less understanding of why physical education teachers retain, or change, teaching approaches not only to achieve the learning outcomes identified for the curriculum they are teaching, but also to improve pupils' learning experiences.

However, there seems to be one requirement for physical education teachers to be able to develop their pedagogy: reflection. For example, Calderhead and Shorrock (1997) highlighted that acquiring new content or pedagogical knowledge requires, among other things, the ability to reflect on and learn from experience. Reflection needs to be developed in ITE. Turner-Bissett (1997) highlighted the impact on student teachers' development of knowledge of self which is an important requisite for higher levels of reflection. Likewise, Grossman et al. (1989) and McDiarmid et al. (1989) identified the need for student teachers to identify, examine and reflect upon their own experiences and how they have shaped their perspective of content within the subject area, and to acknowledge the influences that those beliefs have on what they learn and what they teach. Rossi and Cassidy (1999) stressed the importance of teacher educators in the development of student teachers' ability critically to evaluate the conventions and routines they have absorbed during their own education and while on school placement as part of their ITE course. This requires student teachers to challenge some of the curriculum models they have encountered through the process of critical analysis. However, in order to reach this level of conceptual awareness, student teachers need to understand, for example, the unique experiences each NCPE area of activity can offer pupils, and to have considered what the overall aims of physical education are and how it can contribute to a pupil's personal, social, moral, spiritual and cultural development. Tinning et al. (2001) suggested that there are two questions that provide a point of focus for higher levels of reflection: 'What are the implications of what I choose to teach?' and 'What are the implications of how I teach?'. The extent to which physical education teachers and student teachers address these questions is unclear.

Despite this need for reflection, Kirk (1986) criticised ITE programmes for focusing too much on a technical orientation to teaching with too little focus on an inquiry perspective. The extent to which this perspective is used on ITE courses is not clear. It has been suggested (Schempp and Graber, 1992) that if teacher educators want to change the status quo, they must challenge existing perspectives and beliefs. Such a change is more likely if teacher educators have an innovative orientation towards physical education and if they agree on a shared technical culture and professional ideology (Graber, 1993; Lawson, 1983a, 1983b). If teacher educators have a conservative orientation towards physical education and see current practice as unproblematic, they are likely only to reinforce what the majority of student physical education teachers have learned prior to ITE. As Schempp and Graber (1992: 336) noted 'in the absence of a vigorous dialectic in teacher education, little is likely to change. Only when recruits encounter teacher educators with alternative orientations is a dialectic likely to emerge and enable change to take place'. The model of ITE in place in England at the present time may not encourage the development of reflective skills.

Some studies (O'Sullivan, 1996; Wilson and Berne, 1999) have focused on how teachers learn to teach, particularly how, what and under what conditions learning takes place (Borko and Putnam, 1996; Richardson, 1996; Wideen et al., 1998). Feiman-Nemser and Floden (1986: 513) emphasised that 'understanding the organisation of teachers' knowledge refines our appreciation of uses by showing how different forms of knowledge permit different kinds of performances'. Feiman-Nemser and Remillard (1996: 63) recognised 'that understanding more about teachers as learners, what they need to know and how they learn their craft, can help in clarifying the role of formal teacher education in learning to teach'. Calderhead (1996: 709) focused on 'how teachers make sense of their professional world, the knowledge and beliefs they bring with them to the task; and how teachers' understanding of teaching, learning and children, and the subject matter informs their everyday practice are important questions that necessitate investigation of the cognitive and affective aspects of teachers' professional lives'. It is important that consideration is given in ITE courses to how teachers learn to teach.

Although developing reflection is important in ITE, the process needs to be continued throughout a teacher's career. Student teachers interact with, and learn from, experienced teachers from the time they start their ITE course and are, therefore, influenced by their values and beliefs. Ennis and Chen (1995) highlighted the importance of the first ten years of teaching in the formation of a teacher's value orientations. Value orientations become more stable, and are less likely to change, with 10–20 years' teaching experience. However, by the time teachers have 20 years of experience their values and beliefs are firmly established and are very unlikely to change. As disciplinary mastery is the most traditional of the five value orientations identified by Ennis and colleagues, it is likely to be the orientation adopted by experienced teachers. Ennis and Zhu (1991) hypothesised that inexperienced teachers are more likely to favour an orientation associated with socio-cultural goals.

Beginning teachers, therefore, need support and mentoring in order to protect them from conservative elements within their school (including experienced teachers with whom they work) otherwise the perspectives and practices acquired during their ITE course are likely to be washed out. They also need a high level of support to address problems and questions with their teaching or questions concerned with top-down innovations (Evans and Penney, 1994; Faucette, 1987). Further, powerful and intensive forms of in-service training also need to be provided for practising physical education teachers.

Further, Green (2000; 2002) identified different dimensions incorporated into physical education teachers' 'philosophies'. It is likely that teachers who hold philosophies which include different dimensions find it difficult to develop pedagogies that enable a range of learning outcomes to be achieved and which meet the needs of pupils. Thorburn and Collins (2003: 185) suggested that 'the attempt to achieve multiple aims within the same programme of study just adds to the complexity of decision-making on teaching methods'. Thus, student and beginning teachers need to reflect on the importance, and implications, of 'philosophies' they hold, rather than just take these for granted. If they are not challenged in their thinking, then it is unlikely that change will result.

Although Alexander and Luckman (2001) highlighted the use of less directed teaching approaches in sport education they warned that the focus on pupil-led organisation may encourage teachers to settle for, what Placek (1983) called, 'the busy, happy and good' approach to teaching, rather than seriously attempting to promote learning. This led them to suggest that 'what is needed is not just more research on sport education applications. The physical education research agenda may benefit from a concern with another question: Under what conditions will otherwise skilled, knowledgeable and thoughtful teachers commit themselves to the achievement of learning in physical education?' (1983: 263). There will be no change without engaging teachers in identifying the need for change and then carrying it out.

REFERENCES

Abrahams, A. and Collins, D. (1998) 'Examining and extending research in coach development', *Quest*, 50: 59–79.

Alexander, K. and Luckman, J. (2001) 'Australian teachers' perceptions and uses of the sport education curriculum model', *European Physical Education Review*, 7 (3): 243–67.

Amade-Escot, C. (2000) 'The contribution of two research programs on teaching content: "pedagogical content knowledge" and "didactics of physical education" ', *Journal of Teaching in Physical Education*, 20: 78–101.

Borko, H. and Putnam, R. (1996) 'Learning to teach', in D.C. Berliner and R.C. Calfree (eds), *Handbook of Educational Psychology*. New York: Macmillan. pp. 673–708.

Calderhead, J. (1996) Teachers: Beliefs and Knowledge, in D.C. Berliner and R.C. Calfree (eds), *Handbook of Educational Psychology*. New York: Macmillan. pp. 709–25.

Calderhead, J. and Shorrock, S.B. (1997) *Understanding Teacher Education*. London: Falmer Press.

Capel, S. and Katene, W. (2000) 'Secondary PGCE PE students' perceptions of their subject knowledge', *European Physical Education Review*, 6 (1): 46–70.

Curtner-Smith, M.D. (1999) 'The more things change the more they stay the same: factors influencing teachers' interpretations and delivery of National Curriculum Physical Education', *Sport, Education and Society*, 4 (1): 75–97.

Curtner-Smith, M.D. (2001) 'The occupational socialization of a first-year physical education teacher with a teaching orientation', *Sport, Education and Society*, 6 (1): 81–105.

Curtner-Smith, M.D. and Meek, G.A. (2000) 'Teachers' value orientations and their compatibility with the National Curriculum for Physical Education', *European Physical Education Review*, 6 (1): 27–45.

Department for Education (DfE) (1995) *Physical Education in the National Curriculum*. London: HMSO.

Department for Education and Employment and Qualifications and Curriculum Authority (DfEE/QCA) (1999) *Physical Education: The National Curriculum for England*. London: HMSO.

Department of Education and Science (DES) (1985) *The Curriculum From 5 to 16: Curriculum Matters 2. An HMI Series*. London: HMSO.

Department of Education and Science and the Welsh Office (DES/WO) (1992) *Physical Education in the National Curriculum*. London: HMSO.

Dewar, A. and Lawson, H.A. (1984) 'The subjective warrant and recruitment into physical education', *Quest*, 36: 15–25.

Dodds, P., Placek, J., Doolittle, S., Pinkham, K., Ratliffe, T. and Portman, P. (1992) 'Teacher/coach recruits: background profiles, occupational decision factors, and comparisons with recruits into other physical education occupations', *Journal of Teaching in Physical Education*, 11: 161–76.

Doolittle, S.A., Dodds, P. and Placek, J.H. (1993) 'Persistence of beliefs about teaching during formal training of preservice teachers', *Journal of Teaching in Physical Education*, 12, 355–65.

Ennis, C.D. and Chen, A. (1995) 'Teachers' value orientations in urban and rural school settings', *Research Quarterly for Exercise and Sport*, 66: 41–50.

Ennis, C.D., Chen, A. and Ross, J. (1992) 'Educational value orientations as a theoretical framework for experienced urban teachers' curricular decision making', *Journal of Research and Development in Education*, 25: 156–64.

Ennis, C.D. and Mueller, L.K (1991) 'Description of knowledge structures within a concept-based curriculum framework', *Research Quarterly for Exercise and Sport*, 62 (4): 309–18.

Ennis, C.D., Mueller, L.K. and Hooper, L.M. (1990) 'The influence of teacher value orientations on curriculum planning within the parameters of a theoretical framework', *Research Quarterly for Exercise and Sport*, 61: 360–68.

Ennis, C.D. and Zhu, W. (1991) 'Value orientations: a description of teachers' goals for student learning', *Research Quarterly for Exercise and Sport*, 62: 33–40.

Evans, J. (1992) 'A short paper about people, power and educational reform. Authority and representation in ethnographic research subjectivity, ideology and educational reform: the case for physical education', in A. Sparkes (ed.), *Research in Physical Education and Sport: Exploring Alternative Visions*. London: Falmer Press. pp. 231–47.

Evans, J. and Clarke, G. (1988) 'Changing the face of physical education', in J. Evans (ed.), *Teachers, Teaching and Control in Physical Education*. London: Falmer Press. pp. 125–45.

Evans, J., Davies, B. and Penney, D. (1996) 'Teachers, teaching and the social construction of gender relations', *Sport, Education and Society*, 1 (2): 165–83.

Evans, J. and Penney, D. (with Bryant, A.) (1993) 'Physical education after ERA?', *British Journal of Physical Education Research Supplement*, 13: 2–5.

Evans, J. and Penney, D. (1994) 'Whatever happened to good advice? Service and inspection after the Education Reform Act', *British Educational Research Journal*, 20 (5): 519–33.

Evans, J., Lopez, S., Duncan, M. and Evans, M. (1987) 'Some thoughts on the political and pedagogical implications of mixed sex grouping in the PE curriculum', *British Educational Research Journal*, 13 (1): 59–71.

Evans, J. and Williams, T. (1989) 'Moving up and getting out: the classed and gendered opportunities of physical education teachers', in T. Templin and P.G. Schempp (eds), *Socialization into Physical Education: Learning to Teach*. Indianapolis, IN: Benchmark Press, pp. 235–51.

Faucette, N. (1987) 'Teachers' concerns and participation styles during in-service education', *Journal of Teaching in Physical Education*, 6: 425–40.

Feiman-Nemser, S. and Floden, R.E. (1986) 'The cultures of teaching', in M.C. Wittrock (ed.), *Handbook of Research on Teaching*. New York: Macmillan. pp. 505–25.

Feiman-Nemser, S. and Remillard, J. (1996) 'Perspectives on learning to teach', in F.B. Murray (ed.), *The Teacher Educator's Handbook: Building a Knowledge Base for the Preparation of Teachers*. San Francisco, CA: Jossey-Bass, pp. 63–91.

Flintoff, A. (1995) 'Anti-sexist practice in physical education', in L. Milosevic (ed.), *Fairplay? Gender and Physical Education*. Leeds: Leeds Education Authority.

Flintoff, A. (2003) 'The School Sport Co-ordinator Programme: changing the role of the physical education teacher', *Sport, Education and Society*, 8 (2): 231–50.

Graber, K.C. (1993) 'The emergence of faculty consensus concerning teacher education: the socialization process of creating and sustaining faculty agreement', *Journal of Teaching in Physical Education*, 12: 424–36.

Graber, K. (1995) 'The influence of teacher education programs on the beliefs of student teachers' general pedagogical knowledge, pedagogical content knowledge, and teacher education course work', *Journal of Teaching in Physical Education*, 14: 157–78.

Green, K. (1998) 'Philosophies, ideologies and the practice of physical education', *Sport, Education and Society*, 3 (2): 125–43.

Green, K. (2000) 'Exploring the everyday 'philosophies' of physical education teachers from a sociological perspective', *Sport, Education and Society*, 5 (2): 109–29.

Green, K. (2002) 'Physical education teachers in their figurations: a sociological analysis of everyday 'philosophies'', *Sport, Education and Society*, 7 (1): 65–83.

Grossman, P.L., Wilson, S.M. and Shulman, L.E. (1989) 'Teachers of substance: subject matter knowledge for teaching', in M.C. Reynolds (ed.), *Knowledge Base for the Beginning Teacher*. New York: Pergamon.

Hargreaves, A. (1989) *Curriculum and Assessment Reform*. Milton Keynes: Open University Press.

Harris, J. and Penney, D. (2002) 'Gender, health and physical education', in D. Penney (ed.), *Gender and Physical Education: Contemporary Issues and Future Directions*. London: Routledge.

Hendry, L.B., Shucksmith, J., Love, J.G. and Glendenning, A. (1993) *Young People's Leisure and Lifestyles*. London: Routledge.

Her Majesty's Inspectorate (HMI) (1987) *Quality in Schools: The Initial Training of Teachers*. London: HMSO.

Hutchinson, G.E. (1993) 'Prospective teachers' perspectives on teaching physical education: an interview study on the recruitment phase of teacher socialization', in S. Stroot (ed.), *Socialization into physical education* [monograph], *Journal of Teaching in Physical Education*, 12: 344–54.

Jewett, A.E., Bain, L.L. and Ennis, C.D. (1995) *The curriculum process in physical education* 2nd edn. Madison, WI.: Brown and Benchmark.

Kane, J. (1976) 'The schools curriculum inquiry', in J. Kane (ed.) *Curriculum Development in Physical Education*. London: Granada. pp. 70–96.

Kirk, D. (1986) 'A critical pedagogy for teacher education: toward an inquiry-oriented approach', *Journal of Teaching in Physical Education*, 5: 230–43.

Kirk, D. (1993) *Defining Physical Education: The Social Construction of a School Subject in Post-war Britain*. London: Falmer Press.

Laws, C. and Aldridge, M. (1995) 'Magic moments, myth or millstone – the implementation of national curriculum physical education', *British Journal of Teaching Physical Education Research Supplement*, 16: 2–12.

Lawson, H.A. (1983a) 'Toward a model of teacher socialization in physical education: the subjective warrant, recruitment, and teacher education (part 1)', *Journal of Teaching in Physical Education*, 2 (3): 3–16.

Lawson, H.A. (1983b) 'Toward a model of teacher socialization in physical education: entry into schools, teachers' role orientations, and longevity in teaching (part 2)', *Journal of Teaching in Physical Education*, 3 (1): 3–15.

Lawson, H.A. (1986) 'Occupational socialization and the design of teacher education programs', *Journal of Teaching in Physical Education*, 5: 107–16.

Lortie, D.C. (1975) *School Teacher: A Sociological Study*. Chicago, IL: University of Chicago Press.

MacDonald, D., Kirk, D. and Braiuka, S. (1999) 'The social construction of physical activity at the school/university interface', *European Physical Education Review*, 5 (1): 31–51.

McDiarmid, G.W., Ball, D.L. and Anderson, C.W. (1989) 'Why staying one chapter ahead doesn't really work: subject specific pedagogy', in M.C. Reynolds (ed.), *Knowledge Base for the Beginning Teacher*. New York: Pergamon.

Mawer, M. (1996) *The Effective Teaching of Physical Education*. London: Longman.

Mawer, M. (1999) 'Teaching styles and teaching approaches in physical education: research developments', in C. Hardy and M. Mawer (eds) *Learning and Teaching in Physical Education*. London: Falmer Press.

Mosston, M. and Ashworth, S. (2002) *Teaching Physical Education*, 5th edn. San Francisco: Benjamin Cummings.

Murdoch, E. (2004) 'National Curriculum for Physical Education 2000 – where are we so far?: A consideration of some of the concepts that are challenging us in the revised curriculum', in S. Capel (ed.), *Learning to Teach Physical Education in the Secondary School: A Companion for the Student Physical Education Teacher*, 2nd edn. London: RoutledgeFalmer.

National Curriculum Council (NCC) (1992) *Physical Education: Non-Statutory Guidance*. York: NCC.

O'Bryant, C.P., O'Sullivan, M. and Raudensky, J. (2000) 'Socialisation of prospective physical education teachers: the story of new blood', *Sport, Education and Society*, 5 (2): 177–93.

O'Sullivan, M. (1996) 'Failing gym is like failing lunch or recess: two beginning teachers' struggle for legitimacy', *Journal of Teaching in Physical Education*, 8: 227–42.

Office for Standards in Education (OFSTED) (1995a) *Physical Education. A Review of Inspection Findings 1993/94*. London: HMSO.

Office for Standards in Education (OFSTED Wales) (1995b) *Report by HMI. Survey of Physical Education in Key Stages 1, 2 and 3*. Cardiff: OHMCI.

Penney, D. and Evans, J. (1995) Changing structures; changing rules: the development of the 'internal market', *Social Organisation*, 15: 13–21.

Penney, D. and Harris, J. (1998) 'The National Curriculum for Physical Education: have we got it right?', *British Journal of Physical Education*, 29 (1): 7–10.

Placek, J. (1983) 'Conceptions of success in teaching: busy, happy and good?', in T. Templin and J. Olsen (eds), *Teaching Physical Education*. Champaign, IL: Human Kinetics. pp. 46–56.

Placek, J.H., Doolittle, S.A., Ratliffe, T.A., Dodds, P., Portman, P.A. and Pinkham, K.M. (1995) 'Teacher recruits' physical education backgrounds and beliefs about the purposes for their subject matter', *Journal of Teaching in Physical Education*, 14: 246–61.

Richardson, V. (1996) 'The role of attitudes and beliefs in learning to teach', in J. Sikula, T. Buttery and E. Guyton (eds), *Handbook of Research on Teacher Education*. New York: Macmillan, pp. 102–19.

Rink, J. (2001) 'Investigating the assumptions of pedagogy', *Journal of Teaching in Physical Education*, 20: 112–28.

Rossi, T. and Cassidy, T. (1999) 'Knowledgeable teachers in physical education: a view of teachers' knowledge', in C.A. Hardy and M. Mawer (eds), *Learning and Teaching in Physical Education*. London: Falmer Press.

Schein, E.H. (1988) *Organizational Culture and Leadership*. San Francisco: Jossey-Bass.

Schempp, P. (1989) 'Apprenticeship of observation and the development of physical education teachers', in T.J. Templin and P. Schempp (eds), *Socialization into Physical Education: Learning to Teach*. Indianapolis, IN: Benchmark Press, pp. 13–38.

Schempp, P.G. and Graber, K.C. (1992) 'Teacher socialization from a dialectical perspective: pre-training through induction', *Journal of Teaching in Physical Education*, 11: 329–48.

Scottish Qualifications Authority (SQA) (1999) *Arrangements Document Higher still Physical Education: Higher Level*. Dalkeith. Edinburgh: SQA.

Scraton, S. (1992) *Shaping up to Womanhood: Gender and Girls' Physical Education*. Buckingham: Open University Press.

Shulman, L. (1986) 'Those who understand: knowledge growth in teaching', *Educational Researcher*, 15: 4–14.

Shulman, L. (1987) 'Knowledge and teaching: foundation of a new reform', *Harvard Review*, 57: 1–22.

Solmon, M.A. and Ashy, M.H. (1995) 'Value orientations of pre-service teachers', *Research Quarterly for Exercise and Sport*, 66: 219–30.

Sparkes, A.C. (1987) ' "Strategic rhetoric": a constraint in changing the practice of teachers', *British Journal of Sociology of Education*, 8 (1): 37–54.

Sparkes, A.C. (1991a) 'Curriculum change: on gaining a sense of perspective', in N. Armstrong and A. Sparkes (eds), *Issues in Physical Education*. London: Cassell, pp.1–19.

Sparkes, A.C. (1991b) 'Exploring the subjective dimension of curriculum change', in N. Armstrong and A. Sparkes (eds), *Issues in Physical Education*. London: Cassell, pp. 20–35.

Sparkes, A.C. (1992) 'The changing nature of teacher's work: school governors and curriculum control of physical education', in N. Armstrong (ed.), *New Directions in Physical Education, Volume 2: Towards a National Curriculum*, Champaign, IL.: Human Kinetics, pp. 1–31.

Templin, T.J. (1979) 'Occupational socialization and the physical education student teacher', *Research Quarterly for Exercise and Sport*, 50: 482–93.

Thorburn, M. and Collins, D. (2003) 'Integrated curriculum models and their effects on teachers' pedagogy practices', *European Physical Education Review*, 9 (2): 185–209.

Tinning, R., Macdonald, D., Wright, J. and Hickey, C. (2001) *Becoming a Physical Education Teacher: Contemporary and Enduring Issues*. Melbourne: Prentice Hall.

Turner-Bissett, R.A. (1997) 'Subject matter knowledge and teaching competence,' PhD dissertation, University of Exeter.

Underwood, G. (1988) *Teaching and Learning in Physical Education*. London: The Falmer Press.

Van Maanen, J. and Schein, E.H. (1979) 'Toward a theory of organizational socialization', in B. Staw (ed.), *Research in Organizational Behavior Volume 1*. Greenwich, CT: JAI Press. pp. 209–61.

Waddington, I., Malcolm, D. and Cobb, J. (1998) 'Gender stereotyping and physical education', *European Physical Education Review*, 4 (1): 34–46.

Watkins, C. and Mortimore, P. (1999) 'Pedagogy: what do we know?', in P. Mortimore (ed.), *Understanding Pedagogy and its Impact on Learning*. London: Paul Chapman. pp. 1–19.

Wideen, M., Mayer-Smith, J. and Moon, B. (1998) 'A critical analysis of the research on learning to teach: making the case for an ecological perspective on inquiry', *Review of Educational Research*, 68 (2): 130–78.

Wilson, S. and Berne, J. (1999) 'Teacher learning and the acquisition of professional knowledge: an examination of research on contemporary professional development', *Review of Research in Education*, 24: 173–209.

Wilson, S. M., Shulman, L.S. and Richert, A.E. (1987) '150 different ways of knowing: representations of knowledge in teaching' in J. Calderhead (ed.), *Exploring Teachers' Thinking*. London: Cassell.

Wright, J. (1995) 'A feminist post-structuralist methodology for the study of gender construction in physical education: description of a study', *Journal of Teaching in Physical Education*, 15 (1): 1–24.

Zeichner, K.M. and Tabachnik, B.R. (1981) 'Are the effects of university teacher education "washed out" by school experience?', *Journal of Teacher Education*, 32 (2): 7–11.

8 Model-based Teaching and Assessment in Physical Education: The Tactical Games Model

David Kirk

Leading American educational researcher Mike Metzler (2000) observes, in his book *Instructional Models for Physical Education*, that most instruction in physical education is based on content. The various forms of physical activity that make up physical education programmes are, he suggests, the organising centre for teaching. Conventionally, we start with content such as basketball or gymnastics or swimming, and determine our teaching strategies, tasks, sequences of learning experiences, assessment techniques, and so on, from there. He also claims that the ways in which we teach swimming or volleyball or archery tend to be much the same regardless of the age and experience of the students, at least with secondary school age students.

We might add to Metzler's observations studies in the UK by Green (1998), Curtner-Smith (1999), Penney and Evans (1999), Mawer (1999) and others that show that, despite several significant changes to physical education brought about by the National Curriculum, teachers continue to use only one or two teaching styles, the most common of which (to use Mosston's language) is the direct or command style (Mosston and Ashworth, 1986). These studies reveal that teachers use the same limited number of teaching styles irrespective of the content, the learning outcomes they hope to achieve, and an analysis of their students' readiness to learn.

This research evidence is rather damning for physical education in an era where increasingly in school systems around the world teachers are being held accountable for their work on the basis of student learning outcomes. In this context, assessment has become a major challenge for physical education teachers. High stakes examinations such as the A Level in England, and equivalents in countries such as Australia and Scotland, have been around for some time. But the recent requirement in England and Wales for mandatory reporting for the first time in physical education of student progress at the end of Key Stage 3 is just one example of a trend towards assessment as a regular feature of education across the curriculum and across age groups, not just in prestigious academic subjects or in high stakes exam situations.

Teachers are working to meet these new challenges in various ways, and there is evidence of quality practice at various levels of the education system in the UK (Qualifications and Curriculum Authority (QCA), 2003a; Office for Standards in Education (OFSTED), 2003). The research suggests, however, that these quality practices in school physical education need to become more widespread (Curtner-Smith, 1999; Penney and Chandler, 2000). How can we as a profession, as a community of physical education practitioners, learn collectively from the work of our outstanding teacher colleagues to meet the challenges of what we teach, how we teach and how we know we are achieving our aspirations for our students?

It is these three questions of content, teaching styles and assessment that I want to address in this chapter. I will take a lead from Metzler's (2000) proposals for how we should meet these challenges. He argues that rather than start from any one factor alone such as content or teaching style, we need instead to consider both of these factors equally with a range of others, including intended learning outcomes, the context and teaching environment, and a student's developmental stage and readiness. He proposes that the way forward for the physical education profession is to practice what he calls model-based teaching. I will begin by explaining what he means by this notion of model-based teaching, and then address the issue of what forms of assessment might be appropriate and viable within this approach. I will then conclude with two examples of how content, teaching styles and learning outcomes and assessment can be organised in the Tactical Games Model, which is one of the seven instructional models Metzler presents in his book, and in the National Curriculum for Physical Education (NCPE) schemes of work (QCA, 2003b).

WHAT IS MODEL-BASED TEACHING?

According to Metzler, the distinctive feature of model-based teaching is that content and teaching styles are matched closely to intended learning outcomes, with due consideration of the key factors of student experience and characteristics, and school and policy contexts. For example, two secondary school physical education teachers may be about to begin a unit of soccer, but they each have different learning outcomes in mind for their classes. In the case of Teacher A, the intention is to promote higher level technique development with independent student progression. In the case of teacher B, the intention is to develop students' tactical knowledge and the appropriate use of skills in game situations. In each case, argues Metzler, the teachers will choose a different instructional model, even though they are teaching the same content. With his emphasis on independent student learning of techniques, teacher A could choose what Metzler calls the Personalised System of Instruction. With her emphasis on tactics and skills, teacher B could select the Tactical

Games model. The decision on how to teach is in these examples not based on the unit content alone, but additionally on the teacher's aspirations for the learning outcomes of his and her students and other salient factors.

Is the conventionally most commonplace teaching style of direct instruction ever appropriate within a model-based approach to teaching? Metzler argues that it is, and indeed suggests that direct instruction is an instructional model in its own right. Imagine a situation in which I have 25 eight-year-olds by myself who are about to begin a unit of swimming, and all are non-swimmers. My intended learning outcome is that they will learn to swim, but clearly I must first of all ensure that the children remain safe at all times. In this context, during the introductory lessons of a unit, I am unlikely to use a guided discovery teaching style! A Direct Instruction model might be entirely appropriate as I establish the various routines required to ensure the intended learning outcomes associated with safe behaviour in and around the pool. Once again, in this example we can see that intended learning outcomes and contextual factors are, along with content, the primary considerations in determining teaching style.

An instructional model is then an irreducible cluster or chunk of teaching styles, content and intended learning outcomes and allied contextual considerations. In other words, the instructional model rather than content or teaching style alone becomes the organising centre for the construction of a physical education programme. Metzler describes seven instructional models in his book, some of which have already been mentioned. The seven are:

1. Direct Instruction.
2. Personalised System for Instruction.
3. Cooperative Learning.
4. Sport Education.
5. Peer Teaching.
6. Inquiry Model.
7. Tactical Games.

These models are merely examples of how content and teaching styles can be matched with learning outcomes, and Metzler argues that there is a need for multiple models in physical education since teachers typically attempt to realise a range of physical, cognitive and affective learning outcomes through physical education programs. Contrary to popular mythology, our subject is complex and many-sided, and it is, therefore, demanding of learners. We need the range of instructional models that reflect this complexity and help us fulfil our aspirations for our students.

Metzler lists some good reasons why model-based teaching may be a fruitful way forward for physical education, among them the increased possibility of success in realising our aspirations for student learning when we match these closely with content and teaching styles. He also demonstrates that all of the models he lists already have strong research to support their effectiveness and he notes that a good instructional model will always include benchmarks for a teacher to know if he or she is using the model correctly and if the intended learning outcomes are being realised.

So what does a specific instructional model look like? In the next part of this chapter, I want to look in detail at one form of model-based teaching in physical education, the Tactical Games model, before moving on to consider how assessment might fit within this model and model-based teaching more broadly. This model has been around in one form or another since the early 1980s, and so will be familiar to most readers. It has also become popular beyond England, its country of origin, and is informed by a growing research base, particularly in the USA and Australia.

THE TACTICAL GAMES MODEL (OR TGFU OR GAME SENSE)

The term 'tactical games model' is the American term for the notion of Teaching Games for Understanding (TGfU) first developed by Thorpe et al. (1986) at Loughborough University in the late 1970s and through the 1980s. The Australians prefer to use the term Game Sense, which they coined in the 1990s in a sports coaching context. Whichever of these three terms we use, they refer essentially to the same instructional model.

First, a short summary of the original ideas behind TGfU will provide an introduction to the key features of the model. Bunker and Thorpe (1982) had observed that much teaching and coaching of games was dominated by the development of techniques within highly structured lessons. They also observed that, in school physical education, the development of techniques took up the majority of lesson time with little time left over to actually play the game. Even when game play was included in lessons, teachers and coaches rarely made connections between the technique practices and how and when these techniques should be applied in game play. A common complaint voiced by teachers and coaches was that the techniques apparently learned laboriously in lessons and training sessions break down in game play.

Their solution to this perceived problem was to develop an alternative approach to games teaching and coaching that assisted players to learn the tactics and strategies of game play in tandem with skill development. They made an important distinction between a technique and a skill. A technique is a means of executing movement efficiently and within the rules of a game for a specific purpose, but is practised and performed outside an actual game context. An example of a technique is the lateral pass in rugby, often practised unopposed or in drills. A skill is the appropriate practice and performance of a technique in a game situation (Thorpe, 1990). In the case of the lateral pass, the ideal 'textbook' technique becomes a skill when speed, direction and spin are modified to produce a catchable pass in a given situation. Thorpe et al. (1986) were concerned primarily with the development of these two key features of game play, tactics and skills.

At the heart of their approach was the use of modified games. All games teaching and coaching that aim to achieve tactical and skill learning outcomes take place within the framework of game play. Games are modified to suit the developmental level of the players. Modifications are made to rules, playing area, and equipment and seek to assist the player to make appropriate decisions about what to do and how to do it in game forms that exaggerate one or more aspects of the game, and usually also simplify some of the skills. For example, a teacher might use a 2v1 non-kicking game in a 10m × 10m box to help rugby players understand some basic strategies for beating a defender, such as committing the defender to tackle before off-loading a pass to her team-mate, making a dummy pass, or using a side-step to evade the defender. A 4v2 game played in a wide box (say 30m × 20m) can encourage players to use the spaces out wide to get past defenders, or the same game in a narrow box (20 × 30m) can encourage them to run from deep and with pace in order to evade or break through a tackle. Other modifications to skills such as touch tackling and specific conditions can be used to exaggerate particular game situations. Of key importance is that any modified game form must retain the essential feature of the full game, such as the objective of scoring a try in rugby, if learning is to transfer from one game form to another. As players improve, game forms can become more challenging and complex.

This introduction to the origins of TGfU provides some clues to the essential characteristics of the Tactical Games model. A teacher would normally select the Tactical Games model when the key learning outcomes are to develop understanding and use of tactics and skills in game play. The teaching styles most likely to be useful for the purpose of developing understanding are guided discovery and problem solving, involving the teacher in using the Socratic method (Butler, 1997) of question and answer. Indeed, the Australian version of the model recommends a sequence of activities in a lesson that include warm-up, modified game, questions and challenges, back to modified game, further questions and challenges and progression of game. Encouraging players to think for themselves, to come up with their own solutions and to try them out may be a more effective means of developing understanding than simply telling the players what to do (Australian Sports Commission (ASC), 1997). With these learning outcomes in mind, and using these teaching styles, the content of lessons is primarily modified games. In other words, players learn to play games by playing games, albeit in modified form.

Guided discovery and problem solving teaching styles are not necessarily easy to use, especially for teachers who have used mainly directive and practice styles. Guided discovery and problem solving require the teacher to structure the learning tasks – in this case modified games – very carefully. They also require the teacher to step back, to intervene only occasionally, to use question and answer to guide learners towards a solution, and to hand over to players a degree of responsibility for learning. Our own research using the Tactical Games model (Brooker et al., 2000) taught us that even the most willing teacher has to undergo a period of considerable adjustment in order to learn to use these teaching styles effectively. For some teachers, stepping back may feel like an abrogation of their role as teacher where they are always out in front, directing the class. Our research, along with the work of Inez Rovegno (see Rovegno et al., 2001), and Linda Griffin (see Griffin et al., 2001) also suggests that the teacher must be very knowledgeable about particular games, and must be able to think creatively and divergently to select or invent modified games that work in their own local situations with their students. Fortunately, there are already some good textbooks and other resources available to assist teachers to construct good modified games (for example, Griffin et al., 1997; Wein, 2001; Launder, 2001; Department of Education, Ireland, no date).

The research on the Tactical Games model has suggested why the directive teaching style has persisted for so long, even when it has been shown to be inappropriate for realising some learning outcomes. The directive style is a very effective means of managing classes of children. Especially in primary schools, where generalist teachers typically lack in-depth knowledge of particular games, a technique-based directive approach is favoured because the teacher can ensure that all children remain safe, busy, relatively happy and good. It may be also that children themselves are familiar and comfortable with this directive style and have little experience of any other form of teaching in physical education. These are some of the reasons why we still see so many so-called games lessons where children spend most of their time passing basketballs or hockey balls back and forwards to each other in straight lines. The lesson is safe, the teacher can see all of the children, and the teacher can argue that the children are learning the basic techniques of the game. This may be so. But one thing we can be sure of is that they are not learning to play the game.

So the Tactical Games model is not necessarily easy to use. But overviews of the research already completed on the model shows that it can improve students' ability to play games (Rink et al., 1996; Metzler, 2000; Kirk and MacPhail, 2000), though it is also important to note that results from research studies have not been as conclusive as they might due to conceptual and methodological problems that are now beginning to be resolved (Kirk, 2001a). One of the major strengths of the model identified by Metzler is that this approach provides students with authentic learning tasks in the form of modified games, in contrast to technique drills that can bear little resemblance to the game. This feature of authenticity holds important implications for assessment within the Tactical Games model.

ASSESSMENT FOR LEARNING WITHIN THE TACTICAL GAMES MODEL

Assessment has been a fraught subject for physical educators (Kirk, 2001b). Part of the difficulty of assessment derives from the complexity and multidimensional character of the subject, where we seek to achieve learning outcomes across the cognitive, psychomotor and affective domains. There are batteries of validated tests that can be used in physical education classes, but these tend to relate only to the psychomotor domain, and sometimes barely adequately at that. Written tests, essays and research projects have also been used widely to measure learning in the cognitive domain. The real challenge of assessment in the context of model-based teaching is when authentic learning involves the interaction of all three domains. This is most definitely the case with learning to play games.

Metzler (2000: 357) notes that tactical knowledge developed through the Tactical Games model can be demonstrated in the cognitive and psychomotor domains. Although researchers have used paper and pencil tests in some studies, revealing one of the methodological problems I alluded to earlier, Metzler (2000) argues that the true test of learning the tactics and skills of a game is their demonstration in game situations. While it is certainly desirable to ask students to think about and discuss tactical problems, the authentic test of their learning will be the game performance itself. In short, the measurement of authentic learning requires authentic assessment.

The literature suggests that authentic assessment requires participation by both teachers and learners, and that learners should be given a degree of responsibility for making judgements about their own and their peers' learning (Kirk and O'Flaherty, 2003). There are at least two ways in which teachers and learners together might assess game performance authentically, either by using a checklist approach such as the Game Performance Assessment Instrument (GPAI) (Oslin et al., 1998) or by using a set of criteria and standards, as in the case of the Senior Physical Education programme in Queensland, Australia, and in the case of the NCPE in England and Wales. Both approaches could indeed be used together, since the GPAI provides useful quantitative information on player decision making and the appropriate selection of skills that can inform teachers' and learners' interpretations of criteria. However, even using the GPAI, teachers and learners are ultimately required to interpret the information they collect and exercise their own judgements about the level and quality of game performance and the learning the performance demonstrates. The Queensland approach in particular makes this process of judgement explicit.

A CRITERION-BASED APPROACH: THE QUEENSLAND SENIOR PE SYLLABUS

The Queensland Senior Physical Education Syllabus (Board of Senior Secondary School Studies (BSSSS), 1998) requires teachers to design assessment tasks that generate information in relation to three assessment criteria, which are acquiring, applying and evaluating knowledge in physical education.

1. Acquiring refers to abilities such as gathering, recalling, recognising and comprehending information.
2. Applying refers to abilities such as interpreting, analysing, implementing and manipulating information.
3. Evaluating refers to abilities such as predicting, synthesising, justifying and appraising information (BSSSS, 1998: 5–6).

Teachers are asked to judge the extent to which each of these criteria is met. To do this, they employ five standards' statements for each criterion ranging from very high achievement to very low achievement. Many of the assessment tasks test the acquisition, application and evaluation of skills and strategies together rather than in isolation. In this high stakes examination context, it might be argued that learners have less involvement than they might in contributing to assessment processes (Brooker and Macdonald, 2001). They do, nevertheless, very quickly come to know and use the assessment criteria in relation to their own performance, even though this happens informally for the most part.

An example from the Queensland syllabus of a combined physical and oral assessment task in golf looks like this:

> Students engage in a one-hole walk-and-talk task. They play the hole and explain the situation, their judgments and the decisions they make as they play. They may talk about club selection based on their assessment of the accuracy and distance they know they can achieve with particular clubs, the influence of the terrain, weather, and the state of play in the match. They might also provide an assessment of their performance of strokes and explanations for the outcomes of shots. (BSSSS, 1998: 29)

An example from the syllabus of a physical assessment task in basketball is as follows:

> Students demonstrate offensive ... skills and tactics in a 3 on 3 half-court game. They demonstrate their ability to evaluate game-play through the selection of appropriate individual and team skills and strategies in relation to an analysis of their opposition's strengths and weaknesses. (BSSSS, 1998: 28)

The Queensland criterion-based approach has been influential in the development of a similar approach adopted and developed within the NCPE.

A QUASI CRITERION-BASED APPROACH: THE NCPE SCHEMES OF WORK

In the case of the NCPE, I have used the term 'quasi' criterion-based approach because the NCPE does not use the term 'criteria' and does not employ a set of standards in the same systematic fashion as the Queensland syllabus requires. This may be because the same approach is used across Key Stages 1–4, rather than in a high stakes examination context alone. What are called 'criteria' in the case of the Queensland syllabus are called 'objectives' in the NCPE. Standards are expressed as 'expectations' at three levels of 'most pupils will', 'some pupils will not have made so much progress and will', and 'some pupils will have progressed further and will'. Judgements about which level best fits any individual learner will be made as each pupil participates in the activities and core tasks (more of which below).

The objectives in the schemes of work closely recall the Queensland criteria, and are as follows:

- acquiring and developing skills;
- selecting and applying skills, tactics and compositional ideas;
- knowledge and understanding of fitness and health;
- evaluating and improving performance.

In relation to each of these learning objectives, the schemes of work list possible teaching activities and learning outcomes. By way of example, the learning objectives, possible teaching activities and learning outcomes for Unit 6: Invasion Games are set out in Table 8.1 (opposite):

The main vehicle for assessment is the use of a series of core tasks, set out in each unit of the scheme of work (QCA, 2003b). For Unit 6: Invasion Games, there are three core tasks. The core tasks are intended to provide a focus for learners' activities in the unit. Crucially, they also, simultaneously and consistent with the Queensland approach, provide a medium for authentic assessment. For example, Core Task 1 focuses on the objective of acquiring and developing skills and involves: 'Four attackers versus two defenders (progress to 4v3). Attackers start with the ball from a safe exclusion zone near their own goal. They attempt to score in one of three goals. Defenders can score in one large goal, shooting from outside the exclusion zone. After each goal the attackers restart from the exclusion zone.' Core Task 2 seeks to progress game play from Core Task 1, with a particular focus on selecting and applying skills and tactics, involving: 'Three attackers versus three defenders (progress to four defenders). Attackers start with the ball in their own third of the pitch and try to score in the defenders' goal. The defenders attempt to "gain" possession and score in one of two goals, wide on the wings of the pitch.' Core Task 3 provides a further development of Core Tasks 1 and 2, testing the objectives of selecting and applying, and evaluating: 'In small-sided versions of the games (4v4, 5v5, 6v6, 7v7) pupils plan for effective team play, applying tactics with understanding of the principles of attack, defence and transpossession.' These three core tasks can be varied and adapted to include different kinds of invasion games, sizes of playing area and different equipment. Their key purpose is to provide both a template for organising learning to play invasion games and evidence over time of the progression of learning in relation to the key objectives and learning outcomes.

ASSESSMENT SCENARIOS AND MODIFIED GAMES

Taking this criterion-based approach to assessment, it is possible to map the assessment scenarios (in this case modified games) directly on to the main learning experiences (in this case modified games). As learning progresses, so the assessment scenarios and learning experiences can become more sophisticated. But the essential features of game play – such as moving the ball quickly into space, deceiving an opponent, selecting and deploying appropriate skills and tactics, and so on – remain the bases on which learning is judged. One of the key principles from the authentic assessment literature is that students should never encounter an assessment item for the first time when it really matters, that is, as summative

Table 8.1 *Learning objectives, possible teaching activities and learning outcomes for Unit 6: Invasion Games*

Learning objectives	Possible teaching activities	Learning outcomes
Acquiring and developing skills		
◆ To improve the consistency, quality and use of skills in the games played	◆ Ask pupils to play small-sided versions of the selected game, keeping the rules and organising themselves into teams with positions and roles	◆ Use an increasing range of personal techniques consistently, accurately and fluently while playing small-sided games
◆ To adapt and develop their skills	◆ Help pupils consolidate the basic techniques and teach new techniques. Explore ways in which pupils anticipate the flight or movement of the ball and learn the importance of feints and acceleration when trying to outwit an opponent	◆ Adapt skills to different situations
◆ To apply more specific techniques in the activities undertaken	◆ Help pupils investigate techniques employed when attacking, e.g. *control and protection of the ball, progression and shot*, and consolidate defensive techniques, e.g. *mark, cover, intercept and tackle*	
Selecting and applying skills, tactics and compositional ideas		
◆ To organise themselves as a team and select and apply strategies consistently and effectively	◆ Talk to pupils about patterns of play in attack and defence, and teach the pupils how to make decisions about when and where to pass	◆ Organise themselves as a team to attack and defend and play in different positions
◆ To adapt strategies and tactics used in one game and apply them to a different one	◆ Help pupils explore the basic principles of attack, e.g. *width, speed and support to keep possession and make progression*, the basic principles of defence, e.g. *delay, denial of space, pressure and cover to regain possession*, and the skills and techniques to put the principles into operation. Help the pupils to recognise patterns of play	◆ Select and use a range of tactics and strategies and apply them successfully in different games
	◆ Help pupils consolidate their understanding of simple tactics and explore the way these tactics can be adapted to small-sided games	◆ Explain the similarities between the different invasion games played

Table 8.1   Continued

Learning objectives	Possible teaching activities	Learning outcomes
Selecting and applying skills, tactics and compositional ideas (continued)		
	◆ Listen to pupils say why tactics may succeed in one invasion game and fail in another. Help them to adapt their tactics to the current invasion game	
	◆ Ask pupils to explore simple game plans that increase the chances of successful outcomes in attack and defence	
Knowledge and understanding of fitness and health		
◆ To prepare for and recover from exercise safely and effectively and to know the principles used	◆ Listen to pupils talk about their understanding of the way in which strength, stamina and suppleness can be improved by playing invasion games	◆ Describe what they need to do to improve their own fitness
	◆ Help consolidate pupils' knowledge of warm-up and cool-down activities relevant to invasion games	◆ Design and carry out warm-up and cool-down routines safely and effectively
◆ To recognise the benefits to their health of regular exercise and good hygiene and the benefits of being active in games	◆ Ask pupils to refine their own warm-up routines, e.g. *mobilise, raise the body temperature and stretch*	◆ Explain why these activities are important
	◆ Talk to pupils about different ways of improving performance in invasion games, e.g. *draw upon knowledge of training in athletics to improve speed or acceleration*	◆ Recognise and describe how games affect their health and fitness
	◆ Help pupils understand the importance of specificity in training	
Evaluating and improving performance		
◆ To make effective evaluations of strengths and weaknesses in their own and others' performance	◆ Ask pupils to analyse their own and others' strengths and weaknesses and to identify aspects of technique that need to be improved. Teach them how to 'read' a game	◆ Explain the range of decisions they have to make in a game

Evaluating and improving performance (continued)

◆ To make suggestions to improve play, e.g. on *attack and defence tactics*

◆ Help pupils explore different ways of observing and analysing performance and recognise what is effective and what needs improving

◆ Talk to pupils about the ways they think both the games and their own play can be improved. Listen to what they think they need most help with, then invite ideas on how to adapt and vary the games

◆ Talk to pupils about their knowledge of rules and develop their ability to officiate small-sided games

◆ Identify their own and others' strengths and weaknesses

◆ Implement practices to improve their performance

◆ Identify aspects of technique that require practice and improvement

◆ Assess and comment on the ways in which they can improve, e.g. *attack and defence tactics*

Source: QCA Standards site *www.standards.dfee.gov.uk*

judgements are being made (Piotrowski and Capel, 2000). In other words, authentic assessment is more accurately perhaps described as assessment for learning, since the construction of modified game scenarios provide constant and ongoing feedback on student progress to learners and teachers. The criteria upon which student learning will be judged are the same criteria upon which learning experiences are constructed. The Queensland and NCPE examples show that once criteria for assessment have been agreed, it is not difficult for knowledgeable observers to reach a consensus on the standard of play, even though some preliminary negotiation will inevitably take place.

CONCLUSION

In this chapter I have provided little more than a brief introduction to how model-based teaching in physical education might provide a framework for forms of assessment that permit teachers and learners to make both formative and summative judgements about the progress of learning (Piotrowski and Capel, 2000). The instructional model I have used as an example is the Tactical Games model, since there is already a reasonably well known body of research evidence, craft knowledge and practical experience to illustrate the implementation of this model. I suggested that the real advantages of taking a model-based approach to teaching and learning is that our organising centre for curriculum planning is learning outcomes, content, teaching styles and appropriate contextual factors taken together as a unit, rather than any one of these factors in isolation. Since learning outcomes are closely matched to content and teaching styles, it is then possible to map criteria for assessment directly on to criteria for learning and teaching.

Of course there is much more that needs to be said about model-based teaching and assessment that I have not been able to cover in this chapter. I have considered only an instructional model that is concerned with game tactics and skills as learning outcomes. But as I noted near the beginning of this chapter, physical educators ambitiously attempt to achieve learning outcomes across the entire range of cognitive, psychomotor and affective domains. So how the notions of model-based teaching and assessment might apply across physical education programs need to be worked through.

There is also much to be said about the purely technical and practical implications of assessment for learning within model-based teaching. There remains the not inconsiderable task of collecting, recording and reporting evidence of learning (Physical Education Association United Kingdom (PEA UK), 2000). Arguably, model-based teaching should help teachers to reduce the administrative burden of these processes since only information salient to the learning and assessment criteria is to be generated. Nevertheless, lack of time emerges as a ubiquitous threat to the extent to which teachers can fulfil these tasks of collecting, recording and reporting, particularly on an ongoing basis. Much imagination and lateral thinking is required to address these issues.

At the same time, I suggest that model-based teaching is an idea worth exploring further as a means of meeting the challenge of assessment in physical education, particularly in ways that contribute to the progression of student learning. As I've argued elsewhere with Mary O'Flaherty (Kirk and O'Flaherty, 2003), it is important that we do not become too focused on assessment and fail to consider our concept of learning that provides a rationale for assessment in the first place. The era of using a superficial concept of enjoyment as a rationale for physical education, of positioning physical education as an antidote to the otherwise overly academic curriculum, and of the directive teaching method of keeping kids 'busy, happy and good', is over. In any case, we sell ourselves short with these traditional practices, when physical education has so many rich educational experiences to offer young people. Model-based teaching, I suggest, is worth exploring as one potential means of moving us closer to realising the rich learning outcomes that physical education might provide.

ACKNOWLEDGEMENT

Thanks to Mary O'Flaherty for her feedback on this chapter. All shortcomings, however, remain my responsibility.

REFERENCES

Australian Sports Commission (1997) *Games Sense: Developing Thinking Players*. Canberra: Australian Sports Commission..

Board of Senior Secondary School Studies (BSSSS) (1998) *Physical Education: Senior Syllabus*. Spring Hill, Brisbane: BSSSS.

Brooker, R. and Macdonald, D. (1999) 'Did *we* hear *you*? Issues of student voice in a curriculum innovation', *Journal of Curriculum Studies*, 31 (1): 83–98.

Brooker, R., Kirk, D., Braiuka, S. and Bransgrove, A. (2000) 'Implementing a game sense approach to teaching Year 8 basketball', *European Physical Education Review*, 6 (1): 7–26.

Butler, J. (1997) 'How would Socrates teach games? A constructivist approach', *Journal of Physical Education, Recreation and Dance*, 68 (9): 42–7.

Bunker, D. and Thorpe, R. (1982) 'A model for the teaching of games in the secondary school', *Bulletin of Physical Education*, 10: 9–16.

Curtner-Smith, M.D. (1999) 'The more things change, the more they stay the same: factors influencing teachers' interpretations and delivery of the National Curriculum physical education', *Sport, Education and Society*, 4 (1): 75–98.

Department of Education, Ireland (no date) *Games for Understanding: A Manual for Teachers*. Cork: DoE, Ireland.

Green, K. (1998) 'Philosophies, ideologies and the practice of physical education', *Sport, Education and Society*, 3 (2): 125–43.

Griffin, L.L., Dodds, P., Placek, J.H. and Tremino, F. (2001) 'Middle school students' conceptions of soccer: their solutions to tactical problems', *Journal of Teaching in Physical Education*, 20 (4): 324–40.

Griffin, L.L., Mitchell, S.A. and Oslin, J.L (1997) *Teaching Sport Concepts and Skills: A Tactical Games Approach*. Champaign, IL: Human Kinetics.

Kirk, D. (2001a) 'Future prospects and directions for TgfU', Keynote Address to the International Conference on Teaching Games for Understanding, Waterville Valley, New Hampshire, August.

Kirk, D. (2001b) 'Learning and assessment in physical education', Keynote Address to the Physical Education Association of Ireland, Ennis, October.

Kirk, D. and O'Flaherty, M. (2003) 'Learning theory and authentic assessment in physical education'. Paper presented to the Annual Conference of the British Educational Research Association, Edinburgh, September.

Kirk, D. and MacPhail, A. (2000) *The Games Sense Approach: Rationale, Description and a Brief Overview of Research*. Leeds: Human Kinetics.

Launder, A.G. (2001) *Play Practice: The Games Approach to Teaching and Coaching Sports*. Champaign, IL: Human Kinetics.

Mawer, M. (1999) 'Teaching styles and teaching approaches in physical education: Research developments', in C.A. Hardy and M. Mawer (eds) *Learning and Teaching in Physical Education*. London: Falmer. pp. 83–104.

Metzler, M. W. (2000) *Instructional Models for Physical Education*. Boston: Allyn and Bacon.

Mosston, M. and Ashworth, S. (1986) *Teaching Physical Education* (3rd edn). Columbus: Merrill.

OFSTED (2003) *Good Assessment Practice in Physical Education*. HMI 1481. *http://www.qca.org.uk/ca/5-14/afl/ subject_guidance_pe.asp*

Oslin, J.L., Mitchell, S.A. and Griffin, L.L. (1998) 'The Game Performance Assessment Instrument (GPAI): development and preliminary validation', *Journal of Teaching Physical Education*, 17 (2): 231–43.

Penney, D. and Chandler, T. (2000) 'Physical education – what future(s)?', *Sport, Education and Society*, 5 (1): 71–88.

Penney, D. and Evans, J. (1999) *Politics, Policy and Practice in Physical Education*. London: Spon.

Physical Education Association United Kingdom (PEAUK) (2000) *Assessment, Recording and Reporting in Physical Education: Guidance for Teachers*. Reading: PEA UK.

Piotrowski, S. and Capel, S. (2000) 'Formal and informal modes of assessment in physical education', in S. Piotrowski and S. Capel (eds), *Issues in Physical Education*. Routledge/Falmer: London.

Qualifications Curriculum Authority (2003a) < *http://www.qca.org.uk/pess/* >

Qualifications Curriculum Authority (2003b) < *http://www.standards.dfes.gov.uk/schemes2/phe/* >

Rink, J.E.R., French, K.E. and Tjeerdsma, B.L. (1996) 'Foundations for the learning and instruction of sport and games', *Journal of Teaching in Physical Education*, 15 (4): 399–417.

Rovegno, I., Nevett, M., Brock, S. and Barbiaz, M. (2001) 'Teaching and learning of basic invasion game tactics in fourth grade: a descriptive study from a situated and constraints theoretical perspective', *Journal of Teaching in Physical Education*, 20 (4): 370–88.

Thorpe, R. (1990) 'New directions in games teaching', in N. Armstrong (ed.), *New Directions in Physical Education, Volume 1*. Leeds: Human Kinetics. pp. 79–100.

Thorpe, R., Bunker, D. and Almond, L. (1986) *Rethinking Games Teaching*. Loughborough: Loughborough University.

Wein, H. (2001) *Developing Youth Soccer Players*, Champaign, IL, Human Kinetics.

9 | Examinations: A 'New Orthodoxy' in Physical Education?

Ken Green

Arguably the most dramatic development in secondary physical education (PE) in the UK over the past 30 years has been the growth, not to say explosion, of General Certificate of Secondary Education (GCSE) and Advanced (A) level examinations (Carr, 1997; Green, 2001; MacKreth, 1998; Reid, 1996a; Stidder and Wallis, 2003). While other developments in PE during the same period – such as health-related exercise (HRE) – have also had significant ramifications for the way in which the subject is conceptualised and practised, a lineage for such developments can be traced in the historical development of the subject (see, for example, Harris, this volume; Kirk, 1992). Examinable PE, by contrast, can be said to represent something of a step-change. Indeed, some would argue that the growth of examinable PE is indicative of not only a 'new orthodoxy' (Reid, 1996a, 1996b) among physical educationalists regarding the nature and purposes of PE but also the 'future direction' of the subject (Stidder and Wallis, 2003). It is for these reasons that this chapter will focus upon one aspect – GCSE and A level examinations – of the broader topic of assessment in PE. To this end, the chapter briefly charts the growth and development of GCSE and A level PE in England before exploring the claim that a process of academicisation has culminated in the emergence of a new academic orthodoxy in the subject.

THE EMERGENCE AND DEVELOPMENT OF EXAMINATIONS

Examinations[1] emerged as a significant aspect of formal education in the second-half of the nineteenth century (Brook, 1993). The Oxbridge universities, in the first instance, and then the Public and Grammar schools, were central to the rapid development of school-leaving examinations (Black, 1998; Brook, 1993) as a means of enabling the recruitment of young men to the professions, from among the rapidly expanding numbers of 'educated' school-leavers, on merit rather than favour or patronage. Thus, school leaving examinations in particular, and the public examination system in general, developed in England via the universities and the examination boards which they controlled (Black, 1998).

The introduction of mass education at secondary level, following World War II, brought with it an increasing demand for appropriate formal educational qualifications in a context of technological advance and economic development (Banks, 1971; Black, 1998). Examinations were introduced into the new state run school system at the end of primary and secondary education respectively (Brook, 1993). The local education authority 11-plus served to select for the various forms of secondary schooling while the General Certificate of Education (GCE) Ordinary (O) and Advanced (A) levels enabled entry into more specialised and professionalised areas of the job market and higher education respectively (Banks, 1971). Subsequent pressures 'to provide school leaving certification through examinations for all pupils' (Black, 1998: 14) led to the introduction of the Certificate in Secondary Education (CSE) into Secondary Modern schools in the 1960s and, in the process, the extension of examinations to cover the whole of the secondary sector. The two-tiered system of CSE and GCE was replaced by a unified examination – the General Certificate of Secondary Education (GCSE) – in 1987. More recently, the revision of the post-16 qualification has ushered in the AS (Advanced Secondary) and A2 examinations as replacements for the established A level examination.[2]

Unsurprisingly, given its longstanding associations with games 'playing' and physical exercise, PE has been a relatively late arrival on the examination scene. Indeed, it has taken a concerted effort on the part of an examination lobby within the PE subject-community to convert not only their non-PE colleagues and headteachers but also the PE profession itself. Despite the rapid growth of examinable PE in recent years, the evidence to suggest that the majority of physical educationalists have, indeed, been persuaded of the merits of examinable PE is compelling but by no means unequivocal (Green, 2001).

THE GROWTH AND DEVELOPMENT OF EXAMINATIONS IN PE

Carroll (1994, 1998) has charted the emergence and proliferation of examinations in PE from a period of innovation in the early 1970s, via successive phases of consolidation in the mid- to late 1970s and rapid and sustained growth in the 1980s, to a widespread expansion and acceptance of GCSE PE and A level PE and Sports Studies during the 1990s. To this might be added a further stage, since 2000, wherein GCSE and A level courses have been broken down into two parts: short and full courses. In the case of A level PE, for example, the first year now involves separate certification at what is known as Advanced Subsidiary (AS) level while the second year of study – A2 – completes the A level syllabus. The one year AS level in PE – known as the 'short course' – is ostensibly set at the same standard as a full A level but contains half the content.

The last decade or so, in particular, has witnessed substantial growth in examinable PE both in terms of pupil examinees and exam centres. A 1998 report from the Office for Standards in Education (OFSTED) referred to 'the rapid growth of GCSE PE', which more than doubled in the five-year period up to 1997, as 'a strong feature of secondary PE' (OFSTED, 1998: 1). By 2003, the total number of entries for GCSE PE stood at approximately 110,900 (see Table 9.1) (Department for Education and Skills (DfES), 2004a). For its part, A level PE experienced equally swift expansion: from 35 candidates at its inception in 1985 to over 11,000 by 1998 (MacKreth, 1998), 13,000 a year later (Department for Education and Employment (DfEE), 2000a) and almost 19,000 (18,931) in 2003 (see Table 9.2) (DfES, 2004b). These figures represent a 221 per cent growth in GCSE PE between 1990 and 2003 and a 2,863 per cent growth for A level PE over the same period (see Table 9.3).

Table 9.1   *Comparison of growth of total GCSE entries in England in selected subjects between 1997–1998 and 2002–2003*

	1997–1998†	2002–2003‡	Percentage change
Art and Design	183,200	190,300	+3.88
Biological Sciences	38,100	42,700	+12.07
Business Studies	88,500	83,100	−6.10
Chemistry	36,600	40,900	+11.75
English	520,800	577,400	+10.87
French	307,400	304,500	−0.94
Geography	236,200	200,100	−15.28
History	189,200	194,800	+2.96
Mathematics	537,900	613,400	+14.04
Music	38,300	47,600	+24.28
Physical Education	**84,200**	**110,900**	**+31.71**
Religious Studies	94,200	114,000	+21.02
TOTAL	4,626,700	5,030,500	+16.26

†Figures have been rounded up or down by the authors or the DfES.
‡Based upon provisional figures.
Sources: Carroll, 1998; MacKreth, 1998; DfES, 2004a.

It is readily apparent that GCSE and A level PE have become more and more widely available in England. The 'unprecedented growth' (Stidder, 2001a: 25) in examinable PE over the last decade has, it seems, been reinforced by the rapid expansion of secondary schools designated as Specialist Sports Colleges – the vast majority of which appear to offer examinable PE at least to GCSE level (Stidder, 2001a, 2001b). The emergence and rapid growth of GCSE and A level PE has, as one might expect, thrown up a number of more or less significant issues.

Table 9.2 *Comparison of growth of total A level entries in England in selected subjects between 1997–1998 and 2002–2003*

	1997–1998	2002–2003	Percentage change
Art and Design	27,840	35,384	+27.10
Biological Sciences	42,826	45,773	+6.88
Business Studies	25,612	33,560	+31.03
Chemistry	32,269	32,319	+0.15
English	73,700	88,259	+19.75
French	18,152	13,544	−25.39
Geography	36,324	31,475	−13.35
History	31,627	37,265	+17.83
Mathematics	54,980	51,438	−6.44
Music	5,429	7,834	+44.30
Physical Education	**12,027**	**18,931**	**+57.40**
Religious Studies	6,235	10,260	+64.55
TOTAL	605,320	686,472	+13.41

Sources: Carroll, 1998; MacKreth, 1998; DfES, 2004b.

Table 9.3 *Total entries for GCSE and A level PE in England 1990–2003*

	GCSE PE	A Level PE
1990	34,529	639
1992	42,026	2,600†
1994	50,400†	6,000†
1996	80,645	9,732
1998	84,200†	12,027
1999	94,100†	13,030
2003	110,900†	18,931‡
Percentage growth		
1990–2002	221%	2,863%

†Figures have been rounded up or down by the authors or the DfEE/DfES.
‡For comparative purposes this figure does not include Advanced Subsidiary (AS) level entries.
Sources: Carroll, 1998; MacKreth, 1998; DfEE, 2000a, 2000b; DfES, 2003a, 2003b, 2004a, 2004b.

ISSUES IN EXAMINABLE PE

Issues, by definition, are 'live' or current. Thus, some issues related to examinable PE – such as a lack of appropriate resources (for example, in the form of suitable text books) for theory work (Carroll, 1991) – appear to have been sufficiently resolved for reference to them in the PE press, for example, to have dissipated if not quite disappeared. Others, however, persist, and this is is particularly true for issues to do with the gendered nature of the subject, standards of attainment and, perhaps most significantly, the implications for conventional PE of the ostensible academicisation of the subject.

Gender and examinable PE

Its dramatic growth notwithstanding, examinable PE remains heavily gendered (Flintoff and Scraton, this volume; Penney et al., 2002). This is manifest in the significantly greater popularity among boys than girls of GCSE and A level PE – at a ratio approaching 2:1 (DfES, 2003a, 2003b). The difference in take-up may well reflect a difference in appeal and this, in turn, may in part be attributable to the gendered nature, not to say bias, to be found in PE, in general, and in the examinable form of the subject, in particular. The latter ranges from 'gender bias' in text books (Stidder, 2001a) through to the ways in which physical characteristics (especially strength and size) can be 'embedded' in the practical aspects of GCSE and A level PE when and where 'physical performance is central to the assessment programme' (MacDonald and Brooker, 1999: 185). Alongside this is the potentially gendered nature of the knowledge presented in examinable PE, especially in the form of the physical activities selected or, at least, made available and the tendency to marginalise or reject aesthetic activities on the basis that 'boys in particular would reject the subject if an aesthetic activity were to be included' (MacDonald and Brooker, 1999: 186). Despite such issues, and the fact that approximately twice as many boys as girls enrol for GCSE PE, it is worthy of note that girls continue to out-perform boys in terms of attainment (OFSTED, 2002).

Standards of attainment

Perhaps unsurprisingly, standards of attainment in examinable PE, especially at GCSE level, are a particularly acute concern for the government's inspection and advisory service: OFSTED. This is reflected in OFSTED's subject reports for PE. While more and more pupils are gaining a GCSE PE qualification, standards of attainment (especially in the theoretical aspects of the programmes) continue to be a 'cause for concern' for OFSTED. This has been a persistent theme in the relatively brief history of examinable PE. In 1991, Carroll (1991: 144) commented upon the need for PE teachers 'to become more familiar with the theoretical content [and] depth required' in examinable PE. Despite subsequent claims of 'a much closer relationship of theory to practical participation' (McConachie-Smith, 1996) the reality, according to OFSTED, is quite different. The continuing 'gap between achievement in the theoretical and practical aspects of the course' (OFSTED, 2002: 2) – as well as the perceived need to raise achievement in GCSE theory – highlighted in OFSTED's *Subject Report for Physical Education 1999/2000* (OFSTED, 2001), remains a very live issue with OFSTED in its 2002 report. In this regard, it is interesting to note that, despite its claims that 'the good standards of attainment in GCSE (PE) highlight the improvements made in recent years', OFSTED also observe that 'there has been no increase in the proportion of candidates gaining higher grades' (OFSTED, 2002: 1). OFSTED's enduring concern with the standards of achievement in the theoretical elements of GCSE PE is particularly noteworthy in relation to a move among the PE profession to 'redress the balance of theory and practical' within A level PE: 'which is now effectively 80 per cent theory and 20 per cent practical' (Green, 2002: 34). This, Green (2002: 34) comments, makes A level PE 'somewhat off-putting to our practically oriented students'.

The impact of examinations on curricular PE

An additional issue is the marked trend towards GCSE PE becoming separated from, rather than integral to, curricular PE. Stidder and Wallis (2003: 43) note the Qualification and Curriculum Authority's (QCA) observation that although 'the average time allocation for "core" PE in key stage four varies between one and two hours a week', pupils who take GCSE PE 'receive an additional two hours'. While, on the face of it, GCSE PE in England serves a similar role to that in Wales – insofar as it goes 'some way towards protecting PE time for Years 10 and 11' – a good deal of this time is not spent 'in actual sports participation' (Sports Council for Wales (SCW), 2002: 16). In effect, the growth of examinations in PE has meant that 'non-examination or "core" programmes of physical activity are competing for timetable space with other forms of PE' (Stidder and Wallis, 2003: 41). In addition, and as PE teachers in England (Green, 2001) have reported, the bureaucracy associated with providing examinable PE 'places additional burdens on PE departments' in a variety of ways ranging from detracting from extra-curricular provision to placing additional pressure on PE department budgets by using up resources that might otherwise have been spent on sporting equipment and resources.

Having alluded to some of the more salient contemporary issues surrounding examinable PE, I now want to explore what might be seen as an over-arching or enduring issue, namely, the purported academicisation of PE (Green, 2001; Reid, 1996a, 1996b) and its ramifications for the nature and purposes of the subject.

EXAMINATIONS, THE ACADEMICISATION PROCESS AND THE 'NEW ORTHODOXY' IN PE

Alongside the significant growth of examinable PE (relatively as well as absolutely) several developments – in particular the proliferation of PE/Sports Science programmes at degree level (Carroll, 1998) – and the widespread acceptance and adoption of 'academic' justifications for PE in curriculum and assessment documentation and policy (see, for example, OFSTED, 1998; Qualifications and Curriculum Authority and Department for Education and Employment (QCA and DfES), 1999a, 1999b, 1999c) suggest that a process of academicisation has gathered pace within school PE programmes over the past two decades (Reid, 1996a, 1996b). This process is said to be reflected in the steadily increasing concern on the part of PE teachers with examinable PE (Carroll, 1998; Green, 2001).

Academicisation is probably best defined in terms of an increasing emphasis upon the theoretical study of physical activity and sport, in both absolute and relative (that is to say, at the expense of practical activities) terms. For some commentators (see, for example, Carroll, 1994, 1998; Reid, 1996a), this process is viewed as indicative of – almost tantamount to – the emergence and consolidation of what has been referred to as a 'new orthodoxy' (Reid, 1996a) in PE; a sea-change in teachers' 'philosophies'[3] (Green, 2000) towards an acceptance (at a conceptual as well as a practical level) of a theoretical or intellectual core at the heart of PE.

From the 1960s onwards, the pre-eminent form of theorising about the nature and purposes of education came to be that of liberal educational philosophy. This postwar philosophical tradition in Britain – associated, particularly, with the work of Richard Peters and Paul Hirst in the 1960s and 1970s – provided the template for much subsequent academic reflection upon, analysis of, and justification for, PE *vis-à-vis* the rest of the formal school curriculum (Arnold, 1997; Carr, 1997; McNamee, 1998, this volume; O'Hear, 1981; Reid 1996a, 1996b, 1997). The so-called 'Peters-Hirst' approach (Carr, 1997) to philosophising about education is based upon the premise that education is fundamentally concerned with knowledge of a valuable kind and that such knowledge is, in turn, necessarily theoretical or intellectual. On this view, what distinguishes education from other forms of socialisation or even mere training is its concern with the 'initiation of pupils into a broad range . . . of forms of rational knowledge and enquiry' (Carr, 1997: 196), which are inevitably intellectual. A corollary of this perspective is that the acquisition of (theoretical) knowledge can only be manifested, and its acquisition assessed, in written or spoken form (Reid, 1996a, 1996b). On this conceptualisation, education is interpreted as being essentially *academic* (Reid, 1996b).

The dominance from the 1960s (Reid, 1996b, 1997; Carr, 1997; McNamee, 1998, this volume; Parry, 1998) of the analytical (Peters-Hirst) conception of education in theory and practice presented those teachers and academics who favoured the 'traditional' *de facto* PE curriculum – in the practical, games-oriented form it had developed – with a profound dilemma. PE had either to 'undergo a radical change of identity and redefine itself as an academic subject in the school curriculum, or else acknowledge its incorrigibly marginal status' (Reid, 1997: 6). Consequently, to many physical educationalists at all levels, from teaching through to academia, it has become increasingly evident since the early 1970s[4] that, 'if the possession of academic credentials is a condition of entry to the mainstream (curriculum)', then physical educationalists were (and, for that matter, remain) obliged to direct their subject away from 'the familiar idea of the teaching and learning of practical physical activities' (Reid, 1996b: 95) – which are necessarily made problematic by the aforementioned conceptions of knowledge and education – and towards 'academic' aspects of PE. That is to say, towards intellectual development of one sort or another 'through' sport (especially the allegedly scientific dimensions of the study of sport) rather than the 'practice' of sport. If PE is not concerned with the acquisition and mastery of theoretical knowledge, the argument goes, it is by the very nature of education non-academic and thus non-educational.

According to Reid (1996a), a consequence of the broad acceptance of the 'standard' liberal educational view of PE has been repeated calls for a greater emphasis upon 'theory' within the subject (see, for example, OFSTED, 1998), which is likely to occur at the expense of unreflective practice or 'playing'. What he describes as an emergent 'new orthodoxy' has, according to Reid (1996b: 102), sought to 'redefine physical education in terms of the opportunities which it provides for theoretical study'. In so doing, he argues, it has implicitly accepted the superiority of the kinds of knowledge that are expressed predominantly in written or verbal forms rather than by practical demonstration (Reid, 1996a, 1996b). Thus, the rapid growth of examinations coupled with their continued expansion (Carroll, 1998; MacKreth, 1998) appears to lend weight to the claim that the academic (or 'standard') view of education, which has flourished in education at all levels since the 1960s, is in the ascendancy within PE and is, indeed, tantamount to a 'new orthodoxy' at the level of PE teaching.

In this manner, PE might be said to have joined other school subjects on the academic 'treadmill' identified in Dore's (1976, 1997) work on the alleged *Diploma Disease* and, in the process, is becoming more, rather than less, like other (academic) subjects. In one sense, the development of the physical 'education' curriculum to incorporate the *sine qua non* of academic education – the examination – should not be viewed as surprising. After all, many teachers are broadly familiar with the argument that PE is fundamentally about education 'through' as well as 'in' the physical. In this vein, Mason (1995: 3) pointed to 'broad agreement' among the secondary school heads of PE in her national study that ' "PE" is a wider concept than "sport" ' because it 'is part of the education of the whole child whereas "sport" is an activity undertaken to provide that education'.

In expressing such views (Green, 2001; Mason, 1995), teachers have done no more than take their lead from the various academic conceptualisations of PE to be found in a range of official and semi-official documentation (Department of Education and Science/Welsh

Office (DES/ WO), 1991) and academic sources (Carr, 1979; Laker, 1996; Munrow, 1972; Stidder and Wallis, 2003) over the past quarter of a century or so, as well as in debates within various groups among the subject-community. Indeed, already well-developed attempts to establish the academic credibility of the subject were epitomised by the conceptualisation of PE – as the education of young people 'in and *through* the use and knowledge of the body and its movement' [emphasis added] – built into the template for National Curriculum Physical Education (NCPE), *Physical Education for Ages 5 to 16* (Department for Education and Science (DES)/Welsh Office (WO), 1991: 5). In this definition, the requisite theoretical or intellectual component has two discernible dimensions: first, knowledge, in the form of underlying principles, 'about' the performance of physical activities ('*in* the use and knowledge of the body'); and, second, knowledge about other areas of allegedly valuable knowledge, such as health-related exercise (HRE) or ethical behaviour ('*through* the use and knowledge of the body') that PE is held to be well (according to some, uniquely) placed to deliver. In this regard, it is worthy of note that in seeking, among other things, 'to clarify the learning associated with the subject' (Penney, 2000: 137), the 1999 review and revision of NCPE (QCA and DfEE, 1999a) described the 'distinctive contribution' of PE as involving 'learning about and *through* physical activity areas which require different ways of *thinking*, selecting and applying skills' (QCA and DfEE, 1999b; emphasis added).

Having traced the rapid growth of examinable PE and explored some of the more salient issues surrounding the topic, I now want to focus upon how this significant development might best be explained as well as what it tells us, if anything, about possible shifts in physical educationalists' views of their subject; that is to say, in the form of a 'new orthodoxy'.

EXPLAINING THE GROWTH AND DEVELOPMENT OF EXAMINABLE PE

The case for examinable PE

The case for examinable PE (see, for example, Carroll, 1994; Fisher, 1991; Green, 2001; Stidder and Wallis, 2003), as presented by physical educationalists (as either academics or teachers) over the years, can be broadly divided into two parts: the surface-level or rhetorical justifications and the deeper-lying motivations or reasons. On the surface, that is to say, at the level of rhetoric at least, the case for examinable PE (as presented by teachers and academics) seems to revolve around three different types of justification:

1. Opportunities for those 'practically-minded' pupils with ability in and/or keeness for PE and sport (who may also be less 'academically able'), to study an area to their liking and one that enables them to obtain a qualification that may, in turn, have vocational 'spin-offs' – a justification often presented in terms of the promotion of equal opportunities.

2. Opportunities for schools to (a) attract students keen to pursue an increasingly popular examination subject, while (b) motivating and, thus, it is claimed, endearing less-able pupils to the school.

3. Opportunities for PE teachers and departments to improve the academic and professional standing or status while, at the same time, establishing the alleged centrality of the physical as well as the intellectual to the process of education.

The more prosaic reasons offered by PE teachers as justifications for their own support for the development of examinable PE include 'a break from the teaching in the gym' and on the playing fields, 'a chance to teach something more intellectually demanding and interesting', 'an alternative source of income' (from examining) and, most pertinently, a necessary step towards career enhancement (Green, 2001). In the case of the latter justification, one of the less obvious but more compelling constraints on PE teachers – towards embracing examinable PE – has, indeed, to do with the career benefits they, and particularly those relatively new to the profession, perceive as accruing from being involved with examinable PE. Teachers in Green's (2001) study, for example, perceived an increasingly direct association between teaching examinable PE and job prospects – to the extent that they perceived their career prospects would be hampered significantly by not being involved in teaching examinable PE.

In this vein, rhetorical explanations for the rapid growth of examinable PE (see, for example, Carroll, 1991, 1994, 1998) have tended to be couched in what might best be described as the purposive, not to say functionalist, terms occasionally associated with educational perspectives on assessment (Yates et al., 1997). When viewed from a more detached perspective, however, reasons for the significant increase of academic examinations in PE may be somewhat more complex than the surface level justifications provided by teachers and PE academics suggest. Rather than representing 'a growing acceptance of the value of examinations in physical education' (Carroll, 1991: 141), or even, for that matter, a widespread acceptance of a 'new orthodoxy' at a philosophical level (Reid, 1996a, 1996b), it may be more accurate to describe developments in examinable PE as the outcome of conjuncture of several interrelated processes; in effect, a coming together of the wider academicisation process with practical responses by PE teachers and academics to a number of practical concerns notable among which was the threat of marginalisation in relation to teachers' concerns for professional status. I want now, then, to say a little more about the circumstances and process that together, it is argued, have created a context which has constrained PE teachers towards examinable PE.

The academicisation of PE

As indicated earlier in this chapter, a process of academicisation has been apparent in PE for a quarter of a century or more. In this respect, developments in examinable PE in secondary schools can be seen to reflect developments in tertiary institutions (MacDonald et al., 1999), one noteworthy dimension of which has been the emergence of undergraduate PE and Sports Science degrees, that have come to form the main career route (when supplemented with a postgraduate teaching qualification) into PE for would-be teachers of the subject (MacDonald et al., 1999). A consequence of this development has been an increase in the proportion of secondary PE teachers whose predispositions or habituses (Nash, 1999; van Krieken, 1998) are suffused with strong attachments to an academic ideology (Green, 2000) and an attendant commitment to the supposed value of theoretical knowledge and examinations in PE.

The professionalisation of PE

A further process, that of professionalisation, is intimately related to the academicisation process and has manifested itself within PE in relation to the perceived threat of 'marginalisation' of the subject and the 'broad problems of legitimation' (Yates et al., 1997: 436) faced by physical educationalists at all levels, but particularly in schools. In this regard, Houlihan and White (2002: 15) observe that 'the position of sport, games and PE in the curriculum has always been contested and the status of PE teachers insecure'. For numerous commentators since the 1970s, PE teachers and academics have become increasingly concerned with the academic credentials of PE in direct proportion to their growing concern with the marginal professional status of PE (see, for example, Hendry, 1976; Evans and Williams, 1989; Kirk, 1992; Baker et al., 1996; Green, 2000); a trend they perceive as having been exacerbated by the arrival of a national curriculum and the identificafion of core and foundational subjects therein (Kirk, 1992; Green 2000).

Against a backdrop of low status for PE and its practitioners within the world of education (Houlihan, 1991), it is somewhat unsurprising to find PE teachers enthusiastically embracing examinations in an attempt 'to bring about the redefinition and re-evaluation' (Eggleston, 1990: 63) of their marginalised, poorly-esteemed subject. As Eggleston (1990: 62) says of professional subject associations in general, the history of physical education associations in the UK appears predominantly to be a history of 'struggle to redefine the subject in question as one that is examinable at school, college or university'. For a number of academic commentators (see, for example, Alexander et al., 1996; Green, 2001; Houlihan, 1991; Reid, 1996a, 1996b), the dramatic growth of examinable PE is best viewed against the 'backdrop of subject marginality' (Alexander et al., 1996: 23) not only in the UK but also worldwide (Hardman, 1998; Hardman and Marshall, 2000): 'PE on most continents is viewed as marginal to the central purposes of schooling and to sport in the culture generally' (Alexander et al., 1996: 26).[5] Thus, according to Houlihan (1991) and Reid (1996a, 1996b, 1997), among others, the quest for educational status is deeply implicated in the rise to prominence of examinable PE.

The educational status of PE as a secondary school subject has, then, been a long-standing issue for physical educationalists at all levels (Fitzclarence and Tinning, 1990). Concern –

one might even describe it as a preoccupation to the point of distraction – with achieving academic respectability, in terms implicit in academic subjects, became a steadily growing issue in the PE subject-community from the 1960s onwards. Hendry (1976), Evans and Williams (1989) and Kirk (1992) have all highlighted physical educationalists' deeply-felt concern with professional status. It was apparent from the comments of teachers in Green's (2001) study that many of them saw their professional status – as well as the degrees of autonomy associated with that status – as central to their perceptions of themselves and the subject they taught. Examinable PE has been, and continues to be, perceived by teachers as having the potential to raise the status of PE teachers and their departments, especially where they are involved with A level PE (Green, 2001). It is, perhaps, significant that there is a very real sense among teachers that the more demanding the theoretical aspect of the work the greater the status attached to the subject, both in the eyes of colleagues and pupils (Green, 2001).

An additional aspect of the process of professionalisation within PE, that serves to encourage or constrain PE teachers towards examinable PE, is what might be referred to as workplace socialisation; that is to say, the manner in which the culture of the (secondary school PE) workplace – and especially their perceptions of necessary pragmatic responses to the constraints of their everyday work situations – have become internalised by teachers. Notable among these constraints are the expectations of significant others within and without the school setting (such as headteachers, heads of department, parents and the inspection and advisory service OFSTED) as well as the structurally generated pressures on teachers to academicise PE in order to demonstrate their educational worth and professional status, alluded to earlier.

The educational market place

Developments in education generally, in the late 1980s, can be seen to have reinforced the academicisation of PE. The internal market created by the Education Reform Act of 1988 (Gorard et al., 2003) heightened pressures towards competition between schools which were increasingly able to control their own income and expenditure, not least by competing for potential pupils as if vying for a market share. Headteachers, school governors and physical educationalists themselves have become acutely aware of the financial implications of examinable PE, especially in terms of pupil recruitment. Headteachers are particularly appreciative of the recruitment potential of examinable PE – especially with youngsters beyond the age of compulsory schooling; for example, at A level (Green, 2001). The development of GCSE and then A level examinations in PE have enabled schools to keep and recruit more pupils and, in particular, financially lucrative sixth-formers (Green, 2001). Headteachers and PE teachers have also identified the scope for practically-oriented pupils to achieve hitherto unexpected examination success in PE, with the concomitant benefits for school status and profile that may result (Green, 2001).

An additional constraint towards the academicisation of PE has been the explicit support for examinable PE in national and school OFSTED reports. Shaw et al. (2003: 70) observe that 'students' examination performance is commonly taken to be an important measure of a school, not least by governments and OFSTED'. Comments from teachers in Green's (2001) study suggested that OFSTED inspectors were keen to encourage teachers to maintain and extend examinable PE. When placed alongside OFSTED inspectors' informal comments to teachers themselves, the formal observations to be found in OFSTED school reports – to the effect, for example, that results in A level PE were 'very encouraging' – could be seen as tangible evidence of OFSTED's keenness to support the academicisation process in PE (see, for example, OFSTED, 1998) and inclination to encourage such a development where it was lacking.

CONCLUSION

The growth of examinations in PE – in the form of GCSE and A level – has, it is argued here, resulted from a combination (or configuration) of circumstances: prominent among which are PE teachers' desire for increased professional status alongside the marketisation of education generally, as well as the practical day-to-day benefits examinable PE is perceived as having. Rather than simply representing a shift in teachers' views of their subject towards a more academic conception of PE, the rapid growth of examinations in PE is more adequately understood as representing teachers' response to a perceived threat and a clear opportunity. The threat came in the form of the 'cinderella status' (McNamee, this volume) and clear implications for the esteem of PE, and, therefore, PE teachers, of the increasingly hegemonic 'cognitive imperialism' (McNamee, 1998) of the intellectual and, thus, academic conception of education associated with educational theorising from the 1960s onwards. At the same time, examinable PE can be seen, at least in part, as a response by teachers to the informal sanctions associated with OFSTED's (1998) perceptions of 'good practice' in PE; namely, the development of an academic strand to the subject at secondary school level. Opportunity came with the advent of the educational market after the Education Reform Act of 1988. In this respect, examinable PE has undeniably become a 'power resource' (Mennell, 1998: 70) for those in the PE subject-community – a power resource that many PE teachers and academics have been quick to appreciate and exploit.

Thus, far from indicating a substantial and straightforward shift in PE teachers' 'philosophies' – towards the theory and, concomitantly, away from the practice of PE – the growth in examinations is more adequately explained in terms of a particular conjuncture of several interrelated processes; notably the academicisation and professionalisation of PE. While theoretical justifications are frequently utilised and, indeed, hotly debated (e.g. Reid, 1996a, 1996b, 1997; Carr, 1997; McNamee, 1998; Parry, 1998) by those – especially at the academic level – keen to bolster the place of PE in the curriculum, those at the grass roots level (PE teachers) tend to have more prosaic, more pragmatic, reasons for favouring examinable PE which reflect their perceptions of contextual pressures of a practical kind (Green, 2001). A neat summary of some of these dimensions of what they and many other physical educationalists take to be the potential benefits of the development of examinations in PE, was provided by Stidder and Wallis (2003: 43) recently while outlining what they took to be the 'case for' such a development:

> the potential elevation of the status and kudos of the subject in the eyes of significant others, in particular peers in the teaching profession, the likelihood of increasing pupil numbers . . . in terms of finance, staffing and time allocation . . . as a marketing tool for influencing the size and nature of intake to a school . . . possible enhancement of application for Sportsmark, Sportsmark Gold or Sports College status . . . a significant contribution to a school's overall examination percentages.

All in all, PE teachers have, over recent decades, become increasingly inclined – at a philosophical or, rather, ideological (Green, 2003) – level to make claims for an academic, intellectual dimension to physical *education*. However, it is noteworthy that this ideological transformation does not signal a decisive shift in their perceptions of an appropriate balance between the supposed physical and intellectual dimensions of the subject in favour of the latter, such that we can justifiably talk of a consensus in 'philosophy' and practice; it does not, in effect, justify the claim that the rapid rise in the popularity of examinable PE is part of a process that threatens to bring with it a 'redefinition of sport away from "sport as skill" and towards "sport as knowledge"' (Houlihan, 1991: 240). Examinable PE, it seems, has not quite yet become 'the opiate of PE teachers', to paraphrase Broadfoot (1979) (cited in Green, 2001). Nor, for that matter, does a broad consensus around the benefits of examinable PE explain, in a causal manner, its rapid expansion. Quite the reverse: the growth is better explained, it is argued, in terms of practical constraints leading to philosophical changes in the sense that PE teachers have been quick to recognise the more obvious status-related personal and professional benefits of examinable PE and have been supported, for the most part, by headteachers who have also stood to gain from the development. In this regard, constraints towards the academicisation of PE over the last decade or so have, in many respects, reflected the increasing pressures on schools, their governing bodies and headteachers – evident since the introduction of market principles to the education system (Gorard et al., 2003) – to seek any available market advantage in order to survive, let alone flourish. It is also worth remembering that the academicisation of PE has been occurring since the mid-1960s; driven in no small measure by PE teachers' desires to demonstrate their academic credentials and professional status.

Nevertheless, whereas the 'old' orthodoxy of 'traditional PE' – with its emphasis upon team games – can be said to represent mere agreement or consensus at an ideological level among PE teachers, the academicisation of PE may well be described as an *emerging* orthodoxy inasmuch as PE teachers feel increasingly constrained to 'go along' with the development regardless of any reservations they may have concerning the nature and purposes of PE.

It is worth noting that examinable PE has by no means been an unmitigated success in terms of status and credibility. There have been unintended and seemingly unforeseen consequences. The struggle for professional status and security has shaped, and continues to shape, the 'Catch-22' situation PE teachers find themselves in – damned if they do examinable PE, damned if they do not. It is also noteworthy that the seemingly inexorable growth of examinable PE camouflages a strong element of resistance: the dominance of examinable PE is by no means complete. There are evidently some PE teachers who feel themselves 'demeaned' by 'the hierarchical dominance, or positioning, of propositional over performative knowledge' (McNamee, this volume).

Some teachers in Green's (2001) study reported that not only did they not welcome examinable PE but that there was no internal pressure in their schools nor, for that matter, in their departments for such a development. In this regard, it was interesting to observe teachers at several schools in the study identifying themselves and their departments (and, usually, their schools) as possessing more 'traditional' views on the virtues of PE in terms of an emphasis on competitive sport – and particularly team games – of the kind well documented elsewhere (see, for example, Penney and Harris, 1997). In effect, headteachers in academically successful schools appear less likely to encourage – or even, at times, allow – the development of examinable PE (Green, 2001). Headteachers in such schools can clearly afford to concentrate on 'proper' academic subjects without risking penalising themselves in terms of recruitment or academic results. Perhaps unsurprisingly, it was the case that most of the schools resisting the development of examinations in PE in Green's (2001) study were relatively advantaged and successful schools.

In the early 1990s, Fitzclarence and Tinning (1990) suggested that three themes remained unresolved and problematic despite the apparent popularity of examinable PE among pupils and teachers alike; they were: the nature of essential or worthwhile knowledge in PE, the educational status of PE as a school subject, and the place of physical activity within an examinable 'academic' subject. In 2004, while the juggernaut that is examinable PE rolls on, such issues endure.

NOTES

1 The term 'examination' is more conventionally used to refer to physically and temporally segregated assessment activities. Nevertheless, it is being used here in a more generic sense to refer to formal, nationally recognised assessments in PE – specifically, the more academic forms of assessment (such as GCSE and A level) rather than other forms of externally accredited courses such as the vocational forms (such as City and Guilds, BTEC and GNVQ) and national governing body and sports leader awards that have begun to develop since the Dearing review of assessment in the National Curriculum (Carroll, 1998). At the same time, references to examinable PE will also be taken to include A level Sports Studies. Examination is being used instead of the more conventional term 'assessment' because of its more common currency among teachers in the study referred to, as well as within academic and professional literature in the PE subject-community.

2   At the time of writing, the UK government had established a Working Group for 14–19 Reform, to consider, among other things, the development of an English baccalaureate-style qualification – the equivalent of the continental baccalaureate designed to suit English circumstances – to be available at several levels, recognise a wide range or portfolio of activities and achievements and facilitate simpler and more transparent progression thorugh different 14–19 programmes (DfES, 2003c).

3   The term 'philosophy' indicates the aphoristic or everyday views of PE teachers upon the nature and purposes of their subject (Green, 2003).

4   A trend that corresponded with the emergence of a graduate teaching profession (Kirk, 1992) alongside what Dore (1997: 15) refers to as the changing 'social definition of the purpose of schooling' and the attendant qualification spiral.

5   The trend towards the academicisation of PE in the UK is a trend also evident in other countries. With regard to Australia, MacDonald et al. (1999: 38) observe: 'In the school sector, perhaps the most significant development in recent years has been the emergence and consolidation of examinable . . . physical education.'

REFERENCES

Alexander, K., Taggart, A. and Thorpe, S. (1996) 'A spring in their steps? Possibilities for professional renewal through sports education in Australian schools', *Sport, Education and Society*, 1 (1): 23–46.

Arnold, P.J. (1997) *Sport, Ethics and Education*. London: Cassell.

Baker, J.A.W., Hardman, K. and Pan, D.W. (1996) 'A perceptual mapping approach to determine an appropriate descriptor for our field', *European Physical Education Review*, 2 (2): 75–81.

Banks, O. (1971) *The Sociology of Education*. London, Batsford.

Black, P.J. (1998) *Testing: Friend or Foe? The Theory and Practice of Assessment and Testing*. London: Routledge.

Broadfoot, P. (1979) *Assessment, Schools and Society*. London: Methuen.

Brook, V. (1993) 'The resurgence of external examining in Britain', *British Journal of Educational Studies*, 21 (1).

Carr, D. (1979) 'Aims of physical education', *Physical Education Review*, 2 (2): 91–100.

Carr, D. (1997) 'Physical education and value diversity: a response to Andrew Reid', *European Physical Education Review*, 3 (2): 95–105.

Carroll, B. (1991) 'Examinations and assessment in physical education', in N. Armstrong (ed.) *New Directions in Physical Education 1*. Champaign, IL: Human Kinetics. pp. 137–60.

Carroll, B. (1994) *Assessment in Physical Education: A Teacher's Guide to the Issues*. London: Falmer Press.

Carroll, B. (1998) 'The emergence and growth of examinations in physical education', in K. Green and K. Hardman (eds.), *Physical Education: A Reader*. Aachen: Meyer & Meyer Verlag. pp. 314–32.

Department for Education and Employment (DfEE) (2000a) *Statistical Bulletin Number 0412000*. http//:www.dfee.gov.uk/statistics.

Department for Education and Employment (DfEE) (2000b) (personal communication).

Department of Education and Sciences/Welsh Office (DES/WO) (1991) *Physical Education for Ages 5–16. Proposals of the Secretary of State for Education and the Secretary of State for Wales*. London, DES/WO.

Department for Education and Skills (DfES) (2003a) *GCE/VCE, A/AS Examination Results for Young People in England, 2001/02 (Provisional)*. http//:www.dfee.gov.uk/statistics.

Department for Education and Skills (DfES) (2003b) *National Curriculum Assessments for Key Stage 3 (Revised), GCSE/GNCQ Examination Results (Provisional) and Associated Value Added Measures for Young People in 2001/02*. http//:www.dfee.gov.uk/statistics.

Department for Education and Skills (DfES) (2003c) *Extending Opportunities, Raising Standards*. London: DfES.

Department for Education and Skills (DfES) (2004a) *GCSE Results of 15-year-olds in All Educational Establishments, by the end of 2002/2003, Subject and Grade*. www.dfes.gov.uk/rsgateway/DB/SFR/s000442/tab009.shtml.

Department for Education and Skills (DfES) (2004b) *GCE A level Examination Results of all Students in all Schools and Colleges by Subject and Grade in 2002/03*. www.dfes.gov.uk/rsgateway/DB/SFR/s000441/tab007a.shtml.

Dore, R.P. (1976) *The Diploma Disease. Education, Qualification and Development* (1st edn). London: Allen & Unwin.

Dore, R.P. (1997) The *Diploma Disease. Education, Qualification and Development* (2nd edn). London: Allen & Unwin.

Eggleston, J. (1990) 'School examinations – some sociological issues', in T. Horton (ed.), *Assessment Debates*. Buckingham: Open University Press. pp. 57–67.

Evans, J. and Williams, T. (1989) 'Moving up and getting out: the classed and gendered opportunities of physical education teachers', in T. Templin and P. Schempp (eds.), *Socialization into Physical Education: Learning to Teach*. Indianapolis, IN: Benchmark Press.

Fisher, S. (1991) 'Justifying, promoting and establishing qualifications in PE', *Bulletin of Physical Education*, 27 (2): 25–6.

Fitzclarence, L. and Tinning, R. (1990) 'Challenging hegemonic physical education: contextualizing physical education as an examinable subject', in D. Kirk and R. Tinning (eds.), *Physical Education, Curriculum and Culture. Critical Issues in the Contemporary Crisis*. London, Falmer Press. pp. 169–92.

Flintoff, A. and Scraton, S. (this volume) 'Gender and Physical Education', in K. Green and K. Hardman (eds), *Physical Education: Essential Issues*. London: Sage Publications. pp. 161–79.

Gorard, S., Taylor, C. and Fitz, J. (2003) *Schools, Markets and Choice Policies*. London, RoutledgeFalmer.

Green, K. (2000) 'Exploring the everyday "philosophies" of physical education teachers from a sociological perspective', *Sport, Education & Society*, 5 (2): 109–29.

Green, K. (2001) 'Examinations in physical education: a sociological perspective on a "new orthodoxy" ', *British Journal of Sociology of Education*, 22 (1): 51–73.

Green, K. (2003) *Physical Education Teachers on Physical Education. A Sociological Study of Philosophies and Ideologies*. Chester: Chester Academic Press.

Green, N. (2002) 'A level physical education', *British Journal of Teaching Physical Education*, 33 (3): 34.

Hardman, K. (1998) 'To be or not to be? The present and future of school physical education in international context', in K. Green and K. Hardman (eds.), *Physical Education. A Reader*. Aachen, Meyer and Meyer Verlag. pp. 353–82.

Hardman, K. and Marshall, J.J. (2000) 'The state and status of physical education in schools in international context', *European Physical Education Review*, 6 (3): 203–229.

Harris, J. (this volume) 'Health-related exercise and physical education', in K. Green and K. Hardman (eds), *Physical Education: Essential Issues*. London: Sage Publications. pp. 78–97.

Hendry, L.B. (1976) 'Survival in a marginal role: the professional identity of the physical education teacher', in N. J. Whitehead and L.B. Hendry (eds), *Teaching Physical Education in England – Description and Analysis*. London: Lepus. pp. 89–102.

Houlihan, B. (1991) *The Government and Politics of Sport*. London: Routledge.

Houlihan, B. and White, A. (2002) *The Politics of Sports Development. Development of Sport or Development Through Sport?* London: Routledge.

Kirk, D. (1992) *Defining Physical Education. The Social Construction of a School Subject in Postwar Britain*. London: Falmer Press.

Laker, A. (1996) 'Learning to teach *through* the physical . . .', *British Journal of Physical Education*, 27 (3): 18–22.

MacDonald, D. and Brooker, R. (1999) Assessment issues in a performance-based subject: a case study of physical education, in P. Murphy (ed.), *Learners, Learning and Assessment*. London: Paul Chapman Publishing. pp. 171–90.

MacDonald, D., Kirk, D. and Braiuka, S. (1999) The social construction of the physical activity field at the school/university interface, *European Physical Education Review*, 5: 31–51.

McConachie-Smith, J. (1996) 'Physical education at Key Stage 4', in N. Armstrong (ed.), *New Directions in Physical Education: Change and Innovation*. London: Cassell. pp. 82–93.

McNamee, M. (1998) 'Philosophy and physical education: analysis, epistemology and axiology', *European Physical Education Review*, 4 (2): 75–91.

McNamee, M. (this volume) 'The nature and values of physical education', in K. Green and K. Hardman (eds.) *Physical Education: Essential Issues*. London: Sage Publications. pp. 1–20.

MacKreth, K. (1998) 'Developments in A level physical education', *The British Journal of Physical Education*, 29: 16–17.

Mason, V. (1995) *Young People and Sport*. London: The Sports Council.

Mennell, S. (1998) *Norbert Elias: An Introduction*. Dublin: University College Press.

Munrow, A.D. (1972) *Physical Education. A Discussion of Principles*. London: Bell & Hyman Limited.

Nash, R. (1999) 'Bourdieu, habitus, and educational research: is it all worth the candle?', *The British Journal of Sociology of Education*, 20: 175–87.

Office for Standards in Education (OFSTED) (1998) *Secondary Education 1993–97. The Curriculum*, < http:// www.opengov.gov.uk >.

Office for Standards in Education (OFSTED) (2001) *Secondary Subject Reports 1999/2000: Physical Education*. London: OFSTED.

Office for Standards in Education (OFSTED) (2002) *Secondary Subject Reports 2000/01: Physical Education*. London: OFSTED.

O'Hear, A. (1981) *Education, Sociey and Human Nature. An Introduction to the Philosophy of Education*. London: Routledge & Kegan Paul.

Parry, J. (1998) 'Reid on knowledge and justification in physical education', *European Physical Education Review*, 4 (2): 70–4.

Penney, D. (2000) 'Physical education, sporting excellence and educational excellence', *European Physical Education Review*, 6 (3): 135–50.

Penney, D. and Harris, J. (1997) 'Extra-curricular physical education: more of the same for the more able?', *Sport, Education and Society*, 2 (1): 41–51.

Penney, D., Houlihan, B. and Eley, D. (2002) *Specialist Sports Colleges National Monitoring and Evaluation Research Project: First National Survey Report*. Institute of Youth Sport: Loughborough University.

Qualifications and Curriculum Authority and the Department for Education and Employment (QCA and DfES) (1999a) *The Review of the National Curriculum in England. The Secretary of State's Proposals*. London: QCA.

Qualifications and Curriculum Authority and the Department for Education and Employment (QCA and DfES) (1999b) *The Review of the National Curriculum in England. The Consultation Materials*. London: QCA.

Qualifications and Curriculum Authority and the Department for Education and Employment (QCA and DfES) (1999c) *Physical Education: The National Curriculum for England and Wales*. London: QCA.

Reid, A. (1996a) 'The concept of physical education in current curriculum and assessment policy in Scotland', *European Physical Education Review*, 2 (1): 7–18.

Reid, A. (1996b) 'Knowledge, practice and theory in physical education', *European Physical Education Review*, 2 (2): 94–104.

Reid, A. (1997) 'Value pluralism and physical education', *European Physical Education Review*, 3 (1): 6–20.

Shaw, I., Newton, D.P., Aitkin, M. and Darnell, R. (2003) 'Do OFSTED inspections of secondary school make a difference to GCSE results?', *British Educational Research Journal*, 29 (1): 63–75.

Sports Council for Wales (SCW) (2002) *Swimming Against the Tide? Physical Education and Sports Provision in Secondary Schools in Wales*. Cardiff: SCW.

Stidder, G. (2001a) 'Curriculum innovation in physical education at Key Stage 4: a review of GCSE results in one English secondary school', *Bulletin of Physical Education*, 37 (1): 25–46.

Stidder, G. (2001b) 'Who's for exams? A review of GCSE PE results in one English secondary school 1997–2000', *British Journal of Teaching Physical Education*, 32 (3): 46–48.

Stidder, G. and Wallis, J. (2003) 'Future directions for phsyical education at Key Stage 4 and post-16: some critical questions', *British Journal of Teaching Physical Education*, 34 (4): 41–7.

Van Krieken, R. (1998) *Norbert Elias*. London: Routledge.

Yates, L., Butterfield, S., Brown, S. and Baudelot, C. (1997) 'Review symposium: education, assessment and society: a sociological analysis', *British Journal of Sociology of Education*, 18: 435–9.

10 | Gender and Physical Education

Anne Flintoff and Sheila Scraton

This chapter identifies key issues and debates in gender and physical education (PE), and how these have influenced policy and practice over the past three decades. We have structured the chapter into three key sections: equal opportunities and access; femininities, masculinities and sexualities; and bodies, identities and difference. Although these sections are not contained within specific time frames, they do reflect shifts in emphasis and understanding about gender relations over this period of time.

Before introducing the three key areas, we briefly introduce the different theoretical strands of feminist thought that have sought to understand and explain gender inequality in PE. It is important to recognise that these theories underpin the particular issues that have emerged, but also that theory moves on and develops as a result of empirical research and professional practice. Feminism has always recognised that theory can inform practice, just as practice must be the cornerstone of theory.

Feminist discourse has sought to understand and explain gender relations, highlighting inequalities between men and women, girls and boys, and has proposed strategies for change. There has been the development of many different feminisms and strands of feminist thought, each focusing on specific areas and issues (Scraton and Flintoff, 1992; Scraton and Flintoff, 2002). Although we cannot explore feminist theories in detail in this chapter, nevertheless it is important to highlight some of the key concepts and issues that underpin the diverse strands of feminist thought. It is also important to recognise that these strands should not be viewed as having clear boundaries or as totally distinct from each other. Theories are fluid and dynamic, and reflect gender relations themselves that are not static and change over time. However, it is also important to note that at no point is one theory totally replaced by another. We still have liberal feminist thought today as well as feminists who take a radical, socialist or poststructuralist theoretical and political stance.

The main strands of feminist thought that have impacted on PE are liberal, radical, socialist, and poststructuralist. Another important strand of feminism – black feminism – has had very little impact on PE research, policy and practice. We will return to this in more detail later in the chapter when we identify areas for future research. In PE, liberal feminism has focused on the gendered differentiation of activities offered to boys and girls; different socialisation of girls and boys into gender-specific activities; stereotyping and attitudes, and unequal access to facilities and opportunities. Radical feminism is more concerned with underlying structural power relations that are the result of the systematic maintenance of male power through patriarchy, whereby men as a group dominate women as a group. Radical feminists centralise sexuality as the major site of men's domination over women through the social institution of heterosexuality. In PE the focus has been on how girls learn and develop a female physicality that emphasises appearance, presentation and control (desirable 'femininity') whereas boys are encouraged to develop physical strength, aggression and confidence in their physical prowess (desirable 'masculinity') (Cockburn and Clarke, 2002; Scraton, 1992). Radical feminists have also contributed to our understanding of lesbianism and homophobia in PE (Clarke, 1997, 1998, 2002, 2004). Socialist feminist analysis draws on a radical focus on sexuality, and the relations between gender, class and 'race'. Socialist feminism has shifted the emphasis from solely concentrating on girls' and women's experiences to looking more critically at gender relations. In PE this has developed into work on boys and masculinities (Bramham, 2003; Fleming, 1991; Parker, 1996; Skelton, 1993). More recently, the development of poststructural feminism has centred attention on difference and diversity, emphasising the plurality of femininities and girls' experiences, together with masculinities and boys' experiences. As yet, poststructural analysis in PE is under-developed, although there has been some work on language (Wright, 1996, 1997); bodies (Garrett, 2004; Paechter, 2003a, 2003b) and queer theory (Sykes, 1998). Contemporary concerns on health and the body have also begun to be explored within PE and schooling although only a limited amount of the work focuses specifically on gender issues (Clarke, 2004; Garrett, 2004; Oliver and Lalik, 2004; Rich et al., 2004).

EQUAL OPPORTUNITIES AND ACCESS

Early debates in gender and PE during the 1970s and early 1980s focused on equal opportunities and issues of access. A key concern was the differential access to activities on the PE curriculum offered to girls and boys. Leaman's (1984) research and others, such as ILEA (1984), were influential in analysing the curriculum in PE, showing how girls were socialised into 'female' activities, for example, netball and gymnastics, and boys into 'male' activities, for example, football and cricket.

Drawing on the traditions of liberal feminism, there were a number of school-based curriculum projects developed at this time, aimed at challenging the sex differentiated curriculum, sex stereotyping by teachers, and improving girls' access and opportunities. For example, the Schools Council's Sex Discrimination project[1] sought to challenge the sex-differentiated curriculum in schools by showing the impact of this on girls' future career choices and trajectories. A related initiative, the Girls into Science and Technology (GIST) project, aimed to encourage more girls to continue science and technical craft subjects when these became optional at secondary school, and encouraged teachers to adopt 'gender fair' interaction in classrooms (see Kelly, 1985; Weiner, 1994).

In PE, this generated discussion and action around single sex and mixed sex groupings. Mixed sex groupings were perceived to be a key vehicle for enabling girls to have equal access to curriculum activities. PE was one of the few subjects on the curriculum where pupils had been traditionally taught different activities in single sex groupings, building on a long gendered history of curriculum differentiation (see Fletcher, 1984; Kirk, 1992). The training of specialised women PE teachers began in the late nineteenth century, in separate colleges, with a distinctive 'female tradition' and culture (Fletcher, 1984). This emphasised the importance of physical activity for women's health and well-being, and incorporated a child-centred approach, drawing on a broad range of physical activities including dance, gymnastics and games. In contrast, men's specialist teacher training in PE in England began some 30 years later, and grew out of different roots, influenced by militarism and competitive team games (Kirk, 1992). The development of separate training for women PE teachers challenged some gendered expectations of women's physical capabilities and gave them access to sport and physical activities previously denied to them. However, this separate tradition was also underpinned by powerful gendered ideologies of femininity and physicality that continued to influence and shape a separate girls' PE curriculum.

Given the strong tradition of separate and gendered provision, it is not surprising that moves towards mixed sex PE were not straightforward. Research showed that although mixed sex PE provided equal access for boys and girls to *certain* activities, this did not necessarily remove gender inequalities. In practice, the curricular activities offered in mixed PE tended to be traditional 'boys' activities in which girls had less experience and skills (Talbot, 1990). Rarely did mixed PE open up access for boys into traditional 'girls' activities. Consequently, gendered stereotypes were left largely unchallenged, and were often reproduced by the teachers involved (Evans, 1989; Evans et al., 1985; Flintoff, 1995; Scraton, 1992, 1993).

Concerns about the sex differentiated PE curriculum and mixed PE have not necessarily gone away, even with the introduction of a compulsory National Curriculum for Physical Education (NCPE) in 1992 and its subsequent revised versions in 1995 and 1999 (Flintoff, 1990; Green and Scraton, 1998; Penney, 2002a). Although one of the stated principles underpinning the introduction of a national curriculum into all subjects areas, was to ensure that all children 'regardless of their sex, ethnic origin and geographical location, have the same access to broadly the same good and relevant curriculum' (DES, 1987: 4), this has not been the case in practice in the NCPE. As Penney (2002a) highlights, the Interim Report from the NCPE working party (DES, 1991) included a strong section on equal opportunities in PE, which was cut to a minimum in the final Orders that went to schools (DES, 1992). Despite the lack of explicit attention to gender, she argues that the NCPE is nevertheless openly gendered, citing the flexibility inherent within the policy, as well as the privileging of games over other activities, as key dimensions. Not only is there a strong discourse of sport central to the NCPE (whereby games activities, rather than activities such as dance, or gymnastics, are privileged), but the flexibility of the NCPE framework allows a gender differentiated curriculum to continue (Penney, 2002a; Penney and Evans, 1999). For example, although all pupils are required to study invasion, net and striking fielding games in each of the first three key stages of education (5–14 yrs), teachers can, and do, continue to offer specific games to boys (more usually those with high status in society, such as rugby, cricket, and football) and others to girls (netball, hockey, rounders) in single sex lessons (Evans et al., 1996). Other activities on the NCPE that have the potential to challenge sex stereotyped attitudes and behaviours have either been marginalised, e.g. outdoor and adventurous activities (see Humberstone, 1993) and dance (see Hargreaves, 1994), or are themselves delivered in gender specific versions (for example, health related fitness (Harris and Penney, 2002)). In addition to a focus on the curriculum, concerns about equal access and opportunities have also been highlighted in extra-curricular PE provision. As Penney and Harris (1997) note, because there has always been a strong link between curriculum content and the established pattern of extra-curricular PE provision, this has resulted in school teams in stereotypically gendered sports (mainly invasion games) forming the mainstay of this provision. Aside from the range of activities on offer, other research (for example, Office for Standards in Education (OFSTED), 1995) has also shown that girls have tended to have fewer opportunities available to them in extra-curricular provision.

Issues of equal opportunities and access have also been raised in relation to PE teachers' training and their careers. Clearly teachers are crucial agents in both the reproduction and challenging of gender in schools. Research into initial teacher education (ITE) has highlighted the significance of the curriculum. In her research into England teacher education, Flintoff (1993a) found that a sex-differentiated curriculum was not restricted to schools but was also prevalent in the practical elements of ITE programmes. Many male and female PE teachers, therefore, remain differentially skilled in their confidence, ability and commitment to deliver across a broad range of activities (Evans et al., 1996; Flintoff, 1995; Waddington et al.,1998). Flintoff (1993b) also found that there was little evidence of student teachers being enabled to understand and challenge gender relations in their teaching as a consequence of their involvement in the theoretical aspects of their courses. Here and elsewhere, for example in Australia and North America, ITE programmes in PE are dominated by the 'hard' sciences and sports performance discourse, with space for social sciences and discussions about equity issues marginalised or excluded (Dewar, 1990; Wright, 2002b). The considerable change to teacher education policy and practice in England over the last ten years has only contributed to a practical, competence-based view of teaching becoming more prominent (see Furlong et al., 1996). A 'national curriculum' of initial teacher *training* (rather than education) introduced by the Teacher Training Agency (TTA) in 1998 now lays out the 'national standards' that all trainees need to accomplish, focusing on teachers' operational roles within the classroom with a down-playing of theoretical perspectives and social contexts (TTA, 2002). As a result, issues of equality and social justice occupy only a tenuous and marginal position in the contemporary teacher training curriculum (Coffey and Delamont, 2000; Mahony, 2000; Mahony and

Hexhall, 1997). Other studies have shown that although not formally part of the educative process, nevertheless, gender issues influence students' experiences of, and success on, school-based practice elements of their training (Flintoff, 1994; Laker et al., 2003). Going further, the work of Brown and Rich (Brown, 1999; Brown and Rich, 2002; Rich 2001) argue that gender is so central a part of PE teachers' identities that it becomes a key aspect of their pedagogical strategies. Student teachers were shown to possess a limited range of gendered resources including modes of communication; subject knowledge; movement skills and narratives of the self – so that they become complicit with, rather than challenging of, the existing gender order in schools in their teaching.

In relation to teachers' career trajectories, work in the 1980s showed that men were more likely to occupy the overall head of department positions, even though the departments might still operate with a head of girls' PE, or as separate men's and women's departments (Evans and Williams, 1989). Sikes (1988) argued that men teachers are advantaged in promotion and career opportunity because of the link between masculinity, sporting performance and dominant perceptions of teaching competence in PE. Although there is little recent empirical evidence of the impact of gender on teachers' careers and promotion, it appears that women's access to key decision-making roles in PE remains limited. For example, Waddington et al.'s, (1998) research in Nottinghamshire showed that only 17 per cent of heads of departments were women, and in Penney et al.'s (2002) survey of Specialist Sports Colleges, just 30 per cent of directors of PE and sport were women.

Clearly there has been a significant focus on equal opportunities and access in work on gender and PE over the past three decades. Most of the work has focused on the inequalities faced by girls and young women and many of the issues highlighted in this section are enduring themes that have continued into the twenty-first century. However, parallel with this liberal approach to gender and PE has been a more radical focus that has sought to understand unequal gender power relations in PE policies and practices.

FEMININITIES, MASCULINITIES AND SEXUALITIES

An important strand of more radical feminist work in PE has explored how images and ideas of femininity are constructed and reproduced in and through PE. This work is important because it recognises that issues of gender are not just about different opportunity and access, but more about how ideologies of femininity and masculinity are constructed as unequal power relations. In other words, what we understand about masculinity at any one time is always defined in relation to femininity. These ideas are not just relational but also hierarchical where one set of attributes and associated activities (men's) are viewed as more important than the others (women's).

In an extensive study of girls' PE, Scraton (1992) showed how ideologies of femininity were produced and reproduced through PE practice. The study focused on teachers' attitudes and expectations relating to girls' capabilities and interests. For example, teachers had clear ideas about appropriate activities for girls based on historical and traditional expectations of their physical capabilities. These underpinned the curricular and extra-curricular opportunities made available to the girls, but also influenced teachers' expectations of girls' behaviours, their dress for PE and the teachers' pedagogical practice. This study also began to problematise universal conceptions of femininity, and difference across class and ethnic backgrounds. These more complex theoretical and empirical debates around difference have been taken up more recently, and are discussed further in the section on Bodies, Identities and Difference.

In the early 1990s, Scraton identified PE kit and compulsory showers as significant factors that contribute to some girls' negative perceptions and experiences of PE. These have been identified in more recent research as continuing to impact on girls' and young women's PE experiences (Cockburn and Clarke, 2002; Youth Sport Trust (YST)/Nike, 1999). In England, a traditional PE kit of short skirt, tee-shirt and 'PE knickers', continues to be seen as problematic by many girls and young women. On one hand, its revealing nature potentially puts girls' and young women's bodies on display and opens up opportunities for unwanted and uncomfortable heterosexual, male gaze and comment. On the other, the wearing of PE kit is viewed by some girls and young women as childish and in conflict with their developing adult, heterosexual femininity. Although there has been some change in this policy in some schools, in others, female PE teachers still see a traditional PE kit as important for maintaining standards and projecting a 'respectable' female image.

Part of a respectable female image is linked to perceptions of *heterosexual* femininity. There is little work that takes a radical feminist perspective within PE focusing on girls' and young women's experiences. Nevertheless, there is work that looks at the impact of dominant discourses of heterosexual femininity more generally in schooling (Epstein, 1994; Epstein and Johnson, 1998; Lees, 1993). Lees' work in particular has been very influential in recognising the pressures on young women to negotiate a respectable heterosexual femininity and avoid being labelled a 'slag', a 'drag' or a 'lezzie'. Radical feminist work is more prevalent in sport, where women who show an interest or success in sport are often labelled as lesbian. Griffin (2002) shows how this label is constructed as negative, operates to control women's sporting behaviours, and prevents many women from seeing sport as an appropriate activity.

In PE, radical feminist work has, to date, focused on lesbian teachers' experiences (Clarke, 1997; 2002; Squires and Sparkes, 1996; Sykes, 1998). Clarke's (2002) work shows how lesbian teachers adopt coping strategies to negotiate homophobia and heterosexism, and often to conceal their lesbian identity. These include strict self-censorship, avoiding personal conversations, distancing themselves from changing rooms and shower facilities, and 'playing' the heterosexual.

Much of the work discussed so far in this chapter has concentrated on understanding and exploring the impact of gender relations on girls' and women's experiences of PE and sport.

However, by the late 1980s, there was a growing recognition of the need for a more comprehensive understanding of men and masculinity and their role in gender power relations. At this time Connell's (1987) early work was most influential for analysing the concept of masculinity, showing how masculinities are constructed in relation to one another, and in relation to femininities. Connell (1987) describes hegemonic masculinity as an 'idealised' form of masculinity and shows that although few men live up to this ideal, nevertheless, very large numbers of men become complicit in sustaining this hegemony. In western societies, this ideal continues to centre around physical strength, dominance, competition and heterosexuality. As Connell argues, male power is linked to male physicality: 'The social definition of men as holders of power is translated not only into mental body images and fantasies, but into muscle tensions, posture, the feel and texture of the body. This is one of the ways in which the power of men becomes "naturalised"' (Connell, 1987: 85). Writers such as Messner (1992), Messner and Sabo (1990), McKay et al. (2000), and Whitson (1990) have taken the concept of hegemonic masculinity and have shown the close links between this idealised masculinity and sport. PE and sport have increasingly been recognised as key sites where boys and men can 'perform' masculinity.

The 'performance' of masculinity is not only linked to an idealised male physicality but also to a heterosexuality constructed around unequal power relations between men and women. As Curry (2002) argues in his research on men's locker room talk, this talk can reinforce hegemonic masculinity and male privilege. Men's talk reveals how masculine identity is affirmed through homophobic comment and conversations that both denigrate women and men who are perceived as different. In PE, Bramham (2003), Fleming (1991) and Parker (1996) all show how hegemonic masculinity operates to reproduce particular kinds of behaviours and attitudes, and how boys who do not conform are subjected to verbal and physical abuse. Bramham (2003), for example, identifies the importance of boys being 'one of the lads', having a laugh or being 'hard'. Boys are expected to demonstrate that they are competitive, aggressive, tough, heterosexual, brave and have other attributes associated with a hegemonic masculinity.

The work on masculinity highlights not only the inequalities between men and women, but also, the centrality of power relationships between different groups of men. Hegemonic masculinity exists in relation to subordinated masculinities, such as gay masculinity, working-class masculinity, or black masculinity. However, while the complex inter-relationships between gender, race and class, and the experiences of black and minority ethnic pupils have been explored in relation to schooling more broadly (see, for example, Mac an Ghail, 1988, 1994, 1996; Mirza, 1992; O'Donnell and Sharpe, 2000) they remain under-researched within PE, particularly in relation to black masculinities. This point is explored further in the section below.

BODIES, IDENTITIES AND DIFFERENCE

During the 1990s and since the millennium, the body has taken on increased significance in social and cultural analysis. However, within feminist work, few writers and researchers have focused on the significance of sporting bodies (Hall, 1996). Although the body is central to sport and physical education, it has received little critical social analysis in relation to education and schooling (Paechter, 2003a, 2003b). In a recent study, Paechter (2003a, 2003b) concentrates on children's bodies in schooling and explores PE as an arena in which they learn and construct dominant and subordinate masculinities and femininities. She argues that bodies do matter to pupils' gendered identities and shows how different forms of PE, sports and fitness support the development and perpetuation of gendered forms of bodily usage. She suggests that PE must look to alternative activities in order to encourage more open, communicative and connective body pràctices. It is only by moving away from traditional PE activities that gender stereotyped bodily usages can be resisted and challenged. Whitson (1994) comes to similar conclusions in his research into the relationship between physical and social power. Concentrating more on sport rather than PE he emphasises how girls and boys, women and men, learn to live their bodies in gendered ways. He highlights how gendered subjectivities are embodied by individuals as they move through childhood and into adult sexual identities. However, Whitson argues that sport can also be a site for the empowerment of women whereby their bodies become skilled and forceful subjects capable of challenging gendered power relations. He goes on to consider the potential of 'new' sports or physical activities in this process such as aerobics, outdoor activities and dance. These activities, he argues, encourage power to be embodied in ways not necessarily tied to domination or gender. This notion of empowerment through physical activity has increasingly become a focus of feminist research into sport as reflected in the work of McDermott (1996, 2002) focusing on women's outdoor experiences and Gilroy (1997) within more formal team sport settings.

Whitson, in writing about embodiment and empowerment a decade ago, drew theoretically on the early structural feminist writings of people such as Iris Young (1979) and Catherine Mackinnon (1987), whereas Paechter takes a more overtly post-structuralist approach. Indeed, it is with the advent of poststructuralist discourse that the body has become much more significant in feminist work both in relation to schooling and PE. Within this work the writings of Foucault have been particularly influential (Hall, 1996) drawing on his ideas around the concepts of discourse, surveillance and technologies (Garrett, 2004). As Garrett acknowledges in relation to her use of Foucault to understand young Australian women's lived embodied experiences in and around physical activity: 'His theories have been useful and relevant . . . in helping to reveal the ways in which young Australian women's bodies are constructed and inscribed with knowledge that impact on self-understanding and involvement in physical activity' (Garrett, 2004: 141).

Garrett (2004) argues that poststructural analysis which sees the importance of language and discourse, together with a recognition of the body as a material entity, is the best approach to understanding the ways in which young women come to have and experience a gendered embodiment in PE. She argues that there are at least three types of bodies constructed within and through PE: the bad body, the comfortable body and the different body. Her conclusions have resonance with the work of Whitson and Paechter in that she argues that PE needs to help pupils challenge narrow and restricted gender discourses that serve to limit physical opportunities for any individual. Her work is interesting because it uses empirical data from young women in their final year of schooling and presents their 'physical stories'. These stories demonstrate the complexity and interconnectedness of bodies, gender and physical identity and identifies how social and discursive practices of sport and PE can serve to inscribe bodies and impact on 'lived' bodily experiences.

In addition to focusing on the body and identities, post-structuralist discourse also provides conceptual challenges to the macro universalistic approaches of liberal and structural feminist accounts (Scraton and Flintoff, 2002). Poststructural feminism argues for the deconstruction of the term 'woman' and a recognition of the diversity of femininities. However, debates about difference and the problems of a universal theorising relying on the accounts of white feminists have long been a focus of attention by black feminists (Hill-Collins, 1991; Hooks, 1982, 1984, 1989). Yet within the literature and research on gender and PE (or indeed gender and sport) difference, beyond that between women and men or girls and boys, has largely gone unexplored (Lovell, 1991; Raval, 1989; Scraton, 2001).

Benn's (1996, 2002) and Zaman's (1997) research focuses on the experiences of Muslim women thus recognising the complex interplay of gender, race, *and* religion. Both studies centralise difference, identifying the western and masculine definition of sport, and racism, and Islamophobia as major issues. Benn's (1996, 2002) research explores the different life experiences, opportunities and constraints for Muslim women entering teacher training in PE. She shows that while PE is seen as an important part of Islam, many of the traditional practices of PE have to be adapted or changed in order to successfully incorporate the religious needs of the women in their university course. The Muslim young women in Zaman's (1997) study also identify positively with exercise and physical activity. However, as in Benn's research, the organisation and presentation of activities in a non-Islamic culture posed problems for them (see also De Knop et al., 1996). These studies are important for recognising specific constraints for Muslim women posed by western constructions of sport and PE. It is these constructions that serve to exclude particular groups of girls and women. These studies help to shift the focus of 'the problem' away from individuals and their religion and/or ethnicity, to a recognition that the structure and organisation of PE and sport needs to be challenged.

Although not specifically on PE, Wray's (2002) work on Pakistani Muslim women and physical activity extends beyond a focus on equal opportunities and issues of access and constraint to look in more detail at the complex constructions of different femininities. Using participation observation and discussion groups, she explores in detail the women's experiences and perceptions of participation in exercise classes. In doing this she shows how their bodily identities are constructed within specific cultural and historic circumstances. She concludes that femininities need to be understood as 'constructed and experienced through racialised power relations that regulate ethnic identity in western society' (Wray, 2002: 137).

As noted earlier, work on masculinity has highlighted the centrality of power relations between different groups of boys and men. Just as Wray's work suggests the importance of addressing racialised power relations between different femininities, Fleming's (1991) work focuses on similar issues relating to racialised power and masculinities. He shows the diversity of Asian masculinities constructed and experienced within PE. In his ethnographic study of 50 Asian boys at one secondary school, he identifies four broad categories of behaviour and general demeanour in PE. Although these boys had very different experiences of, and responses to PE, nevertheless, the common denominator for all boys was the pervasiveness of racism, and racial stereotyping about their participation and abilities.

CURRENT POLICIES AND FUTURE RESEARCH QUESTIONS

In the final section of the chapter, we now turn to look at current policies and practices, and highlight future research directions and questions for gender and PE. Recently, there has been the introduction of a number of new policies in England designed to raise standards in PE, and increase young people's participation levels, as part of a national strategy – the *Physical Education and School Sport Clubs Links Strategy* (PESSCL) (Department for Education and Skills (DfES), 2003). In providing new opportunities for PE and sport, these new policies require critical evaluation in relation to gender. What kinds of activities and opportunities will they offer to young people, and which young people will benefit? What is the potential for these new policies to break down or change existing gender relations in PE? For example, two important strands of this strategy are the introduction of Specialist Sports Colleges[2] and the School Sport Coordinator Programme[3]. Initial research shows, positively, that the curriculum in many sports colleges has been broadened to get a better balance between games and other activities on the NCPE (Penney et al., 2002). What the research does not show, however, is whether this wider range of activities is offered to both girls and boys, or perhaps more importantly, what is the nature of pupils' experiences in these classes. Although there is evidence that the Nike Girls into Sport project has produced some innovative practice in relation to girls' PE in sports colleges, as mentioned earlier, overall, it appears that teachers in sports colleges are no more likely than PE teachers elsewhere to address gender inequalities in their practice (YST/Nike, 1999).

A second key strand is the School Sport Coordinator programme, again very much in its early stages. While increasing the number of opportunities for young people to take part in PE and sport, some initial evaluations are noting the difficulties in some partnerships in attracting under-represented groups of youngsters, particularly girls and pupils from ethnic minority backgrounds (OFSTED, 2002; Flintoff, 2002; Flintoff, 2003). Although these recent initiatives are focused on providing more opportunities in PE and sport for young people, the nature of these opportunities is such that gendered differences remain largely unaddressed. These are early evaluations of the first phase of the programme, but highlight the importance of monitoring which young people are accessing and benefiting from the programme. All eight work strands of the national strategy: specialist sport colleges; school sport coordinators; professional development; step into sport; school-club links; gifted and talented; swimming; Qualifications and Curriculum Authority (QCA) PE and sport investigation, will require careful monitoring and evaluation in relation to gender.

Throughout the chapter we have shown the ways in which issues of gender have been researched and debated. Over the last three decades our understandings of gender have developed and become more theoretically sophisticated. In over viewing key research in gender and PE, it becomes clear that there are still important issues to be addressed within contemporary PE.

Gender, physical education and health

Young people's activity levels and health raise important questions for professionals working in PE and sport. In the UK Sport (2003) strategy *Framework for Women and Sport*, Sue Campbell, the interim chair, notes: 'If we are to seriously address the rising concerns for the health of our young people then there must be open and equal opportunity for everyone to participate and progress, regardless of their gender, ability or cultural background' (UK Sport, 2003:2).

There continues to be clear evidence that girls and young women are less likely to take part in physical activity and sport compared with boys and young men (see, for example, Rowe and Champion, 2000; Sport England, 2003). However, our knowledge remains largely limited to quantitative data identifying participation rates. We still need to know, in qualitative terms, how gender (including questions around expectations of femininity, physicality, identities, bodies) impacts on girls' and young women's experiences of PE and sport. It is insufficient to focus on access and opportunity alone, and research is needed to determine what encourages girls and young women to engage in positive and empowering, physical experiences both within and outside school (Flintoff and Scraton, 2001). The link between active lifestyles and health is now well acknowledged so that gendered patterns of inactivity are of concern.

Similarly, in the twenty-first century, concerns about obesity are becoming more prevalent. However, debates about obesity, body image and physical activity also raise important gender issues. The social construction of an ideal femininity and masculinity can influence young people's self-perceptions and esteem, and affect how others interact with them. As Evans et al. (2004) note, PE teachers are influential in constructing and reproducing discourses of health, obesity and the body that are also gendered and require critical analysis and investigation.

Difference and diversity

Our theoretical understanding of gender has become more sophisticated over the last three decades, with a recognition of the importance of understanding and exploring difference and diversity. However, there are still large gaps in our knowledge and understanding of different girls' and young women's experiences in PE, as well as those of boys and young men. There remains a tendency – in both research and in policy and practice – to either talk about 'girls' or 'boys' experiences of PE as if they were homogeneous groups, or as Penney (2002b) has highlighted, to take a 'single issue approach' where the focus is on *either* gender, *or* 'race'/ethnicity, *or* ability, and so on. Although recognising some dimension of difference, Penney (2002b) rightly notes that a further problem with 'single issue' research is that *particular* issues become identified as requiring action, whereas others are ignored. For example, research in PE remains largely silent on issues of ethnicity, sexuality and disability. We need to know more about the ways in which pupils' (and teachers') *multiple* identities are constructed and experienced within PE, and importantly, how the structural organisation of PE and sport may serve to exclude or marginalise some groups of young people. We know very little, for example, about the physical activity experiences of black or South Asian young women, either in or out of school, or how racialised aspects of gender relations may impact on these experiences.

The introduction of the third NCPE in 2000 explicitly establishes 'inclusion' as a key focus for contemporary PE practice (DfES, 1999). All teachers are asked to pay 'due regard' to three principles of inclusion. Although useful, as Penney (2002b) notes, there is little guidance to help teachers apply these principles and alter their practice to be inclusive, and specifically no advice on the complexities of addressing issues of gender (or any other form of) equity. The silence about gender in this policy text is mirrored more widely in professional debates. Gender issues in PE appear to have largely disappeared from the professional agenda in favour of a focus on 'different' differences – for example, children with special educational needs or those with talent in PE and sport (see, for example, Bailey and Morley, 2003; Vickerman, 2003). Research on special educational needs or talent development in PE is both worthwhile and necessary, but there are gender issues that need to be addressed within these areas. For example, how may abilities be socially constructed and gendered? We need to know more about how PE teachers understand the challenge of 'inclusion', the extent to which gender issues are part of this, and the kinds of resources (their knowledge base as well as strategies) they draw on in order to provide inclusive opportunities in their teaching.

High quality PE and school sport

One of the key work strands of the national PE and sport strategy is the QCA's research project that aims to examine the nature and benefits of 'high quality' PE. What counts as high quality PE is an important question for the twenty-first century. The document

Learning Through PE and Sport (DfES, 2003) outlining the national strategy suggests: 'High-quality PE and school sport produces young people with the skills, understanding, desire and commitment to continue to improve and achieve in a range of PE, sport and health-enhancing physical activities in line with their abilities' (2003: 3).

It goes on to suggest that where there is high quality PE, young people 'show a strong commitment to making PE and sport an important and valuable part of their lives in both the school and community', and who 'enjoy PE and school and community sport'. The danger of this kind of definition is that it focuses entirely on the young people, and not on the nature of the PE provision. It is then only too easy to 'explain away' a lack of commitment to PE on the part of some girls and young women as being 'their' problem. If we are to engage those young people (and in particular girls and young women) who currently neither enjoy nor are committed to PE, we will need a critical reappraisal of the curriculum and pedagogy practices in relation to gender. For example, Penney and Evans' (1999) research has identified the dominance of an elite sporting discourse within the NCPE and a marginalisation of activities such as gymnastics, dance and outdoor education. We need to know how this curriculum is experienced by different girls and young women, and what kinds of pedagogical practice are successful in helping them to develop active lifestyles in and out of school. Other trends within PE, such as the increasing take up of examinations, raise questions linked to gender. Penney et al. (2002), for example, show that increasing numbers of young people in sports colleges are engaging in examination courses in PE and dance but that the take up is strongly gendered. Almost twice as many boys than girls are opting to take examination courses in PE, with girls mainly opting to take examination courses in dance. We need to know more about why this is the case, and investigate the implications of these gender imbalances for pupils' future careers and opportunities in PE and sport. Contemporary PE 'knowledge' continues to be strongly gendered – how it will develop and change in the future will require critical evaluation.

Teachers' professional development and careers

Teachers play an important role in reinforcing or challenging gender relations in PE. The content and nature of their initial and ongoing professional development in relation to gender remains a significant element for critical appraisal. Despite the detailed knowledge now available about the social construction of gender through PE and sport, very little of this is included in the ITE curriculum (Wright, 2002b). As the routes into teaching become increasingly diverse, it is difficult to see how this situation will improve in the future. The newly developed continuing professional development programme for PE teachers, currently in its pilot stage, has an opportunity to provide a balance between scientific knowledge about performance in *activities* and social knowledge about *children and young people* and their education, and by so doing, challenge the dominance of scientific discourse in PE. We will need to carefully evaluate the impact of this new programme on teacher development, but we also need to know more about the nature of programmes that have successfully engaged teachers in problematising and challenging gendered PE practices (see, for example, Wright, 2002a). More detailed studies on the philosophies, identities and pedagogies of ITE staff and of those teachers in school with responsibility for coordinating school-based elements of courses are also required.

While ITE and continuing professional development opportunities remain crucial to help teachers appreciate and acknowledge difference and diversity, in their pedagogy, the kinds of people choosing to enter the profession in the first place is significant. National strategies aimed at widening university participation to previously under-represented groups have yet to impact on ITE cohorts that remain remarkably homogeneous, particularly in PE. PE students tend to be good at sport themselves, positively orientated towards the values of sport (and, therefore, generally conservative) and from a limited range of social and cultural backgrounds. The numbers of students from minority ethnic backgrounds are extremely low, despite strategies to attract such young people into teaching (see, for example, teacherworld.org.uk). A more diverse PE profession would not just reflect the school populations teachers will work with, but help challenge the homogeneity of PE culture, both in ITE and in schools. Benn's (1996, 2002) work is an important starting point in exploring how different femininities are constructed in ITE PE, and identifying what we can learn from the experiences of minority ethnic students.

Finally, the national PESSCL strategy opens the way for career development opportunities and for new, decision-making roles in PE. The kinds of PE and sport opportunities that are promoted and developed under the new strategy will have implications for teachers' career progression. There is a need for research that builds on and updates the work of Sikes (1988) and which seeks to explore the relationships between contemporary conceptions of PE and school sport and gendered career progressions.

This chapter has provided a comprehensive overview of the key issues and debates in gender and PE, and how these have impacted on policy and practice. As we noted at the beginning of the chapter, although presented in sections that represent shifts in emphasis and theoretical understanding over the last three decades, all three sections address issues that remain significant for contemporary policy and practice in PE. What is also clear, however, is that it has been debates about access and opportunity, emanating from a liberal feminist perspective, rather than other theoretical understandings of gender that have been the most influential in PE. Nevertheless, there have been other important questions raised about femininities, masculinities, identities, and bodies and these will need to be addressed if we are to provide a high quality PE capable of addressing some of the participation, lifestyle and health issues of today's diverse young people.

NOTES

1   The Schools Council was the main curriculum development body in the UK between 1964 and 1982 (see Weiner, 1994).

2   Specialist Sports Colleges were introduced in England in 1997 by the Labour government, although the broader specialists schools initiative was originated by the previous Conservative government. Specialist Sports Colleges are maintained secondary schools in England that receive additional funding from the DfES to raise standards in PE and sport within its own school, in a local family of schools and in the community. To apply, schools are required to raise £50,000 from private sector sponsorship and submit a four-year development plan.

3   The School Sport Coordinator Programme is an English initiative designed to increase sporting opportunities for young people by developing and enhancing links between school PE and sporting opportunities in the wider community. The programme is based on a group of schools working together in a 'partnership', with a sports college at the 'hub', to develop PE and sporting links with each other and the community. The first phase of School Sport Coordinator Programme development started in September 2000 and there are now plans to increase the number of partnerships to 3,000 by the end of 2005.

REFERENCES

Bailey, R. and Morley, D. (2003) 'Towards a model of talent development in PE', paper presented at the annual conference of the British Educational Research Association, Edinburgh, September.

Benn, T. (1996) 'Muslim women and physical education in initial teacher training', *Sport, Education and Society*, 1 (1): 5–21.

Benn, T. (2002) 'Muslim women in teacher training: issues of gender, "race" and religion', in D. Penney (ed.), *Gender and Physical Education: Contemporary Issues and Future Directions*. London: Routledge.

Braham, P. (2003) 'Boys, masculinity and PE', *Sport, Education and Society*, 8 (1): 57–71.

Brown, D. (1999) 'Complicity and reproduction in teaching physical education', *Sport, Education and Society*, 4 (2): 143–59.

Brown, D. and Rich, E. (2002) 'Gender positioning as pedagogical practice in physical education', in D. Penney (ed.), *Gender and Physical Education: Contemporary Issues and Future Directions*. London: Routledge.

Clarke, G. (1997) 'Playing a part: the lives of lesbian physical education teachers', in G. Clarke and B. Humberstone (eds), *Researching Women and Sport*. London: Macmillan Press.

Clarke, G. (1998) 'Queering the pitch and coming out to play: lesbians in physical education and sport'. *Sport, Education and Society*, 3 (2): 145–60.

Clarke, G. (2002) 'Difference matters: sexuality and physical education', in D. Penney (ed.), *Gender and Physical Education: Contemporary Issues and Future Directions*. London: Routledge.

Clarke, G. (2004) 'Threatening space: (physical) education and homophobic body work', in J. Evans, B. Davies and J. Wright (eds), *Body Knowledge and Control: Studies in the Sociology of Physical Education and Health*. London: Routledge.

Cockburn, C. and Clarke, G. (2002) 'Everybody is looking at you! Girls negotiating the "femininity deficit" they incur in physical education', *Women Studies International Forum*, 25 (6): 651–65.

Coffey, A. and Delamont, S. (2000) *Feminism and the Classroom Teacher: Research, Praxis and Pedagogy*. London: RoutledgeFalmer.

Connell, R.W. (1987) *Gender and Power*. Cambridge: Polity Press.

Curry, I. (2002) 'Fraternal bonding in the locker room: a profeminist analysis of talk about competition and women', in Scraton, S. and Flintoff, A. (eds), *Gender and Sport: A Reader*. London: Routledge.

De Knop, P., Theeboom, M., Wittock, H. and De Martelaer, K. (1996) 'Implications of Islam on Muslim girls' sports participation in western Europe. Literature review and policy recommendations for sport promotion'. *Sport, Education and Society*, 1 (2): 147–64.

Department for Education and Skills (1987) *The National Curriculum: A Consultation Document*. London: HMSO.

Department of Education and Science (1991) *Physical Education for Ages 5–16 Years: Proposals to the Secretary of State of Education and Science*. London: HMSO.

Department of Education and Science (1992) *Physical Education in the National Curriculum*. London: HMSO.

Department for Education and Employment (1999) *Physical Education: The National Curriculum in England*. London: Department for Education and Employment/Qualifications and Curriculum Authority.

Department for Education and Skills (2003*) Learning through PE and Sport: A Guide to the Physical Education, School Sport and Club Links Strategy*. Nottingham: DfES Publications.

Dewar, A. (1990) 'Oppression and privilege in physical education: struggles in the negotiation of gender in a university programme', in D. Kirk and R. Tinning (eds) *Physical Education, Curriculum and Culture: Critical Issues in the Contemporary Crisis*. Basingstoke: Falmer.

Epstein, D. (ed.) (1994) *Challenging Lesbian and Gay Inequalities in Education*. Buckingham: Open University Press.

Epstein, D. and Johnson, R. (1998) *Schooling Sexualities*. Buckingham: Open University Press.

Evans, J. (1989) 'Swinging from the crossbar: equality and opportunity in the physical education curriculum', *British Journal of Physical Education*, 20 (2): 84–7.

Evans, J., Lopez, S., Duncan, M. and Evans, M. (1985) 'Some thoughts on the political and pedagogical implications of mixed sex groupings in the physical education curriculum', *British Educational Research Journal*, 13 (1): 59–71.

Evans, J. and Williams, T. (1989) 'Moving up and getting out: the classed and gendered career opportunities of physical education teachers', in T. Templin and P. Schempp (eds), *Socialisation into Physical Education: Learning to Teach*, Carmel, Benchmark Press.

Evans, J., Davies, B. and Penney, D. (1996) 'Teachers, teaching and the social construction of gender relations', *Sport, Education and Society*, 1 (2): 165–83.

Evans, J., Davies, B., and Wright, J. (2004) *Body Knowledge and Control: Studies in the Sociology of Physical Education and Health*. London: Routledge.

Fletcher, S. (1984) *Women First: The Female Tradition in English Physical Education 1880–1980*. London: Athlone Press.

Fleming, I. (1991) 'Sport, schooling and Asian male youth culture', in G. Jarvie (ed.), *Sport, Racism and Ethnicity*. London: Falmer.

Flintoff, A. (1990) 'PE, Equal opportunities and the national curriculum: crisis or challenge?', *European Physical Education Review*, 13 (2): 85–100.

Flintoff, A. (1993a) 'Gender, PE and initial teacher education', in J. Evans (ed.), *Equality, Education and Physical Education*. London: Falmer.

Flintoff, A. (1993b) 'One of the boys? Gender identities in physical education initial teacher education', in I. Siraj-Blatchford (ed.), *'Race', Gender and the Education of Teachers*. Buckingham: Open University Press.

Flintoff, A. (1994) 'Keeping gender on the agenda: PE teacher education in the 1990s', in *Working Papers in Sport and Society, Vol. 3, 1994/5*. Warwick Centre for the Study of Sport in Society: University of Warwick.

Flintoff, A. (1995) 'Anti-sexist practice in secondary physical education', in L. Milosevic (ed.), *Fairplay: Gender and Physical Education*. Leeds: Leeds Education Authority.

Flintoff, A. (2002) 'An evaluation of an out of school hours learning in PE and Sport programme, Interim Report', *Bulletin of PE*, 38 (2): 99–110.

Flintoff, A. (2003) The School Sport Coordinator Programme: Changing the role of the physical education teachers? *Sport, Education and Society*, 8 (2): 231–50.

Flintoff, A. and Scraton, S. (2001) 'Stepping into Active Leisure? Young women's perceptions of active lifestyles and their experiences of school PE', *Sport, Education and Society*, 6 (1): 5–21.

Furlong, J., Whitty, G., Barton, L. and Barrett, E. (1996) 'From integration to partnership: changing structures in ITE', in R. McBride (ed.), *Teacher Education Policy: Some issues Arising from Research and Practice*. London: Falmer.

Garrett, R. (2004) 'Gendered bodies and physical identities', in J. Evans, B. Davies and J. Wright (eds), *Body Knowledge and Control: Studies in the Sociology of Physical Education and Health*. London: Routledge.

Gilroy, S. (1997) 'Working on the body: links between physical activity and social power', in G. Clarke and B. Humberstone (eds), *Researching Women and Sport*. London: Macmillan.

Green, K. and Scraton, S. (1998) 'Gender, co-education and secondary physical education: a brief review', in K. Green and K. Hardman (eds), *Physical Education: A Reader*. Aachen: Meyer and Meyer.

Griffin, P. (2002) 'Changing the game: homophobia, sexism and lesbians in sport', in S. Scraton and A. Flintoff (eds), *Women and Sport: A Reader*. London: Routledge.

Hall, M.A. (1996) *Feminism and Sporting Bodies: Essays on theory and practice*. Leeds: Human Kinetics.

Hargreaves, J. (1994) *Sporting Females: Critical Issues in the History and Sociology of Women's Sports*. London: Routledge.

Harris, J. and Penney, D. (2002) 'Gender, health and physical education', in D. Penney (ed.), *Gender and Physical Education: Contemporary Issues and Future Directions*. London: Routledge.

Hill Collins, P. (1991) *Black Feminist Thought: Knowledge, Consciousness and the Politics of Empowerment*. London: Routledge.

Hooks, B. (1982) *Ain't I A Woman? Black Women and Feminism*. Boston Massachusetts: South End Press.

Hooks, B. (1984) *Feminist Theory: From Margin to Centre*. Boston Massachusetts: South End Press.

Hooks, B. (1989) *Talking Back: Thinking Feminist, Thinking Black*. Boston, Massachusetts: South End Press.

Humberstone, B. (1993) 'Equality, Physical education and outdoor education – ideological struggles and transformative structures?', in J. Evans (ed.), *Equality, Education and Physical Education*. London: Falmer.

ILEA (Inner London Education Authority) (1984) *Providing Equal Opportunities for Girls and Boys in Physical Education*. London: ILEA College of Physical Education.

Kelly, A. (1985) 'Changing schools and changing society: reflections on the Girls into Science and Technology project', in M. Arnot (ed.), *Race and Gender: Equal Opportunities in Education*. Oxford: Pergamon.

Kirk, D. (1992) *Defining Physical Education: The Social Construction of a Subject in Postwar Britain*. Basingstoke: Falmer Press.

Laker, A., Craig, J. and Lea, S. (2003) 'School experience and the issue of gender', *Sport, Education and Society*, 8 (1): 73–89.

Leaman, O. (1984) *Sit on the Sidelines and Watch the Boys Play: Sex Differentiation in Physical Education*. London: Longman for Schools Council.

Lees, S. (1993) *Sugar and Spice: Sexuality and Adolescent Girls*. London: Hutchinson.

Lovell, T. (1991) 'Sport, racism and young women', in G. Jarvie (ed.), *Sport, Racism and Ethnicity*. London: Falmer.

Mac an Ghaill, M. (1988) *Young, Gifted and Black*. Buckingham: Open University Press.

Mac an Ghaill, M. (1994) *The Making of Men: Masculinities, Sexualities and Schooling*. Buckingham: Open University Press.

Mac an Ghaill, M. (1996) *Understanding Masculinities*. Buckingham: Open University Press.

Mackinnon, C. (1987) *Feminism Unmodified: Discourses on Life and Law*. Cambridge, MA: Harvard University Press.

Mahony, P. (2000) 'Teacher education policy and gender', in J. Salisbury and S. Riddell (eds), *Gender, Policy and Educational Change: Shifting Agendas in the UK and Europe*. London: Routledge.

Mahony, P. and Hexhall, I. (1997) 'Sounds of silence: the social justice agenda of the teacher training agency', *International Studies in Sociology of Education*, 7 (2): 137–56.

McDermott, L. (1996) 'Towards a feminist understanding of physicality within the contexts of women's physically active and sporting lives', *Sociology of Sport Journal*, 13: 12–30.

McDermott, L. (2002) 'A qualitative assessment of the significance of body perception to women's physical activity experiences: revisiting discussions of physicalities', *Sociology of Sport Journal*, 17 (4): 331–63.

McKay, J., Messner, M. and Sabo, D. (2000) *Masculinities, Gender Relations and Sport*. Thousand Oaks, California: Sage.

Messner, M. (1992) *Power at Play: Sports and the Problem of Masculinity*, Boston: Beacon Press.

Messner, M. and Sabo, D. (eds) (1990) *Sport, Men and the Gender Order: Critical Feminist Perspectives*. Leeds: Human Kinetics.

Mirza, H. S. (1992) *Young, Female and Black*. London: Routledge.

O'Donald, M. and Sharpe, S. (2000) *Uncertain Masculinities: Youth, Ethnicities and Class in Contemporary Britain*. London: Routledge.

Office for Standards in Education (OFSTED) (1995) *Physical Education and Sport in Schools: A Survey of Good Practice*. London: HMSO.

Office for Standards in Education (OFSTED) (2002) *The School Sport Co-ordinator Programme: Evaluation of Phases 1 and 2, 2001–2003*. London: HMSO publications.

Oliver, K. and Lalik, R. (2004) 'The beauty walk': interrogating whiteness as the norm for beauty in one school's hidden curriculum', in J. Evans, B. Davies and J. Wright (eds), *Body Knowledge and Control: Studies in the Sociology of Physical Education and Health*. London: Routledge.

Parker, A. (1996) 'The construction of masculinity within boys' PE', *Gender and Education*, 8 (2): 141–57.

Paechter, C. (2003a) 'Reconceptualising the gendered body: learning and constructing masculinities and femininities in school', paper presented at the annual conference of the British Educational Research Association, Edinburgh, September.

Paechter, C. (2003b) 'Power, bodies and identity: how different forms of physical education construct varying masculinities and femininities in secondary school', *Sex Education*, 3 (1): 47–59.

Penney, D. (2002a) 'Gendered policies', in Penney, D. (ed.), *Gender and Physical Education: Contemporary Issues and Future Directions*. London: Routledge.

Penney, D. (2002b) 'Equality, equity and inclusion in physical education', in A. Laker (ed.), *The Sociology of Sport and Physical Education*. London: Routledge.

Penney, D. and Evans, J. (1999) *Politics, Policy and Practice in Physical Education*. London: E and FN Spon.

Penney, D. and Harris, J. (1997) 'Extra curricular physical education: more of the same for more of the able? *Sport, Education and Society*, 2 (1): 41–54.

Penney, D., Houlihan, B. and Ely, D. (2002) *Specialist Sports Colleges National Monitoring and Evaluation Research Project: First National Survey Report*. Institute of Youth Sport: Loughborough University.

Raval, S. (1989) 'Gender, leisure and sport: a case study of young people of South Asian descent – a response', *Leisure Studies*, 8: 237–40.

Rich, E. (2001) 'Gender positioning in teacher education in England: new rhetoric, old realities', *International Studies in Sociology of Education*, 11 (2): 131–54.

Rowe, N. and Champion, R. (2000) *Young People and Sport: National Survey 1999*. London: Sport England.

Scraton, S. (1992) *Shaping Up to Womanhood: Gender and Girls' Physical Education*. Milton Keynes: Open University Press.

Scraton, S. (1993) 'Equality, co-education and physical education in secondary schooling', in J. Evans (ed.), *Equality, Education and Physical Education*. London: Falmer.

Scraton, S (2001) 'Re-conceptualising race, gender and sport: the contribution of black feminism', in Carrington, B. and McDonald, I. (eds), *Racism and British Sport*. London: Routledge.

Scraton, S. and Flintoff, A. (1992) 'Feminist research and physical education', in A. Sparkes (eds), *Research in Physical Education and Sport: Exploring Alternative Visions*. London: Falmer Press.

Scraton, S. and Flintoff, A. (2002) 'Sports feminism: the contribution of feminist thought to our understandings of gender and sport', in S. Scraton and A. Flintoff (eds), *A Reader in Gender and Sport*. London: Routledge.

Skelton, A. (1993) 'On being a male PE teacher: the informal culture of students and the construction of hegemonic masculinity', *Gender and Education*, 5 (3): 291–303.

Sikes, P. (1988) 'Growing old gracefully? Age, identity and physical education', in J. Evans (ed.), *Teachers, teaching – and control in – physical education*. Lewes: Falmer.

Squires, S.L. and Sparkes, A. (1996) 'Circles of silence: sexual identity in physical education and sport'. *Sport, Education and Society*, 1 (1): 77–101.

Sport England (2003) *Young People and Sport National Survey 2002*, London, Sport England.

Sykes, H. (1998) 'Turning the closets inside/out: towards a queer-feminist theory in women's physical education', *Sociology of Sport Journal*, 15: 154–73.

Talbot, M. (1990) 'Equal opportunities and physical education', in N. Armstrong (ed.), *New Directions in Physical Education, Volume 1*. Leeds: Human Kinetics.

Teacher Training Agency (2002) *Qualifying to Teach: Professional Standards for Qualified Teacher Status and Requirements for Initial Teacher Training*. London: Teacher Training Agency.

UK Sport (2003) *UK Strategy Framework For Women and Sport*, London: UK Sport.

Vickerman, P. (2003) 'Inclusion confusion? Official line perspectives on including children with special educational needs in physical education', paper presented at the annual conference of the British Educational Research Association, Edinburgh, September.

Waddington, I., Malcolm, D. and Cobb, J. (1998) 'Gender stereotyping and physical education', *European Physical Education Review*, 4 (1): 34–6.

Weiner, G. (1994) *Feminisms in Education: An Introduction*. Buckingham: Open University Press.

Whitson, D. (1990) 'Sport in the construction of masculinity', in M. Messner and D. Sabo (eds), *Sport, Men and the Gender Order: Critical Feminist Perspectives*. Leeds: Human Kinetics.

Whitson, D. (1994) 'The embodiment of gender: discipline, domination and empowerment', in Birrell, S. and Cole, S. (eds), *Women, Sport and Culture*. Leeds: Human Kinetics.

Wray, S. (2002) 'Connecting ethnicity, gender and physicality: Muslim Pakistani women, physical activity and health', in S. Scraton and A. Flintoff (eds), *Gender and Sport: A Reader*. London: Routledge.

Wright, J. (1996) 'The construction of complementarity in PE', *Gender and Education*, 8 (1): 61–79.

Wright, J. (1997) The construction of gender contexts in single sex and co-educational physical education lessons', *Sport, Education and Society*, 2 (1): 55–72.

Wright, J. (2002a) 'Changing gendered practices in physical education: working with teachers', *European Physical Education Review*, 5 (3): 181–97.

Wright, J. (2002b) ''Physical education teacher education: sites of progress or resistance', in D. Penney (ed.), *Gender and Physical Education: Contemporary Issues and Future Directions*. London: Routledge.

Young, I. (1979) 'The exclusion of women from sport: conceptual and existential dimensions', *Philosophy in Context*, 9: 44–53.

Youth Sport Trust/Nike (1999) *The Girls in Sport Partnership Project*. Institute of Youth Sport: Loughborough University.

Zaman, H. (1997) 'Islam, well-being and physical activity: perceptions of Muslim young women', in G. Clarke and B. Humberstone (eds), *Researching Women and Sport*. London: Macmillan.

11 | Social Class, Young People, Sport and Physical Education

Ken Green, Andy Smith and Ken Roberts

A great deal is known about the relationship between social class and education and, to a lesser extent, about social class, leisure and sport. Very little, however, is known about the relationship between social class and physical education. It is our intention in this chapter to begin to tease out the significance of social class for our understanding of physical education and, more specifically, how 'the class divisions that arise in economic life are liable to spill over' (Roberts, 2001: 21) into other areas of young people's lives that have implications for physical education: such as their leisure lifestyles, sporting abilities and dispositions, and so forth.

Social class has proved to be related to virtually all areas of life so it is no surprise to find that class is related to leisure in general, and sports participation in particular. However, within leisure there are exceptions (watching TV, for example) and other uses of leisure where the predictive power of class is relatively weak (for example, gambling). This also applies to certain sports such as angling and football. Might it, then, be possible, via physical education, to weaken the link across the whole of sport? Indeed, might it be possible for physical education to have a positive impact upon the likely involvement of young people from all social class backgrounds in sport and physical activity beyond school and into adult life? Before we examine these issues we want to say a few words about recent economic changes and their consequences for social class and class-based inequalities in Britain.

ECONOMIC CHANGE, SOCIAL CLASS AND INEQUALITIES

If social class depends upon the ways in which people earn their livings – that is to say, on their occupations – then 'changes in employment are bound to change the class structure' (Roberts, 2001: 80); and, indeed, they have. New technologies and wider processes of globalisation have, as Roberts (2001: 79) observes, 'ushered in new, post-Fordist economic times' characterised by 'greater flexibility (of labour markets, jobs and workers); more precarious, non-standard employment (temporary, part-time and self-employment); higher unemployment; pressure on those in jobs to do more; and wider income inequalities'. These changes in the social class structure of Britain have led to renewed attempts to design up-to-date social classifications (see Roberts, 2001). For present purposes, however, we need only offer a few summary comments on the significance of such changes for our understanding of social class in relation to life in the UK in general and education and physical education in particular.

Recently, Collins (2003) has recounted Beck's (1992) argument that in the (supposedly) postmodern, individualised societies typical of the West, 'the concept of class is terminally crumbling' inevitably to be 'replaced by individual values and behaviours centred around consumption' (2003: 69). Writers such as Beck (1992), Giddens (1991), Lash and Urry (1994), among others, have suggested that 'as the era of mass consumption disappears' lifestyles become not only 'more and more diverse' (Tomlinson, 2003: 98) but also more and more significant than the old social markers of class, ethnicity and gender. For most sociologists, however, it is axiomatic that the much-heralded claims of an end to class – in the sense of a disappearance of class distinctions of any note – are simply not supported by the evidence. Most would agree with Armour's (2000: 71; citing Travers, 1999) observation that 'postmodernist suggestions that social class is no longer a relevant concept are "at odds with our everyday experience" '. Roberts (1999) points out that while some areas of social experience – leisure, for example – are, indeed, more *individualised*, money remains at the root of many obvious differences: in health and education, for example. In relation to leisure, in particular, economic inequalities 'rather than alternative ways of life' continue to lie at the heart of 'the main differences between uses of leisure in different strata' (Roberts, 1999: 87). In short, 'the kind of individualism that has spread in these post-Fordist times' continues to be of 'a structured variety' (Roberts, 2003: 23) – structured, among other things, by social class. Despite the overall 'upgrading' of the UK workforce, and the growth in absolute terms of the middle class, 'many young people remain very close to where they started out in life' in social class terms. To the extent that they do so, their biographies become individualised in a relatively 'passive' manner as they 'make the best of available opportunities' (2003: 24).

It is true that, by degrees, old class formations may have been undermined by social and economic changes in recent decades, and the working class has become more fragmented or disorganised. Nevertheless, not only do class inequalities 'remain very much alive' they are, in fact, wider than ever when 'judged by income differentials' (Roberts, 2001: 80). While Britain is undoubtedly 'a far more prosperous country now than in the 1960s, nevertheless 'a substantial section of the working class has not shared the benefits' (Roberts, 2001: 108). Even though they are no longer as strong as they have been in the past, class differences remain huge: 'The most wealthy one per cent of the population holds approximately a sixth, and the bottom 50 per cent holds hardly any of all personally-held wealth' (Roberts, 2001: 1). All in all, there has been a clear polarisation of income levels in Britain since 1980 as 'the less advantaged sections of the population have become even more disadvantaged' (Roberts, 1995: 2). Poverty, according to Collins (2003: 68), is at the 'core of (social) exclusion' with 23 per cent of British people potentially classified as 'in poverty' in 2001. In relation to young people, one million chidren are said to be in a state of poverty currently in Britain with nearly 10 per cent of children experiencing 'severe and persistent poverty lasting five years or more' (Carvel, 2003: 10).

Social class is evidently 'related to people's wealth, health and education' (Roberts, 2001: 6) and, for that matter, many other aspects of their lives. The effects of class range from the ages at which people marry, how they vote and church attendance through to risks of criminal conviction (Roberts, 2001). To this list, we might add playing sport and experiences of physical education. The poorest million children are more likely, among other things, 'to miss meals or be unable to join in play activities' (Carvel, 2003: 10) while children in severe poverty appear 'five times as likely as other children to be excluded from simple social activities like having a friend around for tea . . . or even having a hobby' (2003: 10).

Before exploring the significance of social class for leisure, sport and physical education in greater detail, we want to say something about social class as a concept.

DEFINING SOCIAL CLASS

In academic as well as popular thinking, attempts to define social class tend to have an economic base. In other words, 'all concepts of class group together people with similar ways of making their livings, that is, in similar occupations' (Roberts, 2001: 21). Sugden and Tomlinson (2002: 312) observe that 'few would disagree' with the broad notion of social class as an 'economically grounded concept'. 'In the most general of senses', they suggest, 'class is the social and cultural expression of an economic relationship' (2002: 312). They add that classes 'are made up of people who are similarly placed in terms of the contribution they make to economic production, the command over resources this gives them and the lifestyles which this helps to generate'. In short, the concept of class revolves around work and market situations as well as life-chances (Roberts, 2001). Hence the tendency to refer to socio-economic status as a synonym for social class. Social classes are essentially socio-economic groupings based upon occupation, labour market experiences, education and housing (Roberts and Brodie, 1992).

Notwithstanding the centrality of economic position to class, it is important to bear in mind that people are said to have at their disposal social, cultural and physical, as well as economic, resources (Collins with Kay, 2003; Field, 2003; McDonald, 2003; Roberts, 2001; Shilling, 1998). There are, in other words, social, cultural and physical dimensions to class.

The social and cultural dimensions of class

The social dimension of class (often referred to as social 'capital') is conceptualised as 'the intangible resources of community, shared values and trust upon which we draw in daily life' (Field, 2003: i) and, thus, 'consists of social relationships' in which one can invest: 'by building up a circle of friends' and colleagues, for example (Roberts, 2001: 218). People can draw upon their social capital when they need to do so and this is especially useful in sporting and leisure contexts. The cultural dimension of class (or cultural capital), on the other hand, 'consists of the skills, knowledge, beliefs and values that we acquire in our particular social milieux' (Roberts, 2001: 218) and serves as a kind of 'coinage' of 'cultural currency' (Field, 2003: 14). Kew (1997: 150) describes cultural capital as 'a product of specific class-based lifestyles' and summarises Bourdieu's (1984) view that 'early socialisation experiences and conditionings, and the social networks within which these are gained, have a crucial effect upon an individual's outlook, attitudes and values, disposition, tastes and preferences' (1997: 150) in a whole range of cultural practices including sport and physical activity.

Cultural capital is 'built up gradually' and, in the same way that economic resources can be passed-down the generations, so too, it is said, can social and cultural resources (Field, 2003; Roberts, 2001). 'At all subsequent life stages, and in all spheres of life' Roberts observes, 'the cultural capital that individuals bring to their situations affects their opportunities'. While it is something that we all possess, however, 'the crucial differences are not so much in the amounts, but the types, and how valuable they prove to be' (2001: 218) – in educational and sporting terms, in the case of physical education.

Notions of cultural and social dimensions to class help us, then, to appreciate that while economic resources lie at the heart of social class, social and cultural relations and resources help 'create and reproduce inequality' (Field, 2003: 14): money is not the sole reason for the less well-off having 'a narrower range of tastes and activities' (Roberts, 2001: 86) – in sporting terms in particular. Middle- and upper-class people typically possess wider ranging social networks as well as cultural interests in addition to greater disposable income. For this reason, it is unsurprising to find that the middle- and upper-classes' breadth of interests owes a good deal to their education as well as their wide-ranging social networks. Hence, the aphorism, 'People who work together also play together' (Roberts, 2001: 82). Indeed, Collins (2003: 69) argues that taking part in sport *requires* social capital: it 'requires confidence, skills, knowledge, ability ... [and] a group of supportive friends and companions, including some who share the same desire to take part'. Collins' employment of the term social capital covers both social *and* cultural resources for, as previously indicated, while the social dimension of class is usually taken to indicate relationships with others that can prove beneficial in one way or another, the cultural dimension represents the skills, knowledge, and so forth that give one, as it were, a head start in particular social contexts: put more succinctly, *who* you know as well as *what* you know. In this vein, Kew (1997) suggests that some sports – he probably had in mind such things as polo and sailing and, to a lesser extent, fencing, golf, skiing and sub-aqua – remain more or less socially exclusive whether or not they continue to be cost exclusive. Wilson (2002: 5) observes that findings from the General Social Survey in the USA suggest that 'those who are richest in cultural capital and those who are richest in economic capital are most likely to be involved in sports generally' and that 'these tendencies are independent of one another'. Interestingly, he adds that whereas economic capital has no bearing on involvement in what he refers to as 'prole' or working-class sports, 'those richest in cultural capital are least likely to be involved' in such sports.

The physical dimensions of class

The bodily or physical manifestations of social class position are often referred to as physical capital (McDonald, 2003; Shilling, 1998). It is probably more adequate, however, to view physical capital as an aspect of cultural capital; that is to say, a dimension of *what* people know – in terms of their physical skills and abilities as well, one might add, as their physical condition and health.

According to McDonald (2003: 171), the body is pivotal 'in understanding the relationship between, class, sport and PE'. In other words, 'How we manage our bodies in terms of diet and exercise, how we carry our bodies in terms of posture and deportment, how we present our bodies in terms of clothing, and how we use our bodies in social and physical activities, carry significant social and class meanings' (McDonald, 2003: 170). In effect, people's physical skills, experiences and even condition shape their predispositions towards new or familiar activities and give rise to their tastes in, among other things, sporting activities: 'distinctive practices are not arbitrary or accidental' (McDonald, 2003: 170) but arise out of their 'class-based' physical capacities and related dispositions.

For Shilling (1998), Kirk (2004) and Evans (2004) the physical dimensions of behaviour betray 'an individual's class dependent social location and orientation to the world' (Kirk, 2004: 52). The ways in which young boys and girls from different social classes hold particular views of what sports and physical activities it is 'cool' to be involved in (Sport England, 2003a) – that is to say, socially appropriate or normative – as well as how they want their bodies to look are, on this view, an expression of the cultural dimensions of social class and are reinforced by the activities of physical education and the expectations of physical education teachers. Similarly, particular 'sets of body techniques' (Shilling, 1998: 247) or 'skills' in particular sports will tend to bestow particular and differing amounts of social kudos and, thus, possess differential value in terms of cultural resources or capital. The point here is that particular social class locations make it more or less likely that involvement in differing kinds of sport and physical activity (such as skiing or weight-lifting, rugby union or rugby league) will lead to young people acquiring particular forms of physical capital – physical skills, abilities and attributes that have symbolic value and can prove to be valuable social, cultural and even economic resources. In this regard, it is argued that young people's bodies have been, and continue to be, socially constructed in the sense that the (historically and socially specific) programmes of sports and/or physical activities (from military drill through team games to 'body management' activities such as aerobics and health-related fitness) that they experience at their various class-based (Kirk, 1992, 1998) or class-differentiated (Gorard et al., 2003) schools has led to young people developing particular skills and particular views of their bodies which serve to reinforce social class positions and orientations. The point is that social class does not just impact upon 'choice and preferences' (Evans, 2004: 102) in sport and physical activity, it also has a substantial impact upon individuals' physical capabilities (Evans, 2004): in other words, their skills and abilities.

The physical dimension of social class also incorporates physical condition and health. As long as 'socio-economic status remains positively related to health' (Roberts and Brodie, 1992: 117), physical capital will have implications for health generally and health-related exercise in particular. 'Poorer households in poorer communities', for example, 'are less likely to have access to healthy, affordable food and suitable recreational facilities' (Royal College of Physicians et al., 2004: 21). Middle-class children have healthier diets and become generally stronger and healthier than working-class youngsters. In terms of health-related exercise, it is apparent that physical activity is associated with social class and, in particular, income and educational attainment: in all age groups, 'people of higher socio-economic status take part in more physical activity' (Wanless, 2004: 99). Low educational attainment is particularly associated with higher levels of inactivity (Wanless, 2004) and, as if to compound their more sedentary lifestyles, the children of working-class families tend to lack safe places to play or exercise (Royal College of Physicians et al., 2004). One of the major contemporary public health concerns in the western world, namely the rise in overweight and obesity (Wanless, 2004), is a condition 'exacerbated by low socio-economic status' (Royal College of Physicians et al., 2004: 21); not least because, as Hutton (2004) observes, obesity is closely linked not so much to current status but rather the social class into which individuals are born. 'The real drama' in levels of obesity and, for that matter, smoking, he adds (Hutton, 2004: 30), 'is the rise among unskilled, semi-skilled and skilled manual women'. All in all, in terms of the relationship between class and physical capital, it is clear that some groups have more scope for choice, in health-related matters, than others (Roberts and Brodie, 1992) with the upshot that economic deprivation is strongly correlated with relatively poor physical condition and overall health (Roberts and Brodie, 1992; Townsend et al., 1988). Although active involvement in sport and physical activity can make a difference to individual's health it 'will not eradicate or necessarily even lessen' the inequalities associated with social class (Roberts and Brodie, 1992: 119).

From this consideration of the economic, social, cultural and physical dimensions of social class we turn now to the relationship between social class and education.

SOCIAL CLASS AND EDUCATION

The relationship between social class and education is firmly and incontrovertibly established. As Roberts (2003: 15) observes, those researching young people's lives rarely have difficulty in 'identifying a bottom group that is set apart by its frequent truancy, seriously disturbed family and housing histories, chronic unemployment, early parenthood and/or repeat offending'. At the beginnning of the twenty-first century there remains 'a strong statistical relationship between educational qualifications and social class' (Kew, 1997: 147). In this regard, it is worthy of note that 'the general upgrading of the occupational and social class structures since the 1970s has been accompanied by a general rise in children's and young people's educational attainments' (Roberts, 2001: 107). In general, young people from higher socio-economic classes 'tend to have "better" education-al life chances in terms of examination results and full-time further education' (Meighan with Siraj-Blatchford, 2003: 346). This, as we shall see later, is significant in terms of the development of an attachment to sport and physical activity among young people. In addition, middle- and working-class children, it is claimed, have differing experiences of school – for example, in terms of academic success, development of self-esteem and social and cultural capital – which place them at greater or lesser advantage in leisure terms, generally, and in sporting terms, in particular.

Viewed over time, there is little doubt that educational reform has 'widened the opportunities of working-class children and boosted their educational attainments' (Roberts, 2001: 215). Nonetheless, Gorard at al. (2003) observe that whether one refers to such a process as 'polarisation' or 'stratification' it is evident that the more disadvantaged sections of society, the children of the lower socio-economic groups, are becoming concentrated in particular schools: often referred to as 'sink' or 'ghetto' schools. The apparent 'growth in social stratification between schools' (Gorard et al., 2003: 16) seems an inevitable, if unintended, consequence of increased market forces in the education system in the UK since the 1988 Education Reform Act. Whether as a result of market forces or residential segregation and associated 'catchment area' patterns, it seems that English schools, in particular, 'are more socially differentiated than any others in Europe' (Gorard et al., 2003: 19).

A variety of leisure and sporting benefits of being middle-class are associated with education. Levels of educational experience and attainment appear to be 'the most important component of social class for influencing participation/non-participation' (Kew, 1997: 147). In effect, 'education is more important than labour market experience in accounting for overall class variance' (Roberts, 1995: 2). In this regard, Furlong et al. (1990: 222) found that 'young people who were in education tended to have the most active and varied leisure experiences' while Collins and Kay (2003: 248) point to research across Europe demon-strating social class gradients in sports participation and associated evidence that 'people with a higher level of final education were less likely to drop out of sport, having been more likely to take it up in the first place'. In short, the longer a young person stays in full-time education the higher their rate of participation in sport and physical activity is likely to be (Coalter, 1996; Coalter et al., 1995; Roberts, 1995, 1996a, 1996b) and the more likely he or she is to become 'locked in' to sport on a regular basis in their adult lives (Roberts and Brodie, 1992). More specifically, education appears, as Coalter et al. (1995: 70) observe, 'to be the most important component of social class because those who remain in full-time education after the statutory leaving age are more likely to have the free time and more likely to be provided with opportunities for free participation in a wide range of sports'. In this respect, Collins (2003: 71) highlights 'the combined advantage enjoyed by full-time students who have access to facilities and clubs which are often subsidised and who come disproportionately from social groups ABC1'.

SOCIAL CLASS AND LEISURE

While something of a 'leisure democracy' can be said to exist nowadays, 'in the sense that members of all social strata do similar things in their leisure', this, it is important to note, is not the same as leisure equality (Roberts, 1999). Economic capital (in the form of disposable income) continues to lie at the root of the main differences between social class groupings' uses of leisure: differences that 'are basically and blatantly inequalities rather than alternative ways of life' (Roberts, 1999: 87). In this regard, Roberts observes that 'It is more accurate to speak of leisure as class-related than class-based'; that is to say, 'It has become more difficult than in the past to identify qualitatively distinct leisure patterns that are typical of entire social classes or even specific occupations. The main differences are now *quantitative* and are maintained primarily through financial inequalities' (Roberts, 1999: 85; emphasis added). 'The higher strata are not distinguished by their exclusive tastes so much as by their sheer variety': the less well-off simply have 'a narrower range of tastes and activities' (1999: 86). It is, then, the 'omnivorousness' of the middle-classes rather than any specific tastes that sets them apart from the working class contemporarily: nowadays the middle classes 'do more of most things, except watch television' (Roberts, 2001: 157).

It is in this sense that class-based inequalities can be said to remain in the leisure sphere: 'The better off are able to do more of everything that costs money, and there is much more variety in their leisure' (Roberts, 1999: 85). Managers and professionals, for example, 'spend four times as much on leisure goods and services' (Roberts, 2001: 7) and are twice as likely to engage in such leisure activities as going to the cinema, visiting wine bars and taking holidays away from home: 'Moving from the base to the top of the socio-economic hierarchy, levels of leisure participation become progressively higher. The better paid groups take part in more activities, participate in them the most frequently and/or spend the most money on each occasion' (Roberts, 1999: 85). This applies in all the main types of leisure activity, including sport and physical activity, that normally cost money for, 'the long arm of the job exerts some of its most powerful leisure effects via pay'. It is salutory to remind ourselves, at this point, that 'roughly a third of all households are car-less and take no holidays away from the home' (Roberts, 2001: 108).

All in all, economically better-off groups not only have wider leisure opportunities, they tend to do more in leisure terms – and we might say the same thing of sport.

SOCIAL CLASS AND SPORT

In any discussion of the impact of particular social dynamics, such as class, on sports participation it is important to appreciate that there has been a clear trend towards increased participation in sport and physical activity among young people and adults in Western Europe since the 1980s (De Knop et al., 1996) and that the increase has been especially noticeable among young people. In Norway, for example, 'sport is a popular activity among youths' (Sisjord and Skirstad, 1996: 180), while in Sweden, Kristen et al. (2003: 25) report the 'dominance' of sport in the lives of both young people and adults, with the 'sports movement' being the country's 'largest and most vigorous popular movement'. Indeed, in Scandinavian countries, generally, levels of participation among both young people and adults are said to be relatively high (DCMS/Strategy Unit, 2002), with participation in Finland especially so (DCMS/Strategy Unit, 2002; National Public Health Institute, 2001). In Flanders and the Netherlands, 'young people participate in large numbers' (De Knop and De Martelaer, 2001: 41) with 'more and more teenage boys and girls in Flanders' becoming 'involved in leisure-time sports participation' (Scheerder et al., forthcoming). Breedveld (2003) notes that even though membership in sports clubs and associated involvement in competitive and team sports declined in the 1990s in Belgium, general participation in sport and physical activity overall has increased. In Spain (Gonzalez-Diaz, 2003), participation is said to have increased and broadened while in Portugal, 'increasing numbers of young people have taken part in sport since the mid-1970s' (Goncalves, 1996: 202). It seems, then, that the vast majority of young people *are* taking part in sport and physical activity reasonably regularly both in and out of school across western Europe, and particularly so in the northern western European countries.

Adult participation in sport

Despite the evident widespread growth in participation in sport and physical activity, there is, as Evans (2004: 102) observes, 'compelling evidence' of 'the salience of social class in structuring sport, if not determining a person's choice, preferences and opportunities in sport in the UK and elsewhere'. Various sociological studies of sport (see, for example, Coakley, 2001; Collins, 2003; Kew, 1997; Scheerder et al., forthcoming) demonstrate that 'active sports involvement is correlated with social class characteristics' (Scheerder et al., forthcoming: 1) and, as a consequence, the higher the social class, the greater the rate of participation and overall involvement in sport and physical activity among adults (Coakley, 2001; Donnelly, 1996; DCMS/Strategy Unit, 2002; Sports Council for Wales (SCW), 2002; Wilson, 2002). In short, a large body of research demonstrates that social class continues to be 'a key discriminator of participation' (SCW, 2002: 4) in sport and physical activity.

In the UK, the SCW (2002: 11) report observed that on all the major measures of participation, 'there is a clear relationship between likelihood to participate and social class'.

'This', they added, 'is consistent with the supposition that social deprivation has a strong impact on participation' in sport and physical activity. In England, while participation rates for male and female unskilled manual workers are 34 per cent and 19 per cent respectively, at the other end of the socio-economic scale the figures are 61 per cent and 67 per cent for male and female professional workers (Department for Culture, Media and Sport (DCMS)/Strategy Unit, 2002). In Wales, the SCW (2002) reports socio-economic groups A and B to be more than twice as likely to participate than group E in outdoor and indoor games and activities. Evidently, people from economically disadvantaged groups are the least likely to be in sport to begin with and are more likely to reduce participation. Indeed, lower-class groups play fewer sports and thus their sports careers are 'slightly more vulnerable' to drop-out (Roberts and Brodie, 1992: 58).

It is not only *rates* of participation but also *forms* of participation and *numbers* of sports participated in that social class impacts on. Scheerder et al. (forthcoming) observe that in Belgium – as with the rest of Europe – sports and physical actvities such as golf, fencing, sailing, skiing, squash and tennis are more common among the middle- and upper-classes while boxing, angling, weight-lifting and karate, for example, are more popular among lower socio-economic groupings. In terms of numbers of sports, Roberts and Brodie (1992) point out that working-class men and women tend to be involved in fewer sports and physical activities. At the same time, it is not only *what* people do (in terms of specific sports and activities) and *how much* they do it but, also, *where* they play sport is influenced by social class – with the middle-and upper-classes more likely to play sport in voluntary or commercial sporting and physical activity venues while the lower or working classes are more likely to inhabit local authority-run centres.

Young people and participation in sport in and out of school

The British government's recent strategy document *Game Plan* (DCMS/Strategy Unit, 2002: 13) observes that 'young white males are most likely to take part in sport and physical activity'. To age, ethnicity and gender we need to add, social class, and specifically *middle*-class. Having said this, in the SCW's recent study of young people of secondary school age (11–16 years), using free school meals as a proxy measure led them to conclude that socio-economic status 'had only a minimal impact upon the likelihood and level of sports participation' (SCW, 2003a: 4) among school-age youngsters in Wales in 2001. This, they suggested, was the case with curricular and extra-curricular physical education and whether rates of participation were either occasional (at least once) or regular (more than ten times over the year) (SCW, 2003b). By contrast, in their 2002 study, Sport England (2003b: 104) found that 'pupils living in the top 20 per cent of deprived areas in England [were] less likely to have taken part in extra-curricular sport[1] (37 per cent versus 44 per cent of young people who did not live in the top 20 deprived areas)'. Similarly, another recent SCW study found that, in terms of young people's involvement in sport and physical activity in their leisure time (in the form of either extra-curricular physical education and/or spare time sports clubs), the mean number of activities undertaken, by those who did participate, was marginally lower for those receiving free school meals and thus, by extension, working-class (SCW, 2001). With this in mind, it is worth reminding ourselves of Roberts and Brodie's (1992) observation that while social class impacts on the likely involvement of young people in sport and physical activity in the first place, its impact upon committed participants is minimal and largely restricted to kinds and amounts of involvement. In this respect, as with leisure participation, the main class differences among sports participants lies not so much in whether they do sport or not but, rather, in the particular sports they do and the general 'styles' of participation including who individuals choose to play with, the clubs they belong to and the centres they use (Roberts and Brodie, 1992).

The sporting benefits of being young and middle class

Middle-class parents often go to great lengths to ensure that that their off-spring enjoy a breadth of abilities and advantages: the middle-classes 'invest heavily in the cultivation of the physical capital of their off-spring from a very early age' (Evans, 2004: 101). In doing so, they not only 'inculcat(e) "the right" attitudes, values, motivations, predispositions, representations but also the right physical capital in terms of skills, techniques and understanding' (Evans, 2004: 101). And the sporting benefits of being middle class are not simply related to the 'here and now' of participation. As implied by the notions of social and cultural dimensions of class, the benefits tend to be enduring, particularly in terms of ongoing participation in sport and physical activity throughout the life-course – an issue that is demonstrably important to PE teachers (Green, 2003). Middle-class parents, Roberts and Brodie (1992) suggest, are not only more likely to possess the material resources, or economic capital, to enable their off-spring to engage in sport; they are also more likely to be in a position to pass on their social and cultural capital by virtue of being already actively involved themselves and inclined to pass their 'love of sport' on. Hence, young people on middle-class life courses are the most likely to be introduced to a wider range of sports and are the most likely to continue to participate at times in their lives when their participation is most vulnerable to disruption.

It is apparent, then, that although income and wealth are likely to be the most important mediating variables in some of the sporting things that class predicts – such as skiing, ocean yachting and even golf – class is also related to people's predispositions and the importance they attach to sport and physical activity *per se* as young people and adults. Thus, being a more prominent feature of middle-class leisure lifestyles sport is, as a consequence, more likely to be a feature of the abilities, experiences and predispositions of middle-class young people. While young people as a whole are experiencing a broader diet of sporting activities in physical education than previous generations they, nevertheless, continue to be introduced to various sports and physical activities according to their social class, sex and ethnicity.

SOCIAL CLASS, GENDER AND ETHNICITY

There are two overall points to be made regarding the relationship between class, gender and ethnicity. First, although social class is important this is not necessarily at the expense of other social dynamics, such as gender and ethnicity. Second, there are interactive effects: class-related inequalities are frequently 'compounded by other social characteristics' (Evans, 2004: 102) and, in particular, gender and ethnicity. These interactive effects can be seen, for example, in the case of black males' prominence in football, boxing and track athletics. Thus, the main significance of social class appears to be the way in which – in conjunction with other key dynamics – it adds to the likelihood of variation in participation, and more so in some sports than others: for example, swimming, golf, keep-fit and cycling (Coalter, 1996). In short, young people's sporting and leisure involvement continues to be subject to the social dynamics of social class, gender and ethnicity, both in isolation and in configuration: 'The scale of class variation differs substantially between age and sex groups, and between different kinds of sport activity' (Roberts, 1995: 3).

Despite this, Roberts (1999) notes how, over the course of the last decade or so, we have witnessed a *blurring* of class, gender and, to some extent, ethnic differences in the kinds of sports and physical activities participated in, as well as variety within all social groups. Although sports participation continues to be related to age, sex and social class (Farrell and Shields, 2002), 'it is no longer true that all or nearly all participants are young, male and middle-class' (Roberts, 1996a: 54). While young people (especially young males) on middle-class life trajectories continue to have higher levels of sports participation than working-class youngsters, the main social class differences are no longer in whether young people play any sport, but how much, how many and how often.

SOCIAL CLASS AND PHYSICAL EDUCATION

What, then, are the implications of an understanding of the relationships between social class, education, leisure and sport for physical education? They are, we suggest, several fold. First, in terms of education, middle-class youngsters are more likely to display the characteristics of 'ideal pupils' and, in being compliant in the education process (Meighan with Siraj-Blatchford, 2003), are more likely to acquiesce in the process of physical education. Added to this, sport, like valuing academic success, is a more prominent feature of middle-class lifestyles and, consequently, is more likely to be a cultural resource that middle-class young people bring to school and to physical education lessons in particular. They are more likely to have the skills, abilities and experiences that will make them more, rather than less, likely to be involved with and successful in the sports and physical activities characteristic of school physical education. In this respect, young people on middle-class life courses are the most likely to be introduced to a wider range of sports and physical activities by their parents, including those from the range of activity areas (such as swimming, dance, outdoor and adventurous activities) that they are obliged to engage with in National Curriculum Physical Education lessons. In particular, middle-class youngsters are more likely to be comfortable with the typical activities that constitute 'traditional' curricular and extra-curricular team-based games. This is, of course, particularly true for middle-class, white, boys. In this manner, secondary school physical education will probably serve to 'identify and endorse' (Evans, 2004: 99) the sporting and physical abilities that the parents of middle-class youngsters have invested in differentially. Young people with the experiences, abilities and tastes acquired 'by virtue of' their social class 'may be more or less "able" and willing' (Evans, 2004: 101) to take part in various sports and physical activities: male physical education teachers in deprived neighbourhoods, for example, can frequently be heard to bemoan the fact that 'all they (the lads) want to do is play football' (Green, 2003).

CONCLUSION

Notwithstanding the economic and social changes in recent decades, and associated claims that we are witnessing the birth of a postmodern society in the western world, class cultures and divisions are evidently surviving the surrounding economic and political changes (Roberts, 2001): social class persists as a form of inequality. Nevertheless, as with leisure, involvement in sport and physical activity is more adequately described as class-related rather than class-based in the sense that there has been a democratisation of sporting involvement. This is not the same, however, as equality: the middle-classes not only do a wider variety, they also do more of most sporting and physical activities. This inevitably gives the sons (especially) and daughters of the middle-classes a head start in curricular and extra-curricular physical education and further reinforces the already not inconsiderable social and cultural benefits of being middle class.

We opened this chapter by noting that while social class has proved to be related to virtually all areas of life there are exceptions within leisure and sport. This led us to ask the rhetorical question of whether it might, then, be possible, via physical education, to weaken the link across the whole of sport. At first sight, the evidence looks promising; not least because, as we have indicated, among compulsory school-age children the relationship between class and sport participation is rather weak (perhaps unsurpringly since they are all constrained to do school sport). Yet, despite this, there is no escaping the realisation that the class–sport relationship strengthens later on, for a number of reasons. First, the differential stay-on rates in education: 'middle-class children have benefitted academically much more than working class counterparts from the expansion of school and university over the past 20 years' (Evans, 2004: 102). Second, middle-class social and cultural capital gives middle-class youth greater 'staying power'; in effect, they are more likely to develop the kind of wide sporting repertoires (Roberts and Brodie, 1992) that appear to 'lock' people into sport and physical activity throughout the course of their adult lives. Although the relationship between class and sports participation can appear weak while youngsters are at school, it tends, nevertheless, to be reinforced by the process of physical education. Third, middle-class youth tend to possess broader experiences of sport and physical activity and tend also to be 'better' at sport (judged by the origins of elite sports players): they have greater physical capital. Finally, in monetary terms, it remains the case that 'economic inequalities lead inexorably to inequalities in leisure' (Roberts, 2001: 171) and the middle-classes, young and old, can afford more money to do the sports and physical activities (such as attend health and fitness gyms and join sports clubs) that cost money.

So, *can* secondary school physical education hope to make any difference in the long run? Put another way, can PE do anything to supplement, even extend, the physical and cultural resources of working-class youngsters in a manner that might increase the likelihood of their continued involvement in sport and physical activity beyond school and into adult life? Perhaps, indirectly, over time, it might – by increasing the volume of upward mobility from the working-class – however, upward mobility is fundamentally contingent upon changes in the class structure. Either way, the middle classes have a tendency to take 'at least equal advantage' of educational opportunities (Roberts, 2001: 215). More directly, it may be that exposure to the six activity areas that constitute National Curriculum Physical Education enables young people from working-class backgrounds to acquire the broader repertoire of skills and interests that characterise young middle-class males in particular. In doing so, it may be that physical education can build upon interest in sport and physical activity apparent in the leisure lives of all young people (Sport England, 2003a). Young people's leisure activities are said to be 'identity conferring' (Roberts, 2003: 15). So, while young people of school age consider 'sport to be cool' (Sport England, 2003a) and a prominent aspect of their leisure lives (Sport England, 2003b), an opportunity clearly exists. In this regard, one might hold out hope for the impact of the recently emerged and rapidly increasing number of secondary schools identified as Specialist Sports Colleges on the future sporting involvement of young people (Penney et al., 2003). However, to the extent that they show a tendency to group and stratify pupils in physical education lessons in terms of 'gifted and talented' and 'low attainers' (Evans, 2004), class-based sporting advantages and disadvantages will be exacerbated rather than nullified or even undermined by physical education lessons in these schools.

So, can secondary school physical education make a difference? The answer, in short, is not unexpected: it may do but it probably will not; that is to say, it is extremely difficult for schools, let alone particular subjects such as physical education, to countervail against wider social processes, of which social class continues to be a more, rather than less, prominent feature. This is likely to be particularly so if, as appears to be the case, we are witnessing a growing social stratification within the state school system in the UK, with working-class children becoming concentrated in 'sink' or 'ghetto' schools (Gorard et al., 2003).

All told, while the immediate cause of differences in physical education and, for that matter, sport and physical activity generally, may be physical, cultural or social the underlying sources of all such class-based inequalities continue to lie in the economic domain.

NOTES

1   The Sport England surveys of young people between 1994 and 2002 refer to 'out of lessons' sport and physical activities, a category which includes participation during extra-curricular physical education (Sport England, 2003b). Extra-curricular physical education is defined, along with Penney and Harris (1997: 42), as 'the provision of activities outside of the formal PE curriculum, most often after school and at lunch times, but also in some schools, at weekend and/or before school (by PE teachers)'.

REFERENCES

Armour, K. (2000) ' "We're all middle class now": sport and social class in contemporary Britain', in R. L. Jones and K. M. Armour (eds), *Sociology of Sport. Theory and Practice*. Harlow: Pearson Education. pp. 68–82.

Bourdieu, P. (1984) *Distinction. A Social Critique of the Judgement of Taste*. London: Routledge.

Beck, U. (1992) *Risk Society: Towards a New Modernity*. London: Sage.

Breedveld, K. (2003) 'Sport and social capital. Good hopes and high fears', in I. Hartmann-Tews, B. Rulofs and S.A. Luetkens (eds), *Sport and Social Order: Challenges for Theory and Practice. Proceedings of the 2nd World Congress of Sociology of Sport, 2002*. p. 26.

Carvel, J. (2003) 'Drive against child poverty "fails to help the poorest" ', *The Guardian*, 2 September 2003, p. 10.

Coakley, J. (2001) *Sport in Society: Issues and Controversies*, 7th edn. Boston: McGraw-Hill.

Coalter, F. (1996) *Trends in Sports Participation*. Position Paper prepared for the Sports Council. Institute for Leisure and Amenity Management annual conference, Birmingham, 1996.

Coalter, F., Dowers, S. and Baxter, M. (1995) 'The impact of social class and education on sports participation: some evidence from the General Household Survey', in Ken Roberts (ed.), *Leisure and Social Stratification*, 1995. Eastbourne, LSA Publications, no. 53.

Collins, M. (2003) 'Social exclusion from sport and leisure', in B. Houlihan (ed.), *Sport and Society. A Student Introduction*. London: Sage Publications. pp. 67–88.

Collins, M.F. with Kay, T. (2003) *Sport and Social Exclusion*. London: Routledge.

De Knop, P. and De Martelaer, K. (2001) 'Quantitative and qualitative evaluation of youth sport in Flanders and the Netherlands: a case study', *Sport, Education and Society*, 6 (1): 35–51.

De Knop, P., Skirstad, B., Engstrom, L.-M., Theebom, M. and Wittock, H. (1996) 'Sport in a changing society', in P. De Knop, L.-M. Engstrom, B. Skirstad and M.R. Weiss (eds), (1996) *Worldwide Trends in Youth Sport*. Champaign: Human Kinetics. pp. 8–14.

Department for Culture, Media and Sport (DCMS)/Strategy Unit (2002) *Game Plan: A Strategy for Delivering Government's Sport and Physical Activity Objectives*. London: DCMS/Strategy Unit.

Donnelly, P. (1996) 'Approaches to social inequality in the sociology of sport', *QUEST*, 48: 221–42.

Evans, J. (2004) 'Making a difference: education and "ability" in physical education', *European Physical Education Review*, 10 (1): 95–108.

Farrell, L. and Shields, M.A. (2002) 'Investigating the economic and demographic determinants of sporting participation in England', *Journal of the Royal Statistical Society*, 165: 335–48.

Field, J. (2003) *Social Capital*. London: Routledge.

Furlong, A., Campbell, R. and Roberts, K. (1990) 'The effects of post-16 experiences and social class on the leisure patterns of young adults', *Leisure Studies*, 9: 213–24.

Giddens, A. (1991) *Modernity and Self-Identity: Self and Society in the Late Modern Age*. Cambridge: Polity Press.

Goncalves, C. (1996) 'Portugal', in P. De Knop, L.-M. Engstrom, B. Skirstad and M.R. Weiss (eds), *Worldwide Trends in Youth Sport*. Champaign: Human Kinetics. pp. 193–203.

Gonzalez-Dias, A. (2003) (personal communication).

Gorard, S., Taylor, C. and Fitz, J. (2003) *Schools, Markets and Choice Policies*. London: RoutledgeFalmer.

Green, K. (2003) *Physical Education Teachers on Physical Education. A Sociological Study of Philosophies and Ideologies*. Chester: Chester Academic Press.

Hutton, W. (2004) 'The fat of the land', *The Observer*, 15 February 2004.

Kew, F. (1997) *Sport. Social Problems and Issues*. Oxford: Butterworth-Heinemann.

Kirk, D. (1992) *Defining Physical Education: The Social Construction of a School Subject in Postwar Britain*. London: Falmer Press.

Kirk, D. (1998) *Schooling Bodies: School Practice and Public Discourse, 1880–1950*. London: Leicester University Press.

Kirk, D. (2004) 'Towards a critical history of the body, identity and health. Corporeal power and school practice', in J. Evans, B. Davies and J. Wright (eds), *Body Knowledge and Control. Studies in the Sociology of Physical Educatoion and Health*. London: Routledge. pp. 52–67.

Kristen, L., Patriksson, G. and Fridlund, B. (2003) 'Parents' conceptions of the influences of participation in a sports programme on their children and adolescents with a disability', *European Physical Education Review*, 9 (1): 23–41.

Lash, S. and Urry, J. (1994) *Economies of Signs and Space*. London: Sage.

McDonald, I. (2003) 'Class, inequality and the body in physical education', in S. Hayes and G. Stidder (eds), *Equity and Inclusion in Physical Education and Sport*. London, Routledge. pp. 169–83.

Meighan, R. with Suiraj-Blatchford, I. (2003) *A Sociology of Educating*. (4th edn). London: Continuum.

National Public Health Institute (2001) *Health Behaviour and Health Amongst the Finnish Adult Population*.

Penney, D. and Harris, J. (1997) 'Extra-curricular physical education: more of the same for the more able?', *Sport, Education and Society*, 2 (1): 41–54.

Penney, D., Houlihan, B. and Eley, D. (2003) *Specialist Sports Colleges National Monitoring and Evaluation Research Project: First National Survey Report*. Loughborough: Institute of Youth Sport.

Roberts, K. (1995) 'School children and sport', in L. Lawrence, E. Murdoch and S. Parker (eds), *Professional and Development Issues in Leisure, Sport and Education*, Publication No. 56. Brighton: Leisure Studies Association. pp. 337–48.

Roberts, K. (1996a) 'Young people, schools, sport and government policy', *Sport, Education and Society*, 1 (1): 47–57.

Roberts, K. (1996b) 'Youth cultures and sport: the success of school and community sport provisions in Britain', *European Physical Education Review*, 2 (2): 105–15.

Roberts, K. (1999) *Leisure in Contemporary Society*. Wallingford: CABI Publishing.

Roberts, K. (2001) *Class in Modern Britain*. Basingstoke: Palgrave.

Roberts, K. (2003) 'Problems and prioroties for the sociology of youth', in A. Bennett, M. Cieslik and S. Miles (eds), *Researching Youth*. Basingstoke: Palgrave. pp. 13–28.

Roberts, K. and Brodie, D. (1992) *Inner-City Sport: Who Plays and What Are the Benefits?* Culemborg: Giordano Bruno.

Royal College of Physicians, Royal College of Paediatrics and Child Health, Faculty of Public Health (2004) *Storing up Problems: The Medical Case for a Slimmer Nation. Report of a Working Party*. London: Royal College of Physicians.

Scheerder, J., Vanreusel, B., Taks, M. and Renson, R. (forthcoming) 'Social stratification patterns in adolescents' active sports participation behaviour: a time trend analysis 1969–1999', *European Physical Education Review*.

Shilling, C. (1998) 'The body, schooling and social inequalities: physical capital and the politics of physical education', in K. Green and K. Hardman (eds), *Physical Education: A Reader*. Aachen: Meyer and Meyer Verlag. pp. 243–71.

Sisjord, M.-K. and Skirstad, B. (1996) 'Norway', in P. De Knop, L.-M. Engstrom, B. Skirstad and M.R. Weiss (eds), *Worldwide Trends in Youth Sport*. Champaign: Human Kinetics. pp. 170–83.

Sports Council for Wales (2001) *Widening the Net? Young People Participation in Sport 1999/2000*. Cardiff: Sports Council for Wales.

Sports Council for Wales (SCW) (2002) *Adult Sports Participation and Club Membership in Wales 2000/01.* Cardiff: SCW.

Sports Council for Wales (SCW) (2003a) *Secondary School Aged Children's Participation in Sport in 2001.* Cardiff: SCW.

Sports Council for Wales (SCW) (2003b) *Young People's Participation Year 2001 Data: Research and Evaluation Section.* Cardiff: SCW.

Sport England (2003a) *Young People and Sport in England 1994–2002.* London: Sport England.

Sport England (2003b) *Young People and Sport in England, 2002. A Survey of Young People and PE Teachers.* London: Sport England.

Sugden, J. and Tomlinson, A. (2002) 'Theorizing sport, class and status', in J. Coakley and E. Dunning (eds), *Handbook of Sports Studies.* London: Sage Publications. pp. 309–21.

Tomlinson, M. (2003) 'Lifestyles and social class', *European Sociological Review*, 19 (1): 97–111.

Townsend, P., Davidson, N. and Whitehead, M. (1988) *Inequalities in Health.* London: Penguin.

Wanless, D. (2004) *Securing Good Health for the Whole Population. Final Report.* London: Department of Health.

Wilson, T. C. (2002) 'The paradox of social class and sports involvement', *International Review for the Sociology of Sport*, 37 (1): 5–16.

12 | 'Race' and Physical Education, Sport and Dance

Tansin Benn

Addressing racism and physical education provides the opportunity to examine ways in which one subject of a national curriculum in a plural society can lead to polarised experiences for pupils, both celebration and disengagement, harmony and tension, inclusion and exclusion. It is only through critical debate that parents, students, teachers and other adults working with children in schools can address their own prejudices, broaden their knowledge of difference and review how they educate young people. This chapter initially addresses the underpinning complexities of any work in this area, for example, in definition of terms such as 'race', ethnicity and culture. It then offers a justification for the joint consideration of sociological literature from sport and dance, as key arenas of cultural significance and expression, as an approach to inform thinking about racism and physical education. Using this framework, there follows a synthesis of relevant literature on the physical education, sport and dance experiences of young people of African-Caribbean heritage and those of South Asian heritage. The latter is predominantly informed by a case study of the author's own research into the physical education experiences of South Asian Muslim girls and women. The chapter concludes with suggesting a further research agenda to promote ongoing debate.

UNDERPINNING COMPLEXITIES: DEFINITION, DATA AND MULTIPLE DISADVANTAGE

This chapter focuses on issues of racism defined, by McDonald and Hayes (2003: 156) as existing 'where a group of people is discriminated against on the basis of racial and/or cultural characteristics that are held to be inherent within them as a group'. This definition allows for the complexity of overlapping identities, for example, being Asian and Muslim, and acknowledgement of the fact that 'race' does not operate alone in processes of discrimination. The debate will also be limited to issues faced by 'black' people, in this context used to include those of South Asian or African-Caribbean heritage[1], since they represent around 80 per cent of the UK's minority ethnic community (Gillborn and Mirza, 2000). Historical and contemporary evidence demonstrates that there is a constant need to raise questions about barriers for black children and teachers set in a wider societal context of prejudice and discrimination (Grosvenor, 1999; Faust et al., 2000; Majors, 2001).

The need for change in an education system that has disadvantaged black pupils has been championed by many in education since the Rampton Report (1981) and the Swann Report (1985), with more recent calls for action in the Macpherson Report (1999) that resulted from The Stephen Lawrence enquiry. Any exploration of 'race' and cultural diversity in education is complex for three reasons:

1. Definition is problematic.

2. Systems for monitoring and gathering information to increase understanding of issues such as disadvantage and under-achievement are inadequate and inconsistent.

3. The inter-relationship of multiple areas of disadvantage, for example, ethnicity and class, gender, religion or disability have only recently been addressed.

The struggle to clarify definitions can lead to increased understanding, not least of the complexities involved in the debate. To indicate its problematic nature researchers often use the term 'race', retained in parenthesis. It remains a useful political tool to denote prejudice and discrimination that is still targeted at people because of phenotypical features and genetically transmitted traits such as skin colour. McDonald and Hayes (2003: 155) called this a crude form of biological racism. Cultural racism, which can embody biological racism, arises when distinctiveness of groups is seen as incompatible resulting in 'us' and 'them' tensions with the aim of condemning or excluding those who are different. Examples of this can be seen in the treatment of some asylum seekers and Muslims. The overlapping complexities can be seen in the racialisation of religion, especially in the experiences of the majority of British Muslims who are of Asian heritage. Therefore the term racism as meaning racial and/or cultural discrimination is useful in the context of this chapter and the examples to be used.

'Ethnicity' is a more inclusive term than 'race' because it denotes ways in which people define themselves into groups but there are issues about what characteristics define an ethnic group and how they differ from other groups. 'Ethnic groups' are protected under the 1976 Race Relations Act, and defined as those sharing 'a long history and a cultural tradition of their own, which they and outsiders regard as characterising them as a distinct community' (Runnymede Trust 1997: 57). But while Sikhs and Jews are protected under this law, Muslims are not. Issues of protection on grounds of religion are complicated but are enshrined under Article 13 of the European Union Treaty of Amsterdam (1997). Recent Employment Equality regulations in force in the UK from December 2003 which will protect people on the grounds of religion or belief in vocational training and employment, could have serious implications for initial teacher training in physical education. These will be addressed later.

Although 'culture' has been described as one of the most complex words in the English language, it does include learned and transmitted knowledge, attitudes and behaviours that operate at the deepest levels of human meaning and significance. The term is ascribed to define particular frames of culture, for example 'South Asian cultures'. In a conference on South Asian Dance, Ranjit Sondhi highlighted the complexity of the term and the need to resist any notion of culture as 'set in aspic':

> There is, and always has been, in all cultures, a tension between tradition and modernity, between continuity and change. In this sense, cultural identities have always been dynamic, fluid, ambiguous and elusive . . . However, there are tacit dimensions in South Asian cultures that are deep-rooted and resistant to change. (Sondhi, 2000: 7)

From the notion of culture the term 'cultural diversity' evolved as a more inclusive term than ethnicity because it does not have legal limitations. Figueroa (1993) suggested differences in language, dialect and religion were embraced by the term. The term also allowed for the possibility of a more 'alive', fluid sense of cultural identity, supporting the vision of cultures being dynamic, influencing and being influenced by the cultures of others, what Hall (1992; cited in Jenkins, 1997:30) calls 'cultures of hybridity'. In an increasingly globalised world diasporic groups face a 'double-bind' situation of striving to retain preferred values and meanings within groups while needing to share a sense of belonging to other groups. An illustration of the degree to which diasporic Muslim women in 'the West' share similar tensions in their 'double-bind' situation are evident in experiences recounted from Australia, USA, UK and Europe (Jawad and Benn, 2003).

The inadequate and inconsistent systems for collating firm evidence about numbers and achievement of minority groups, flaw attempts to gain the clarity that can guide policy and strategy (Parekh, 2002: xviii). For example, difficulties experienced by Gillborn and Mirza (2000) on attempting to gather a national perspective were compounded by inconsistencies in presentation of data. Among many problems was the fact that no single ethnic classification was used. Some local education authorities (LEA) preferred a range of headings while others combined all 'black' groups under one heading. Despite the limitations of the data it was possible to state that although 'ethnic inequalities in attainment vary from one area to another . . . distinct patterns of inequality are consistently visible', and that African-Caribbean, Pakistani and Bangladeshi pupils are particularly disadvantaged in the 'youth education, labour and training markets [increasing] the likelihood of social and economic exclusion in later life' (Gillborn and Mirza, 2000: 27).

In a city such as Birmingham, England – recently identified as one of two cities likely to become the first majority 'black' city in the UK by 2010 (BRAP, 2003) – recognition of the impact of multiple identities, for example, South Asian and Muslim, is crucial. Two thirds of 'Black Birmingham is an Asian Birmingham' and the majority are of Islamic heritage, with their origins in Pakistan or Bangladesh. They are already disadvantaged in many ways (BRAP, 2003: 14):

> Pakistanis and Bangladeshis already experience disproportionate levels of poverty and exclusion from labour markets within the city. Given the recent revival in islamophobia, it is important to

> consider the impact of anti-muslim feeling on those communities, as well as employers, education and training providers and the community of learners.

Serious consideration of multiple identities is a relatively recent phenomenon but crucial to recognising the impact of complex overlays of prejudice, discrimination and disadvantage (Carrington and McDonald, 2001; Parekh, 2002; Penney, 2002; BRAP, 2003). Crude ethnic categories such as 'white' or 'Asian' can lead to misleading claims about educational success and failure and invisibility of key overlapping facets of identity, for example, race and class, gender, disability, age, religion. In discussing the marginalisation of black women in feminist discourse Scraton cites Mirza who suggests: 'The invisibility of black women speaks of the separate narrative constructions of race, gender and class: it is a racial discourse, where the subject is male; in a gendered discourse, where the subject is white; and a class discourse, where race has no place (Mirza, 1997; cited in Scraton, 2001: 171).

There is a strong call for recognition of 'interlocking multiple axes of oppression' or 'intersectionality' of social identities that moves beyond simple 'additive' discourse and recognises the social and historic contexts of disadvantage (Scraton, 2001). An example of this will be the case study used later in the chapter which identifies the multiple axes of race, gender and religion contributing significantly to the vulnerability of Asian Muslim girls and women in the UK at this particular time.

From the above complexities identified in definition, data inaccuracies and issues of multiple axes of disadvantage, it is not surprising that there are no easy answers to facilitating both respect for cultural difference and improved social integration. The Cantle Report (2002) commissioned after the 2001 riots in Oldham, Burnley and Bradford, highlighted many of the problems which underpinned the discontent which led to the disturbances:

> While the physical segregation of housing estates and inner city areas came as no surprise, the team was particularly struck by the depth of polarisation of our towns and cities. The extent to which these physical divisions were compounded by so many other aspects of our daily lives, was very evident. Separate educational arrangements, community and voluntary bodies, employment, places of worship, language, social and cultural networks, means that many communities operate on the basis of a series of parallel lives. These lives do not seem to touch at any points, let alone overlap and promote any meaningful interchanges. (Cantle, 2002: 9)

The team concluded that ignorance of other's communities could lead to fear and exploitation by extremist groups, which undermines community harmony and division. As a result of the report local and national government strategies have moved to promoting 'community cohesion'. In schools such strategies will be linked to educating young people about difference, about valuing and respecting the diversity of society: 'there is an urgent need to promote community cohesion, based upon a greater knowledge of, contact between, and respect for, the various cultures that now make Great Britain such a rich and diverse nation' (Cantle, 2002: 10).

While such principles are embedded in 'citizenship', it is clearly a cross-curricula opportunity and physical education is one subject through which such principles can be addressed.

In summary, the first section has identified the complexities of any engagement with issues of racism, evolving definitions of key terms used in the area such as 'race', ethnicity and culture and the paucity of accuracy in any data that might illuminate the national picture. Finally, the need to acknowledge the impact of multiple identities was highlighted as significant in any attempt to increase understanding of the complex issues addressed in this chapter.

PHYSICAL EDUCATION, SPORT AND DANCE

In order to inform subsequent sections on the physical education experiences of young people of African-Caribbean and South Asian heritage, this section provides a justification for the joint consideration of sociological literature from sport and dance. Both are key arenas of cultural significance and highly pertinent to the subject of physical education. This approach is proposed to broaden thinking about racism and physical education, perhaps eliciting new questions and directions for future research. One reason for this approach is the dearth of empirical literature available about the experiences of black children in the physical education context. The intention is not to reduce physical education to sport and dance but to recognise that, in popular culture, both activity areas are seen to contribute success and high profile for black people. This has impacted on teachers and children in schools in a way that has been both advantageous and disadvantageous to black children.

Sport and dance have enjoyed different but related histories as significant cultural arenas and in sharing UK educational history within physical education for over 100 years. Currently political initiatives are driving physical education in a 'sport' direction, for example, in the sport-dominated discourse of Specialist Sports Colleges[2], School Sport Coordinators and Sportsmark awards for good practice. Consideration of work on race in sports sociology might be relevant to critical thinking about the school situation. The relatively under-developed area of dance sociology (Thomas, 1995) is beginning to inform understanding of the black experience. Balancing attention between sport and dance in this chapter goes some way to redressing an imbalance as the subject of physical education moves increasingly towards a 'sport hegemony' with, 'the interests of sport now occupying a highly privileged position in the school curriculum' (Penney and Evans, 1999: 126–7).

Other reasons for the unusual combining of literature from sociology of sport and dance approach arise from recognition of the many similarities the areas share, not least being the importance of physicality and centrality of the body. They are both important in what Gilroy (1997: 25) calls 'the politics of performance-centred expressive culture'. Other factors include their socially constructed natures, existence across time and space, cultural significance and links to identity. In England, sport and dance are politically managed as part of Britain's cultural fabric through the Department of Culture, Media and Sport (DCMS) (see critique of current practice in Parakh, 2002: 160–75). Both dance and sport have national and local management structures; they benefit through lottery financing and have parallels in the needs and paths of talented youngsters who might make it to elite athlete/artist levels (Linschoten and Kleipool, 2001). Sport and dance have common trends in academicisation, scientisation and medicalisation[3], for example, through the overlapping of Sport Science/Dance Science, Sport Medicine/Dance Medicine fields (Wyon, 2001). Finally, they are inescapably linked in the education context through the 'art-form model', a conceptual framework of process-based learning around 'planning, performing and evaluating', that underpins the whole national curriculum for physical education, which is largely attributable to clarity of thinking that evolved among the dance lobby (Smith-Autard, 2002). It is also interesting that research in both arenas is growing fastest in the USA.

In the UK, spheres of education and the professional sports and dance worlds have grown closer. Trends towards equality of opportunity, outreach, networking and partnerships have ensured schools have increased accessibility to elite athletes and artists, their skills, and motivational value. One example is the Sport England 'Sporting Champions' scheme. For dance companies, having a good education policy is linked to release of funding. The knowledge and skills of professional coaches, athletes and artists are recognised, valued, and increasingly affordable from the school's perspective as government money flows through numerous schemes into schools (for example Specialist Colleges, Creative Partnerships[4] and *Physical Education, School Sport and Club Links* (PESSCL)).[5] Sports people can increasingly see education work as an important part of their careers and for many professional artists, work in education becomes a major contributor to their survival. Such links have been beneficial, demystifying the 'elite', democratising 'high art' and raising vocational and aspirational opportunities for children. While all young people benefit from such experiences the popular association between success and black athletes and artists in some sports and dance forms makes the debate interesting in the context of this chapter. Do these developments have particular relevance or benefits for black children and for all children in an increasingly diversified society? While anecdotal evidence would support the targeting of such schemes, for example, utilising leading black sports people and dance artists to enhance the self-esteem of black children, there is little empirical evidence.

PHYSICAL EDUCATION, SPORT AND DANCE: YOUNG PEOPLE OF AFRICAN-CARIBBEAN HERITAGE

In 1997, the Office for Standards in Education (OFSTED) identified meeting the needs of ethnic minority children in primary and secondary physical education as a weakness (Clay, 1997). Government concerns about the recruitment and retention of ethnic minority teachers in the profession are constant and recurrent themes. The impact of physical education traditions and practices on black pupils and teachers is under-researched. Empirical research into the experiences of African-Caribbean children in education rarely goes beyond crude quantitative measures that indicate low performance in academic examinations and over-representation in suspensions, expulsions and groups identified with emotional and behavioural difficulties (Gillborn and Gipps, 1996). Concerns in the sport, arts and education literature predominantly relate to how stereotyping can damage the life-chances of black children and how such arenas can be used to both perpetuate and challenge constraining racist thinking (in this section the term black refers specifically to people of African-Caribbean heritage). Carrington and McDonald (2001) highlight the contradictory position of sport. They criticise the lack of research in the UK that avoids pathologising black communities and blackness. They point out the inaccuracies and over-simplification in both Hoberman's (1997) claims that sport reproduces racism and Allison's (1998: 12) version of the popular view of 'sport-as-positive-force ideology', demonstrating the need to consider historical and social context in any search for understanding: 'Sport, like many other cultural arenas, is a site for contestation, resistance and struggle, whereby dominant ideologies are both maintained and challenged at particular historical points and in specific social contexts' (Carrington and McDonald, 2001: 12). In such statements dance can easily be substituted for sport because of the many similarities outlined above.

The cultural links between dance and sport are even clearer when reviewing the discourse of the early versions of the National Curriculum for Physical Education (NCPE). Just as traditional British team games featured prominently in the games discourse of the NCPE the statement 'traditional dances from the British Isles' also appeared in 1995 (Department for Education (DFE)). The phrase was generously interpreted by Jobbins as 'hopefully (including) the great richness of styles that are present in the British culture today' (1995: 2). Subsequent versions of NCPE have moved to a more inclusive language of generic games concepts that can be applied in diverse ways, and a dance language of 'different times, places and cultures', using different styles and forms. In practice, dance has moved further to address diversity than games, which retains a privileged position being deeply rooted in the historic significance of sport in British society (Penney and Evans, 1999).

Much of the literature related to race, sport and physical education has been well summarised by Carrington and McDonald (2001), Chappell (2002) and McDonald and Hayes (2003). The significance of visibility of difference by skin colour (Polley, 1998) and the apparent 'belief that blackness and Britishness are mutually exclusive categories' (Carrington and McDonald, 2001: 2) have led to a preoccupation for some researchers with finding explanations for the success of black athletes. The difficulties of researching this area, and the discrediting of much that has been done, have resulted in pseudo-scientific thinking perpetuating what Coakley (1994: 243) calls the 'race logic'. That is, the ideology rooted in colonial days as a way of justifying abuse of black people, of black *physical* supremacy, and white *intellectual* supremacy, where 'the mind' was more highly valued than 'the body' making whites superior to blacks. Such thinking 'eventually became institutionalised in the form of complex racial ideology about skin colour, intelligence, character and physical skills'. Chappell (2002: 93) reinforces ways in which such ideologies are sustained in contemporary consumer culture through the use of black bodies as icons of physicality:

> The modern world is awash with images of black athletes. The physical talents of black people and the media generated images that sustain them encourage the idea that blacks are biologically different, and more specifically that black athletes are superior to white athletes . . . sustain[ing] the traditional view of blacks having physical attributes which allow them to excel at sport.

Gilroy (1997: 25) sees the growth of the black sports arena (at the expense of some arenas of black dance) and preponderance of images of black sporting bodies, as part of a changing 'black public sphere transformed by the catastrophic state of black urban life in the overdeveloped countries'.

What has been discredited as 'race science' were attempts to explain black athletic success biologically, for example, in terms of bone differences, physique proportions, limb length, speed and strength (Kane, 1971). It is recognised that much research in this area was flawed, often anecdotal, with suspect motivations (Carrington and McDonald, 2001). But it fuelled the ideology that black people were stronger and physically more capable than others. The 1995 'resurrection' of the black supremacy theory by Roger Bannister, an eminent scientist and athlete, with speculation about longer heel bones, better power–weight ratios and elasticity in muscle fibres, gave renewed 'legitimacy' to such 'speculative atheoretical rhetoric' with profoundly damaging results. Such explanations have become 'embedded in many of the stereotypes that exist. When they, in turn, permeate the consciousness of coaches, teachers and even athletes themselves, the impact of scientific racism is very severe' (Fleming, 2001: 112).

In terms of 'self-fulfilling prophecies' black supremacy is deemed to contribute to what is called 'white flight', for example, the relative absence of white athletes in the athletic sprinting arena which is dominated by black athletes. The same 'self-fulfilling prophecy' has enhanced the commitment of some black athletes to excel in other forms of sport and dance. The key problem is the linking of ideologies of physical supremacy with anti-intellectualism, which has happened since Social Darwinist[6] views of white supremacy were used to justify use and abuse of power around the world. The resultant 'all brawn no brains' theory continues to contribute to educational under-achievement of black children. They could be good at sport but were considered inferior intellectually and, therefore, limited in their ability to succeed in academic or other life arenas. The dangers of such thinking are obvious but persist despite revelations of the inadequacies of these biologically determinist views (Cashmore, 1982, 1996; Edwards, 1972, 1973; Lewontin, 1993).

Accounts of leading black sportsmen on the significance of encouragement from physical education teachers to focus on sport, sometimes at the expense of academic subjects, fuelled concerns that teachers were contributing to under-achievement of African-Caribbean pupils (Carrington, 1983; Cashmore, 1982; Chappell, 1995). The popularity of physical education often led to its use in schools as a form of 'social control' whereby the threat of removal of black pupils from teams, clubs or physical education lessons would improve behaviour and achievement elsewhere. At the end of the 1980s, Bayliss (1989) summarised ways in which racial stereotyping impacted on physical education. Myths abounded that affected interactions between teachers and black pupils, for example: African-Caribbean pupils were poor swimmers because they had heavy bones; blacks were good at sport because slavery weeded out the weak; all blacks had a natural sense of rhythm and, therefore, were good at dance and blacks were good at boxing because they could absorb a heavier beating (Bayliss, 1989). It is disappointing, then, that ten years later biological racism still appears to underpin thinking in physical education which may be impacting on the under-achievement of black pupils: 'The physiological mythology surrounding blacks in sport seems deeply entrenched within the physical education profession. This evokes a set of beliefs on behalf of teachers and pupils which maintains a mutually reinforcing and vicious circle' (Hayes and Sugden, 1999; cited McDonald and Hayes, 2003: 162).

At the same time it cannot be denied that sport and dance have been arenas for expressing black cultural resistance to racism and exposing prejudices and discrimination in social structures. An example of this was in the 'Black power' demonstrations of Tommy Smith and John Carlos on the medal rostrum in the 1968 Mexican Olympics, another was the 'theatre' Muhammad Ali made of the boxing ring to make his statements on race and religion. In terms of dance, black companies were started that have challenged myths and exclusion from mainstream dance opportunities, for example, the contemporary Phoenix black, male UK company of the 1970s challenged stereotypes on many levels, and the Dance Theatre of Harlem in USA countered myths that black people could not do ballet:

> Arguably, colour has been and continues to be the critical reason for the widespread exclusion of the black dancer from ballet. It is the dance form which appears to most visibly side-line black dancers, and it is the most powerful global dance form. The ballet has been based on symmetry, harmony, and 'concepts of beauty and grace,' and a black dancer could break up the 'pretty ensemble effect'. (Emery, 1988: 319)

Despite efforts by major companies, for example, the Royal Ballet and Birmingham Royal Ballet, to encourage youngsters from poor and ethnic minority areas into the world of ballet (for example, the Royal Ballet's 'Chance to Dance scheme' and Birmingham Royal Ballet's 'Dance-Track' project[7]) black dancers are under-represented in ballet companies. They are more visible in the professional arenas of the USA, in the modern dance genre and, of course, black dance forms such as hip-hop. Literature still indicates professional black dancers continue to struggle, for example, against critics who comment 'about innate ability rather than applied work, about mysterious qualities of performers and over-emphasis on the physicality of dancers. Dancers have to fight these stereotypes in order to establish themselves as serious creative artists using their rich African-American heritage' (Adair 1992: 180). This serves to constrain choices, life direction and rewards for black dancers.

Similarly, a search for explanations of over- and under-representation of black athletes in different sports has fascinated sports sociologists. Over-representation of black athletes in some sports such as boxing, athletics and basketball and under-representation in others such as golf, are explained on socio-economic grounds related to costs and accessibility of necessary spaces and equipment. In dance there are also areas of over- and under-representation, with black dancers being most successful in dance styles rooted in popular culture that started in the dance-halls and ballrooms before moving into theatre forms (Emery, 1988). The significance of multiple identities and disadvantage in terms of colour, class and gender cannot be underestimated in understanding such issues.

The 'glass ceiling' theory recognises the predominance of black athletes as performers and lack of presence of that expertise in coaching or managerial positions (Coakley, 1994). The same phenomenon occurs in dance (Lenhard, 1997) where it is difficult to 'make it' into professional ranks or positions such as choreographer, particularly for black women: 'There are very few well-known black female dancers or choreographers working in the Western theatre' (Adair, 1992: 162). The phenomenon of 'stacking' identified 'racist positioning' of black players in American football in playing positions requiring particular speed and strength as opposed to white players being positioned in 'thinking central' positions which required vision and leadership. In theatre dance, historically, black characters were often the 'entertainers' cast in 'stereotyped roles of comic stooge and "exotic primitive" ' (Adair, 1992: 192). Marginalising black dancers happened in two ways, in representing black people in 'non-serious' roles and in barring black dancers from some companies because of skin colour. For example, the then London Festival Ballet's reason for not accepting blacks into the company in 1986 was because 'one black swan in the corps would look odd' (Onwurah, cited in Adair, 1992: 167).

The social mobility theory has been used to explain, for example, the over-representation of black men in boxing as it has been seen for some as a 'way out of the ghetto' (Sugden, 1987). A contemporary example might be the visibility of success and wealth gained by some black sports people, such as ex-footballer, Ian Wright, in television. A more critical approach also reveals that while many black youngsters might be inspired or channelled into sporting activities the numbers who 'make it' to the top are small: 'Since at least the 1970s sport has been a route to fame and fortune for numerous black sportsmen and women and yet for thousands of others it continues to conceal deep inequalities, racist beliefs, and to be a path to failure and disappointment' (Jarvie, 2000: 336).

The relative invisibility of black women's issues and experiences in the sociology of sport and dance are recognised and serve to illustrate the complexity of interplay between race, gender and other categories of disadvantage (Scraton, 2001; Adair, 1992). Adair recognised the centrality of dance in many black cultures, the different aesthetic of dance forms, the hierarchical valuing of white western dance forms over black dance forms, the separateness of black and white dance audiences and particular problems for black female dancers: 'it is harder for black women who are up against the Western standards of beauty and "ideal" proportions and the sexism and racism which those standards illustrate' (Adair, 1992: 171).

Many areas of sport and dance epitomise gender polarised views of 'masculine appropriate' or 'feminine appropriate' activities but these do not act alone to constrain life chances. We might consider the power of the film *Billy Elliot* if the ballet-struck boy had been black as well as from a poor socio-economic home dominated by hegemonic masculinity and patriarchal attitudes.

In summary, the relevance to physical education is clear. It would be naïve to suggest that prejudice and discrimination do not permeate the school environment through deep-rooted cultural beliefs and attitudes of some parents, children, teachers, governors and visitors. The visibility and cultural significance of sport and dance impact on us all and have an increasingly central place in the changing face of physical education. For young people of African-Caribbean heritage the fact is that many world famous black athletes and dancers have 'made-it' in some sports and popular dance forms, and explanations of their success have long been sought. But 'race science' has been discredited and the anti-intellectualism that accompanied the 'physical supremacy' theory has proved damaging to some young people. Other more subtle forms of prejudice and discrimination have been recognised which affect the life chances of black people. Schools do provide the only guaranteed access to all facets of physical education, sport and dance, to artists and sports professionals. Schools become an important arena for respecting difference, encouraging potential, for providing positive role models and opportunities, to experience breadth of activities, within an equity framework concerned with justice and fairness. While a macro view of the experiences of black African-Caribbean people has been taken to identify how prejudice and discrimination can permeate physical education and key related activities, the problems with generalisations and homogenization are recognised. The following section counters this to some extent in that very different experiences of South Asian women's perspectives on physical education, sport and dance will be considered, initially through the author's 'case study' research into the physical education experiences of South Asian Muslim women.

PHYSICAL EDUCATION, SPORT AND DANCE: YOUNG PEOPLE OF SOUTH ASIAN HERITAGE

This section will draw initially on the author's own research into the physical education experiences of a group of predominantly South Asian Muslim girls and women. The intention is to offer a 'micro' perspective of a group who encountered different physical education, sport and dance stereotypes to those discussed above. Their experiences do illustrate ways in which complex overlays of gender, religious, cultural and racial ideologies have been experienced in physical education, at primary, secondary and higher education stages, and offer some solutions to more positive inclusion. The section will conclude with wider reference to diversity of physical education, sport and dance experiences in the British South Asian community.

Since the mid-1990s the author has conducted qualitative research into the life experiences of Muslim women, as they passed through higher education on a primary teacher training programme. During this time interviews, observations and diaries were kept through which respondents recalled and captured their perceptions of physical education in their own lives, as they trained to teach the subject, and as they moved out into local schools in the role of student-teacher then teacher. Muslims in Britain are predominantly of South Asian heritage and 75 per cent of the respondents in this study declared themselves as British Asians. With the exception of one white woman the others were black and of African-Asian or African-Caribbean heritage; aspects of the ongoing research have been published elsewhere (Benn, 1996, 2000a, 2000b, 2002; Jawad and Benn, 2003).

Participation in physical activities is not unislamic (Naciri, 1973; Sfeir, 1985; Sarwar, 1994; Daiman 1995). In fact there are many common features between the cultures of Islam and physical education such as attention to hygiene and cleanliness, belief in the importance of exercise, qualities such as perseverance and self-discipline, and practices such as common separation of the sexes around puberty. Where tensions can arise lies, not so much in the activities, as in the traditional physical education practices of kit, changing/showering arrangements, exercise during the month of Ramadan and timing of extra curricular activities that clash with Mosque teaching or other family commitments (Carroll and Hollinshead, 1993). Muslim requirements for modesty in dress, covering the body, arms and legs and avoiding public nudity, even in same-sex situations, have led to the kit/showering/changing issues in physical education. During Ramadan no eating or drinking between sunrise and sunset is allowed, making excessive exercise, or the chance of swallowing water in swimming, problematic for some. Response of local education authorities to the needs of Muslim communities has varied, for example, Birmingham local authority has responded, at different times, to requests from strict Muslim areas to provide single-sex swimming environments for primary schools despite this being a cultural rather than religious requirement prior to adolescence. Other Muslim communities within the same city have been happy with school provision, requiring no changes to be made to accommodate Muslim children.

Attempts to accommodate the needs of Muslim pupils have moved beyond pathologising the community and ignoring institutional racism (Siraz-Blatchford, 1993), and there is more shared knowledge about the needs of Muslim pupils (Parker-Jenkins, 1995). Two-way dialogue is essential in developing knowledge and understanding between Islamic and state education requirements. For example, school/community dialogue about the purpose and nature of dance in education might be one way forward in dispelling fears about the subject in some Muslim communities. In the author's research the popular perceptions of the families of respondents matched that suggested in the literature (Hiskett, 1989), that some

Muslims see dance only as being about displays of sexuality and 'provocative movement' to pop music and, therefore, unworthy of a place in education (Sarwar, 1994). Similarly, in some Islamic sects, music is considered a distraction from the higher order pursuits required of someone on the Islamic path towards oneness with Allah. In such cases state/Islamic requirements may be irreconcilable and alternative solutions may need to be sought.

The Muslim women's own recollections of primary school life and physical education were mainly positive but not in relation to 'PE kit' or general awareness of their needs. Kit issues arose as sources of negative experiences at both primary and secondary levels for the respondents themselves. As adult student-teachers, placed in primary schools for teaching practice, they were highly conscious of Islamic requirements and very aware of the lack of knowledge about Islamic requirements among staff. Students did encounter instances of very young infant children, unable to understand much English having just arrived in the country, crying and refusing to undress for physical education. There was no evidence of sympathy or understanding on the part of the teacher and children were forced to comply without any explanation that they could understand. The respondents interpreted the children's anxieties in relation to the mismatch with concerns for modesty and body covering some would be encountering at home.

Strict kit regulations were sometimes unhelpful and rigidly non-negotiable which angered the Muslim women. The simple 'allowance' of a track-suit would have solved a dress code issue but some schools regarded track-suits as 'safety-risks' and, therefore, would not allow the children to wear them. There were many times when the Muslim student-teachers were upset that ten- and eleven-year-olds, who had gone through or were approaching puberty, were changing in the primary classroom in a public and mixed-sex environment. A small number of schools provided screens or gave permission for the girls or boys to go to the toilets to change but the latter strategy does raise issues of supervision and safety which could be problematic in an increasingly litigious physical education environment.

Some of the Muslim women's recollections of secondary school experiences highlighted problems with the areas of showers, kit, extra-curricular activities and Ramadan, identified by Carroll and Hollinshead (1993). Most respondents had enjoyed physical education and some were aware that their teachers understood and accommodated their needs. One respondent was the only Muslim pupil in her school and her teacher enabled her to meet all religious requirements and participate in physical education: 'I was the only Muslim in my school, a mixed school, and I was allowed to do whatever I needed to, I could adapt the uniform. They said they would rather me do PE with jogging bottoms than not do PE at all' (Shazia).

Some respondents were allowed to wear track-suits under games skirts which was completely acceptable. Others were in more traditionalist departments where 'coping strategies' for lack of concessions to requests to wear track-suits included 'pulling the socks up and skirts down', and taking 'sick-notes' often meant parents colluding in excluding their children from participating in physical education. Swimming had caused the biggest problems and where mixed-sex swimming was expected some parents wrote to exempt their children. Not all respondents were similarly affected by religious requirements. One, who had not adopted hijab because of her modernist perspective of being Muslim, saw it as her role to fit in with society and had no problems participating in mixed-sex physical education lessons. Most, however, were in single-sex secondary schools or had experienced sex-segregated lessons and that had contributed to their enjoyment.

The high-profile of inclusion has improved the situation for Muslim pupils in physical education. The obligation of teachers to meet the religious and cultural needs of pupils was first enshrined in the national curriculum implemented in 2000 (Department for Education and Employment/Qualifications and Curriculum Authority (DfEE/QCA), 1999). The statement includes additional information that refers explicitly to the needs of Muslim pupils, requiring teachers to remove barriers to learning, facilitate participation and, for example, to 'provide appropriate physical activity and opportunity for learning in times of fasting' (DfEE/QCA, 1999: 36). Kit accommodation has tended to move towards the acceptance of track-suits to enable more girls to feel able to participate comfortably in physical education. The wearing of short games skirts during the difficult adolescent years was never just an issue for Muslim girls. There is still no consensus about allowing the wearing of the hijab in physical education but most teachers are supportive provided the head scarf is tied safely. This is not the approach taken elsewhere in Europe, for example a law in France has banned the wearing of all religious symbols in state schools, including the hijab (Henley, 2003; Vaisse, 2004). In some UK schools traditional practices such as showering after every lesson have become optional. Separate cubicle spaces in new-build schools have helped with issues of modesty and privacy in changing. Teachers can accommodate needs during Ramadan by planning imaginatively and utilising different ideas, Sport Education, which encourages multiple role-skilling in terms of, for example, management, coaching and umpiring etc; and similarly, dance-roles such as choreographer, 'teacher' and critical spectator can be equally as important as performer. More public swimming baths are able to provide all-female sessions so, where schools are willing to negotiate and organise, pupils can be taught swimming in single-sex, all-female, environments where necessary. Tensions will still exist around the provision of single-sex teaching and many Muslim parents try to find places for their daughters in single-sex schools. Practices in mixed-sex schools vary in terms of secondary physical education, with some providing co-educational experiences and others separate-sex experiences. Issues surrounding practices for changing and provision in mixed-sex primary schools are unlikely to change.

It is interesting, then, with the improvement of knowledge and accommodating strategies in secondary schools, that most Muslim women, on entering the physical education higher education environment in the UK will not meet the same degree of provision that accommodates Muslim requirements. The co-educational drive of physical education has reversed the once sex-segregated training of secondary specialist physical education teachers. The author herself started her higher education career as a lecturer in the women's specialist

Anstey College of Physical Education which opened in 1897 (Crunden, 1974) and was one of the last single-sex institutions to be phased out in 1985. If a Muslim woman wanted to train to teach physical education today she would have to participate in a mixed-sex course, a realisation which would be prohibitive for some. Such barriers to vocational training might well prove discriminatory in the future if someone challenged under the recent Employment Equality legislation in force in the UK from December 2003 which protects people on the grounds of religion or belief in *vocational training* as well as employment.[8]

In the primary sector all teachers have to deliver physical education, therefore, training should be part of initial and continuing training for every primary teacher. Provision of same-sex environments and staffing are 'not considered an issue' in some institutions and 'would be problematic' in pragmatic terms elsewhere, for example, where there is only one member of PE staff (Benn, 2002). The history of the author's current 'primary training' institution, as a centre that took deliberate actions to encourage more ethnic minority students into teacher training following government directives (Department for Education and Science (DES), 1989), faced many unforeseen changes when increasing numbers of Muslim women entered (Benn, 1996). Cultural changes include providing single-sex accommodation, meeting halal dietary requirements, providing a Muslim prayer room, honouring of religious festivals, and changes in provision of physical education. From responses to the author's 2002 national survey of training institutions it appears this is the only primary teacher training course in the country which can 'consciously' accommodate the physical education needs of Muslim women, that is target groupings and staffing in relation to student-identified need. All female groups did occur sometimes in other institutions but 'by accident' rather than design, as the majority of primary trainees are female. As schools make improved efforts to remove barriers to participation in physical education on religious grounds, it is possible that more Muslim pupils will come through the system with positive attitudes, wanting to teach the subject. Barriers to provision in higher education will have to be addressed and it is recognised that the needs of Muslim men, very similar to those of Muslim women, have not been addressed at all.

While the above examples from research into physical education experiences of Muslim women were included because the majority of British Muslims are of South Asian heritage, not all South Asian people are Muslim. Whereas dance is problematic for some Muslims it is a source of high esteem, cultural identity, career routes and celebration in others. Indeed, dance styles reflect South Asian identity for some groups and ongoing efforts to bring the essence of different styles, along with their cultural heritage, into education have been at the forefront of some of Britain's most highly regarded artists, for example, Chitraleka Bolar who is Artistic Director of Chitraleka Dance Company.[9] Her style is Bharatanatyam, which is rooted in Hinduism and regarded as, 'the most celebrated art form of South India . . . an extremely precise dance style where a huge repertoire of hand movements is used to convey moods and expressions' (Navadisha, 2000: 23). Chitraleka has been in demand in UK schools for over 20 years because of her skills to use the classical art form creatively and share her identity and art form in an accessible way with children and teachers. But the richness of Indian dance is vast and covers a range of styles from classical to folk including Kathak (Storyteller) from North India, Kathakali, just for men, developed in Kerala, south-western coastal state, Manipuri from the north-eastern state of Manipur and Odissi, originally from the eastern coastal state of Odissi (Navadisha, 2000).

One of the most valued contributions of dance in education is its power to communicate, using movement as a medium of expression, a form of communication about people, lives, and the world in which we live. To continue with the example of Indian dance, not only do dance forms represent the richness of difference they also represent the fluidity of culture as 'modernity' brings change and challenge at the boundaries of cultural meaning. Ways in which choreographer Shobana Jeyasingh has used Indian and contemporary styles in examining issues of Indian and British identity express both hybridity and complexity in continually evolving new identities. In referring to her work 'Making of Maps', Roy (1997: 77) suggests:

> Although 'Making of Maps' is a 'personal map of an Indian dancer living in Britain', it is not limited by those beguilingly simple but manifestly inadequate linguistic terms ('Indian', 'Britain'): instead its starting point is their interdependent complexity, and in the process of transgressing the border between them it transfigures their relation from fixed and separate categories into one that is more fluid, mobile and contingent.

All of this is far removed from the sporting stereotypes of Asian females as passive and frail (Chappell, 2002: 103) and the damaging cultural deficit model which blames absence from sport on cultural constraints and oppression of women (Scraton, 2001: 179; Hargreaves, 1994: 259). Because of concerns about the health of the South Asian population in Britain and the low South Asian participation rates in sporting activities,[10] focused projects have emerged to address specific needs and barriers to participation. While there are no religious laws that stop Muslims, Hindus or Sikhs from participating in physical activities, sport does not have the same high profile cultural significance in those communities. Different perceptions of the body and of gender roles contribute to their 'absence' as do fears of harassment, racism and attack (Hargreaves, 1994: 258–60). When the international sporting arena is addressed women from Muslim countries are virtually invisible because 'they represent and reinforce radical and westernised ideas about women and women's bodies which threaten established gender values and relations' (Hargreaves, 1994: 232). Muslim sports feminists are bringing about change and major events are now being held for women from Muslim countries, which meet Islamic requirements, but for 'female eyes' only without photographic or television record.

More has been written about the experiences of South Asian boys and men in physical education and sport but as Chappell (2002) points out this is little compared with the research interest in black African-Caribbean sportsmen. There is also much less visibility of Asian sporting heroes in the consumer culture that thrives on the popularity of sport. While badminton, hockey and cricket have been seen as successful arenas for Asian players there are dangers when physical education teachers steer youngsters in these directions and close other doors, or indeed channel Asian pupils away from sport (Chappell, 2002: 103–4). The relative ostracisation of Asians from mainstream football has been attributed to myths such as lack of physical stamina, academic preferences and other cultural priorities. The experiences of overt racist abuse, violence and marginalisation by selectors, coaches, players and spectators are largely ignored (Johal, 2001). The separatist response of establishing a vibrant South Asian footballing culture provides an opportunity 'to protect themselves from racial abuse and still partake of the sport' (Johal, 2001: 165), it also perpetuates side-lining of talent from mainstream opportunities and rewards from Britain's most lucrative sport.

In schools and elite level sport prejudice is never far from the surface. For example, Conservative MP Norman Tebbit's 'cricket test' which suggested that ethnic minorities cannot call themselves English until they support England at cricket and not the team from their migrant home; and Henderson's now (in)famous *Wisden Cricket Monthly*, comment that black and Asian sportsmen were biologically and culturally different making them 'foreign' players who would never be able to 'give their all' for England because they could not feel Englishness (Henderson, 1995). The resultant backlash and successful libel cases of Malcolm and DeFreitas, named in the article, brought global condemnation (Marqusee, 2001: 125). On the contrary, South Asian athletes have contributed significantly to elite British sport, and, alongside the major contribution of African-Caribbean athletes: 'The inclusion of Asian and black communities into the lived cultures of contemporary Britain, including Britain's sporting cultures, has decidedly reshaped questions of local, national and international identity for *all* Britons' (Carrington and McDonald, 2001: 4).

Fleming's 1990's research into the school-based experiences of South Asian males found that sport and physical education provided opportunities for the racial bullying and abuse of South Asian pupils by dominant white males. Although these incidents were differentially experienced and responded to, in relation to the class, religion, and linguistic background of those involved, they represent the 'pervasive impact of racism in all its guises' (Fleming, 1991, 1994, 1995; cited in McDonald and Hayes, 2003: 162).

In summary, the diversity of physical education, sport and dance experiences recounted here under 'South-Asian heritage' illustrate the importance and need for more in-depth qualitative studies that can increase understanding and respect for difference:

> Most studies of school PE and sport focus on the impact of racial ideologies on the experiences and delivery of school PE and sport, and, given the differential experiences of Britain's ethnic minorities, we would expect that ideologies of experiences of racism are expressed in a diversity of ways. (McDonald and Hayes, 2003: 160)

The diverse attitudes identified about dance are attributable to religious and cultural differences. In addition to the influences of faith on participation in physical education, sport and dance, there are different experiences for males and females, and in terms of other influences not discussed here such as class. The physical education 'stereotypes' of Asian girls and boys are damaging and constraining, the search for sociological explanations of barriers to participation and strategies for positive change need to continue.

In conclusion, cultural diversity provides a challenge to everyone involved in education. The high cultural value of dance and sport activities, associated with British physical education for over 100 years, has been used to demonstrate where and how dominant ideologies operate at elite levels and can impact on teachers and pupils in schools. Teachers have a responsibility to understand diverse needs, to motivate and educate for life-long involvement in physical activity, to provide activities that are attractive and desirable in environments where all feel comfortable to participate. This sometimes requires local solutions to local challenges, maximising the potential of communities and ways in which they can celebrate both distinctiveness and togetherness.

In a fast-moving, image-dominated, technologically-driven society, the tendency remains to attribute stereotypical qualities to people on the basis of what we see, body shape, gender, age, skin colour or clothes, and multiple combinations of these. The particular significance of racial discrimination in the area of physical education, and associated arenas of sport and dance, has been the focus of this chapter. Schools are sites that can both perpetuate and challenge damaging labelling. Current directions towards closer school/professional links, for example, through sport and dance, give teachers new opportunities to socially reconstruct values, attitudes and behaviour through the experiences and links that are fostered and developed. Education is a centre of 'cultural capital' (Bourdieu, 1986), but the dominant culture can permeate and quickly fade the highly valued cultural capital of diverse groups. In addition to knowledge and awareness of diverse cultural practices teachers also need a critical approach to traditional values, beliefs and practices to identify barriers that can be removed to provide a more inclusive ethos.

Parekh (2002) spoke about the importance of the 'listening school' which responds to the needs of its community. Recent research for school improvement in physical education has moved to seeking localised solutions to specific situations (for example, NIKE/YST Girls in Sport Project (Kirk et al., 2001)). Policy, strategy and action need to be informed by understanding of the underpinning issues. This is a key challenge in the area of addressing issues to do with racism in physical education, sport and dance. Teachers need more support through initial teacher training and continuing professional development opportunities to increase their knowledge and understanding of cultural diversity and to address their own school-based issues related to this area. Education for citizenship is high on current agendas and the cultural significance of physical education makes this a good vehicle to encourage social and moral responsibility and involvement with community, respecting and sharing in differentially valued cultural practices. Building on a framework of the Runnymede Trust (1997), Parekh (2002: 247) calls for qualities essential to eradicating racial discrimination, open as opposed to closed views of 'the other'. Open views include regarding 'the other' as interacting, contributing, sharing some values and aims, being different but of equal worth, sincere not hypocritical, self-critical, open to combating discrimination and exclusion. The challenge is to foster open views of diversity through education, one significant medium is through physical education and its cultural arenas of sport and dance.

FURTHER RESEARCH

Sociological explanations can be helpful in the arena of physical education because they make us ask important questions about human beings and the societies that they form. The following questions are examples of possible further research into the area:

◆ What are the effects of skin colour on selection and career development of teachers?

◆ What is the impact of a teacher's identity on pupils?

◆ How do skin colour, religious and cultural beliefs of parents, teachers and pupils influence choices and behaviour in physical education?

◆ How can physical education become more inclusive of cultural diversity?

◆ What does it mean to provide a broad and balanced physical education in a multicultural society?

◆ How can schools celebrate diversity in a meaningful not tokenistic way?

◆ How can teachers empower black children, raise self-esteem, identify and develop talent where it exists, through physical education, without prejudicing other facets of development and life chances?

◆ Does curriculum content need to change to become more appropriate in a culturally diverse country?

◆ As physical education 'expands' beyond the school, which partnerships, projects, role-models are selected? Why and how is their effectiveness measured?

◆ What are the actual physical education, sport and dance experiences of young black African-Caribbean or South-Asian heritage children?

NOTES

1   As defined by Parekh (2002: xxiv) South Asian refers to people with origins in Pakistan, Bangladesh and India, African-Caribbean to those with origins in Africa or the Caribbean.

2   Specialist Sports Colleges are part of a government strategy to raise standards in secondary schools by awarded 'specialist college' status to schools who make successful bids. Schools can select specialism in a number of fields, for example, sport, peforming arts, languages, technology. *www.tctrust.org.uk*.

3   These terms are used in figurational sociology to denote long-term processes of change, for example, 'medicalisation' refers to the process of 'making medicine and the labels "healthy" and "ill" *relevant* to an ever increasing part of human existence . . . an expansion of the number and range of human conditions which are held to constitute "medical problems", a label which, once attached, is sufficient to justify medical intervention' (Waddington and Murphy, 1992: 37).

4 Creative Partnerships is a creative teaching and learning programme funded jointly by Department for Education and Skills (DfES), Department for Culture, Media and Sport (DCMS) and Arts Council England (ACE) running between 2002–2006. It enables partnerships between creative organisations and schools to develop creative teaching and learning across the curriculum. Initially £40 million is being used over two years in 16 pilot areas and Birmingham is one of these. *www.creative-partnerships.com.*

5 Physical Education, School Sport and Club Links (launched 2 October 2002) is a national strategy funded by the Department for Education and Skills (DfES) *www.dfes.gov/uk/pess*, and the Department for Culture, Media and Sport (DCMS) *www.culture.gov.uk.* It aims to improve standards in physical education and school sport within and beyond the curriculum through eight programmes. The £459 million available from 2003–2006 is on top of £686 million being invested to improve school sport facilities across England. Publication from *dfes@prolog.uk.com.*

6 Social Darwinism was a theory that developed from Charles Darwin's theory of human evolution which accredited higher significance to mental traits than physical traits and white-skinned people as more 'civilised' than black-skinned people (Coakley, 1994: 243).

7 'A Chance to Dance' was a Royal Ballet Education project to identify and develop talent 'to reflect the multi-ethnic nature of British society today' (Clarke, 1993: 169–71). 'Dance Track' is an educational project which has run since 1997, in Birmingham Royal Ballet, involving sponsored training of talented children identified from a number of primary schools in Birmingham who would not normally have the opportunity to develop dance training *www.brb.org.uk.*

8 Equality Challenge Unit Guidance on legislation that outlaws discrimination on the grounds of religious belief – Employment Equality Regulations (Religion and Belief) 2003, *www.ecu.ac.uk.*

9 Chitraleka Dance Company is based at the University of Birmingham and its Artistic Director, Chitraleka Bolar, from Kerala, South India, has been working as an Artist in Britain for over 20 years. In addition to her own performance and choreography work she is one of the leading teachers of Bharatanatyam classical Indian dance and is Chairperson of the Bharatanatyam branch of the ISTD (Imperial Society of Teachers of Dance) which manages development of learning in the private dance sector across the country. Her professional focus has turned increasingly to state schools and her current production, a 'Sci-Art' venture called 'The Story of C (Carbon) can be adapted for schools interested in the science/art links, the styles and creative approaches taken or the Indian roots of the artists, music and dance. *www.chitraleka.ac.uk.*

10 See Sports Council (1993) *Sport in the Nineties: New Horizon*, 31. London: Sports Council; and Sports Council (1994) *Black and Ethnic Minorities in Sport: Policy and Objectives*, 15. London: Sports Council.

REFERENCES

Clarke, M. (1993) 'A Chance to Dance', *The Dancing Times*, November 1993: 169–171.

Adair, C. (1992) 'Black power – black dance', in *Women and Dance, Sylphs and Siren*. London: McMillan. pp 160–181.

Allison, L. (1998) 'Biology, ideology and sport', in L. Allison (ed.), *Taking Sport Seriously*. Aachen: Meyer and Meyer.

Bayliss, T. (1989) 'PE and racism: making changes', *Multicultural Teaching* 7 (2): 19–22.

Benn, T. (1996) 'Muslim women and physical education in initial teacher training', *Sport, Education and Society*, 1 (1): 5–21.

Benn, T. (2000a) 'Valuing cultural diversity: the challenge for physical education', in S. Capel and S. Piotrowski (eds), *Issues in Physical Education*. London, Routledge.

Benn, T. (2000b) 'Towards inclusion in education and physical education', in A. Williams (ed.), *Primary School Physical Education*. London: Falmer Press.

Benn, T. (2002) 'Muslim women in teacher training: issues of gender, 'race' and religion', in D. Penney (ed.), *Gender and Physical Education*. London: Routledge.

Bourdieu, P. (1986) 'The forms of capital', in J. Richardson (ed.), *Handbook of Theory and Research for the Sociology of Education*. New York: Greenwood Press.

BRAP (2003) Furthering education, furthering equality? A report for the Birmingham Race Action Partnership.

Carrington, B. (1983) 'Sport as a side-track. An analysis of West Indian involvement in extra-curricular sport', in L. Barton and S. Walker (eds), *Race, Class and Education*. London: Croom Helm.

Carroll, B. and Hollinshead, G. (1993) 'Equal opportunities: race and gender in physical education: a case study', in J. Evans (ed.), *Equality, Education and Physical Education*. London: Falmer Press. pp. 154–69.

Cantle, T. (2002) *Community Cohesion: A Report of the Independent Review Team*. London: Home Office.

Carrington, B. and McDonald, I. (eds) (2001) *'Race', Sport and British Society*. London: Routledge.

Cashmore, E. (1982) *Black Sportsmen*. London: Routledge and Kegan Paul.

Cashmore, E. 2nd edition (1996) *Making Sense of Sport*, London: Routledge.

Chappell, R. (1995) 'Racial stereotyping in schools', *BAALPE Bulletin*, 31 (4): 22–28.

Chappell, B. (2002) 'Race, ethnicity and sport', in A. Laker (ed.), *The Sociology of Sport and Physical Education*. London: Routledge. pp. 92–109.

Clay, G. (1997) 'Standards in primary and secondary physical education: OFSTED 1995–1996', *British Journal of Physical Education*, 28 (2): 5–9.

Coakley, J. (1994) *Sport in Society Issues and Controversies*. London: Mosby.

Crunden, C. (1974) *A History of Anstey College of Physical Education 1897–1972*. Warwickshire: Anstey College of Physical Education.

Department for Education and Science (DES) (1989) *Circular 24/89 Initial Teacher Training: Approval for Courses*. London: HMSO.

Department For Education (DFE) (1995) *Physical Education in the National Curriculum*, London: HMSO.

Department For Education and Employment (DFEE)/Qualifications and Curriculum Authority (QCA) (1999) Physical Education – The National Curriculum for England. London: DFEE/QCA.

Daiman, S. (1995) 'Women in sport in Islam', *Journal of the International Council for Health, Physical Education, Recreation, Sport and Dance*, 32 (1): 18–21.

Edwards, H. (1972) 'The myth of the racially superior athlete', *Intellectual Digest*, 2: 58–60.

Edwards, H. (1973) 'The black athletes: twentieth-century gladiators for white America', *Psychology Today*, 7: 58–60.

Emery, L.F. (1988) *Black Dance 1619 to Today*. New Jersey: Dance Horizons.

Faust, A., Grosvenor, I. and Schaechter, J. (2000) ' ''I feel like I come from somewhere else''. An examination of the way social exclusion impacts on African Caribbean pupils', *Education and Social Justice*, 3 (1): 9–16.

Figueroa, P.(1993) 'Equality, multiculturalism, antiracism and physical education in the National Curriculum', in J. Evans (ed.), *Equality, Education and Physical Education*. London: Falmer Press.

Fleming, S. (2001) 'Racial science and South Asian black physicality', in B. Carrington and I. McDonald (eds), *'Race' Sport and British Society*. London: Routledge. pp 105–20.

Gillborn, D. and Gipps, C. (1996) *Recent Research on the Achievements of Ethnic Minority Pupils*. Report for the Office for Standards in Education. London: HMSO.

Gillborn, D. and Mirza, H.S. (2000) *Educational Inequality: Mapping Race, Class and Gender, a Synthesis of Research Evidence*. London: OFSTED.

Gilroy, P. (1997) 'Exer(or)cising power: black bodies in the black public sphere', in H. Thomas (ed.), *Dance in the City*. London: MacMillan.

Grosvenor, I. (1999) ' ''Race'' and Education', in I. Grosvenor and D. Matheson (eds), *Introduction to Educational Studies*. London: David Fulton. pp. 70–83.

Hargreaves, J. (1994) *Sporting Females*. London: Routledge.

Henderson, R. (1995) *Is it in the Blood?* WISDEN, *Cricket Monthly*, July 1995, pp. 9–10.

Henley, J. (2003) 'France to ban pupils' religious dress: outlawing headscarves at school is persecution, say Muslims', *The Guardian*, 12 December 2003, p. 17.

Hiskett, M. (1989) *Schooling for British Muslims: Integrated, Opted-out or denominational?* London: Social Affairs Unit.

Hoberman, J. (1997) *Darwin's Athletes: How Sport has Damaged Black America and Preserved the Myth of Race.* Boston: Mariner Books.

Jarvie, G. (2000) 'Sport, racism and ethnicity', in J. Coakley and E. Dunning, (eds), *Handbook of Sports Studies.* London: Sage. pp. 334–43.

Jawad, H. and Benn, T. (eds) (2003) *Muslim Women in the United Kingdom and Beyond.* Leiden: Brill.

Jenkins, R. (1997) *Rethinking Ethnicity: Arguments and Explorations.* London: Sage.

Jobbins, V. (1995) Conference 94, Cultural Diversity and Dance Education, in *Dance Matters*, 12: 2.

Johal, S. (2001) 'Playing their own game: a South Asian football experience', in B. Carrington and I. McDonald (eds), *'Race', Sport and British Society.* London: Routledge. pp. 153–69.

Kane, M. (1971) 'An assessment of black is best'. *Sports Illustrated*, 18 January.

Kirk, D., Fitzgerald, H., Claxton, C. and Haywood, D. (2001) 'Moving towards girl-friendly physical education', paper presented at 14th International Congress of the International Association of Physical Education and Sport for Girls and Women, Alexandria, Egypt, October.

Lenhard, E. (1997) 'Many blacks in ballet still face glass ceiling, expert says', in *Dance Magazine, June*, pp. 148–52.

Lewontin, R.C. (1993) *The Doctrine of DNA – Biology as Ideology.* London: Penguin.

Linschoten, R. and Kleipool, A. (2001) 'The dancer as athlete', in *Not Just Anybody*, advancing health, well-being and excellence in dance and dancers. Conference Report Toronto/The Hague, November 1999, Ontario, Canada, pp. 77–92.

McDonald, I. and Hayes, S. (2003) ' "Race", racism and education', in S. Hayes and G. Stidder, (eds), *Equity and Inclusion in Physical Education and Sport.* London: Routledge. pp. 153–168.

MacPherson, W. (1999) *The Stephen Lawrence Inquiry: Report of an Inquiry by Sir William Macpherson of Cluny,* London: The Stationary Office.

Majors, R. (ed.) (2001) *Educating our Black Children.* Routledge: London.

Marqusee, M. (2001) 'In search of the unequivocal Englishman', in B. Carrington and I. McDonald (eds), *'Race', Sport and British Society.* London: Routledge. pp. 121–32.

Naciri, M. (1973) *The Islamic position in sport, in Sport in the Modern World – Chances and Problems* in, Scientific Congress, Munich Olympics, Berlin: Springer Verlag.

Navadisha (2000) *Navadisha 2000: A Conference for South Asian Dance Today – New Directions.* SAMPAD, MAC, Cannon Hill Park, Birmingham.

Parekh, B. (2002) *The Parekh Report – The Future of Multi-ethnic Britain.* London: Profile Books.

Parker-Jenkins, M. (1995) *Children of Islam.* Stoke-on-Trent: Trentham Books.

Penney, D. (ed.) (2002) *Gender and Physical Education.* London: Routledge.

Penney, D. and Evans, J. (1999) *Politics, Policy and Practice in Physical Education.* London: E & FN Spon.

Polley, M. (1998) *Moving the Goalposts: A History of Sport and Society Since 1945.* London: Routledge.

Rampton Report (1981) *West Indian Children in our Schools.* London: Stationery Office.

Roy, S. (1997) 'Dirt, noise, traffic: contemporary Indian dance in the western city; modernity, ethnicity and hybridity', in H. Thomas (ed.), *Dance in the City.* London: Macmillan.

Runnymede Trust (1997) *Islamophobia – A Challenge For All Of Us.* London: Runnymede Trust.

Sarwar, G. (1994) *British Muslims and Schools.* London: Muslim Education Trust.

Scraton, S. (2001) 'Reconceptualising race, gender and sport', in B. Carrington and I. McDonald (eds), *'Race', Sport and British Society.* London: Routledge. pp. 170–87.

Sfeir, L. (1985) 'The status of Muslim women in sport: conflict between cultural traditions and modernisation', *International Review for Sociology of Sport*, 20 (4): 283–304.

Siraj-Blatchford, I. (1993) 'Ethnicity and conflict in Physical Education – a critique of Carroll and Hollinsheads' case study', *British Educational Research Review*, 19 (1): 72–82.

Sondhi, R. (2000) 'A global cultural overview', in *Navadisha 2000 New Directions – A Conference for South Asian Dance Today* SAMPAD, MAC, Cannon Hill Park, Birmingham B12 9QH <*www.sampad.org.uk*>.

Smith-Autard (2002) *The Art of Dance in Education*. 2nd edn. London: A & C Black.

Swan Report (1985) *Education for All*. London: HMSO.

Sugden, J. (1987) 'The exploitation of disadvantage: the occupational sub-culture of the Boxer', in J. Horne, D. Jary and A. Tomlinson (eds), *Sport, Leisure and Social Relations*. London: Routledge and Kegan Paul.

Thomas, H. (1995) 'Formulating a sociology of dance', *Dance, Modernity and Culture*. London: Routledge.

Vaïsse, J. (2004) Veiled Meaning: The French Law Banning Religious Symbols in Public Schools. U.S. France Analysis Series. March 2004. Washington: The Brookings Institution. www.brookings.edu.

Waddington, I. and Murphy, P. (1992) 'Drugs, sport and ideologies' in E. Dunning and C. Rojek (eds), *Sport and Leisure in the Civilizing Process*. London: Macmillan. pp. 36–64.

Wyon, M. (2001) Dance: the role of the sport scientist. *SportsCare News*, National Sports Medicine Institute UK, 23, Summer. Cambridge: Burlington Press. pp. 12–13.

13 | Inclusion, Special Educational Needs, Disability and Physical Education

Andy Smith and Nigel Thomas
(2005)

The inclusion of pupils with special educational needs (SEN) and disabilities in mainstream schools has increasingly become a central feature of national and international policy towards education in recent years. In the context of physical education (PE) in England, this commitment to 'inclusion' manifested itself in the form of a statutory statement in the revised National Curriculum for Physical Education (NCPE) 2000 (Department for Education and Employment/Qualifications and Curriculum Authority (DfEE/QCA), 1999). In the light of these developments, the purpose of this chapter is to explore some of the aspects of the complex inter-relationships and issues that surround the inclusion of pupils with SEN and disabilities in PE. More specifically, we seek to provide a brief review of the following themes and issues:

◆ SEN, special needs and disability;

◆ the history of educating pupils with SEN and disabilities in mainstream schools;

◆ the revision of the NCPE 2000 and the emphasis placed upon inclusion;

◆ concepts of integration and inclusion;

◆ the suitability of sports and physical activities in the NCPE for pupils with SEN and disabilities;

◆ teacher training and continuing professional development;

◆ the role of learning support assistants in PE;

◆ assessing pupils with SEN and disabilities in NCPE; and

◆ the experiences of pupils with SEN and disabilities in PE.

SPECIAL EDUCATIONAL NEEDS, SPECIAL NEEDS AND DISABILITY

In the UK, as elsewhere, there is a tendency on the part of teachers, policy makers, government officials and academics (see, for example, Vickerman et al., 2003) to conflate the terms SEN, special needs and disability and use them interchangeably even though they may be used to refer to different things and used in different ways in different contexts. We will deal with each of these in turn.

SEN is a legally defined term that refers to the school-based learning needs of pupils that arise from a wide range of difficulties – including cognitive, physical, sensory, communicative or behavioural difficulties as well as those who are perceived to be specially gifted in one way or another[1] – and is used to identify (typically in a statement of SEN) those pupils for whom some kind of special educational provision needs to be made (Audit Commission, 2002; Department for Education and Skills (DfES), 2001a: 6). More specifically, while pupils with SEN – like all pupils – are not a homogenous group and 'are part of a continuum of learners' (Garner and Dwyfor Davies, 2001: 26) they are typically considered to have a learning difficulty of one kind or another if they:

◆ have a significantly greater difficulty in learning than the majority of children of the same age; or

◆ have a disability which prevents or hinders them from making use of educational facilities of a kind generally provided for children of the same age in schools within the area of the local education authority;

◆ are under compulsory school age and fall within the definitions above or would so do if special educational provision was not made for them (DfES, 2001a: 6).

While this conceptual distinction of learning difficulties is useful insofar as it provides an indication of the criteria that help teachers to identify pupils with SEN, it is equally important to realise that a (falsely dichotomous) distinction also tends to be made between two broad groups of pupils: those with SEN and those with SEN in PE (Department of Education and Science (DES)/Welsh Office (WO), 1991). Typically, the latter refers to almost all pupils with movement difficulties – many of whom will not have a formal statement of SEN under the 1981 Education Act – as well as those who may have an SEN related to some or all aspects of PE, while the former refers to those pupils who may have SEN in subjects such as science or maths but not PE (DES/WO, 1991).

While it is inappropriate and unhelpful to dichotomise between groups of pupils in this manner (not least because some pupils have SEN in PE *and* other subjects in the National Curriculum) it is equally important to appreciate that pupils' experiences of having SEN and/or disability – which are, in turn, circumscribed by age, gender, ethnicity, 'race' and social class – are context-specific and processual in nature; that is to say, their needs and the requisite provision are likely to vary between and within different academic subjects and will change over time. It is also worth noting in this connection that it is not the case that all pupils with SEN are always those who have disabilities and that those with disabilities do not always have SEN. Although it is true to say that pupils with disabilities are typically perceived to have 'special needs' of one kind or another, this is not the same as suggesting that they necessarily have SEN. This is the case not least because, among other things, the former, unlike the latter, is a descriptive term that is not legally defined and 'is generally used to refer to the needs which may be experienced by pupils from particular social groups whose circumstances or background are different from most of the school population' (Fredrickson and Cline, 2002: 34); such as those with disabilities or who have English as an additional language. While this might appear conceptual nit-picking, it is crucial to appreciate that while the term 'special needs' is often used interchangeably with the term SEN this can be confusing since pupils from groups which have special needs do not always have SEN (Fredrickson and Cline, 2002).

In a similar manner to the contested conceptualisation or understanding of the terms SEN and special needs, what is understood by the term 'disability' has also been the focus of intense debate. While there is no universally accepted definition of disability, the various definitions of disability that do exist generally fall into two dichotomised categories: medical or social. Indeed, in Britain, as elsewhere, disability has traditionally been explained from a more individualised or medicalised perspective wherein it is conceptualised as an impairment belonging to an individual, resulting in a loss or limitation of function. Such a conception largely ignores how disability is socially constructed. By contrast, the social explanation of disability tends to focus on the environmental and social barriers which exclude people with disabilities from various aspects of the wider society and correspondingly downplays the importance of impairment in the lives of people with disabilities (Thomas, 2003). While a more medicalised definition of disability has tended to dominate and inform educational policy and practice, nevertheless, since the 1980s in Britain, as elsewhere, there has been a growing appreciation of the significance of the socio-genesis of disability. This shift in understanding is reflected in the historical development of educational policy in Britain.

THE EDUCATION OF PUPILS WITH SPECIAL EDUCATIONAL NEEDS AND DISABILITIES IN MAINSTREAM SCHOOLS: SOME HISTORICAL OBSERVATIONS

The long-term process of inclusion of pupils with SEN and disabilities in mainstream education has increased especially rapidly over the last half-century or so, even though evidence of this can be traced as far back as the mid-1800s (Smith, 2004). In the light of the relatively detailed coverage that this process has received elsewhere (see, for example, DES, 1978; Fredrickson and Cline, 2002; Halliday, 1993), we want to provide a brief historical analysis of the education of pupils with SEN and disabilities in mainstream schools since the introduction of the 1944 Education Act.

Following the 1944 Education Act, pupils with SEN and disabilities were assigned to medically defined categories, including: the physically handicapped, blind and educationally subnormal (Halliday, 1993; Thomas, 2003). Following a medical or psychological assessment pupils were often placed into (segregated) special education in predetermined categories of impairment which, Halliday (1993) suggests, did not consider their individual needs or competencies. Although not a development that was exclusive to Britain – witness the introduction of the *Education of All Handicapped Act* in 1975 and the concept of 'least restrictive environment' in the USA – by the mid-1960s there was growing support for the need to reverse the segregation of those pupils with SEN and disabilities who received their education in special schools towards encouraging their ability to 'access' and be educated alongside their peers in mainstream schools. While this was due in part to policy developments 'internal' to the education profession at this time, the move towards the integration of pupils with SEN and disabilities in mainstream education was also influenced by broader social processes and power struggles between people with disabilities and others within the wider society. These power struggles principally involved the campaigning by various groups – notably the Union of the Physically Impaired Against Segregation (UPIAS) – which focused upon ensuring that people with disabilities have access to the same opportunities as others to participate in various aspects of wider society such as mainstream schools. Indeed, it was argued that the integration of pupils with SEN and disabilities into mainstream schools would facilitate their access to, and participation in, education and social life more generally. This shift in the focus of the debate surrounding the ostensible need for pupils with SEN and disabilities to be educated in mainstream schools was further consolidated throughout the 1970s and 1980s by various important policy developments, most prominent among which were the 1978 Warnock Report and the 1981 Education Act.

Based on the recommendations of the Warnock Report (DES, 1978) – which has come to be regarded as 'the touchstone of the modern era of SEN provision' (Garner and Dwyfor Davies, 2001: 10) and an important landmark in thinking about SEN – the medically defined categories through which the individual child was perceived as the 'problem' some 30 years previously, were replaced with the concept of SEN in the 1981 Education Act to prevent the sharp distinction between two groups of pupils: the handicapped and the non-handicapped. The introduction of the term 'SEN' resulted in a move away from using those categories of handicap which had previously been the basis for the provision of special educational services for those pupils who needed them (such the educationally subnormal, blind and maladjusted) while, simultaneously, greatly extending the range of pupils considered to have SEN. While the previous categories of handicap applied to approximately 2 per cent of the school population – many of whom were educated in special schools – this re-classification of pupils, which apparently focused more fully on their individual needs[2], led to the identification of as many as 20 per cent of children considered to have SEN (some of whom may have disabilities) (DES, 1978).[3] These developments notwithstanding, according to Halliday (1993), the constraints imposed on teachers and schools by the 1981 Act further encouraged what has been a 'partial and gradual transference' of pupils from special to mainstream schools and thus mainstream PE. It has been partial inasmuch as it was typically those pupils with less severe difficulties who were being educated in mainstream schools, while those with more severe difficulties tended to remain in the special school sector (Halliday, 1993; Thomas, 2003).

During the mid-1990s, the commitment towards integrated education (as it had come to be known by this time) and the debate surrounding its feasibility was further intensified by a number of significant developments in policy legislation – most notably the 1993 and 1996 Education Acts, the introduction of the Code of Practice and Salamanca Statement in 1994 as well as the 1996 Disability Discrimination Act. The Salamanca Statement on inclusive education (United Nations Educational, Scientific and Cultural Organisation (UNESCO), 1994), for example, reflected the ostensible commitment by governments worldwide to providing a more inclusive education system and 'equalising opportunities' for all pupils in mainstream education. In Britain, the political commitment to developing a 'more inclusive education system' is made clear in the Green Paper *Excellence for All Children: Meeting Special Educational Needs* (DfEE, 1997) in which the newly-elected Labour government expressed its commitment to the proclamations made in the Salamanca Statement thus:

> We want to see more pupils with SEN included within mainstream primary and secondary schools. We support the United Nations Educational, Scientific and Cultural Organization (UNESCO) Salamanca World Statement on Special Needs Education. This calls on governments to adopt the principle of inclusive education, enrolling all children in regular schools, unless there are compelling reasons for doing otherwise. That implies the progressive extension of the capacity of mainstream schools to provide for children with a wide range of needs (DfEE, 1997: 44).

This commitment by the Labour government to ensuring that all pupils with SEN and disabilities would be educated in mainstream schools 'unless there are compelling reasons for doing otherwise' (DfEE, 1997: 44), has continued to influence the development of subsequent policies including the White Paper *Meeting Special Educational Needs: A Programme of Action* (DfEE, 1998) and the SEN Revised Code of Practice (DfES, 2001). Most recently, the *Special Educational Needs and Disability Act* (Stationery Office, 2001) strengthened the endorsement of inclusion by revising Section 316 of the 1996 Education Act such that mainstream schools are no longer able to refuse a pupil with SEN or a disability on the basis that they cannot meet their needs.

Given this strong policy commitment to inclusion, therefore, it is perhaps unsurprising to find that the extent to which pupils with SEN and disabilities are being included within lessons in mainstream schools has become the focus of a great deal of attention from researchers and policy makers as well as government officials and other professional bodies. What stands out about much of these enquires related to 'inclusion', however, is a general dearth of research which focuses specifically upon the *inclusion* of pupils with SEN and disabilities in *physical education*. Indeed, much of the research that does exist has largely been conducted in the USA (for a review, see Block, 1999) and has tended to focus upon the *integration* of these pupils in a PE setting: that is to say, the assimilation of these pupils into the existing PE environment.

Notwithstanding the dearth of research on inclusion in mainstream schools in Britain, there is a small, but growing, body of research – mainly conducted in English schools – that has begun to explore the suitability of the NCPE for pupils with SEN and disabilities, teacher training and continuing professional development (CPD) and the role of learning support colleagues in PE by examining the perspectives and experiences of teachers and pupils (see, for example, Fitzgerald and Gorely 2003; Fitzgerald et al., 2003a, 2003b; Morley et al., 2003; Penney and Evans, 1995; Smith, 2004; Smith and Green, forthcoming; Vickerman, 2002, 2003). We want, now, to provide a brief summary of this research by focusing in the first instance on the revision of the NCPE 2000 for England which, like the policies discussed above that were much more specifically related to SEN and disability, has the potential to impact upon the education of pupils with SEN and disabilities in mainstream school.

INCLUSION AND THE NATIONAL CURRICULUM PHYSICAL EDUCATION 2000

The revision of the NCPE 2000 for England featured for the first time a detailed, statutory statement on inclusion (DfEE/QCA, 1999) and, in so doing, re-emphasised the centrality of 'inclusion' and 'inclusive practices' in government policy related to education and PE (Penney, 2002). Broadly speaking, this inclusion statement created an expectation that teachers would ensure that all pupils were 'enabled to participate as fully and effectively as possible within the National Curriculum and the statutory assessment arrangements' therein (DfEE/QCA, 1999: 33). More specifically, the statement requires teachers 'to ensure that all pupils have the chance to succeed, whatever their individual needs and the potential barriers to their learning may be' (1999: 3). To this end, teachers in all subject areas, including PE, are now required to plan and teach the National Curriculum with 'due regard' to three principles of inclusion:

1. setting suitable learning challenges;
2. responding to pupils' diverse learning needs;
3. overcoming barriers to learning and assessment for individuals and groups of pupils (1999: 28).

By paying particular attention to these principles of inclusion, teachers are expected to employ differentiated strategies that are appropriate and challenging to all pupils – including those with SEN and disabilities – regardless of how diverse and challenging their levels of ability needs are (Penney, 2002). While research which explores teachers' understandings and conceptualisations of inclusion and the ways in which they inform teachers' practice is still very much in its infancy (Penney, 2002), there have, nevertheless, been some developments in this regard. It is to a consideration of some of these developments that we now turn.

CONCEPTUALISING INCLUSION AND INTEGRATION IN PHYSICAL EDUCATION

Debate surrounding the nature and purposes of inclusion and integration in education generally and PE specifically – as well as its implications for teachers' practice – remains nothing if not a persistent and contentious one (see, for example, Avramidis and Norwich, 2002; Croll and Moses, 2000; Evans and Lunt, 2002; Vickerman, 2002, 2003; Vickerman et al., 2003). Nonetheless – and notwithstanding the tendency by academics and policy makers as well as teachers to use these terms interchangeably (see, for example, Morley et al., 2003; Smith, 2004) in a manner which has led to 'potential confusion in the interpretation of values and principles related to inclusive education' (Vickerman, 2002: 79) – there are some broad areas of agreement on how each relates to the incorporation of pupils with SEN and disabilities in mainstream schools.

In broad terms, it is generally accepted that the *integration* of pupils with SEN and disabilities in mainstream schools involves 'placing' rather than 'including' these pupils in schools and curricula intended for pupils of higher ability (Barton, 1993). In this regard, integration has been considered an assimilation process through which pupils with SEN and disabilities 'fit in' to the existing arrangements in schools (such as the structure of the NCPE) (Barton, 1993; Fredrickson and Cline, 2002). Conversely, what is understood by 'inclusion' in an education context has generated rather more debate than that surrounding 'integration'. Nonetheless, an enduring feature of recent policy in Britain, as elsewhere, is that inclusion 'within the field of education . . . is reflected in the development of strategies that seek to bring about a genuine equalisation of opportunity' (UNESCO, 1994: 11) for all pupils to participate in the same learning contexts in mainstream schools. In contrast, others have noted how inclusion – as a somewhat vague term that masks a number of implicitly ideological connotations – is often conceptualised as a counterpoint to the equally vague notion of exclusion (Garner and Dwyfor Davies, 2001), while the Office for Standards in Education (OFSTED) suggest that the term inclusion refers to 'the process of educating children with special educational needs (SEN) alongside their peers in mainstream schools' (OFSTED, 2003: 4).

Despite the prevalence of such diverse and contrasting views, it seems clear that if we restrict ourselves to debating the substantive issue of what inclusion is at an abstract conceptual level, then this is, in effect, to fail to appreciate or engage in the realities of PE – and the inclusion of pupils with SEN and disabilities therein – as practice (Green, 2003). By failing to do so, these interested parties will not only continue to talk past each other, they will have little or no chance of engaging PE teachers at any level (Green, 2003). This, it is argued, is crucial, for unless one takes into account the realities of teachers' situations as well as their views and practices and the significance of those for the inclusion of pupils with SEN and disabilities in PE, then academics and policy makers as well as government officials are unlikely to have their objectives concerning inclusion met.

In attempting to more adequately engage in the realities of including pupils with SEN and disabilities in PE as practice, Morley et al. (2003) have noted how *vis-à-vis* the rhetoric in several of the policies referred to above, many of the teachers in their study conceptualised inclusion as an 'aspiration' or a 'journey'; that is to say, the teachers often claimed to be working *towards* the 'greater inclusion' of these pupils in PE. In a similar study, Smith (2004) reported how the 'underpinning rationale' of the policy of inclusion in the NCPE for most of the teachers in his study was to ensure that all pupils, including those with SEN and disabilities, have an 'equal opportunity' to participate in PE and that inclusion is best conceived of as a *process* which has a number of intended and unintended consequences. More specifically, it was concluded that while the phrase 'giving equal opportunities' was a more or less common feature of many of the teachers' views on inclusion, as well as a justification for what they did in practice, it appeared that upon closer scrutiny, what they considered inclusion to 'be' was more in keeping with traditional conceptualisations of integration; that is to say, an assimilation process through which pupils with disabilities and SEN are required to 'fit into' the existing PE curriculum as they were already planned (Smith, 2004).

At the time of writing these are the only existing studies that, to the best of our knowledge, have begun to explore teachers' views and practices concerning the inclusion of pupils with SEN and disabilities in PE since the introduction of the NCPE 2000 and, thus, there remains a clear need for future research of this kind. In contrast, a plethora of studies exist examining such issues beyond the context of PE. Croll and Moses (2000), for example, have reported that the views of education officers and headteachers of special and mainstream schools in their study suggested that while 'the principle of inclusion of all children in mainstream ... schools has achieved widespread support, at least at a rhetorical level' (2000: 4), there 'is a basic belief in the desirability of inclusion but no real thought that this is realisable' (2000: 10). The teachers and other professionals in Evans and Lunt's (2002) study also concluded that the inclusion of all pupils with SEN and disabilities was idealistic and unrealistic and, more specifically, was particularly difficult for some pupils who have severe difficulties that are not easily accommodated in mainstream schools.

ARE PUPILS WITH DIFFERENT TYPES OF SPECIAL EDUCATIONAL NEEDS AND DISABILITIES MORE EASILY INCLUDED IN PHYSICAL EDUCATION?

Teachers' ability to include pupils with SEN and disabilities is frequently influenced by the particular types of needs of those pupils. On the whole, there appears to be a growing consensus that pupils with emotional and behavioural difficulties (EBD) and severe learning difficulties of one kind or another tend to 'present teachers and schools with the greatest challenge' (Garner and Dwyfor Davies, 2001: 67) to inclusion (see, for example, Avramidis and Norwich, 2002; Croll and Moses, 2000; Evans and Lunt, 2002; Morley et al., 2003; OFSTED, 2003; Smith, 2004). Morley et al. (2003), for example, have noted that the

Research into inclusion

majority of teachers in their study were somewhat apprehensive towards the inclusion of pupils with various behavioural difficulties in PE. By contrast, the inclusion of pupils with physical and sensory difficulties of various kinds in PE, like many other areas of the curriculum, tend to be viewed more favourably by teachers, not least because these pupils are often perceived to pose less constraint upon their teaching and are more easily included in lessons (Morley et al., 2003; Smith, 2004).

THE SUITABILITY OF SPORTS AND PHYSICAL ACTIVITIES IN NATIONAL CURRICULUM PHYSICAL EDUCATION FOR PUPILS WITH SPECIAL EDUCATIONAL NEEDS AND DISABILITIES

The introduction of the NCPE in 1992 established a broad and balanced curriculum as a statutory entitlement for all pupils in all state schools in England and Wales. While it is intended that all pupils should experience a broad range of involvement in each of the activity areas that comprise the NCPE, it was recognised by the Working Group prior to the implementation of the NCPE that teachers would experience difficulty in 'fully integrating children with (SEN and disabilities) into all aspects of a physical education programme' (DES/WO, 1991: 36). The Working Group acknowledged, moreover, that 'traditional' team games are activities in which teachers might experience particular difficulty in incorporating some pupils with SEN and disabilities (DES/WO, 1991). More specifically, it was suggested that: 'Modifications to conventional games sometimes facilitate access, but the placing of a child with a visual impairment, or with a severe locomotor disability, in a class learning netball or rugby are not likely to be successful' (DES/WO, 1991: 38).

Conversely, the Working Group considered activities that have been increasingly marginalised within the PE curriculum, such as dance, swimming and Outdoor and Adventurous Activities (OAA) (Penney, 2002; Waddington et al., 1997; Waddington et al., 1998), as particularly suitable activities in which many pupils with SEN and disabilities can be more adequately included with their peers in mainstream PE (DES/WO, 1991). It is perhaps not altogether surprising, therefore, to find that recent research has suggested that while pupils with SEN and disabilities may be included in mainstream PE and afforded equal opportunities to participate in the same learning contexts as their ostensibly 'more able' peers, in practice, many of these pupils do not always experience the same range or types of activities in NCPE (Morley et al., 2003; Penney and Evans, 1995; Smith, 2004; Stafford, 1989). On the basis of the available data, teachers have frequently suggested that pupils with SEN and disabilities are often, although not always, excluded from, or take a limited part in, those activities that tend to form the core of PE curricula within schools: namely, competitive sports and team games (Morley et al., 2003; Penney and Evans, 1995; Smith, 2004). The comments of teachers from two recent studies are particularly illustrative in this regard:

> I think the difficult ones to include pupils with disabilities and special needs are team games. It's alright in situations when you are developing skills and fitness but when it comes to the actual game there is not a lot you can actually do. (Smith, 2004: 47)

> The team situations . . . [are] okay with the skills that's fine but when they're actually put into a game situation . . . they get confused, its frustrating for them . . . because they don't know where they're supposed to be within the spatial awareness of things. (Morley et al., 2003: 23)

This is *not* to say however that *all* pupils with SEN and disabilities tend to be excluded from participating in sport and team games specifically and that by implication *all* of these pupils are always more likely to be easily included in more individualised physical activities. Such assertions do not take into account the diverse experiences of these pupils; the abilities and needs of whom are equally diverse. Rather, it is to simply suggest that, broadly speaking, team games as an area of the PE curriculum, do not often easily lend themselves to the inclusion of *some* pupils with SEN and disabilities, while more individual physical activities might not be viewed as being suitable by teachers for *some* of those pupils.

This notwithstanding, the evidence indicates that many teachers often claim that those activities which are ostensibly more conducive to the inclusion of pupils with SEN and disabilities with various difficulties in PE tend to be those more individualised physical activities that are on the margins of the PE curriculum, such as swimming, OAA, gymnastics, badminton and dance (see, for example, Morley et al., 2003; Penney and Evans, 1995; Smith, 2004). Indeed, it seems that the further we move away from more individualised physical activities towards more complex, competitive performance-oriented team sports there tends to be a correlative increase in the likelihood of the exclusion of some pupils with SEN and disabilities – particularly those with more severe difficulties – from all or some aspects of those activities (Smith, 2004).

We might begin to explain this tendency by exploring, among other things (such as teaching style, available facilities, the nature of the group and group size), the rather different pattern of social relationships involved in more individualised physical activities and rather more complex team sports, insofar as the former are more likely than the latter to involve physical movements of a rhythmic nature which, in addition to the intensity and duration of the activity, can be controlled to a much higher degree by the individual participant (Sugden and Talbot, 1996; Waddington, 2000; Waddington et al., 1997; Wright and Sugden, 1999). In more specific terms, it might be suggested that pupils with SEN and disabilities are perhaps more likely to be fully included in those physical activities in which they are able to move in ways that best suit their own physical capabilities and in which they are more able to control the intensity and duration of those movements than they are in more complex team sports, wherein the complex interweaving of the actions of a large number of players and the use of complex movement patterns as well as other physical and psychological skills might militate against their full inclusion in PE (Sugden and Talbot, 1996; Smith, 2004; Waddington, 2000; Waddington et al., 1997; Wright and Sugden, 1999).

Hence, while the specific nature of a pupil's difficulty and the support they receive in lessons can be fundamental in determining what activities they are able to participate in, it would appear that it is the *nature* of the activities provided in the PE curriculum – with its apparent emphasis upon 'performance', 'excellence' and 'skills' (Green, 2003; Penney and Harris, 1997) – that can ultimately preclude many pupils from participating fully with their peers in mainstream PE. Indeed, the alleged 'privileging' of sport over physical activity (Penney and Evans, 1999) in NCPE alongside the provision of a limited and somewhat narrow range of activities for some pupils with SEN and disabilities raises serious questions about the extent to which these pupils are being, or even can be, fully included within the PE curriculum (Smith, 2004).

INITIAL TEACHER TRAINING AND CONTINUING PROFESSIONAL DEVELOPMENT

One of the issues to have attracted most attention over the last 20 years or so has been the adequacy of the initial teacher training (ITT) programmes and continuing professional development (CPD) in preparing teachers for the inclusion of pupils with SEN and disabilities in mainstream schools and thus PE (Avramidis and Norwich, 2002; OFSTED, 2003; Robertson et al., 2000; Vickerman, 2002; Vickerman et al., 2003). In this context, OFSTED (2003) has noted recently that in the light of the growing commitment to educate pupils with SEN and disabilities in mainstream schools, it is not uncommon for many teachers to claim that they 'were being asked to teach children with significant learning needs and manage difficult situations without enough learning' (2003: 24). With regard to PE, Vickerman (2002: 92), for example, has stressed 'a need for the profession to establish a clear and consistent approach to inclusive PE', while against the background of what they perceive as 'the impoverished nature of special educational needs and inclusive education provision' (Robertson et al., 2000: 61) within PE teacher training, Robertson et al., among others (see, for example, Vickerman et al., 2003) argue that in order to more adequately meet the needs of all pupils, especially those with SEN and disabilities, 'inclusion issues' should be embedded throughout all aspects of such training.

Indeed, teachers in many studies have frequently attributed their lack of confidence in including pupils with SEN and disabilities in PE lessons to what they perceive as the 'inadequate' professional training they receive in their ITT and CPD and, as such, often view this lack of training and preparation for meeting these pupils' needs as one of the most constraining influences upon their everyday practices (Morley et al., 2003; Smith and Green, forthcoming). There are three points to be made in this regard. The first is that the provision of training for teachers (through ITT, CPD or other professional courses organised by organisations such as the Youth Sport Trust) is often too brief, superficial, inaccessible and inconsistently delivered. The second point is that much of the formal school-based training that is delivered to teachers tends to be oriented primarily towards 'general issues of inclusion' and is often not always specifically related to PE. The third point is that a small, but growing body of evidence seems to be suggesting that where teachers do receive training that they perceive as being more relevant to PE, this tends to be done on a rather informal *ad hoc* basis at departmental level; that is to say, through discussions with fellow colleagues both within and beyond PE departments in schools (Morley et al., 2003; Smith and Green, forthcoming; Vickerman, 2002, 2003).

Although there is evidence of an increased availability of training that is focused specifically upon preparing teachers to meet the diverse needs of pupils with SEN and disabilities, there is, in our view, a tendency to over-emphasise the significance of training as it impacts on PE as it is experienced by pupils (Green, 2002). While it is perhaps understandable that commentators and teachers are to be found making positive claims regarding the potential claims of training – especially given the current emphasis on 'inclusion' – there would appear to be an implicit and almost taken-for-granted assumption that ITT or CPD that is focused more specifically towards 'inclusion issues' will necessarily influence the 'already established philosophies and practices of would-be (and currently practising) teachers' (2002: 70). Although a lot more could be said in this regard, we want, now, to briefly consider some of the constraints teachers experience through their relationships at the level of the school: namely, the role of learning support assistants (LSAs) and SEN coordinators (SENCOs) in PE.

THE ROLE OF LEARNING SUPPORT ASSISTANTS IN PHYSICAL EDUCATION

According to Garner and Dwyfor Davies (2001: 79) one of 'the most important features of recent SEN policy is the need for teachers to work in collaboration with a range of other professionals' most prominent among which are LSAs;[4] the upshot of which has been that the network of relationships in which PE teachers are involved at the level of the school has become ever more complex. Moreover, as the political commitment towards the inclusion of pupils with SEN and disabilities in mainstream PE has increased, there has emerged a correlative increase in the emphasis placed upon the role of LSAs in assisting teachers.

While it is likely that teachers' views on the kinds of support they receive from LSAs and SENCOs and the consequences of this for their pupils' learning, will vary according to the particular contexts in which teachers find themselves, at present it appears many PE teachers view LSAs as placing a relatively high degree of constraint upon their everyday practice, not least because most of the LSAs they work with are not always – if at all – trained specifically in PE, which is often said to have serious implications for pupils' experiences of PE (Morley et al., 2003; Smith and Green, forthcoming). Teachers have, moreover, also expressed concern at the lack of support they receive from LSAs compared with other ostensibly more academic subjects such as English, maths and science and have stressed that when they do receive such it can sometimes be 'more of a hindrance than a help' (Morley et al., 2003; Smith and Green, forthcoming).

Having said this, and despite the tendency for teachers to be rather critical of the kind and amount of support they receive from LSAs, one study (Smith and Green, forthcoming) has demonstrated how the former have been particularly receptive to the involvement of the latter in lessons, not least because of the practical benefits this had for them. Indeed, it was observed that although the teachers in their study appeared committed to working with LSAs to meet pupils' needs, their primary concern appeared to be one of pragmatism; that is to say, by supporting ostensibly less-able pupils, LSAs let teachers 'off the hook', as it were, and enabled them to 'get on with teaching the other pupils'. One additional way in which LSAs might be viewed as playing a crucial role in this regard, is that of assisting teachers with ensuring the safety of pupils generally, and those with SEN and disabilities in particular, not least because the constraint on teachers to include pupils with EBD and severe learning difficulties alongside those who use mobility devices (such as wheelchairs), for example, is likely to further intensify the pressures experienced by teachers in ensuring the safety of all pupils in lessons (Morley et al., 2003).

ASSESSING PUPILS WITH SPECIAL EDUCATIONAL NEEDS AND DISABILITIES IN PHYSICAL EDUCATION

In the revision of the NCPE 2000 an eight-level scale of descriptions of pupil performance was introduced and it is on the basis of these that teachers are required to ensure that all pupils, including those with disabilities and SEN, are assessed according to the same assessment criteria. In this regard, Penney (2001) has pointed towards the rather prescriptive nature of these statements and the confusion that this has created for teachers in distinguishing between pupils' performance at, and progression between, each of these levels of achievement. It might also be argued that these levels fail to outline how teachers should amend the criteria to more adequately account for the variations between the performances of pupils with and without SEN and disabilities and thus enable them to convey to those students their achievements. Indeed, in a recent study teachers expressed particular concern about their perceived inability (largely because of their lack of training) to make accurate assessments of pupils with SEN and disabilities in secondary school PE and who are seen as working at a level below that normally expected from pupils at Key Stage 3 and 4 (Smith and Green, forthcoming). More specifically, the teachers often suggested that many of these pupils were unable to meet the assessment criteria in the revised NCPE not least because the apparent 'criterion for achievement in PE is being able to perform the activity', and many of the pupils with whom they worked were unable to perform many of the activities being taught.

Notwithstanding concerns regarding the suitability of the NCPE assessment criteria for conveying some pupils' achievements in PE, teachers are, nevertheless, constrained to do so because of the statutory nature of such assessments and the activities that comprise the NCPE. While teachers are able to supplement these criteria with the 'P' scales developed by the QCA – that is, a set of performance descriptions used for recording the achievements of pupils who are working towards level one of the NCPE – that are in many cases a more adequate representation of these pupils needs, as OFSTED (2003: 17) has noted, they are 'not always well known or used in secondary schools'. Beyond the provision of these 'P' scales, however, it remains very much the responsibility of teachers to adapt activities and skills included in the NCPE on the basis of advice and guidance that is available from 'the various organisations concerned either with a specific impairment, or with sport for people with a disability' (DES/WO, 1991: 36) – such as Disability Sport England and the English Federation of Disability Sport – in order to for them to have a substantive impact upon their pupils' experience of PE.

THE PHYSICAL EDUCATION EXPERIENCES OF PUPILS WITH SPECIAL EDUCATIONAL NEEDS AND DISABILITIES

Thus far, we have concerned ourselves primarily with teachers' perceptions and experiences of the inclusion of pupils with SEN and disabilities in PE following the revision of the NCPE 2000. This is due in no small measure to the fact that the extent to which contemporary policy legislation such as the NCPE 2000 and Revised Code of Practice have influenced the everyday PE and sporting experiences of young people with disabilities and SEN remains unclear and is an area to which little research has been devoted (Fitzgerald and Gorely, 2003; Fitzgerald et al., 2003a, 2003b). In seeking to address this largely under researched area and to rectify the failure among those within and beyond the PE subject community 'to explore PE and sporting experiences from the viewpoint of young disabled people' (Fitzgerald et al., 2003b: 178) themselves, Fitzgerald and colleagues have begun to explore the PE experiences of young people with disabilities using focus group interviews, 'free-time' activity diaries and reflective journal methodologies (see, for example, Fitzgerald and Gorely, 2003; Fitzgerald et al., 2003a, 2003b). Broadly speaking, these studies have suggested that, among other things, while pupils with SEN and disabilities were indeed participating in some of the activities in NCPE, they themselves as well as their teachers often perceived the status of the types of activities in which they were involved as inferior compared with those of others in the class (Fitzgerald and Gorely, 2003; Fitzgerald et al., 2003a, 2003b). This perceived difference in status as well as their experiences of PE, was often exacerbated by their involvement in different activities during lessons. It was also not uncommon for pupils with SEN and disabilities to compare their own physical abilities and position within the group to those of others in the class (pupils without SEN and disabilities) and noted, in particular, the ways in which this can lead to their limited involvement in, even exclusion from, PE and team games such as rugby and basketball (Fitzgerald and Gorely, 2003; Fitzgerald et al., 2003a, 2003b). All in all, these findings the authors argue, raise serious questions about the extent to which these pupils are currently being included in PE and, if we wish to more adequately assess the (often unintended) consequences of various inclusion policies in PE, it is imperative that future research begins to explore in greater detail the views and experiences of pupils.

CONCLUSION

In this chapter, we have sought to briefly outline some of the enduring themes and contemporary issues as well as some of the complex inter-relationships that surround the inclusion of pupils with SEN and disabilities in PE following the revision of the NCPE 2000 in England. However, it is worth remembering throughout the course of any analysis such as this, that the introduction of the policy of inclusion in the NCPE is but one additional policy in an already 'crowded policy space' (Houlihan, 2000). Indeed, some would argue that the principles underpinning the policy of inclusion might be constrained as being diametrically opposed to those underpinning policies in which emphasis is placed upon the raising of standards of achievement and increasing competition between schools for pupils, as well as the introduction of national standards of assessment and testing stimulated by the Education Reform Act (Penney and Evans, 1999). It is also important to appreciate that the present commitment to ensuring that, wherever possible, pupils with SEN and disabilities are educated in mainstream schools, is most adequately conceptualised as a long-term process that is 'not only unplanned, but also unfinished' (Goudsblom and Mennell, 1998: 229), and one that has been intensified further by the current government's view of education and thus PE 'as a key to achieving the broader objective of social inclusion' (Houlihan and White, 2002: 85).

We realise that a wide-ranging discussion such as this on a subject that is both complex and broad in its focus, probably throws up as many questions as it provides answers. Nevertheless, it is our contention that to more adequately understand how pupils with SEN and disabilities are being included in *practice* in PE by teachers – and in the hope of producing realistic policies through which the production of undesirable unintended consequences for the pupils and teachers themselves can be minimised – it is imperative that we strive to engage more fully with the realities of PE as practice. More specifically, in order that we can begin to develop our understanding of the complex inter-relationships and issues that surround the inclusion of pupils with SEN and disabilities in PE, it is our view that the production of further theory-guided, empirically-grounded research is crucial if we are to advance our understanding of these issues.

NOTES

1   While this is evidently the case, our focus in the chapter is on the former.

2   In contrast, Bailey and Robertson have claimed that the term 'SEN' 'is very vague, telling us little about the nature of difficulties experienced by a child . . . it is unhelpfully stigmatising . . . [it fails] to recognise individual differences or needs' (2000: 66).

3   Although there are real difficulties in trying to arrive at a precise estimate of the number of pupils with SEN and disabilities in mainstream schools, recently published data suggests that approximately 1 in 5 school children are now considered to have a formally, or informally, identified SEN of one kind or another (Audit Commission, 2002).

4   LSAs are just one potentially constraining influence on teachers practice at the local level. Others that are likely to impose equal, if not more, constraint on teachers and thus affect PE as it is experienced by pupils are: other teaching colleagues (such other PE teachers and SEN Coordinators), headteachers, senior management and even parents and pupils themselves.

REFERENCES

Audit Commission (2002) *Special Educational Needs: A Mainstream Issue*. London: Audit Commission.

Avramidis, E. and Norwich, B. (2002) 'Teachers' attitudes towards integration/inclusion: a review of the literature', *European Journal of Special Needs Education*, 17: 129–47.

Bailey, R. and Robertson, C. (2000) 'Including all pupils in primary school physical education', in R. Bailey and T. Macfayden (eds), *Teaching Physical Education 5–11*. London: Continuum.

Barton, L. (1993) 'Disability, empowerment and physical education', in J. Evans (ed.), *Equality, Education and Physical Education*. London: The Falmer Press.

Block, M. (1999) 'Did we jump on the wrong bandwagon? Problems with inclusion in physical education', *Palaestra*, 15: 3–17.

Croll, P. and Moses, D. (2000) 'Ideologies and utopias: education professionals' views of inclusion', *European Journal of Special Needs Education*, 15: 1–12.

Department for Education and Skills (2001) *Special Educational Needs Code of Practice*. London: DfES.

Department for Education and Employment (DfEE) (1997) *Excellence for All Children: Meeting Special Educational Needs*. London: Stationary Office.

Department for Education and Employment (DfEE) (1998) *Meeting Special Educational Needs: A Programme of Action*. London: DfEE.

Department for Education and Employment/Qualifications and Curriculum Authority (DfEE/QCA) (1999) *Physical Education: The National Curriculum for England*. London: HMSO.

Department of Education and Science (1978) *Special Educational Needs: Report of the Committee of Enquiry into the Education of Handicapped Children and Young People (The Warnock Report)*. London: HMSO.

Department of Education and Science/Welsh Office (DES/WO) (1991) *Physical Education for Ages 5–16. Proposals of the Secretary of State for Education and the Secretary of State for Wales*. London: DES/WO.

Evans, J. and Lunt, I. (2002) 'Inclusive education: are their limits?', *European Journal of Special Needs Education*, 17: 1–14.

Fitzgerald, H. and Gorely, T. (2003) ' "Inclusive" physical education? Insights from young disabled people', paper presented at the British Educational Research Association Annual Conference, Edinburgh, 10–13 September.

Fitzgerald, H., Jobling, A. and Kirk, D. (2003a) 'Listening to the 'voices' of students with severe learning difficulties through a task-based approach to research and learning in physical education', *Support for Learning*, 18: 123–29.

Fitzgerald, H., Jobling, A. and Kirk, D. (2003b) 'Valuing the voices of young disabled people: exploring experiences of physical education and sport', *European Journal of Physical Education*, 8: 175–201.

Fredrickson, N. and Cline, T. (2002) *Special Educational Needs, Inclusion and Diversity: A Textbook*. Buckingham: Open University Press.

Garner, P. and Dwyfor Davies, J. (2001) *Introducing Special Educational Needs: A Companion Guide for Student Teachers.* London: David Fulton.

Goudsblom, J. and Mennell, S. (eds) (1998) *The Norbert Elias Reader.* Oxford: Blackwell.

Green, K. (2002) 'Physical education teachers in their figurations: a sociological analysis of everyday "philosophies" ', *Sport, Education and Society,* 7: 65–83.

Green, K. (2003) *Physical Education Teachers on Physical Education: A Sociological Study of Philosophies and Ideologies.* Chester: Chester Academic Press.

Halliday, P. (1993) 'Physical education within special education provision', in J. Evans (ed.), *Equality, Education and Physical Education.* London: The Falmer Press.

Houlihan, B. (2000) 'Sporting excellence, schools and sports development: the politics of crowded policy spaces', *European Physical Education Review,* 6: 171–94.

Houlihan, B. and White, A. (2002) *The Politics of Sports Development.* London: Routledge.

Morley, D., Bailey, R., Tan, J. and Cooke, B. (2003) 'Inclusive physical education: teachers' views of meeting special needs in physical education', paper presented at the British Educational Research Association Annual Conference, Edinburgh, 10–13 September.

Office for Standards in Education (OFSTED) (2003) *Special Educational Needs in the Mainstream.* London: HMSO.

Penney, D. (2001) 'The revision and initial implementation of the National Curriculum for Physical Education in England', *The Bulletin of Physical Education,* 37: 93–134.

Penney, D. (2002) 'Equality, equity and inclusion in physical education and school sport', in A. Laker (ed.), *The Sociology of Sport and Physical Education: An Introductory Reader.* London: RoutledgeFalmer.

Penney, D. and Evans, J. (1995) 'The National Curriculum for physical education: entitlement for all?', *The British Journal of Physical Education,* 26: 6–13.

Penney, D. and Evans, J. (1999) *Politics, Policy and Practice in Physical Education.* London: E and FN Spon.

Penney, D. and Harris, J. (1997) 'Extra-curricular physical education: more of the same for the more able?', *Sport, Education and Society,* 2: 41–54.

Robertson, C., Childs, C. and Marsden, E. (2000) 'Equality and the inclusion of pupils with special educational needs in physical education', in S. Capel and S. Piotrowski. (eds), *Issues in Physical Education.* London: RoutledgeFalmer.

Smith, A. (2004) 'The inclusion of pupils with special educational needs in secondary school physical education', *Physical Education and Sport Pedagogy.* 9: 37–54.

Smith, A. and Green, K. (forthcoming) 'Including pupils with special educational needs in secondary school physical education: a sociological analysis of teachers' views', *British Journal of Sociology of Education.*

Stafford, I. (1989) 'Everybody active: a sports council national demonstration project in England', *Adapted Physical Activity Quarterly,* 6: 100–08.

Stationery Office (2001) *Special Educational Needs and Disability Act.* London: Stationery Office.

Sugden, D. and Talbot, M. (1996) *Physical Education for Children with Special Needs in Mainstream Education.* Leeds: Carnegie National Sports Development Centre.

Thomas, N. (2003) Sport and disability, in B. Houlihan (ed.), *Sport and Society: A Student Handbook.* London: Sage.

United Nations Educational, Scientific and Cultural Organization (UNESCO) (1994) *The Salamanca Statement and Framework for Action.* Paris: UNESCO.

Vickerman, P. (2002) 'Perspectives on the training of physical education teachers for the inclusion of children with special educational needs – is there an official line view?', *The Bulletin of Physical Education,* 38: 79–98.

Vickerman, P. (2003) 'Inclusion confusion? Official line perspectives on including children with special educational needs in physical education', paper presented at the British Educational Research Association Annual Conference, Edinburgh, 10–13 September.

Vickerman, P., Hayes, S. and Whetherly, A. (2003) 'Special educational needs and National Curriculum physical education', in S. Hayes and G. Stidder (eds), *Equity and Inclusion in Physical Education and Sport.* London: Routledge.

Waddington, I. (2000) *Sport, Health and Drugs: A Critical Sociological Perspective.* London: E and FN Spon.

Waddington, I., Malcolm, D. and Cobb, J. (1998) 'Gender stereotyping in physical education', *European Physical Education Review*, 4: 34–46.

Waddington, I., Malcolm, D. and Green, K. (1997) 'Sport, health and physical education: a reconsideration?', *European Physical Education Review*, 3: 165–82.

Wright, H. and Sugden, D. (1999) *Physical Education for All: Developing Physical Education in the Curriculum for Pupils with Special Educational Needs*. London: David Fulton.

Index